To my wife Joan and my daughter Karen

Copyright © 1973 by Holt, Rinehart and Winston, Inc.
All rights reserved
Library of Congress Catalog Card Number: 72–9887
ISBN: 0–03–086251–5
Printed in the United States of America
3456 038 987654321

Latin Americans

Contemporary peoples
and their cultural traditions

Michael D. Olien

University of Georgia

Holt, Rinehart and Winston, Inc.
New York   Chicago   San Francisco   Atlanta
Dallas   Montreal   Toronto   London   Sydney

Preface

Latin Americans and North Americans share the New World with each other, yet the general United States public has little understanding of Latin culture. The North American tends to have a distorted view of the Latin American, based either upon his own observations made while traveling "south of the border" or upon the stereotypes of the Latin American portrayed in the mass media.

Latin America is rich in natural beauty and cultural traditions stemming from an ancient intellectual heritage that originated centuries before most of North America was settled. These outstanding qualities, however, often do not impress the average North American. Of his lasting memories, the poverty of the countries he visits remains uppermost in his mind. He notices children with distended stomachs due to malnutrition, elderly barefoot men dressed in rags, women collecting scraps of paper and metal to earn money for food, and small shacks that often house many individuals. Yet poverty is only one facet of life in Latin America. Possibly it is the most noticeable aspect of Latin American life to the visitor because he often comes from an "insulated neighborhood" shared with other middle class North Americans much like himself. Yet when was the last time the visitor drove through the impoverished areas of his own community? Each of our North American communities also has its own share of slum areas with inhabitants suffering from malnutrition living in substandard housing.

The mass media also affects the image the North American has of the Latin American. In movies and on television the Latin American is stereotyped in one of two ways. On the one hand he is depicted as a lazy, ignorant peon dressed in white shirt, baggy trousers, and a large sombrero—frequently with bands of bullets crisscrossing his chest. The peon type is usually shown sleeping in the midday sun propped up against the nearest cactus with his burro patiently waiting nearby. On the other hand the Latin American may be characterized as a slick-haired, mustached, superlover or gigolo. Both types are distortions of the Latin American. Pressure has been brought against the movie and television industries by Americans of Latin descent to eliminate the use of these stereotypes. This book also attempts a more representative picture of Latin Americans and their cultural traditions.

Unlike most areas of the world studied by anthropologists, Latin America has not been adequately covered by introductory texts. As a result, instructors find themselves assigning various monographs or collections of readings, and students often complete an anthropology course on Latin America with considerable knowledge of ethnographic facts but with no framework for organizing this data.

The purpose of this book is to cover the anthropology of Latin America adequately for the beginning student, whether undergraduate or graduate. It includes data basic to understanding the temporal, spatial, and cultural setting of the Latin Americans. General patterns are described at the expense of extensive ethnographic detail in hopes that the student will thereby acquire a general framework. More extensive ethnographic detail can be obtained from monographs and handbooks. At the end of each chapter there are suggested readings for this purpose. Bibliographic aids have been included in the appendices.

There appears to be a growing trend in anthropology toward studies of societies by members of those societies. These anthropologists reason that an investigator is more capable of accurately analyzing his own society than an outsider would be. Surely a Latin American anthropologist could provide valuable insights that this book has not covered. Yet I believe there is still an important place in anthropology for the observations of an outsider. While a book about Latin America written by a North American necessarily contains biases, the same would be true of a book written about Latin America by a Latin American. Though the biases may differ, culture conditions our perceptions whether we are interpreting our own society or another.

Latin America is made up of a number of complex societies, each of which includes a variety of subcultures. Because of this diversity, the anthropologist—whether Latin American or North American—can thoroughly understand only one, or at best a few, of these subcultures. Therefore, in order to generalize about Latin America, it is necessary to rely on the studies of others. This study owes a considerable intellectual debt to many other writers. In particular I have found the writings of the historians Charles Gibson and Magnus Mörner, and the anthropologists Richard N. Adams, George Foster, John Gillin, Arthur Rubel, Julian Steward, Arnold Strickon, Charles Wagley, and Eric Wolf, to name only a few, extremely informative.

I wish to extend my gratitude to George and Louise Spindler who offered invaluable suggestions at each stage in the development of this book. I would also like to thank Professors Frederick L. Bates and Wilfrid C. Bailey, of the University of Georgia, for allowing a reduction in my teaching load that made the completion of this book possible. A number of colleagues have been kind enough to allow me the use of their photographs in illustrating the book: Jay D. Edwards, Mary W. Helms, Pedro A. Pequeño-Rossié, Jaroslaw T. Petryshyn, B. E. Pierce, Dean R. Snow, Dwight T. Wallace, Scott Whiteford, Norman E. Whitten, Jr., and Raymond E. Wiest.

Finally, I would especially like to take this opportunity to thank my wife, Joan, for typing the various drafts of this book as well as for her help in editing the manuscript. Surely without her assistance and her encouragement this text could never have materialized.

M. D. O.

Contents

CHAPTER 1

Introduction

回回回回回回回回回回回回回回回回回回回回回回回回回

The New World was the last easily inhabited large landmass to be settled by man. Settlement began no earlier than fifty thousand years ago, possibly as recently as fifteen thousand years ago. The settlers were most likely all the same basic physical type, shared the same Paleolithic (Old Stone Age) culture, and spoke closely related dialects or languages. Over the millennia great diversity developed in this New World population. The physical types began to alter in response to the various environments. Speech patterns diversified into hundreds of languages that were not mutually intelligible. Great cultural and political diversity developed among groups. Some societies developed a high level of sociopolitical integration—that is to say, they created the state, which organized and controlled hundreds of thousands of individuals. Others existed in much the same manner as the hunting and gathering bands that first populated the New World. This cultural and political diversity did not coincide with the boundary lines now separating Latin America from the rest of the New World. The groups living north of the Rio Grande were identical to those immediately south of the border. The growth and spread of civilization in the pre-Columbian New World was limited to central Mexico, the Mayan area, and the Andes.

The Europeans (Spanish and Portuguese) brought a unity to the region now known as Latin America. Control of indigenous New World societies by the Spanish, and to a lesser extent the Portuguese, created a countertrend to the increasing diversity of the Amerind (American Indian).

1

Thus, Iberian domination resulted in unity and a partially new cultural tradition—a "Latin American" cultural tradition, which was a blend of New World and Iberian beliefs and traits.

The period during which the Spanish converted their New World territories into a Spanish domain coincided with the English, and to a lesser extent the French, settlement of the northern regions of the New World. Both the Spanish and English introduced European traditions; however, these varied considerably. The English introduced a Northern European, Protestant, industrial tradition; the Spanish introduced a Mediterranean, Catholic, preindustrial tradition.

The first areas colonized by the Spanish were several of the Caribbean islands. Conquest and settlement spread into Mexico, Central America, and South America. Spain later lost some of the Caribbean islands, as well as British Honduras and the Guianas on the mainland, to other European nations. Yet throughout the Colonial period this entire area developed into an interaction sphere dominated by the Spanish. The economic and ecological conditions experienced under the Spanish extended even to those areas which had come under English, French, or Dutch control. It would therefore be difficult to discuss Latin America without including those areas of the mainland and the Caribbean that today might not technically be defined as "Latin America." It is also necessary to include under the broad cover term "Latin American" those people who have emigrated from the area in large enough groups to form subcultures in the particular societies in which they have settled.

LATIN AMERICA: A CULTURE AREA

Anthropology has divided the world into "culture areas" for the purposes of study. A culture area is a geographical space within which the people share a number of traits at a given point in time. Anthropologists have been primarily concerned with culture areas of the world prior to the expansion of Western Civilization; however, the culture area can also be used to describe contemporary peoples. As a culture area modern Latin America represents a rather broad abstraction. The colonial Iberian tradition seems to be the primary thread uniting the area. Modern Latin America includes Mexico, the Caribbean, and Central and South America. In a culture area as large as this, it is difficult to outline any trait or characteristic applying to *all* of the people living within its geographic boundaries. Latin America is comprised of a number of subcultures. Some are racially distinct groups: Negroes, Orientals, whites, American Indians, and East Indians; others are distinguished by differences in religious beliefs and practices: Catholics, Protestants, Jews, Buddhists, Hindus, and followers of native religions;

still other subcultures are distinguished by their occupations, access to power, social class, and so on. Nevertheless, it is possible to generalize about Latin America as a culture area, keeping in mind that it represents a broad level of abstraction. Latin America can be compared to other culture

The contributions of diverse cultures to the Latin American cultural tradition.

areas of the same general level of abstraction such as "North America," "Oceania," or "Africa."

Subdivisions of the Culture Area   The primary subdivisions of the modern culture area would be the various states that comprise Latin America, for example, Argentina and Mexico. At the same time Latin America can be subdivided into larger, multistate units that share certain ecological, historical, and cultural traits. "South America" includes all states east and south of Panama. "Middle America," as defined by most anthropologists, includes Mexico and Central America. On the other hand some geographers include the Caribbean area as well in the term "Middle America" because of the interaction among these areas during the Colonial period. Others have extended the term "Middle America" to include not only Mexico, Central America, and the Caribbean, but also the northeastern section of South America (Colombia, Venezuela, and the Guianas).[1]

In the United States the term "Central America" is used to include the area from Guatemala through Panama. To the Central Americans, "Central America" refers only to the states that were included in the Federation of Central American States. The Federation did not include Panama, which at the time was part of Columbia. Panama was not established as a separate state until the beginning of the twentieth century. A further complication in the meaning of the term "Central America" is the status of British Honduras. The Guatemalans consider British Honduras a Guatemalan province, Belice. The people of British Honduras conceived of themselves as an independent country allied more with the British islands of the Caribbean and Guyana.

The subdivision, "the Caribbean," creates another problem in terminology. In some classifications only the islands of the Caribbean are included; in others Central America is included. The "Plantation Sphere" of Charles Wagley is defined primarily by traits found in the Caribbean, but includes the northern coast of South America, the east coast of Central America and Mexico, and the Southeast of the United States as well. The "West Indian islands" is a term that includes the Caribbean islands. "The West Indies"—a term once covering a large area during the period of exploration—was in recent years restricted to a federation of ten British Caribbean colonies established in 1957 and lasting until 1962. The term "Antilles" was sometimes used during early exploration. Today the terms "Greater Antilles" and "Lesser Antilles" are used more frequently. The Greater Antilles refers to the large islands: Cuba, Hispaniola, Jamaica, and Puerto Rico. The Lesser Antilles refers to the remaining small islands. The

---

[1] German geographers have generally restricted the term "Mittelamerika" to include only Central America.

Lesser Antilles are further subdivided into the Leeward Islands of the north and the Windward Islands of the south (Pearcy 1965:18).

Several other terms applied to subdivisions of Latin America should be mentioned, although they describe pre-Columbian cultural differences. "Mesoamerica" was an interaction sphere[2] influenced by the civilizations of Mexico and Guatemala. The boundaries to the north extended to the arid regions of northern Mexico approximately three hundred miles north of Mexico City. Mesoamerica extended southward to northwestern Costa Rica (Kirchhoff 1952). At various points in time this area came under the militaristic, religious, and economic domination or influence of the Aztecs, their precursors, and the Maya or their precursors. The "Andean Area" was a parallel interaction sphere that became a center of civilization contemporary with Mesoamerica. Because of the interaction that took place between these two regions, the entire area from Mexico to the Andes has been given the term "Nuclear America."

In Chapters 2, 3 and 4 the major interaction spheres of Latin America are examined. These included the pre-Contact, Colonial, and Modern interaction spheres, major areas in which traits and ideas spread and in which there was similarity in cultural characteristics. During the Pre-Contact period, Mesoamerica and the Andes were the two major interaction spheres. During the Colonial period, the entire area, excluding Brazil, became integrated into basically a single interaction sphere under the control of Spain. Following Independence, four major traditions began to appear. These modern interaction spheres will be referred to as: Amerind-America, Mestizo-America, Afro-America, and Euro-America.

THE ANTHROPOLOGICAL APPROACH TO LATIN AMERICA

Anthropology is the comparative study of man. In studying the human animal in time and space, the anthropologist focuses on the diversity of man from three major points of view: man's biological diversity, man's linguistic diversity, and man's cultural diversity through time. Life in Latin America today cannot be understood fully without knowledge of all these aspects of man; however, the *focus* of this study is one of cultural diversity.

Most cultural anthropological studies of Latin America have been directed toward the Amerinds, in keeping with the traditional anthropologi-

---

[2] An interaction sphere is an area within which contact and communication between peoples take place facilitating the exchange of ideas and artifacts. However, there are regional and local variations as local groups each have unique problems of adaptation to particular environmental niches, population pressures, levels of sociopolitical integration, and so on. (cf. Caldwell 1964, where the concept was first introduced).

cal focus on non-Western man. In recent years, anthropologists have expanded their interests to include a wider range of peoples, such as peasants, urban proletariats, minority groups, elites, plantation workers, and so on. So-called "primitive" societies are no longer viewed as isolated; they are studied as subcultures of larger, complex societies. Many of the major figures of anthropology have been influenced in one way or another by their research in Latin America. Charles Darwin's voyage on board the Beagle (1831–1836) to the west coast of South America provided a basic key to the development of modern evolutionary theory. A trip to Cuba and Mexico in 1855 initiated Edward Tylor's speculation on primitive man. Other dominant figures in anthropology, such as Alfred Kroeber, Melville Herskovits, Claude Lévi-Strauss, Bronislaw Malinowski, Robert Redfield, and Julian Steward, undertook important field research in Latin America, and in part these studies affected their theoretical outlooks.

Other disciplines such as history, sociology, and political science have also contributed to the study of Latin Americans. What, then, is anthropology's unique contribution? The historian, the sociologist, and the political scientist are primarily interested in formal institutions at the national level, such as legal and governmental systems, political parties, labor unions, the educational system, church organization and doctrine, the army, certain organized sports, the distribution of cash crops and of manufactured goods and other commodities, monetary systems, banking and credit (Steward 1950:142). While recognizing the importance of such institutions, the anthropologist has focused on generally ignored local manifestations of these institutions. For example, orthodox Catholicism at the national level or in the capital of a country is quite different from Catholicism practiced in the rural villages. In some villages Amerind or African deities are worshipped alongside orthodox saints. The analysis of national level institutions *as well as* their local manifestations and linkages is necessary for a satisfactory understanding of modern Latin America.

THE ECOLOGICAL SETTING

Of the twenty-one countries on the Latin American mainland, only Uruguay is located entirely within the Temperate Zone, the area between the tropics and the polar circle. Most of the countries lie wholly in the hot middle belt of the earth. However, South America reaches as far south of the equator as Hudson's Bay is north of the equator. The total land area of Latin America is just under eight million square miles. South America accounts for roughly seven million square miles, with Mexico, Central America, and the Caribbean comprising the remainder. Twenty-five percent of Latin America is mountainous; 25 percent is swampy and 10 percent is desert or very dry. Close to three hundred million people inhabit Latin America. The density of population to total land mass is still rather low compared to other populations, yet the area has the highest rate of population increase of any major world region. It is estimated that the population will almost double (five hundred million) by the year 2000, Latin Americans tend to be unevenly distributed throughout the land mass. The people are characteristically grouped together in cluster areas of concentrated settlement, and these clusters, for the most part, remain distinct from each other and are separated by sparsely occupied territory.

The physical diversity of the land is tremendous. While many of the natural features offer great potentials, they are often poorly located or poorly combined with other resources. The Andes of western South America extend almost unbroken by low passes from the Caribbean to the Strait of Magellan forming the world's longest continuous mountain barrier, stifling trade between the east and west coasts. The Amazon is the world's third largest river and contains the world's largest tropical forest in its basin. Yet neither the river nor the forest can be utilized effectively as long as the whole area remains sparsely populated. Brazil has the world's largest and richest supply of iron ore, but the continent is lacking in the coal necessary to process it. Northern Chile possesses the world's only natural source of nitrate, yet the deposits are separated from the seacoast by the steep slopes of an escarpment. While Rio de Janeiro has one of the world's finest natural harbors, the port is surrounded by highlands that make access to the interior of Brazil both difficult and expensive (James 1959: 23–24).

The Latin Americans live in a violent environment. Many of the hundreds of volcanic peaks from Colima in Mexico to Corcovado in southern Chile are active or have been in violent eruption during the past century. The frequent earthquakes that strike the mountainous zones have been closely associated with this volcanic activity. Many Latin American cities have been destroyed, and most other cities within the mountain belt have been devastated at one time or another (Schurz 1964:5).

The various geomorphic regions of Latin America, though linked together physically, are structurally separate. In Mexico the structure and relief is, at least as far south as twenty degrees N., actually a prolongation of North America. The Caribbean together with the isthmian part of Central America belong to a separate structural region of folded and faulted rock that is aligned along an east-west axis. Although Central America links the North and South American continents, it is not closely related structurally to either. South America, which forms a distinct structural entity, is attached physically to Central America by the narrow Isthmus of Panama, which is "much more a barrier between oceans than a link between continents" (Robinson 1967:5–8). In the Caribbean, the Bahamas are primarily coral reefs that are morphologically distinct from the Antilles. The Greater Antilles are a continuation of Central America; the Lesser Antilles form an arc of volcanoes that link up with the Andes.

Rivers have affected Latin American history insofar as the regions vary in the usefulness and extent of their rivers. Those of Mexico and Central America are swift flood streams and of little use except for power and irri-

Irazú Volcano, Costa Rica.

gation. There are no truly navigable rivers north of Colombia, although the
San Juan River on the Nicaraguan-Costa Rican boundary does permit traffic
by small steamers. The west coast of South America also lacks navigable
rivers. East of the Andes, however, some of the great rivers of the world
flow into the Atlantic and the Caribbean: (1) the São Francisco of Brazil
drains the eastern highland region and is navigable, with interruptions, for

Arenal Volcano, Costa Rica. Posts in front of photograph mark graves of
individuals killed during the first eruptions.

MAP 1.1   Modern Latin America.

some one thousand miles; (2) the Magdalena-Cauca of the northern Andes flows into the Caribbean and is navigable for nine hundred miles. This system drains the valleys between the Andes of Colombia, an area of about three hundred and sixty-five thousand square miles, and furnishes the chief routes of communication for the entire region as it has done for centuries. (3) The Orinoco rises in southeastern Colombia and southern Venezuela and flows into the Caribbean. The River is used for navigation for approximately two hundred miles from its delta; (4) the Paraná-Paraguay River system flows into the one hundred and seventy mile estuary of the Río de la Plata, draining an area of about one and one-half million square miles of northern Argentina, Paraguay, southern Brazil, and Uruguay. Small ships are able to sail all the way from Buenos Aires to Asunción, a distance of roughly one thousand miles. Although shorter than the Amazon and its tributaries, the Paraná-Paraguay River system may be the most important in Latin America because it allows the shipment of grain and meat from northern Argentina and lumber and *quebracho* (the source of tannin) from Paraguay. (5) The Amazon and its tributaries drain an area of more than 2.7 million square miles, about 40 percent of all South America including the heart of Brazil, as well as large areas of Surinam, Guyana, French Guiana, Venezuela, Colombia, Ecuador, Peru, and Bolivia. The river is navigable by ocean vessels as far as Manaus, over nine hundred miles from the delta. Smaller ships are able to sail a thousand miles farther west to the town of Iquitos in Peru (Herring 1968:7–10).

The distance from the Mexican-United States border to the tip of South America is approximately six thousand miles, roughly the distance from London to Peking. Mexico and Central America lie west of South America, as does most of North America. South America is actually closer to Africa than it is to the United States. The eastern most point of Brazil is only fifteen hundred and fifty miles from Africa.

Elevation   Altitude plays a very important role in determining the climates of considerable areas of Latin America.[3] In spite of the fact that such a large proportion of the region lies within the tropics, a large area of this tropical territory has a temperate, and in some areas a cold, climate. These climates are related to altitude and are best exemplified in the Andean zone—on the high intermontane plateaus and sierras—although they are present in other highland areas. In the higher elevations of Latin America, people think of climate in terms of altitude rather than latitude.

The higher altitudes possess climates that are classified into vertical zones. Although all the basic elements of weather and climate (temperature,

[3] This section is based on a discussion of elevation in Latin America by the geographer Harry Robinson (1967).

humidity, pressure, and winds) are modified with increasing elevation, temperature is the overriding factor. Three main zones are usually recognized in the higher lands of Latin America: the *tierra caliente, tierra templada,* and *tierra fría.*

The tierra caliente (hot country) is the low country of the higher elevations, usually below three thousand feet, where hot, wet conditions prevail. In effect the tierra caliente is a vertical extension of the conditions that characterize the equatorial lowlands. The tierra templada (temperate country) normally lies between three thousand and six thousand feet but in some regions extends upwards to eight thousand feet. Above the temperate lands is the tierra fría (cold country) beginning at approximately six thousand feet—this is a zone in which frost occurs. The upper limit of the tierra fría is approximately ten thousand feet in equatorial latitudes and somewhat lower farther from the equator. Above the tierra fría lies the zone of alpine pastures known as *paramos* that extend from about ten thousand feet to the snow line at approximately fifteen thousand feet. The snow-capped peaks of the Andes are in a climate of perpetual frost. In these upper regions are located the highest peak in the Western Hemisphere, Aconcagua, on the Chilean-Argentine border, which rises 22,834 feet above sea level, and the largest lake in Latin America, Lake Titicaca, on the Peruvian-Bolivian border, located at 12,507 feet above sea level.

The extreme differences in altitude have also played a role in human biological adaptation in Latin America. In studies of Peruvian Amerinds living at elevations of between eighty-two hundred and seventeen thousand five hundred and ninety feet, Paul Baker (1969) found that there have been genetic adaptions taking place. In this area there is a high birth rate and a high death rate. The death rate is unusually high among females (both in the prenatal and postnatal stages). Birth weights are low, but placenta weights are high to enable the fetus to receive sufficient oxygen. The natives also have high blood flow to extremities during exposure to cold and in the adult males, maximum oxygen consumption is high.

Both the Spanish and blacks have had problems adapting to high altitudes. The Spanish suffered low birth rates, high rates of miscarriages, abortions, and infant deaths. The blacks, who have concentrated in the lowlands, came from an area of Africa in which there was a high incidence of sickle cell anemia. This disease seriously interfered with the oxygen-carrying capacity of the blood at high altitudes, making it even more difficult for the blacks to survive in the upper elevations.

The high uplands and mountain slopes with their "vertical climates" (as they are sometimes referred to) are important from the point of view of human settlement. Because of their lower temperatures in the tropics, they have provided suitable habitats for man in areas that, at lower elevations, are persistently hot and not very attractive. To immigrant Europeans and their descendants these higher elevations have been particularly attractive, as the conditions prevailing in the highlands bear similarities to the temperate climates of the European midlatitudes. It is significant that in the Andean zone the greatest concentrations of population are found in the highlands; in Brazil, too, the most important part of the country is the central portion of the eastern plateau.

Latin America is a cultural and geographical mosaic. To understand the Latin Americans one must be aware of this great diversity. Yet throughout this culture area there is a common cultural tradition originating in the Colonial period that results in a unique way of life characterized as "Latin American." In the chapters that follow, considerable discussion will be devoted to the cultural diversity but always within the framework of a widespread cultural unity. This book, then, is a search for "The Latin Americans"—who they are, what they are, and how they are studied by anthropologists.

CHAPTER 2

The early interaction spheres

𝓁𝓁𝓁𝓁𝓁𝓁𝓁𝓁𝓁𝓁𝓁𝓁𝓁𝓁𝓁𝓁𝓁𝓁𝓁𝓁𝓁𝓁𝓁𝓁𝓁

The colonial culture of Latin America developed from the interaction of
three diverse groups: the Amerinds (American Indians), the Europeans
(Iberians in particular), and the Africans. During the period of conquest
and colonization these groups combined to form a highly variable colonial
Latin American population and cultural tradition.

Latin American culture is neither entirely "Latin" nor "American."
Instead it represents the culmination of the exchange of ideas and cultural
patterns between New World settlers of diverse backgrounds. Each of the
major components of colonial and modern Latin America were derived from
areas in which there had been an intense exchange prior to the colonial
experience. These areas will be referred to as "interaction spheres." Part
of the pre-Columbian New World represented a major interaction sphere,
Nuclear America, which, in turn, was comprised of two regional interaction
spheres: Mesoamerica and the Andes. At the time of the Spanish conquest
and settlement of the New World, the Iberian Peninsula represented a second major interaction sphere, and West Africa prior to and during the era
of the slave trade represented a third major sphere. This chapter examines
the growth of two of these interaction spheres, Nuclear America and Iberia,
and the contributions of each to the creation of Latin America. Chapter 3
describes the Colonial and African interaction spheres and Chapter 4 examines contemporary Latin America in terms of four modern interaction
spheres.

THE PRE-COLUMBIAN INTERACTION SPHERES

The question of the origin of the American Indian led to years of controversy.[1] At present there are still many questions unresolved. The major outline is becoming clearer, however, and there no longer seems to be any' question of where the Amerind originated. All evidence points to eastern Asia and, in particular, Siberia. The problems of when the Amerind migrated into the New World remains a point of contention among prehistorians. Some archaeologists favor a fairly recent entry into the New World—about 14,000 B.C., while others believe man entered North America nearly forty thousand years ago and possibly even earlier. Differences in the interpretation of the archaeological remains are difficult to resolve, due to problems of dating the cultural material left behind by early man. Almost all of the material are pieces of stone which have been modified by man in one way or another. In a very important survey of the artifacts of early man, Alex Krieger (1964) has suggested three stages of development in the New World prior to the use of pottery—the earliest beginning possibly forty thousand years ago. Krieger's stages will be employed in this discussion.

The Early Nomads   The path followed by the early immigrants was from Siberia across the Bering Straits and into Alaska. The earliest migrations probably began during the Pleistocene, or Ice Age, possibly as early as the fourth glacial period. During some of the migrations the area was frozen and a broad land bridge facilitated overland travel. At other times the temperature changed, causing the glaciers to retreat and creating a series of islands between Siberia and Alaska. Yet the distances between these islands were not great. Travel was possible with the use of crude sailing vessels. For the most part the temperatures were extremely cold, and the migrations into the New World might have been impossible had it not been for the earlier invention of tailored skin clothing.

The evidence from the earliest archaeological sites in the New World suggests that the first waves of migrants arrived in the New World with a tool kit similar to that of the Lower Paleolithic (Lower Old Stone Age) in the Old World. The tools were crude and fashioned through the technique of percussion in which a stone (or piece of bone or wood) was struck against another to fashion a particular shape. Pressure flaking, the technique for making thin, flat artifacts, was lacking. As a result, the first inhabitants did not have projectile points. The artifacts which have been discovered are large and heavy. In a few cases artifacts made from the leg bone of animals have also been discovered, as have the remains of simple camp hearths.

---

[1] See Chapter 5 for details of the controversy.

These remains suggest an undifferentiated hunting-fishing-gathering economy. These artifacts have been found from Alaska to the tip of South America. The distribution is discontinuous in that no artifacts of this very early time period have yet been found in Canada, the northwest and southeast of the United States, northern Mexico, Central America, the Caribbean, the central Andes, or the area drained by the Amazon and its tributaries. The earliest dates thus far comes from the Lewisville site in north central Texas, with two dates greater than thirty-eight thousand years ago, and from the American Falls site in southern Idaho, with a date greater than thirty thousand years and possibly as early as forty-three thousand years (Krieger 1964:44).

The preprojectile point stage is represented in Latin America by material found in Baja California, central Mexico, Venezuela, Colombia, and southern South America (the State of Paraná, Brazil, Uruguay, Argentina, Chile, and southern Bolivia). It is probable that remains of early man will be found in other areas of the Latin American mainland. Little is known of these early inhabitants because for many years the attention of the archaeologist had been directed toward the high civilizations. Furthermore, the early groups were very small and nomadic, thus leaving behind no large accumulations of signs of human occupation.

The crudest artifacts from southern South America, while older than ten thousand years in some areas, may actually be more recent in other areas where a very primitive way of life survived as other groups began to advance.

A second stage can be distinguished as new waves of nomads entered the New World and the tool kit of the Amerind began to change and become more specialized. It cannot yet be determined whether the new technology represents a direct importation from Siberia, an independent New World development out of the preprojectile point stage, or a type of stimulus diffusion in which ideas of tool making, rather than the tools themselves, diffused to the New World and were utilized by the early settlers. In any event, about 10,000 B.C. the older percussion tools exhibit greater control over knapping techniques and new types of tools are added to the inventory. Some archaeologists view this period as one in which a change in physical types takes place, with a new type of Mongoloid now migrating to the New World and replacing the other populations. However, the meager skeletal remains are hardly conclusive.

The new artifacts include relatively thin and flat projectile points and knives. Most seemed to have required pressure flaking for their manufacture. (Pressure flaking is performed by gouging fine flakes from a stone core using a small bone point.) Unfortunately for the interpretation of Latin American prehistory, most sites have been found in the United States and Canada. These nomadic peoples specialized in the hunting of large Pleistocene animales which had not yet become extinct in the New World—for example, the mammoth, the mastodon, and the wild horse, as well as an early form of bison.

The archaeological evidence from Mexico and South America for this second stage of hunting and gathering is limited compared to the material which has been discovered in North America. Artifacts have been found in Tamaulipas, Mexico, the Valley of Mexico, Venezuela, eastern Brazil, Chile, Argentina, and Peru. Some of these are kill sites where the animals were slaughtered and butchered; however, these areas were uninhabited. Others, usually caves or rock shelters, represent camp sites. The Latin American sites date from about ten thousand years ago.

Evolving from the early hunting and gathering tradition which had spread throughout the New World were four subsistence specializations. These specializations, representing a third stage of development, appeared in Latin America from about 10,000 to 5000 B.C. as localized responses to ecological changes resulting from climatic fluctuations. Sanders and Marino (1970:33–39) refer to these specializations as the montane hunters and gatherers, the littoral collectors, the tropical lowland hunters and gatherers, and the grassland hunters.

The montane specialization included highland ecological niches which remained rich in mammals for hunting such as deer and cameloids, coupled with a plentiful supply of plant foods. This specialization was predominant in the Andes.

The littoral collectors persisted along the western and northern coastal areas of South America where shellfish, fish, and sea mammals were found in abundance. The archaeological sites show greater permanence of settlement than is true of the highland hunters and gatherers. All of these coastal people probably participated in some type of inland hunting and gathering. Several of the sites suggest incipient cultivation of plant food, particularly in Peru.

Settlement of the tropical lowlands may have been somewhat later than in other areas. By 4000 B.C. at least two different ways of exploiting the environment had developed. The east coast of Brazil was populated by shellfish gatherers, while in the savannas a hunting and gathering tradition was maintained. The tropical forest savannas were generally quite limited in their fauna resources.

A fourth specialization was found in the southern grasslands of Patagonia where a hunting tradition persisted until the Spanish Conquest. The inhabitants of this area hunted the ground sloth and the horse. In early times hunting was done with spears and bolas. Later the bow and arrow replaced the spear.

Becoming Settled Farmers The development of agriculture in the New World was a complex affair with at least three centers of domestication: Mesoamerica, the Andes, and the South American tropical lowlands.

Desert tradition   Incipient cultivation

▤ Montane hunters and gathers
■ Littoral collectors
▨ Tropical lowland hunters and gatherers
▦ Grassland hunters

MAP 2.1 Specializations in occupied areas of Latin America about 5000
B.C. (Adapted from Sanders and Marino 1970.)

There are important crops which make their initial appearance in each of these areas. Once domesticated, plants often spread rapidly throughout the Nuclear American interaction sphere, making it difficult to reconstruct the origin of the various plants.

In western North America the retreat of the glaciers brought about increasing aridity. The various small bands of people who inhabited the vast region from Oregon to Guatemala developed a new specialized "desert culture." These people often dwelled in caves and under overhanging ledges known as rock shelters. They collected whatever was available for food, relying heavily on rabbits, rodents, and insects. Above all they gathered a variety of wild plant foods, particularly seeds. These seeds were ground on milling stones. The various tools and weapon points of flint which form a part of the desert culture seem crudely made in contrast to the beautiful points which had been manufactured by the earlier specialized hunters, the last of whom were continuing to hunt larger game in the prairie areas of eastern North America, the Andes, and in Patagonia. The desert peoples, on the other hand, excelled in the manufacture of basketry, matting, and sandals. Baskets and bags were used to collect and store the wild seeds and plants (M. Coe 1962:44).

An archaeological sequence from Tamaulipas in northeast Mexico suggests that supplementary cultivation emerged about 6000 B.C. among desert peoples who relied mainly on game and wild plant foods such as the agave, the opuntia, and the runner bean. The plants which probably were already domesticated at this time were the bottle gourd, the pumpkin, and the chili pepper. In the Old World the important plants, wheat and barley, were present from the beginning of supplementary cultivation; corn, the most important plant of Mesoamerican agriculture, was not present in the early Tamaulipas material. An early variety of maize (native corn) appeared in Tamaulipas and at Bat Cave, New Mexico, by approximately 3000 B.C. Somewhat later the warty squash appeared. Several thousand years elapsed between the initial cultivation of plants (6000 B.C.) and the appearance of communities in which the main subsistence was derived from food production (1500 B.C.).

In the Tehuacán Valley of Puebla, Mexico, during the period 5200 to 3400 B.C., several species of squash and beans, chili peppers, amaranths, avocados, gourds, cotton, and zapotes, as well as a form of maize, may have been cultivated. At this time the wild ancestor of maize and other plants were still being collected and eaten; in fact, wild plants formed a considerable proportion of the diet of the Mesoamericans until the advent of irrigation about the first millenium B.C.

The earliest cultivated form of maize in Tehuacán was probably only slightly more productive than its wild ancestor. Perhaps the early cultivated variety was slightly modified in the beginning simply because it grew in a better environment produced by man's removal of competing vegetation. Between 3400 and 3200 B.C. a fully domesticated form of maize appeared in Tehuacán but was probably not of local origin. The Colombian and Venezuelan lowlands have been suggested by Sauer (1959) as the source of tropical root crop cultivation—manioc, the yam, and the peanut—which developed sometime before 1000 B.C.

Sanders and Marino (1970:50) suggest the possibility that root crop cultivation may have begun in the lowlands of Mesoamerica, since settled villages were in existence on the Gulf Coast as early as 1500 B.C. It is not yet clear from archaeological evidence whether the villages were supported by locally evolved root crops or by seed crops introduced from the highlands.

Another series of cultivated plants appeared by 2200 B.C. on the Peruvian coast—squash, peppers, gourds, cotton, and achira tubers. These developed in semisedentary marine fishing and shellfish gathering economies which utilized wild plants as well.

While some of the plants thought to have originated in Peru may reflect an early diffusion of cultivated plants from the Mesoamerican region, there is greater likelihood that the Amazonian root crop tradition (manioc, yams, and peanuts) arose independently.

At least four cultivated New World species suggest early transoceanic contacts between the Old World and the New: the jack bean, the bottle gourd, and two species of cotton. While most authorities looked to Asia for possible origins, Karl Schwerin (1970) has suggested that these plants and others may have come to the New World from West Africa.

While new sources of food were being exploited, a new artifact—pottery—made its appearance in the New World. Some of Latin America's earliest pottery has been found on the coasts of Colombia and Ecuador, dating from about 3000 B.C. Evans, Meggers, and Estrada (1959) have suggested that some of this first New World pottery is directly related to the Jomon pottery of Japan. A similar early pottery also appears in Panama at Puerto Hormiga at roughly the same time. These early examples of pottery in Latin America occur first in shell heaps. The Ecuadorian, Colombian, and Panamanian potteries are older than plant cultivation in their respective regions. In Mesoamerica, where the earliest plant domestications were made, pottery does not occur until 2300 to 2400 B.C. In the eastern Amazon the earliest pottery has been dated at 1800 to 2000 B.C. In Peru it appears no earlier than about 1800 B.C. (Willey 1971:264–277).

In Mesoamerica, by 2300 B.C., there were established village farming peoples, equipped with all of the important domesticated plants, houses of wattle and mud daub construction, and pottery. This period of settled village life is generally called the "Formative" period because it serves as the fundamental basis for all subsequent developments in the area. The

Formative period of the New World is analogous to the Neolithic (New Stone Age) period of the Old World even though the Formative occurred much later. Compact settlements, loom weaving, the working of stone by grinding, as well as chipping and the modeling of human fiurines in clay, have been found in both the Formative and the Neolithic periods. The major difference is that animal husbandry never developed to the extent in the Americas that it did in the Old World.

Seven hundred years later a new feature developed in the farming villages—the rise of an elite and the first important ceremonial centers. This marked a transition from the villages-and-center.

The Rise of Civilization   The first ceremonial centers arose on the coast of Peru and in the jungles of the Gulf Coast lowlands of Mexico.

During the period from 2500 B.C. to 1800 B.C., cultivation was firmly established in most coastal valleys of Peru. This was also a period of rapid population expansion due possibly less to agriculture than to the successful exploitation of sea life. On the north central coast, where plentiful sea food was coupled with maize cultivation, the population was especially dense. Some of the villages contained as many as one thousand inhabitants (Lanning 1967:64).

Many of the traits which are characteristic of later Peruvian civilizations make their initial appearance on the north central coast at this time (Lanning 1967:77):

They include pyramids and temples; diversified construction in stone, adobes, and clay; mummy bundles; multiple burials in which secondary individuals were sacrificed to accompany a person of importance; trophy heads . . . ; ceremonial caches; coca chewing with lime carried in gourd bottles and extracted with bone spatulas; snuff tablets and tubes; the development of art in textiles, bone, wood, gourds, stone, and clay; spindles and spindle whorls; composite combs; bone flutes; eye needles; jet mirrors; earplugs; mesh measures; slings; and a great diversity of baskets, bags, mats, beads, pendants, and hairpins.

At Chuquitana, in the lower Chillón Valley, a community has been discovered whose ruins consist of eight large platforms covering an area of 900 by 700 meters. The structures are made primarily of stone blocks set in mud mortar. One of the larger units may have been a temple complex. A date in the 1800 to 1500 B.C. range has been obtained for the latest building phase. Willey (1971:99) suggests that probably more than fifteen hundred people lived together at this site.

Dated at about the same period is the site of Las Holdas in the Casma Valley. Here is a large compound 450 meters long containing seven temple platforms. The ceremonial center spans an area of 700 by 200 yards. The construction is of basalt blocks and mud mortar.

In the highlands the economy was changing from that of hunting and gathering to maize and possibly potato farming. An important highland site of the Formative period is Kotosh. The site consisted of nine groups of ruins, the main parts of which are two mounds, one large (13.7 meters high and 100 meters in diameter) and one small one (6.5 meters high and 30 meters in diameter) (Izumi and Sono 1963:37). One of the earliest structures was a special temple called the "Temple of the Crossed Hands." Beneath one of the large niches in one wall was a pair of crossed hands sculptured from clay.

These early ceremonial centers in the Andes begin prior to the introduction of pottery into the area; however, later phases of building are generally associated with pottery. The first ceramics of the Andean region appeared in the northern highlands between 1800 and 1200 B.C. Between 1200 and 750 B.C. pottery spread rapidly through most of the central Andes.

In Mesoamerica ceremonial centers began to appear a few hundred years later, marking the beginning of a new period—the pre-Classic. Whereas the Andean centers integrated limited areas—possibly a single valley, the centers of Mesoamerica represent the integration of a large part of southern Mexico and Guatemala into a single interaction sphere.

By 1500 B.C., while the central highlands of Mexico developed a tradition of farming villages, often without ceremonial centers, the southern half of Mesoamerica witnessed the rise of a widespread ceremonial tradition which precipitated the development of civilization. The later states of Mexico and the Mayan area seem to have been derived from this earlier development. The name generally identified with this tradition is "Olmec."

The Olmecs inhabited the south Caribbean coast of Mexico in the the present day states of Vera Cruz and Tabasco. This region was the location of at least three major ceremonial centers: San Lorenzo de Tenochtitlán, the earliest (1200–900 B.C.), La Venta, the largest (1000–600 B.C.), and Tres Zapotes, the longest occupied (1000–100 B.C.). At La Venta the most imposing feature was an earth mound 240 by 420 feet at the base and 110 feet high.

The Olmec tradition appears to be one of the primary sources for the first great New World art style. The art style was truly pan-Mesoamerican with ceremonial centers in the central Mexican highlands, the Izapan sites of the Pacific slopes of Chiapas and Guatemala, the highlands of Guatemala, and the valley of Oaxaca all making their own unique contributions to its development. It is difficult to interpret a simple development of the Olmecs in the Gulf Coast area and then a spread of its traits by conquest to other areas of Mesoamerica from the archaeological evidence to date. For one thing the Olmec art style appears full-blown in the Gulf Coast area about 1200 B.C. at the site of the first Olmec ceremonial center. The origin of the art style must have occurred elsewhere. The analysis of Gulf Coast languages through glottochronology (a technique used by linguists to date the separation of related languages) also suggests an intrusion in the Gulf area, about 1200 B.C., of new people driving a wedge between the related Huastec and Mayan languages. Charles Wicke (1971) has hypothesized, on the basis of changes in art styles, that the Olmec tradition may have originated in the mountainous Mixteca Alta region of Oaxaca, but this question of origins is far from resolved. In any case, instead of hypothesizing a direct spread of Olmec culture to the rest of Mesoamerica, it is perhaps more accurate to hypothesize a Mesoamerican interaction sphere in which diffusion, innovation, and the evolution of culture occurs. Some of the important traits of this interaction sphere have their greatest development in the Gulf area. Stone carving occurs in the form of colossal heads up to nine feet tall and weighing four tons, stelae and alters of basalt, as well as celts, figurines, and pendants produced from blue-green jade and serpentine. Yet other important traits appear earlier at other ceremonial centers of the Mesoamerican interaction sphere. Possibly the most important set of traits, appearing first at Monte Albán and later in the Gulf area, is that of a system of writing, the calendar and dot and bar numerals used for counting. All of these elements were at one time thought to have originated with the Maya of the Classic period.

This early Mesoamerican interaction sphere was to influence the other great cultures of Mesoamerica which followed in the period known as the Classic. As Bernal (1969:193) has so aptly remarked:

The end of the Olmec world is not an end but a beginning. It leads

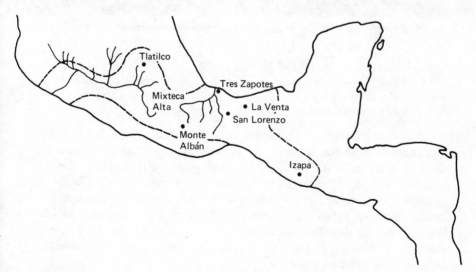

MAP 2.2   The pre-Classic Mesoamerican interaction sphere (1200–1 B.C.).

Danzantes from Monte Albán. Suggested as "Olmec-style" carving.

directly into the Classic world of Teotihuacán, Monte Albán, Tajín and and the Maya. These people were to absorb the Olmec inheritance and push civilization to far higher levels. They would reach a new ledge on the rocky ascent to civilization.

By about 900 B.C. a comparable interaction sphere was developing in the Andes. Just as the locus of the Mesoamerican interaction sphere was the Olmec tradition, the locus of the Andean interaction sphere was the Chavín tradition. The heartland of Chavín was the site of Chavín de Huantar—whether or not this site was the actual origin of the tradition. In any case, many Andean scholars consider the Chavín tradition to have arisen in the northcentral highlands—the location of Chavín de Huantar; although, as with the Mesoamerican interaction sphere, some of the important elements originated elsewhere.

The Chavín art style was reflected primarily in stone carving. The

MAP 2.3   The pre-Classic Andean interaction sphere (900–200 B.C.).

most frequently depicted subjects were hawks, eagles, jaguars, and humans. Almost all mouths, regardless of the creatures depicted, were shown as fanged jaguar mouths. The temples associated with the Chavín style also represent a specific architectural style. Generally the temples were built of high platform mounds, often with wings outlining a center patio. This tradition was also represented by a unique pottery style which spread rapidly over the northern half of Peru.

The impressive Chavín stone carving may have had its antecedent at the site of Cerro Sechín in the Casma Valley, where a temple platform had a facade composed of twenty-two major carved stone monoliths, as well as a number of minor ones. A few artifacts have been found elsewhere in Peru which seem to contain certain Chavín-like as well as Sechín elements. The dating of Cerro Sechín is still debated, and it is possible that it is derived from Chavín rather than antecedent to it.

Just as the previous period in Peru was one of extensive regionalism and isolationism, the development of the Andean interaction sphere represented a period in which ideas and goods were widely spread.

Chavín or Chavín-related designs were reproduced in clay, cloth, wood, bone, stone, and metal. It is within this interaction sphere that the earliest gold work thus far discovered first appears, with Chavín-style decoration.

As with the Mesoamerican interaction sphere, the Andean interaction sphere occurred where life had developed to the level of settled farming villages. No real Chavín influence is found in the southern Andes where the inhabitants had not yet reached this level.

Some Mesoamerican scholars (e.g., Porter 1953; Coe 1962) have suggested that the Chavín tradition was directly influenced by the Olmec. At the site of Tlatilco, in the Valley of Mexico, there are Olmec-like traits as well as a few traits which resemble the Chavín art style. Since the Olmec appears to predate the Chavín, it is thought to be the precursor, possibly as a result of contact by sea. Andean scholars have been less willing to accept this direct diffusion, and the relationships, if any, between Olmec and Chavín traditions are still not very clear.

Olmec and Chavín culture can be said to represent the spread of "great traditions" or possibly a single "great tradition"—across parts of Nuclear America. Most Olmec and Chavín ceremonial centers appear not to have been true cities, although San Lorenzo and the Peruvian sites tended to have been settled by fairly dense populations. For the most part these centers were elite centers composed of large and imposing religious structures, but generally with no large concentrations of population. These two art styles possibly reflect the religious ideologies of the early farming societies of Mesoamerica and the Andes. As panregional great traditions they provided a mechanism of intercommunication, a way of binding together the smaller parts of the social universe of their day into a more unified whole than had heretofore been possible (Willey 1962).

This pattern for civilization, which began in the pre-Classic period, crystalized in the following period called the Classic period, which begins as early as the birth of Christ in some areas of Latin America. The developments which occurred both in the Classic and the later post-Classic periods are analogous to the developments of the early civilizations of the Old World, although the growth of civilizations came about later in the New World. Great public works, unified and evolved monumental art styles, bureaucratic administration strengthened by writing systems (in Mesoamerica), and other techniques were already present by the end of the pre-Classic period. Added to these traits in the Classic period was the development of true cities and truly stratified societies. A major difference between the New World and the Old World was the way in which metallurgy was utilized. Metalworking developed as an art in South America during the pre-Classic period, but the use of metal was primarily as decorative art, whereas in the Old World it became an essential part of the technology of tool and weapon making.

Mesoamerican Civilization   In Mesoamerica, during the Classic period, the area encompassed by the interaction sphere grew. At least four regional cultures developed representing centers of diffusion and innovation within the interaction sphere: Teotihuacán in central Mexico, Monte Albán in Oaxaca, Tajín on the central Gulf Coast, and the Maya of the Yucatán Peninsula, southern Mexico, Guatemala, and Honduras. Each of these regional cultures had been influenced in one way or another by the Meso-

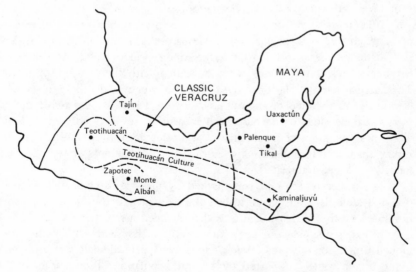

MAP 2.4   The Classic Mesoamerican interaction sphere (1–900 A.D.).

american interaction sphere of the pre-Classic period and each contributed to the expanding interaction sphere of the Classic period.

Teotihuacán society was the most influential force, economically, culturally, and politically, within the Mesoamerican interaction sphere. Teotihuacán began its era of greatness during the transition from the pre-Classic to the Classic period beginning about 1 A.D. and continuing into the seventh century.

The site of Teotihuacán covered an area of eight square miles and consisted not only of some of the largest platform ceremonial mounds of all pre-Columbian America, but of closely-packed, walled, residential structures as well. Teotihuacán was Mesoamerica's first true city. Its population has been estimated as being anywhere from fifty thousand to two hundred thousand inhabitants with the most probable figure falling somewhere in the fifty thousand to one hundred thousand range. Millon (1970:1080), who has recently mapped the site, suggests that the city had a minimum population of one hundred twenty-five thousand and a possible population exceeding two hundred thousand persons at its height.

With the Classic period, the Mesoamerican interaction sphere witnessed a new level of sociopolitical integration. Whereas the internal differentiation of pre-Classic societies appears to have been that of ranked kinship groups, the differentiation within Classic societies was in the form of integration based on stratified social classes.

A new level of integration developed in the Classic period as a response to the problems of control over resources which had resulted from rapid population growth. Competition between groups over resources had led to conflict. The state form of organization evolved as the most effective institution for mediating conflict between groups.

With the rise of Teotihuacán came the formalization of a pantheon of gods which spread through most of Mesoamerica, including the Rain God, the Water Goddess, the Sun God, the Moon Goddess, and the Feathered Serpent. Some of these gods were associated with the growing of maize. The largest temple platform built for the worship of these gods was Teotihuacán's Pyramid of the Sun, rising to a height of over two hundred feet, with the sides of its base each measuring seven hundred feet long. The finest temple and palace art of Teotihuacán was in mural painting rather than sculpture. Distinctive forms of Teotihuacán pottery and clay figurine styles also appeared.

The center of the city was marked by massive ceremonial structures oriented along a main avenue called the "Avenue of the Dead" (a name bestowed by the Aztecs). The city also included a tremendous number of houses and minor palaces—approximately four thousand. Unlike the ceremonial centers of the pre-Classic period, which had a small group of elite living at the center supported by a rural population, Teotihuacán was a true city. In fact it was one of the largest cities of the preindustrial world. At the height of its power it was larger than imperial Rome (Millon 1967:38). Sanders and Marino (1970:57) have noted that the entire Olmec ceremonial center of La Venta would easily fit into the market place of Teotihuacán.

The city's center was carefully planned. Some areas show periods of urban renewal. The apartments (or houses) appear almost always as one-story dwellings. According to Millon (1967:43):

> The architects of Teotihuacán designed apartments to offer a maximum of privacy within the crowded city, using a concept similar to the Old World's classical atrium house. The rooms of each apartment surrounded a central patio; each building consisted of a series of rooms, patios, porticoes and passageways, all secluded from the street. This pattern was also characteristic of the city's palaces. The residential areas of Teotihuacán must have presented a somewhat forbidding aspect from the outside: high windowless walls facing on narrow streets. Within the buildings, however, the occupants were assured of privacy. Each patio had its own drainage system; each admitted light and air to the surrounding apartments; each made it possible for the inhabitants to be out of doors yet alone.

The city was both highly stratified and diversified. The elite probably included both religious and military leaders. The remainder of the population was composed of farmers, artisans of many types, merchants, traders,

Pyramid of the Sun, Teotihuacán.

and soldiers. It is thought that the members of an apartment building may have formed a corporate group based on kin and/or occupation (Millon 1967:43).

Eventually all of central Mexico seems to have come under the domination of Teotihuacán influence. In other areas of Mesoamerica it is not really clear where Teotihuacán cultural and political dominance ceased and its ceramic and artistic elements persisted as mere evidences of influence or trade. Some authorities believe that Teotihuacán was a conquest state or an empire and that its influences were carried directly to such distant places as the Guatemalan highlands and even the Maya lowlands by military might; others emphasize effective control by a priesthood. The site of Kaminaljuyú (in Guatemala) seems to show direct influence. Sanders and Price (1968:168) have suggested that control of Kaminaljuyú allowed Teotihuacán a monopoly over the cacao trade of the Pacific coast plain. In any case, the domination of Mesoamerica by Teotihuacán ended abruptly around 600 A.D. when the city was destroyed, as legend has it, by northern barbarians.

While Teotihuacán grew to considerable political prominence in the Mexican highlands, another center within the Mesoamerican interaction sphere developed in the Maya lowlands. The first settlers of the Mexican-Guatemalan lowlands arrived in the middle of the pre-Classic period. For several centuries they seem not to have been in the main current of developments moving toward civilization elsewhere in Mesoamerica. However, toward the end of the pre-Classic period the population was drawn into these currents. By 300 A.D. they had produced a brilliant, and in some ways unique type of Mesoamerican civilization.

The basic elements of Mayan development were already present at the end of the pre-Classic period. Some of the Mayan characteristics were directly influenced by the interaction sphere of the pre-Classic; others show independent development (cf. W. Coe 1965:1401–1419). According to M. Coe (1966:54), the Classic Maya of the lowlands can be defined by the following traits: an elaborate calendar, hieroglyphic writing, temple pyramids and palaces of limestone masonry, with vaulted rooms, buildings arranged around a plaza, polychrome pottery, and a very sophisticated art style expressed mainly in bas reliefs and in wall paintings. During the first half of the Classic period, from about 300 A.D. to 600 A.D., there were marked influences from outside the area—in particular, the introduction of dating on monuments and writing from the Olmec and the Izapans and Teotihuacán influence in the form of sculpture, pottery styles, and architecture. During the last half of the Classic period, 600 A.D. to 900 A.D., following the fall of Teotihuacán, there was less outside influence. As a result, Mayan art developed its own unique characteristics. It was an art style which was basically naturalistic. Both the Late Classic Maya and the Mochica of Peru, their contemporaries, were interested in capturing the uniqueness of particular individuals in their portraiture.

Unlike Teotihuacán, the Maya Classic sites may not have been true cities—though some scholars believe that they were, others consider them elite ceremonial centers. Major centers such as Uaxactún, Tikal, Palenque, or Naranjo were nuclei for districts subdivided into zones. The average district covered an area of something less than one hundred square miles. The densest concentration of inhabitants was immediately surrounding the major ceremonial structures. The rest of the district was made up of zones which were dependent clusters, consisting of a minor ceremonial center and fifty to one hundred dwellings. The population was supported by slash-and-burn agriculture. This was somewhat less efficient than that of the highland system of irrigation agriculture and hence unable to support a population with the density of Teotihuacán, although Tikal may have had a population of forty thousand. Most of the great Maya centers collapsed about 900 A.D. for reasons which are still unclear. The fall of some of the centers was probably due, in part, to the movement of highland Mexican peoples into the Maya area.

A third center within the Mesoamerican interaction sphere was Monte Albán in the highlands of Oaxaca. According to Sanders and Price (1968: 140), the valley of Oaxaca was the only area of Mesoamerica besides the Mexican central plateau where urbanism was definitely present.

The Classic development of Monte Albán is attributed to a people known as the Zapotec. During the first part of this period Monte Albán was influenced by ideas primarily from the Maya area and later from Teotihuacán. However, as Monte Albán was sufficiently isolated, it was able to grow somewhat independently of events in central Mexico. In the early part of the Classic period there were eighteen or nineteen sites which have been attributed to the Zapotec. By the close of the Classic period there were at least two hundred sites in the valley of Oaxaca (M. Coe 1962: 124).

The site of Monte Albán was constructed on the top of a mountain spur which had purposely been leveled. While the top of the mountain is covered by a ceremonial center, hundreds of small house-platforms cover the sides of the hill (Willey 1966:145).

The major contributions of Monte Albán to the interaction sphere may have been the elaboration of a writing system and calendar already begun in the pre-Classic period. While no codices have survived, glyphs (picture writing) appear frequently in sculpture, on pottery, and painted on walls. Other than a few dates, little has been deciphered.

Monte Albán was also the site of magnificent tombs constructed for the lords of the city. The site was abandoned about 900 A.D., after which

Pyramid of the Great Jaguar, Tikal. (Courtesy of Jaroslaw T. Petryshyn.)

it was used only as a place for burials, first by the Zapotecs and later by the Mixtecs.

Also in the Classic period there arose a tradition on the Gulf Coast known as Classic Veracruz with its center at El Tajín. Classic Veracruz attained its height of development somewhat later than the other three centers of the Mesoamerican interaction sphere. It exhibits influences from

Olmec and Izapa, as well as Teotihuacán.[2] However, Classic Veracruz also added its own unique contributions to Mesoamerica.

One of the major focal points of Classic Veracruz culture was the pre-Columbian ball game, in which two opposing teams attempted to pass a rubber ball through a ring set in the wall using only elbows, hips, or legs. Many scholars feel that a strong case can be made for the origin of the ball game here—or at least along the Gulf Coast. First, the area is abundant in rubber trees, and balls for this game were made of rubber. Too, many ball courts have been found in the area (shaped like the capital letter I), including seven at El Tajín. Although the ball courts are from the Classic period, some of the equipment dates from the pre-Classic. Yokes, *palmas,* and *hachas* made of wood have been discovered and were probably the equipment used by the players in the ceremonial game. The yokes were shaped like horseshoes and worn around the players' waists for protection. The palmas were paddle shaped and fit into the front of the yokes. The hachas may have been markers or scoring devices (Willey 1966:143). Later this equipment was reproduced in stone and widely traded throughout the interaction sphere, possibly also indicating the spread of the ball game.

Andean Civilization   The Classic period in the Andes is marked by the full development of various technical processes, the flourishing of art styles, and the establishment of highly organized and militaristic states. It was also during this period that elaborate irrigation systems developed in many of the coastal valleys. As early as 200 B.C. urbanism began to develop in the Andean area. By the Classic period practically all pre-Columbian techniques of weaving were known, and both cotton and the wool of the llama and alpaca were used extensively. Unlike Mesoamerica, a writing system never developed (Bushnell 1963:70–71).

Metallurgy was well-developed during the Classic period in Peru. All of the pre-Columbian processes and alloys were in use by this period, with the exception of bronze. Gold, silver, copper, and various alloys were used. These metals functioned primarily for making ornaments—except in the Mochica culture of the north coast. The Mochica specialized in metallurgy and objects such as blades for digging sticks, mace heads, and lance points were made from copper (Bushnell 1963:73).

Mochica was the great power of the north coast during the Classic period. The Mochica conquered the Pacasmayo, Chicama, Moche, Virú, Santa, and Nepeña Valleys. Large adobe pyramids and large-scale irrigation works were found throughout the Mochica State. Subsistence was based

---

[2] M. Coe (1962:119) feels the greatest influences may have been those of the Bronze and Iron Age cultures of China.

MAP 2.5 The Classic Andean interaction sphere (200 B.C.–700 A.D.).

primarily on agriculture with secondary emphasis on fishing and herding. The region also was characterized by naturalistic pottery which depicted all aspects of life. This pottery is a major source of information about the Mochica.

The probable capital of the Mochica was the site of Moche. The site consists of a large plaza flanked by two large buildings. One of the buildings may have served as a palace. The second structure is a huge temple platform measuring 228 by 136 meters at the base and 18 meters in height. The structures were constructed of adobe bricks. The Mochica State existed from about 200 A.D. to 700 A.D. From Mochica art and other archaeological evidence, it is apparent that the Mochica were organized into a society which was highly centralized, aristocratically structured, aggressively militaristic, and internally complex (Sanders and Marino 1970:75).

The Nazca culture developed on the south coast of Peru. Like Mochica it also represented a conquest state. At Cahuachi, in the Nazca Valley, a ceremonial center consisting of at least six pyramids, each associated with courtyards, was constructed. Domestic buildings have also been discovered. The Nazca were potters and weavers of considerable skill.

The southern highlands were dominated by Tiahuanaco, a major ceremonial center. Most of the architecture of the site made use of very large stone blocks, some weighing more than one hundred tons. One of the most striking features of the site was a great monolithic gateway cut out of a single block of lava. A number of massive monolithic statues have also been found, the largest being 24 feet in height. The zone of the site has been estimated at 2.5 to 3.0 square kilometers, with a population of five to twenty thousand inhabitants. A considerable part of the site was destroyed in post-Contact times, but there appears to have been some city planning oriented along two wide avenues. The largest structure in the city center is the Akapana, a temple platform measuring 140 by 180 meters at the base and 15 meters high. Most of the monumental structures of the city center were built before 600 A.D.

During the Classic period in the Andean region, there appears to have been less of a single widespread interaction sphere than in Mesoamerica. While some contact probably occurred between the various states, they indicate regional developments with considerable local autonomy.

The Early Post-Classic Period   The fall of Teotihuacán, about 600 A.D., initiated a period of almost three hundred years in which the major sites of the Classic period were destroyed and partially abandoned. During this period three highland centers developed on the central plateau: Cholula, Xochicalco, and Tula. The Late Classic period was a struggle for power between the three highland centers (Sanders and Marino 1970:62), and Tula emerged as the victor.

Pyramid of Quetzalcoatl at Tula, the Toltec capital. (Courtesy of Jaroslaw T. Petryshyn.)

The early post-Classic period represents the spread of Toltec culture from Tula. The Toltec tradition represented a syncretism of the traits of the Mesoamerican interaction sphere of the Classic period; religious elements from Cholula; and traditions which had been carried by invaders from the northern part of Mexico.

Under the Toltecs, the Mesoamerican interaction sphere of the early post-Classic period expanded to integrate new peoples to the north and to the west. While many new elements were added to the interaction sphere, the basic characteristics of the pre-Classic and Classic periods continued to survive in spite of the three hundred years of social upheaval which followed the collapse of Teotihuacán. Whereas during the pre-Classic and Classic periods the interaction sphere had been dominated by priests, the post-Classic society was dominated by militarists, and the post-Classic Mesoamerican focus on warfare, death, and particularly human sacrifice had its roots in Classic Veracruz and Cholula traditions. The Toltecs believed that unless the sun were to rise each morning, the earth would be destroyed. It was rationalized that the only way to assure the rising of the sun was through warfare to provide human sacrifice; however, the practice most likely had political and economic bases.

The influence of Tula was widespread. In northern Yucatán, the Mayan center, Chichen Itzá shows many direct architectural relationships with Tula, as do other sites in highland Guatemala. Tula was destroyed in the twelfth century—a result of continued pressures from the north. The fall of Tula was followed by two centuries of warfare with minor centers attempting to fill the power vacuum left by the Toltecs.

The early post-Classic period in the Andes is marked by the spread of the Tiahuanaco art style and religious symbolism. During this period the central Andes came under the control of a military power known as Huari

Main pyramid at Cholula. Most massive structure of the pre-Columbian world. (Courtesy of Dean R. Snow.)

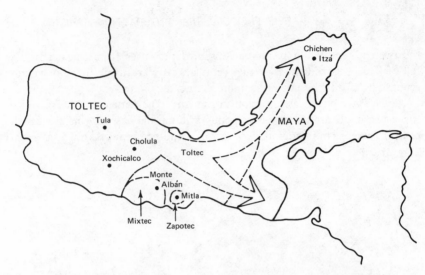

MAP 2.6 The early post-Classic Mesoamerican interaction sphere (900 A.D.–1200 A.D.).

(also spelled Wari). This society had been strongly influenced by Tiahuanaco. Possibly these people had accepted the religion of Tiahuanaco and, in turn, extended its acceptance through conquest. The site of Tiahuanaco was of minor importance by 800 A.D., whereas the site of Huari, in the same time period, encompassed an area of ten square kilometers. The central core of the city of Huari was surrounded by a massive wall built for fortification (Sanders and Marino 1970:78–79). By 750 A.D. the Huari Empire had expanded northward to Cajamarca and the Chicama Valley and southward almost to the Titicaca Basin (Lanning 1967:134). Under the Huari militarists the concept of planned compound architecture was carried to many regions. The great planned cities which followed on the north coast probably originated from Huari expansion (Willey 1971:164).

Tiahuanaco-Huari was followed by the emergence of various states and chiefdoms on the Peruvian coast from 1000 to 1476 A.D. Great urban centers were built. Trade became somewhat more extensive than in the previous period and was facilitated by a network of roads. Also during this period the aboriginal population reached its maximum.

It was during the post-Classic period that the idea of a planned center of population within a compound wall reached its fullest development in northern Peru. The most powerful group of this period was the Chimú Kingdom of the north coast. The mestizo chronicler, Garcilaso de la Vega, in his *Royal Commentaries,* described four coastal empires which had been conquered by the Inca: Chimú in the North; Cuismancu and Chuquismancu on the central coast; and Chincha in the South. Of these four, only Chimú has been substantiated by archaeological evidence. Either the others did not

MAP 2.7 The early post-Classic Andean interaction spheres (700–1400 A.D.).

Pyramid at La Centinela, Chincha Valley, Peru. (Courtesy of Dwight T. Wallace.)

exist or they represented a lower level of sociopolitical integration than that suggested by Garcilaso de la Vega (Lanning 1967:152–156).

The capital of the Chimú Empire was Chan-Chan, a site covering at least six square miles and containing ten or more large walled enclosures. Each compound averaged about twenty acres in area. Chan-Chan was the largest city ever built in pre-Columbian Peru. Within each of these enclosures were large rooms, courtyards, sunken gardens, and numerous small rooms. Tombs that suggest a ruling elite have also been discovered in the enclosures. The grave offerings included large amounts of jewelry made of gold and silver, pottery, feathered cloaks, textiles, and other materials made of bronze and wood (Willey 1971:165). Some Chan-Chan enclosures suggest specific political or economic functions, such as craft specialists, while other enclosures housed the common people. Most of the housing for the masses lay at the fringes of the center. Sanders and Marino (1970:80) suggest the population of Chan-Chan was comparable in size to Teotihuacán or the Aztec capital of Tenochtitlán.

The Chimú constructed smaller versions of Chan-Chan in other north coast valleys to serve as provincial centers. The kingdom was, in part, integrated by a system of transvalley canals, massive fortifications, and an extensive network of roads. These roads formed the basis of the later Inca highway system.

Less integration is seen in the rest of the Andes during this period. In the central coastal area there are large cities similar in plan to Chan-Chan. This area is represented by two different pottery styles: Chancay and Huancho. These pottery styles do not, however, correlate with two "kingdoms" as Garcilaso de la Vega had suggested.

On the south coast and in the highlands there was a general decline of urbanism and the development of a basically rural population with groups of villages held together in shifting alliances. The widest spread pottery styles in the South are Ica and Chincha, both of which developed out of the earlier Huari.

THE LATE POST-CLASSIC PERIOD

The Aztec Rise to Power   A period of population movement and the rise of small city-states followed the decline of the Toltec domination of Mesoamerica. The Aztecs first appear in the historical record about the beginning of the eleventh century A.D. Their legends tell of a simple beginning in a homeland known as Aztlán. These earliest Aztecs are described as poor and barbarous cave dwellers living off the land. Insects, rodents, berries, and other food provided their subsistence. They wandered for many years and eventually called themselves "Mexica" (Padden 1967:2).

The early Mexica wanderers became caught up in the general pattern of population pressure exerted by the nomadic bands of northern and western Mexico toward settled agriculturalists living on the fringes of civilization. The nomads, and some of the agriculturalists as well, are referred to under the general term Chichimec. They eventually conquered a great part of the Valley of Mexico and established their capital at Tenayuca. (Part of their military success can be attributed to the use of the bow and arrow against the spear thrower [*atlatl*] of the agriculturists.) In other city-states, the Chichimecs lived side by side with descendants of the Toltecs. Thus, two life styles coexisted in the Valley of Mexico—the barbaric ways of the Chichimecs and the civilized ways of the Toltec descendants.

The Aztecs appeared in the Valley of Mexico about the middle of the thirteenth century. As newly arrived barbarians, the Aztecs were not welcomed by the settled peoples of the Lake Texcoco region in the Valley of Mexico. Eventually the Aztecs were hired as mercenaries by the Chichimec Tepanecs of Azcapotzalco. The Aztecs were later captured by the Culhuas of Culhuacán, Toltec descendants. The Aztecs adopted some of the traits of civilization while living with the Culhuas. They then fled into the marshes of Lake Texcoco after incurring the wrath of the king of the Culhuas (for flaying his daughter). In the first half of the fourteenth century the settlers divided into two groups—one establishing the center of Tenochtitlán (which ultimately became the center of the Aztec Empire) and the other settling Tlatelolco.

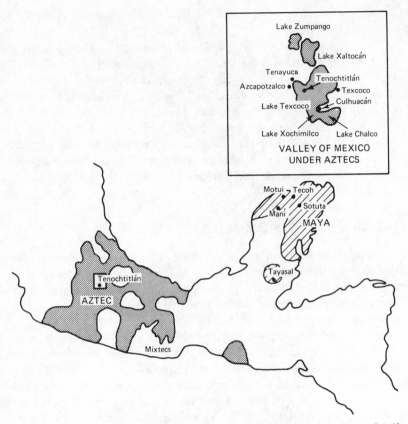

MAP 2.8   The late post-Classic Mesoamerican interaction sphere (at the time of the Conquest). (Adapted from Coe 1962 and 1966.)

By about 1375 the Aztecs felt strong enough to elect their first emperor, Acamapichtli.[3] He appears to have been chosen because his mother was Culhua.[4] Thus the Aztecs could make a claim to Toltec ancestry and be considered one of the civilized, rather than barbaric, groups of the Lake region. Yet the Aztecs were still unable to challenge the power of the Tepanecs of Atzcapotzalco who had grown to become the most powerful people of the Lake region. Moreover, the Tepanecs controlled the source of the Aztec water supply and extracted a heavy tribute from the Aztecs.

By 1428 the Aztecs, under the fourth emperor Itzcoatl (a son of Acamapichtli), were ready to challenge the Tepanecs through the help of allies. The Aztecs formed a Triple Alliance with Texcoco and Tlacopán and defeated the Tepanecs. The Aztecs took the major share of the spoils of battle, as they now represented the major power of the Lake region.

[3] Some accounts suggest that there may have been earlier rulers. The official history, however, establishes Acamapichtli as the first Aztec ruler.
[4] His father was Mexica.

The Aztecs continued to extend their powers over a vast area of central Mexico, so that by 1520 their territory extended from the Pacific coast to the Caribbean coast. Yet enclaves remained within this domain which were never subjugated; primarily, Tlaxcala, Yopotzingo, and Teotitlán del Camino. On its frontiers the border was never able to extend into the Tarascan Kingdom to the west nor to the Mixtec, Coatlicamac, and Chiapenec to the south. The Aztec Empire integrated the largest polity in Mesoamerican history—a population of five to six million and a territory of two hundred thousand square kilometers (Sanders and Marino 1970:64).

The Organization of Aztec Society   During the Aztec's earlier years in the Lake Texcoco region, the society formed a tribe organized on the basis of kin residence groups called the *calpulli*. According to Monzon (1949), the calpulli were probably "conical clans." Sahlins (1968:24) defines the conical clan as, "an extensive common descent group, ranked and segmented along genealogical lines and patrilineal [descent reckoned through father's blood relatives] in ideological bias." The calpulli was also endogamous (i.e., marriage occurred within the calpulli).[5] Common descent was traced to the original settlers of Tenochtitlán. Ownership of land was vested in the calpulli rather than in the individual.

With the founding of Tenochtitlán, a stratified society emerged which was dominated by a group of nobles—individuals who were able to trace their ancestors back to Toltec origins, primarily through King Acamapichtli. The commoners continued to farm calpulli-owned land while the nobles (*pipiltin*) were able to acquire private individually-owned lands through conquest. In many cases the nobles also acquired the conquered peoples who had previously worked the land as serfs and who were, therefore, bound to the land.

Land ownership and service are summarized as follows:

TABLE 2.1

Aztec land under private domain		
	Owner	*Worked by*
Private Property	Pipiltin	Mayeques
Communal Property	Calpulli	Macehualtin

(Derived from Caso 1963:874)

[5] Caso (1954:21), however, defined the calpulli as patrilineal, patrilocal [a residence pattern where husband and wife live with his father], and endogamous clans with territory.

Some land was privately owned by the king and worked by mayeques. Still other land was under public domain entrusted to the king, the temples, or the army and worked by the macehualtin, mayeques, and various tribute payers.

The society was divided into three major categories of individuals: the pipiltin (nobles), the *macehualtin* (the commoners), and the *mayeques* (serfs). There also existed a group of slaves who were either captives of war or individuals who were forced temporarily into slavery in order to repay a debt. A small group of merchants (*pochteca*) and artisans (especially the feather workers, *amanteca*) formed a middle sector between the pipiltin and the macehualtin.

As Aztec society evolved, the distinction between noble and commoner became more marked. During the early years, nobility had allowed some macehualtin access to the pipiltin group through outstanding war feats. However, by the reign of Moctezuma II (1502–1520) such advancement became an impossibility for the commoner. The pipiltin had become a closed group. The differences between noble and commoner were formalized through a series of decrees from Moctezuma II: (1) only nobility could now attend the *calmecac,* a school where boys were trained in rhetoric, history, religion, and astrology as preparation for entry into the priesthood or the civil bureaucracy (Padden 1967:21)—thus, in effect, limiting the priesthood and the bureaucracy to the nobility; (2) persons of commoner stock were removed from all offices and replaced by pipiltin; (3) greater demands were made on the macehualtin in terms of labor, service, and tribute; (4) the food of macehualtin was rationed; (5) macehualtin could eat only from simple clay dishes; and (6) they could wear no cottons or sandles but only a uniform dress made of coarse agave fiber (Padden 1967:85–94). The lot of the commoner became a miserable one:

He was sentenced to death for overtaking a strolling noble, or for looking directly into his face; he was slain for tax evasion or accidental underpayment; he was put to death for incest, adultery, abortion, theft, rape, homosexuality, homicide, second offense drunkenness, for wearing a garment of status mark above his station, for daring to enter a lord's palace, for entering a woodlot belonging to a noble or the state, for felling a tree for fuel; if detected in treason against a lord or the state he was tortured to death, his family and descendants enslaved to the fourth generation, his fields sown with salt, his house pulled down. If none of these sufficed, there was a catchall statute under which any plebeian could be summarily sacrificed to Huitzilopochtli for "insubordination" (Padden 1967:94).

The pipiltin, on the other hand, enjoyed many privileges. They could become drunk and engage in orgies, as long as they did so in private. They became the warriors, priests, and bureaucrats of the Aztec society, and only from their ranks could the successor to the throne be chosen. Conquest land had been plentiful and was given to the pipiltin for their private use; however, during the reign of Moctezuma II, conquest land became scarce. The Aztecs had extended their empire to its limits. Hence the pipiltin, still hungry for more private land, began to encroach on the communal land of the calpulli. Many commoners of the calpulli were forced into serfdom, causing bitter resentment on the part of commoners.

The captives of war began to diminish as the predatory expansion of the Aztecs was brought to a halt, and the pipiltin turned to the commoners once again to fill the sacrificial demands of their bloodthirsty deities. Macehualtin children became the primary victims. Some sources estimate that as many as one child out of every five was sacrificed. Parents who were reluctant to give up their children were themselves sacrificed. For very special occasions, only the nobility could suffice as sacrificial victims.

With the emergence of the pipiltin toward the end of the fourteenth

Modern Mexico City built over the remains of Tenochtitlán.

century, a true state level of sociopolitical integration evolved, headed by an emperor. The conquered states were organized into thirty-eight provinces for the purpose of collecting tribute. Each province had a capital, a governor, a garrison, and taxcollectors (Sanders and Marino 1970:65).

Central Mexico represented a symbiotic region (cf. Sanders and Price 1968) incorporating a variety of specialties and the produce of micro-environments into a single economic system which only a state level of integration could regulate. Highland crops such as grains, wood products, reeds for baskets and mats; lowland crops such as honey, cotton, tropical fruits, cacao; and specialty products such as salt and paper formed the basis of the elaborate redistributive system. Trade was widespread.

On a local level, peasants sold maize, vegetables, and poultry in markets; female vendors sold cooked meals in the streets; merchants sold cloth, skins, pipes, and other objects; fishermen sold daily catches of fish, frogs, and other lake creatures (Soustelle 1970:59). A separate group of traders, the pochteca, were involved in long-distance trade and often served as Aztec spies.

The Maya   The Maya represent another specialization within the Meso-american interaction sphere. Like the Aztecs, the Maya adopted, adapted, and contributed elements to the interaction sphere. With the exception of a three hundred year period (600 A.D. to 900 A.D.), parts of the Mayan area were often influenced by groups from central Mexico. Therefore, it is not surprising that there are many parallels between the Aztecs and Mayans. In each area gods were chosen from the same pantheon of Mesoamerican deities. The calendar system of both areas, as well as the writing systems, evolved from earlier Mesoamericans. On the other hand, the Maya developed their own unique art styles, a more evolved system of writing than the Aztecs, and a different type of settlement pattern.

The origins of the Maya have been inferred from linguistics evidence. The Mayan languages are grouped into the Penutian Phylum and share closest resemblances to the Mixezoque language family whose speakers live adjacent to the Mayan area, the Totonacan language spoken on the east coast of Mexico, and more remotely to other languages of the Penutian Phylum spoken in the northwest coast area of the United States. Glotto-chronology suggests that the Mayan languages split off from the northwest coast languages about five thousand years ago.

The earliest Mayan developments occurred in the Guatemalan highlands. During the reign of Teotihuacán, Kaminaljuyú, on the outskirts of modern Guatemala City, became a major Mexican outpost. In the lowlands, the Mexicans exerted less influence. Yet the largest Mayan center, Tikal, shows evidence of contact with Teotihuacán. With the collapse of Teotihuacán, around 600 A.D., the Mayan society evolved along an independent course for some three hundred years. During this period a stratified state began to appear, dominated by a priesthood. Sanders and Price (1968) have suggested that the development of the Mayan State resulted from contact with the Central Mexican State. While it lacked some of the elements of primary development, it was able to develop a state in response to pressures from the Mexican State. During the Classic period, the major Mayan centers were located in the jungles of the lowlands. By 900 A.D., most of these centers began to decline in importance. Following the collapse of the Toltec Empire, the Yucatán area was settled by remnant Toltec groups who imposed Mexican elements on the Mayan way of life, especially art motifs and religious beliefs. By the time of Spanish contact, the center of the Yucatán Peninsula was abandoned and the Maya were restricted to northern Yucatán and the east and west coasts.

The Nature of Late Post-Classic Mayan Society By Spanish Conquest, the Maya of Yucatán were divided into five or more small states, each with its own ruler and ruling family. The Xiu had their capital at Maní, the Cocom at Sotuta, the Canek at Tayasal, the Chel at Tecoh, and the Pech family at Motul. In each area commoners were ruled by a nobility and a priesthood that were based on hereditary positions. Thus access to the nobility and priesthood was closed to the commoner.

The society was composed of four groups: the nobility (*almehenob*), the priesthood (*ahkinob*), the commoners (*ah chembal uinicob*), and the slaves (*ppencatob*). The top leader of each of the five territories was the civil-religious leader, *halach uinic* ("true man"). The office of halach uinic was passed on from father to eldest son of a single kin group. According to Morley (1956:145), the halach uinic had broad powers: "He probably formulated foreign and domestic policies with aid of a council composed of the leading chiefs, priests, and special councilors (*ah cuch cabob*). He appointed the town and village chiefs (*batabob*), who stood in a sort of feudal relation to him, and the most important of whom were no doubt his close blood relatives." The halach uinic was the highest ecclesiastic authority as well.

Under the halach uinic were the local bureaucrats, the batabob, who exercised executive and judicial authority in their respective towns and villages. Each batabob was commander of his own soldiers. The batabob also served as judge in criminal and civil suits involving members of his community. Beneath the batabob were two or three town councilors (ah cuch cabob).

The highest offices of the priesthood were hereditary and passed from father to son. The high priests were scholars, astronomers, and mathematicians in addition to their regular religious duties. The lower ranking priests acted as diviners. They also conducted human sacrifice and attended to

Wife of Nemesio Xiu, direct ancestor of the royal Xiu dynasty, holding drawing of the genealogical tree of the Tutul Xiu family, which had been given
to the family by Sylvanus G. Morley. (Courtesy of Jaroslaw T. Petryshyn.)

other duties, such as kindling the new fire at the beginning of the New Year.
The priesthood represented a powerful adjunct to the nobility. Hostility
between the two powers may have been reduced because members of each
group were closely related to each other (Morley 1956:155–157).

Distinct from the nobility and the priesthood were the commoners.
They formed the majority of the society. Their lives were centered around
maize farming. They provided the tribute and manpower which supported
the nobles and priests. While the nobles and priests resided at ceremonial
centers, the commoners lived in small hamlets close to their fields—land
owned by their kin groups. M. Coe (1966:146) suggests that there may also
have been a serf group comparable to the mayeques of the Aztecs who
worked the land of the nobility.

Finally, the slaves represented the bottom of the Mayan social hierarchy. Morley (1956:159) lists five conditions under which a person could

become a slave: (1) by being born into slavery, (2) as punishment for theft, (3) as a result of capture in war, (4) by becoming an orphan, and (5) by being sold into slavery to repay a debt.

Both the Aztecs and the Maya shared a basic Mesoamerican calendar system based on a fifty-two year cycle. The basis of this cycle was the interlocking of two cycles: a year of 260 days (thirteen months of twenty days each), and a solar year of 365 days (eighteen months of twenty days—with an additional five day period at the end of the year). It took fifty-two years before the same two days of each calendar appeared together again. For the Maya the calendrical cycles became a greater cultural focus than in Aztec society, and more complex astronomical observations were undertaken. The Maya also used another year of 584 days based on the movement of Venus. M. Coe (1966:162) believes that tables in the Dresden Codex (a Mayan post-Classic document) suggest the Maya also reckoned a year of 780 days based on the movement of Mars, a year of 117 days based on Mercury, and possibly even a year based on the movement of Jupiter. The astronomical information formed the basis of their astrological belief system in which the movement of stars and planets determined one's fate.

Yucatán Maya hut. Probably quite similar to the pre-Contact dwellings. (Courtesy of Jaroslaw T. Petryshyn.)

The Inca Rise to Power   The Incas believed that Atahuallpa, the emperor at the time of the Spanish Conquest, represented the thirteenth Inca emperor. The line of emperors was said to have begun about 1200 A.D. with Manco Capac. The first eight emperors were rulers of a small local domain and Manco Capac was semimythical.

The early Incas wandered from their original homeland, Pacaritambo, and eventually came to settle in the area of Cuzco, which was some eighteen miles away, about 1250 A.D.—approximately the same time the Aztecs arrived on the shores of Lake Texcoco. Like the Aztec, the Inca official history claims that they were a chosen people destined to rule other peoples. The original Incas, called Tambos, carried with them a golden staff which sank into the earth at the exact spot they were destined to settle. Cuzco, the promised land, was already settled by at least two other groups, each more powerful than the Incas. Only after many years of alliances, intermarriage, and warfare were the Incas able to bring the peoples of Cuzco together and under their control. These Cuzco groups were considered Inca even though they originally represented linguistically and ethnically separate groups from the Tambos—the original Incas (see Brundage (1963) for greater detail).

As the Incas came to consolidate their power, problems of internal factions arose from the diverse groups who had only recently become Inca. Throughout the Andes, villages had been raided for tribute but not for political consolidation. Under Viracocha Inca, the eighth emperor, the Inca State was further consolidated and military expansion for some twenty-five miles around Cuzco was implemented. Viracocha Inca's son, Pachacuti, who later became the ninth emperor, was instrumental in defeating another powerful group, the Chanca, wherein the Incas became the dominant people of the Andes. The beginning of the Inca Empire is thought to date from the crowning of Pachacuti in 1438. Under Pachacuti and his son Topa Inca, the Empire reached its height through extensive militarism. The borders were pushed north to Ecuador and south to Chile. Nowhere was there another state capable of withstanding the Incas, not even the powerful Chimú (Rowe 1946:201–209). Under Topa Inca's son, Huayna Capac, the Empire was extended slightly farther. At its maximum, the Inca Empire covered more than one-third of a million square miles (Mason 1957:117).

Following Huayna Capac's death, controversy arose over succession to the Crown. Two sons, Huascar, living in Cuzco, and Atahuallpa, living in Quito, Ecuador, eventually went into battle against each other. Atahuallpa had just defeated Huascar's troops when the Spanish conquistador Pizarro arrived.

The Organization of Inca Society   As with the Aztecs and Maya, the organization of Inca society changed through time. The initial kin-based

MAP 2.9 The late post-Classic Andean interaction sphere (at the time of the Conquest). (Adapted from Steward and Faron 1959 and Lanning 1967.)

society was ultimately overlaid by a stratified society. Yet the kin group-ings survived. The basic kin organization was the *allyu*. Although many writers have described it as a unilineal clan, its structural features seem to resemble the ambilateral conical clan form of organization described for the Aztec calpulli. Like the calpulli, the allyu was endogamous.The members of the allyu traced their descent to a common ancestor, often one of the found-ers of Cuzco, built a cult around him, and kept his mummified body. The allyu was also a land holding group.[6] New allyus were formed as a result of conquest, and each new emperor began a new royal allyu (Mason 1957: 170–172; Rowe 1946:249–269). As the Inca society developed into a con-quest state, a number of new institutions on the state level of organization were superimposed on the original allyu system.

At the head of the Inca political structure was the emperor. The emperor was an absolute ruler with divine right, a descendant of the sun itself. The emperor was succeeded by a son of his principal wife and was chosen for his ability. Members of the emperor's family were chosen for the most important political positions. As the state evolved, a noble class began to emerge in which officials in the administration passed their official posi-tions on to their sons, thus forming a permanent aristocracy.

The nobility was divided into the Inca class and the *curaca* class. The Inca class represented the highest nobility. It included members of the eleven royal allyus, as well as all the inhabitants of the Empire who spoke Quechua as their native language. The latter were Incas by privilege, rather than blood, who were included in the highest nobility because there was not a sufficient number of blood kin of the royal allyus to fill the responsible administrative offices. The curaca (chief) class which represented the lower nobility was made up of independent rulers who had been conquered by the Inca. The privileges of the noble class included exemption from taxes, the right to use a litter or parasol in the manner of the emperor, as well as the right to the produce of certain land granted by the emperor (Rowe 1946:302–308).

The Inca Empire was divided into four quarters (*tawantiñ-soyo*), each controlled by a governor (*apo*) stationed in Cuzco. The four governors (usually close relatives of the emperor) formed a council of state. The office of governor was not hereditary. Each of the four quarters was divided into provinces (*wamañ*) which often corresponded to former conquered tribes or native states. The provinces had capital cities and were administered by provincial governors (*t'oqrikoq*), and the inhabitants of each province wore distinctive headdresses. The provinces were each further subdivided into

---

[6] It seems unlikely that the organization of allyu remained unchanged through time. There were probably many adaptations in response to the development of a state level of socio-political integration.

two or three parts, either moieties (dual kinship divisions) or sections (*saya*), and the sections, in turn, were divided into allyus. The provincial governor was assisted in administering the subunits of the province by a number of curacas (chiefs).

The curacas were classified by the number of taxpayers under their control. The *hono koraka* was chief of a unit consisting of about ten thousand taxpayers; the *picqa-warañqa koraka* was chief of five thousand; the *waranqa* was chief of one thousand; the *picqa-pacaka koraka* was chief of five hundred; and the *pacaka koraka* was chief of one hundred. Each of these offices was hereditary, upon approval from the emperor. The curacas were assisted by two ranks of foremen which they appointed: the *picqa-coñka kamayoq*, who was responsible for fifty taxpayers; and the *coñka kamayoq*, who was responsible for ten taxpayers (Rowe 1946:302–308).

The Inca may never have developed a writing system.[7] Records were kept by tying knots on a mnemonic device called a *quipu*. The quipu consisted of a set of strings on which knots were tied. There was a main cord to which other strings were attached. Knots of various types and positions were made on the attached strings. These knots had numerical values. Different colored string may have been used to denote the object being counted. The Inca also used a kind of abacus for calculation. Garcilaso de la Vega (1961:78–79) describes the quipu and abacus:

Throughout the Empire, all levies and taxes, both exemptions and claims, were recorded by means of knots made in colored cords. They could add, subtract, and multiply with these knots, and in order to determine what was owed to each village, made their allotments on the basis of little pebbles and grains of corn, in such a way that there could be no mistakes in their calculations. Special bookkeepers were appointed for each section, whether it had to do with war or peace, such as taking a census of the vassals, or of levies, herds, laws, and ceremonies, and they were able to give an accounting at any moment, their collections of cords and knots being as clear and exact for them as any books.

The other great class of the Inca State was the commoner class. These were individuals who lived in rural communities. The Incas did not establish urban centers comparable to those of the Aztecs. Even Cuzco, which may have had a population of two hundred thousand, was made up of a number of hamlets.

The commoners provided the labor which supported the noble class. They farmed public land, as well as land assigned to them by the allyu. They were further required to work on public-works projects, serve in the armies, and work as servants to the nobles.

[7] There are recent indications from the work of the German ethnohistorian Thomas S. Barthel that some form of writing may have existed.

Forming a small group, intermediate between nobles and commoners, were the nontaxpayers recruited from the ranks of the commoners who served as accountants, craftsmen, and the Chosen Women.[8] Some of these individuals were called *yana-kona* (servants). Later this term was applied by the Spanish to refer to all Amerinds who did not pay taxes.

The Incas took great measures to organize the people under them. Conquered populations were often relocated in other parts of the empire to reduce the possibilities of renewed uprisings. Inspectors (*tokoyrikoq*) were utilized to constantly check the officials of the bureaucracy. The system of roads begun by the Chimú was utilized and expanded by the Incas to connect all parts of the Empire.

Inca Crafts   While mastercraftsmen, the Incas applied techniques which had already been devised by earlier peoples. They spread the use of bronze throughout the Empire. Inca tools and weapons were cast in both copper and bronze. Their greatest technological skills were in architecture. Stone masonry was of such excellence that many Inca buildings have withstood the ravages of time, the Spanish, and earthquakes. The most important buildings were covered with gold leaf. The Incas were especially fond of gold and sent many expeditions across the Andes into the montaña and beyond in search of gold. When the Spanish kidnapped the emperor Atahuallpa, he was able to fill a room with gold (valued at over eight million dollars) as his ransom.

The Nuclear American Interaction Sphere   Beginning in the Formative period, there had been contacts of various types between Mesoamerica and Peru. The major exchange at this time appears to have been the introduction of maize from Mesoamerica into Peru. There are also a number of similarities between the Olmec and Chavin art styles, which suggest some type of contact. In later periods, metallurgy apparently diffused from northwestern South America to western Mexico. Within the region from Mesoamerica to Peru were found the highest levels of sociopolitical integration in the New World. It was in Nuclear America that a number of basic items first appeared: the domestication of plants, great art styles, monumental architecture, large-scale irrigation projects, metallurgy, writing, cities, and civilizations. The only major New World traits which may not have developed in this area are the domestication of root crops and possibly the first pottery. These traits may have occurred first in Latin America within the circum-Caribbean tradition. In any case, pottery was developed to a fine art

---

[8] Women picked from the villages on the basis of their beauty to become wives of nobles and warriors, as concubines of the emperor, to serve the Sun God, or to be sacrificed on special occasions.

Example of Inca architecture. (Courtesy of Jaroslaw T. Petryshyn.)

within the area from Mesoamerica to Peru. The greatest cultural and technological developments occurred in Mesoamerica and in the Andean area, with the Intermediate area playing only a minor role. This suggests that considerable interaction between Mesoamerica and the Andes may have occurred by the sea rather than over land, in which case the Intermediate area would have been bypassed. Within both the Mesoamerican and the Andean areas there were local traditions, or cotraditions, which during certain periods developed along their own independent lines. At other periods, these cotraditions were unified by the spread of Chavín, Tiahuanaco, and Incan traditions in the Andean area and by the spread of Olmec, Teotihuacán, and Toltec traditions in Mesoamerica.

Marginal Areas of South America The culture history of the regions of South America outside of the Andean and circum-Caribbean areas is less understood. In the Guianas there are ties with the Caribbean, but the region has not been sufficiently explored archaeologically to suggest a clear outline of development. What evidence is available suggests that this area may have been a corridor between the Caribbean and the Amazon, an area of considerable population movement. Village sites have been discovered in Chile and Argentina, but pottery was not present until about 500 B.C. In the protohistoric period, there appears to be Inca influence extending into central Chile. Metal artifacts, however, are not found in this area even though it is rich in copper ore. Copper casting was developed to a considerable skill in Argentina in the La Aguada region, but there seems to be no similar development elsewhere in Argentina.

Few people are found today in the Gran Chaco of Uruguay and Paraguay. The impenetrable jungle growth and desert lands make the area extremely uninviting; there is little archaeological evidence to suggest that this area was ever heavily populated. Evidence available indicates that it was inhabited by nomadic hunters-fishers-gatherers. Where permanent villages existed, they were centered around riverine lowlands.

THE INDIGENOUS POPULATION AT THE DAWN OF EUROPEAN CONTACT

At the time of the Conquest, the Latin American indigenous population occupied different levels of sociopolitical integration. It is difficult to reconstruct an accurate map of the distribution of these groups for several reasons. First, archaeological evidence is varied. In general, most archaeological data have come from the areas of highest development, Mesoamerica and the Andes. Other areas are almost completely unknown—the eastern half of South America, in particular. Second, the date of initial contact of the Europeans with the Amerinds varied from one place to another by as much as a hundred or more years. Little account has been taken of the changes in the native groups as a result of indirect contact with European culture. Many groups felt the effects of the Europeans long before they experienced actual face-to-face contact with the Spanish and Portuguese. Therefore, any attempt to classify the Amerind groups prior to contact can only be partially correct.

Sanders and Marino (1970:118) have attempted to classify the population of Latin America in 1500 A.D. on the basis of levels of sociopolitical integration. The nomadic hunters, gatherers, and fishers lived on the band level. Although these nomadic bands were at one time scattered over the entirety of Latin America, by 1500 A.D. they had been pushed to the most marginal areas of the land by more effective economic systems based on agriculture and more effective political organization, such as chiefdoms and states. When the Spanish arrived in the New World, the nomadic bands remained only in Argentina, southern Chile, part of the Chaco, part of the east coast of Brazil, and in northern Mexico. At the other extreme were the societies organized into complex political units—states. The state form of sociopolitical integration was found in Mesoamerica and the Andes.

Other parts of Latin America were organized into different types of agricultural-based societies. In some areas of Brazil and in the Chaco, people were just beginning to farm. Most of Brazil, parts of lowland Colombia, Venezuela, Honduras, Nicaragua, and the Caribbean Islands off the north coast of South America were organized on the tribal level. The people here were settled village agriculturalists not yet integrated into more effective political units.

The rest of Latin America (Panama, lowland Costa Rica, most of Colombia and Venezuela, as well as the larger islands of the Caribbean) also consisted of agriculturalists but was organized into more complex political and economic units, either tribal confederations or chiefdoms.

THE IBERIAN INTERACTION SPHERE

If, at the time of the Conquest, the Amerind societies of Nuclear America represented the latest carriers of ideas of a highly varied interaction sphere, the same can be said of Iberian conquerors. As Haring (1963:23) has remarked, "No part of Europe had suffered more from the shock of conquest or felt the impact of more diverse races and cultures than had the peninsula of Spain."

The Phoenicians and the Greeks established trade settlements in Iberia between 1000 B.C. and 600 B.C. Both of these peoples contributed to the cultural tradition of Iberia, but neither seems to have been interested in large-scale conquest or colonization. The Celts, on the other hand, were. The Celts began moving into the peninsula as early as 900 B.C. Having been expelled from their former homes in central Europe, they conquered the western areas of Galicia and Portugal. In the east and south the aboriginal peoples held their own. In the central tableland, a more sparsely populated area, a miscegenation of the Celts and the aboriginal peoples formed a population known as the Celtiberians (Atkinson 1960:17–19).[9]

Beginning in 206 B.C., the Romans initiated a policy of extensive "romanization" in Iberia. Roman colonists were relocated in the Peninsula. Within two generations, the miscegenation of Romans and Iberians produced a new population, the "mixed bloods." By 171 A.D., a colony had been founded at Carteia (El Rocadillo) specifically for individuals of mixed parentage, and slowly there took shape a racial stratification of the peninsula closely analogous to that which fifteen hundred years later resulted from the conquest of the New World. The Roman born in Rome, the Roman born in Spain, the offspring of Roman father and native mother, and the native Iberian, each had, in the beginning, his own particular interests and grievances. Gradually the dividing lines between these groups grew blurred.

---

[9] Unless otherwise noted, this section is primarily based upon Atkinson's (1960) account of the history of Spain and Portugal.

Just as earlier Iberians and Celts had given rise to the Celtiberians, so also did the peoples of Rome and Hispania merge into the Hispano-Romans (Atkinson 1960:30). By the third century colonies of Jews and Syrians were established on the South Coast (Livermore 1960:47).

The beginning of the fifth century saw the invasion of a number of Germanic groups. These groups were not united and were easy prey for another group of nomads, the Visigoths. By 456 A.D., the Visigoths had taken over control of most of the peninsula, with the exception of Galicia. Whereas the Romans had come originally in pursuit of the Carthaginians, an enemy that threatened their homeland, the Visigoths sought territory in which to settle and adopted the peninsula as their new homeland. Taking on some of the characteristics of Roman civilization, the Visigoths were able to unify both themselves and the Hispano-Romans into one kingdom. Iberia, which previously ranked merely as a province of alien empires, was now a kingdom in its own right. As a result, the Visigoths were able to command the loyalty of the people to a greater extent than had ever been possible before. Catholicism, which had been introduced into the peninsula under the Romans, became the state religion.

The collapse of the Visigoths came in 710 with the death of the ruler Wittiza. A year later an army of twelve thousand men from North Africa landed at Gibraltar under an Arab leader. The Arabs arrived in the peninsula as worshippers of Allah and his prophet Mohammed. These newcomers were Arabs, Syrians, Moors, and Berbers with only one common cultural denominator—they were all Muslims. Their opponents were not the Hispano-Romans or the Goths, but rather the Christians. The Muslims had their greatest strength in Al-Andalus (Andalusia) while the Christians remained fairly independent in the north. Some Christians remained in Al-Andulas under the Arabs and were known as *mozárabes* (almost Arab), but many more converted to Muslim and were known as *muladíes* (converts). Al-Andalus was a dependency of Damascus; however, in 756 'Abdu'r-Rahman proclaimed himself Emir of Al-Andalus. The dynasty of 'Abdu'r-Rahman ruled Muslim Spain for two and one-half centuries (Livermore 1960:70–71). By 1090, however, Islam was converting greater numbers of people than ever before in North Africa. A new crusade was organized, primarily of Berber tribesmen of the Sahara (who had recently accepted Islam), in order to bring Iberia more closely in line with the empire of Morocco. The Moors attacked with the Berber troops, the *almorávides* (vowed to God), in 1086 and 1090. Al-Andalus became a subject of the Moroccan Empire.

Throughout this long history, the Jewish population of Iberia had grown large. By paying tribute they were able to avoid persecution from the Moors; however, the mozárabes were unable to escape persecution and many were exiled to Africa, while all who could fled north to land held by the Christians. Still another Islamic group entered the peninsula. The *almohades* (unitarians) of the Atlas Mountain area were even more devoted followers of Mohammed and somewhat more primitive than the almorávides. By 1172 they had united Muslim Spain, which had once again began to fragment. These latest peoples introduced new ideas to the already complex culture of the peninsula. They included Berbers, Arabs, and Slavs (Arabized Russians).

About 1200 A.D., the Spanish Christians began to overcome the petty differences which had allowed the Moorish invaders to dominate the country in the first place. As the Christians united, the Moors lost ground, and by 1276 the Moorish Kingdom consisted only of the state of Granada. The Christian kingdoms of Castile and Aragon became more and more powerful. In the year 1469, Ferdinand of Aragon married Isabella, half sister of the king of Castile. By 1479 Ferdinand and Isabella had united Castile and Aragon and embarked on a plan to unify all of the independent kingdoms into a single, powerful country. Ferdinand and Isabella were determined to make Spain a wholly Catholic country. They supported the Spanish Inquisition which, in 1480, began to imprison persons suspected of not believing in Catholicism. Many Jews were killed and many others were expelled from the peninsula. During the reconquest of the peninsula, many Muslims of the north-south frontier were brought north into Galicia as slaves. They intermarried with the existing population and those who converted to Christianity were granted freedom from slavery (Livermore 1960:134). As the Christians began to conquer the south, the Arabized Christians were resettled in the north. A basically Muslim population remained in the southern part of the peninsula. In 1492, the year of the discovery of the New World by Columbus, Spanish troops defeated the Moors at Granada, and Ferdinand and Isabella were able to unify the entire country. When Granada fell, the Moors were given the choice of conversion to Catholicism or expulsion; most accepted conversion. Throughout the long history of conquest on the peninsula, the Basques, living in the Pyrenees, stubbornly held on to their old traditions, many of which dated back to pre-Roman or even pre-Celtic times.

The major interaction of ideas and customs outlined above holds true for Portugal, as well as Spain, with one important exception. In 1440 Portugal initiated the importation of African slaves on a large scale and eventually created a situation in which the southern district of Algarve had more Negroes than whites and most of the nation was dependent upon Negro slave labor (Herring 1968:91).

The Iberian Peninsula, at the time of the discovery of the New World, formed a highly complex interaction sphere. The concept of a "pure Spanish race" certainly has no historical validity. Iberian, Celtic, Roman, Germanic, Slavic, Moorish, Arabic, Berber, Negroid, and many other peoples contributed in various amounts to the population composition of the new states, Spain and Portugal.

The arrival of the Spanish settlers in the New World followed that of the conquistadors. They emigrated from a number of areas in the Iberian Peninsula carrying with them a variety of regional traditions. If the records of Spanish emigration to Chile (Thayer Ojeda 1919:59; cited in Foster 1960:32) are somewhat representative of Spanish New World emigration, the number of settlers from particular provinces changed from century to century. In the sixteenth century most came from Andalusia, New Castile, and Extremadura, in that order. In the first half of the seventeenth century the major migration was from Andalusia, Old Castile, and New Castile; while in the second half of that century the greatest numbers came from Andalusia, Old Castile, and the Basque Provinces. In the first half of the eighteenth century Old Castile and the Basque Provinces ranked first and second, while Andalusia ranked third; and in the last half of the eighteenth century the Basque Provinces ranked first in the number of emigrants, followed by Old Castile and Navarra. Other provinces contributed settlers in smaller numbers.

The Spanish material culture and cultural traditions adopted in the New World come predominantly from Andalusia (primarily the western part) and Extremadura, as well as much of New Castile and the southerly parts of Old Castile and Leon. For example, the Andalusian and Extremaduran type of plow is the only peninsular type used in the New World. Latin American net types and terminology seem to have come from coastal Andalusia. The New World form of fictive kinship, *compadrazgo,* is most similar to the form practiced in Andalusia. These traits represented the informal means of cultural transmission. The reason for the predominance

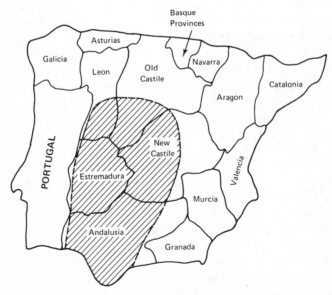

MAP 2.10   Source of Spanish material culture and cultural traditions adopted in the New World.

of traits from these regions in the New World is that the earliest settlers came from the southwest and west central parts of Spain. Many of the New World patterns were being shaped during these early years of contact. The settlers from the north arrived later and had less of an impact on the Colonial interaction sphere (Foster 1960:230). On the one hand the settlers represented informal culture transmission, while on the other, "It is clear that the formally transmitted categories of culture, in which Church and State policy were predominant, are Castilian rather than Andalusian-Extremaduran. This is to be expected, for the obvious reason that Castile was the kingdom of the ruling house and of the administrators and churchmen most concerned with government" (Foster 1960:231).

Many Spanish traits were never transferred to the New World. Others were not adopted by the Amerinds. Where a trait had no Amerind counterpart or the Amerind version was less satisfactory, Spanish traits were often adopted, e.g., new crops, agricultural implements, and domestic animals. However, where there were satisfactory native counterparts, Spanish influence on native culture was less marked, e.g., types of food and practices and beliefs associated with the life cycle (Foster 1960:228).

Both the Nuclear American and Iberian interaction spheres had incorporated highly diverse cultural traditions as a result of extensive predatory expansion immediately prior to the initial Iberian-Amerind contact. In the next chapter it will be shown how these diverse traditions underwent a synthesis during the Colonial period, out of which grew the Latin American cultural tradition.

RECOMMENDED READING

Bernal, Ignacio, 1963, *Mexico Before Cortez: Art, History and Legend.* New York: Doubleday and Company, Inc.
A readable synthesis of Mesoamerican prehistory for the beginner.
————, 1969, *The Olmec World.* Berkeley, Calif.: The University of California Press.
The best available summary on the Olmecs.
Brundage, Burr Cartwright, 1963, *Empire of the Inca.* Norman, Okla.: University of Oklahoma Press.
Andean mythology is utilized to reconstruct Inca history.
Coe, Michael D., 1962, *Mexico.* New York: Frederick A. Praeger, Inc.
A synthesis of Mexican prehistory, emphasizing the role of the lowlands in cultural development. This work should be contrasted with that of Sanders and Price.
————, 1966, *The Maya.* New York: Frederick A. Praeger, Inc.
Most up-to-date summary of Mayan culture history.
————, 1968, *America's First Civilization.* New York: American Heritage Publishing Co., Inc.

A well-illustrated account of the Olmecs. Presents the first nontechnical account of Coe's recent research at San Lorenzo, an important early Olmec center.

Krieger, Alex D., 1964, Early Man in the New World. In Jesse Jennings and Edward Norbeck (eds.), *Prehistoric Man in the New World*. Chicago: University of Chicago Press, pp. 23–81.
The best attempt at interpreting the archaeological data of early man prior to the use of pottery.

Lanning, Edward P., 1967, *Peru Before the Incas*. Englewood Cliffs, N.J.: Prentice-Hall, Inc.
One of the most recent syntheses of Andean material, including data from a number of new sites excavated by the author.

Mason, J. Alden, 1957, *Ancient Civilizations of Peru*. Baltimore: Penguin Books, Inc.
A bit out of date, but still a useful summary of Inca life. Contains one of the most extensive, readily available bibliographies on the Andean civilizations.

Morley, Sylvanus G., and George W. Brainerd, 1956, *The Ancient Maya*. 3rd ed. Stanford, Calif.: Stanford University Press.
Morley's research formed the basis of Mayan studies. The work is still recommended.

Padden, R. C., 1967, *The Hummingbird and the Hawk: Conquest and Sovereignty in the Valley of Mexico. 1503–1541*. New York: Harper & Row, Publishers.
An ethnohistorical account of Aztec history comparing what is known anthropologically with the official Aztec history.

Rowe, John N., 1946, Inca Culture at the Time of the Spanish Conquest. In Julian Steward (ed.), *Handbook of South American Indians*. Washington, D.C.: Smithsonian Institution, Bureau of American Ethnology, Bulletin 143, vol. 2, pp. 183–330.
Remains the basic source on the Inca.

Sanders, William T., and Barbara J. Price, 1968, *Mesoamerica: the Evolution of a Civilization*. New York: Random House, Inc.
Important statement of the "highland school" of Mesoamerican archaeologists. It stresses the growth of civilization primarily as a highland element. Interprets archaeological data by level of sociopolitical integration. A most insightful work.

Thompson, J. Eric S., 1954, *The Rise and Fall of Maya Civilization*. Norman, Okla.: University of Oklahoma Press.
Although some of the interpretations are now out of date, the author presents a readable synthesis of Mayan Classic civilization based on his many years of study in the Mayan area.

Willey, Gordon R., 1966–1971, *An Introduction to American Archaeology*, vol. 1, (*North and Middle America*); vol. 2 (*South America*). Englewood Cliffs, N.J.: Prentice-Hall, Inc.
A long awaited major synthesis of the entire New World. It is the most comprehensive summary available. Volume 2 is the most up-to-date summary of South America. It is well illustrated with maps and extensive photographs.

CHAPTER 3

The colonial interaction sphere

ⅢⅢⅢⅢⅢⅢⅢⅢⅢⅢⅢⅢⅢⅢⅢⅢⅢⅢⅢⅢⅢⅢⅢ

CONTACT AND CONFRONTATION IN NUCLEAR AMERICA

The Law of Cultural Dominance states that "the cultural type that develops more power and resources in a given environmental space will spread there at the expense of indigenous and competing cultures" (Sahlins 1968:2). In Nuclear America the Spanish conquerors found societies organized on basically the same level of sociopolitical integration as Spain. In both areas the people were organized into states. The Spanish had not yet experienced the Industrial Revolution. The Spanish success at replacing the leaders of the native political hierarchies in Nuclear America was based upon superior weapons and a psychological advantage; however, the Spanish did not establish a new cultural type. They merely assumed leadership positions within already established state organizations.

The situation was different in the areas of chiefdoms, tribes, and bands. Here the Spanish state expanded at the expense of these other cultural types. Had the native states remained free from outside contact, they also would have spread into the ecological niches held by the tribes and chiefdoms. On the other hand, some of the areas utilized by the nomadic hunting and gathering bands could not have been effectively exploited by the native states had their level of technology remained unchanged. The Spanish were able to utilize areas that had been marginal to the aboriginal population, such as the grasslands of the Argentine Pampas, only after the introduction of plow agriculture to the New World.

The term "conquest" is only partially appropriate to describe the period of initial Spanish-Amerind contact. In the Caribbean the initial Spanish contact with New World populations resulted in the successful domination of the islanders to the point of their extinction. The Spanish had not yet faced the highly organized, massive populations of Mesoamerica and the Andean area.

Once the Spanish took to the mainland they found a situation quite different from that of the Caribbean islands. In both Mesoamerica and in the Andean area, the empires which the Spanish encountered were basically conquest states. In some areas, the population had come under the domination of the Aztecs or the Incas only a few years before the Spanish arrived. To many of these groups, the Spanish provided an escape from subjugation and were seen as liberators, not conquerors.

In Mexico the Aztecs ruled a confederation of states. As the Aztecs conquered various groups, they forced them to supply tribute. Prisoners were offered as sacrifices to the increasingly bloodthirsty Aztec gods. When it was learned that the Spanish were marching to Tenochtitlán, the Aztec capital, many subjugated natives quickly joined forces with the Spanish. Others, like the Tlaxcalans, had not been conquered by the Aztecs and were only too happy to side with the liberators. By playing one group of natives against another, the Spaniards were able to conquer the Aztecs. As Ralph Beals (1967:452) has observed, "It now seems clear that in areas dominated by or threatened by the Aztec confederacy the 'conquest' was essentially a native insurrection against the Aztecs for which the Spanish provided leadership."

The first contacts between Spanish and Indian in Mesoamerica were quite varied and not always the traumatic conflict that the historians of the Prescott tradition would have us believe.[1] For some groups it was merely the continuation of ancient power struggles with allies or new enemies; for others it was a liberation. Initial contact varied temporally as well. Contact in the Yucatán Peninsula began in 1527, but many groups in the interior of the peninsula had no direct contact until well into the seventeenth or even eighteenth century when missionaries, settlers, traders, travelers, and explorers, as well as soldiers, were involved in the initial contacts—thus lending a different flavor to the contact situation.

In the Andes, the Spanish followed the strategy that Cortes had used in Mexico of pitting one native population against another. The Quechua, as the post-Conquest descendants of the Inca are known, either sided with the Spanish or attempted to resist them, although there tended to be no widespread resistance to the Spanish. The main opposition came from the

---

[1] Historians, beginning with Prescott, have tended to magnify the military tactics of the conquest of Tenochtitlan at the expense of examining other types of initial contacts.

dispersed remnants of the Inca armies, but there was little cooperation between these groups. Instead each local group worked independently of the others for its own particular advantage. It was only in 1536 that Manco Inca, who had been Pizarro's protégé and had learned Spanish military tactics, was able to mold these diverse groups into a fighting force against the Spanish at Cuzco and Lima. Yet less than a thousand Spaniards (190 survivors at the finish of the battle) were able to withstand the siege of Cuzco by 180,000 of Manco Inca's troops. The Spanish were successful partially because of the help they received from other Indians. Besides allying with the Spanish, the Indians were able to infiltrate Manco's troops and learn of his plans of attack.

Whether the initial contact with the Spanish resulted in liberation or traumatic conquest, the contact did bring about wholesale changes in the culture of most native groups. During the Contact period there was a rapid reduction in the total number of natives, as well as an introduction of a number of new traits and ideas. Those who were most resistant to Spanish control were often the ones who most rapidly adopted some of the new traits. Ironically, they did so in order to maintain their pre-Contact identity. For example, Kubler (1949:343–344) describing the Inca who resisted the Spanish remarks that ". . . the group depended heavily upon a commercial and piratical relationship to European culture. The great need for European weapons and horses was satisfied by raiding activities. Other commodities were acquired by a clandestine commerce in tobacco, coca, and precious metals. Its volume is difficult to estimate, but there can be no question that neo-Inca resistance relied upon copious supplies of goods acquired from Europeans and the pacified Quechua. Hence, acculturation was materially advanced by the very fact of resistance."

The early exploration and conquest in the New World was undertaken by private enterprise under license from the Crown. The *encomienda* system was introduced as a method of rewarding those who helped the Crown. Through a formal grant of encomienda, Amerind families (usually the inhabitants of a town or group of towns), were entrusted to the charge of a Spanish colonist who thus became the *encomendero*. At first the encomenderos were permitted to extract both commodity tribute and labor service from the Indians they "held." In this way they derived an income and were able to control labor groups without risk or effort. In return the encomenderos were expected to render military service (a traditional obligation for the privileged, as well as a consequence of the fear of Indian uprisings) and to provide for the Christianization of the Indians committed to their charge. Technically the term encomienda referred to the conditions of trust under which the Amerind peoples were granted to the encomendero; they were "entrusted" to an encomendero's care as a responsibility and favor in return for military and religious obligations on his part (Gibson 1966:49).

The encomienda system had its origin in feudal Europe. Spain had undergone a series of invasions and subjugation herself and was living in a social system that was based upon the privileges of conquest. "The conqueror seized the land, defended it (when he could) from his marauding neighbors, levied tribute (feudal dues) on his vassals, protected them after a fashion, forced them to serve him, and permitted no one to bear arms but himself and his retainers. In practice the feudal system became much more complicated than that, but essentially it divided society horizontally into lord and vassal, master and serf" (Simpson 1950:viii). Ideally the encomienda system was granted to provide tribute, and to a lesser extent labor, for the encomendero. The Crown feared that by assigning the land it would lose control of the New World to the encomenderos. The right to encomienda was restricted in terms of inheritance. Royal legislation established the number of *vidas* (generations) that were to comprise an encomienda's legal duration prior to reversion of the encomienda to the Crown. If the first holder of an encomienda bequeathed it to his son, that encomienda was said to be in the second vida. The grandson of the first holder accounted for the third vida and the great-grandson for the fourth. In New Spain the Crown allowed a third vida in 1555 and a fourth in 1607. In Peru the third vida was legalized in 1629 (Gibson 1966:61–62). In practice the picture was highly complex, for there were many exceptions, violations, and complications. In general, the New World settlers favored inheritance in perpetuity; the Crown opposed it.

The encomienda was just one of the attempts employed by the Spanish to utilize the labor available in the New World. At first some attempts were made at outright enslavement of the Amerind. In general this method was less effective with the Amerind than the African Negro. Besides the encomienda, the Spanish used two other means of extracting tribute, the institutions of *yanacona* (personal servant) and of *mita* (draft labor).

After the Conquest, the Spanish took many of the native specialists, artisans, and servants (the term yanacona was used in Peru) into their personal service, usually as household helpers of different sorts. These individuals became highly acculturated due to their loss of identification with the Amerind community. In Paraguay, a frontier area, the encomienda system amounted to the yanacona system due to the scarcity of subjugated Amerinds and the low level of native sociopolitical integration. Many encomenderos had less than thirty Amerinds under their control—some had as few as two or three. The natives were very poor and were barely able to feed themselves, much less provide tribute. Although the use of the encomienda for personal service was eventually forbidden by the Crown, it continued in Paraguay as the only effective way of controlling the conquered Guaraní Indians. The Spanish conquistadors of Paraguay numbered only a few hundred. Many of the Indians used by these Spanish were women who served as domestics, agriculturalists, wives, and concubines. The second generation of Paraguay was *mestizo* (of white-Amerind admixture), and the mestizo population rapidly grew to dominate the society. Although the Guaraní adapted to the Spanish culture as might be expected, the Spanish also accommodated to several aspects of Guaraní culture. The Spanish retained the system of polygyny (plural wives) which had been practiced by the successful Guaraní. Many of the Spanish, and later the mestizos, had ten or more wives and concubines. The Guaraní language has remained important, even up to the present. It is considered a national language alongside Spanish (Service 1954).

Another means of utilizing the Amerind labor supply was through draft labor known as the *cuatequil* or mita. The nature of the work varied according to the resources of the region. The mita was especially important in mining areas but was also used in agriculture and manufacturing. There were certain tasks the workers were forbidden to engage in. For example in Peru the *mitayos* (mita workers) could not be utilized to search for treasure in pre-Contact graves, in the coca industry, in vineyards, olive plantations, sugar mills and in lumber industries (Montesclaros 1859:25–27, cited in Kubler 1946:371). Ideally the mita was a system in which the employer was to pay the Amerind a standard wage. Work was to be periodic rather than continuous, so that the laborers could return to their villages after working for a stipulated period of time. No more than a few percent of the laborers of any community were to be away on mita labor at any one time. In theory a man would not be called for mita more than four or five times during his active work years. In practice, however, as the native population rapidly declined and the need for labor rapidly increased, an individual might be called as frequently as every five years. Many of the Amerinds died in the mines. Fray Motolinía (Steck 1951:93) described the mining situation at Oaxyecac, Mexico as follows: "Here for half a league round and for a great part of the way one could scarcely walk, except over dead bodies or over bones; and so numerous were the birds and the crows that came to feast on the dead bodies that they greatly obscured the sun." Some natives were too poor to return home and remained in the towns around the mines; others escaped from Spanish domination and retreated into the hinterland.

THE AFTERMATH OF CONQUEST IN THE HIGHLANDS

In the aftermath of conquest a variety of persons, classes, and interests became rivals for control of what had been won. The Indian had now been excluded as a significant competitive element and would ever afterward be held subordinate. The early settlers' fear of Indian revolt proved for the most part groundless, and no Indian uprising was ever more than temporarily successful. The conquest did resolve the question of racial mastery. The postconquest conflicts were not between Spaniards and Indians but among factions of Spaniards, who vied for domination over Indians and over one another (Gibson 1966:48).

The Natives From the point of view of the Spanish Crown, the pacification of the Indian represented only one type of accommodation necessitated by the particular nature of the New World. The systems of personal servants and encomienda were used as rewards for the conquistadors. In general the conquistador was left to his own discretion in administering the Indians. In many, if not most, areas the encomendero was not concerned about the religious welfare of his charges nor about their allegiance to the Spanish Crown, but he was concerned instead with the Amerind's allegiance to himself.

The Crown issued a series of decrees in order to block the conquistadors' exclusive control of the Indians. Beginning in 1530 the enslavement of Indians was increasingly curtailed and continued to survive only in the marginal frontier areas where it was often the only effective weapon of pacification and subjugation of the still unconquered Indians.

After 1549 the Crown attempted to curtail the privileges of the encomendero by no longer allowing him to collect tribute and extract labor. Instead, the encomienda was restricted exclusively to tribute payments. After the sixteenth century the encomienda was displaced in many areas by a tribute system directly administered by the Crown, known as *corregimiento*. As the encomiendas reverted back to the Crown, they were not reassigned to other conquerors but rather were administered by a Crown official, the *corregidor,* who was placed in charge of collecting tribute. While this was a means of curtailing the power of the encomendero, it was also an attempt by the Crown to improve the treatment of Indians. In practice, however, the corregidor was often a worse tyrant than the encomendero. The corregidor was to provide justice for the Indians, protect them from unwarranted abuse, and supervise the collection of tribute. Extortion of the Amerinds by the clergy, the encomenderos, native bosses, and others continued. At the same time, the corregidores turned out to be a worse evil than the situation they were intended to remedy. Their salaries were very small. Therefore they found it necessary to supplement their incomes with precisely the kinds of extortion they had been sent to eradicate. Being Spanish, they viewed their residence among the Indians as an exile. They surrounded themselves, illegally, with superfluous deputies and servants to console themselves (Lorente 1867–1872, vol. 1:20; Aponte 1867:544). According to Herring (1968:165), the corregidores were responsible for the greatest scandals of colonial rule:

> The *corregidor* was tax collector, policeman, and magistrate, and it was easy for him to use his power for his own enrichment. He could col-

lect as he was able, pocket as much as he pleased, commandeer the services of Indians, and farm out their labor to contractors near or far. He
could acquire the best land for himself and rob the Indian of his water
rights at will. He could buy the Indians' wares at whatever price he
chose to pay, and he could sell manufactured goods to them under threat
of slavery or excommunication. We read of *corregidores* who forced
their villagers to buy silk stockings, eyeglasses, and other preposterous
items. The *corregidores* often used Indian chieftains as aides in their
nefarious schemes, and many of these outdid the Spaniards in defrauding
the simple Indians. Even more corrupt than the *corregidores* were the
alcaldes mayores, who were assigned to lesser communities and seldom
received any salary.

After the middle of the sixteenth century, the Crown turned increasingly to a system of compulsory regulated labor, mediated through royal
labor exchanges, to fill applications for labor on the part of individuals. This
was the mita or cuatequil system that persisted up to the end of the
eighteenth century. If a trustee wanted Indian labor, he had to hire it from
a royal labor exchange at the same price as other men competing for the
same labor force, and no trustee could interfere if a royal officer wished to
assign Amerinds from his tributary villages to the enterprises of another
(Wolf 1959:191).

The various mechanisms described above enabled the Spanish to bring
many of the Latin American Amerinds under their effective control. They
were successful perhaps because slavery, tribute, and draft labor all had
their antecedents in pre-Contact times. Although many of the details differed, the basic forms were the same, at least in Mesoamerica and the
Andean areas. This did not mean that the Indians were particularly happy
with their lot. From time to time throughout the Colonial period, and even
into the Republican period, the Indians did revolt.

Some of the revolts were revitalization movements. Others, however,
resulted from the Amerinds' desire for greater access to the institutional
structure of Spanish colonial society. Several examples of revitalization
movements include the Mixton War in the Jalisco-Nayarit area, which took
place from 1538 to 1541, the Tarahumara uprising in northern Mexico,
between 1645 and 1697, and the Caste War of Yucatán in 1847 (Beals
1967:461). In 1610 the Amerinds of Costa Rica's Caribbean lowlands
attacked and burned the only successful Spanish penetration into the lowland, the five-year-old City of Santiago de Talamanca. This was an effective
attempt to drive the Spanish from the lowlands (Olien 1967:53–54). On
the other hand, uprisings that took place around Mexico City in 1692 failed
because the leadership was divided in its goals. Some favored a return to
pre-Spanish life, while others preferred greater access to the Spanish institutional structure (Beals 1967: 461).

The rebellion of José Gabriel Tupas Amaru in the 1780s climaxed a series of popular uprisings in the Viceroyalty of Peru extending back to riots that occurred in Lima, Peru during the 1670s. Most of these revolts involved the mestizos to as great an extent as the Amerinds and generally reflected the animosity of the Indians toward their corregidores. "Indian rebellion was usually conducted within a framework of loyalty to Church and Crown; these institutions were rarely questioned, and the causes of social oppression were identified by the Indians with the minor resident officials" (Kubler 1946:384–385). In 1730 Indians revolted in the Province of Cochabamba when the regional inspector attempted to take a census; while in Asangara, Carabaya, Cotabamba, and Castrovirreina, several corregidores were murdered. In 1734 there was another revolt against a corregidor, this time in Andahuailes. The Tarma Revolt erupted in 1742. The Revolt of Huarochirí began in 1750, in Lima, with a conspiracy among urban Indians. During the revolt a corregidor's lieutenant and his family were murdered (Kubler 1946:385).

Probably the most important and best known uprising in the Viceroyalty of Peru during the late Colonial period was the Revolt of Tupac Amaru. Actually the revolt was a series of connected episodes—the Chayanta rebellion against the extortions of corregidores in Viceroyalty of Buenos Aires from 1779 to 1781; the Siege of Cuzco by Tupac Amaru from 1780 to 1781 for administrative reform; the First Siege of La Paz from March to June 1781; the Second Siege of La Paz from August to October 1781; and a revolt in Huarochirí Province in 1783 (Kubler 1946:385–389). These rebellions operated within the framework of the Spanish institutions. They were not a rejection of Spanish administration as were the rebellions of Manco Inca in the sixteenth century. Instead they were primarily concerned with the abuses of particular individuals. The Tupac Amaru Revolts were also revitalization movements. The leader took his name from the Inca ruler who had been disposed and executed by Viceroy Toledo in the late sixteenth century. Nevertheless, all of these revolts, however troublesome as they may have been to the Spanish Crown, were not, in the final analysis, as serious as the discontent of the creoles.

The Creoles   The creoles were individuals of Spanish descent born in the New World. Eventually the term was extended to include others not of Spanish origin. The creoles represented the greatest threat of competition over New World resources for the Crown. While the first generation of Spaniards may have remained loyal to their ruler, those born in America identified less and less with Spain as the generations passed.

In order to perpetuate loyalty to Spain, the Crown continued to appoint European Spaniards to the most important offices in the Church and the State in the New World. Although the Europeans, or peninsular Spaniards, were relatively small in number, the fact that they held almost all positions of power was a major grievance of the creoles against the Spanish Crown.

The Crown was the absolute authority over all of the New World possessions; however, a number of institutions were established to aid the king in governing the New World and these institutions were manned by the peninsular Spanish.

In 1492 Columbus was made the first Viceroy (vice-king) of the West Indies. His powers were to extend to all lands he expected to discover. In 1503 the Crown established the *Casa de Contratación* (Board of Trade) in Seville to regulate colonial economic affairs. As the administration of the New World became more complex, the Crown established the *Consejo de Indias* (Council of the Indies) to supervise all noneconomic matters (Wilgus and d'Eca 1963:65).

As more of the mainland was brought under Spanish control, the Crown established two Viceroyalties, each with a Viceroy to administer the Spanish-held territory. The Viceroyalty of New Spain was established in 1535 to control Mexico, New Galicia (northwestern Mexico and parts of what became the United States), Central America, the Antilles and eventually the Philippine Islands; the Viceroyalty of Peru was established in 1544 to control all of the South American continent, excepting Portuguese Brazil, the Guianas and the Caribbean coast of Venezuela (Haring 1963:69–93). The administration of the vast territory under the Viceroyalty of Peru became so unwieldy that northwestern South America was established as a separate Viceroyalty, New Granada, in 1717, and the area of Paraguay, Uruguay, and Argentina was established as a separate Viceroyalty, La Plata, in 1776.

The Viceroyalties were divided into smaller administrative units, *presidencias* and captaincies-general. The Viceroys, the presidents, and captains-general were all appointed directly by the Crown. Under these officials were lesser officials: governors, corregidores, and alcades mayores.

Counterbalancing the political powers of these officials was a system of seven courts, *audiencias,* the first established in Santo Domingo in 1511. By the end of the Colonial period, the number had grown to fourteen. Like the major political officials, the members of the audiencias were peninsular Spanish appointed by the Crown. The Viceroy acted as the president of the audiencia. According to Herring (1968:159),

As a court representing the king, it was superior to all other courts within its jurisdiction. In addition to judicial duties, the audiencia was the mouthpiece of the king. Its decisions had final authority subject only to the king's veto, hence it became in effect a legislative agency. Furthermore, the audiencia had administrative and consultative functions.

At the local level the basic instrument of royal authority was the

Viceroyalty
of
New Spain
(established 1535)

Mexico

Viceroyalty
of
New Granada
(established 1717)

Bogotá

GUIANA

BRAZIL

Lima

Viceroyalty
of
Peru
(established 1544)

Rio de Janeiro

Viceroyalty
of
La Plata
(established 1776)

Buenos Aires

MAP 3.1   Spanish viceroyalties in Latin America, 1784. (Adapted from Herring 1968:161.)

cabildo (city council). The cabildo consisted of the appointed offices of *regidores* (councilors) and *alcaldes ordinarios* (magistrates). The duties of the cabildo included such tasks as policing, sanitation, justice, and tax collecting.

Because the actual number of peninsular Spanish was small, the aristocracy of the Spanish colonies in the New World was composed largely of creoles. Some of the leading creole families traced their descent from the followers of the conquistadores. By law the descendants of the conquerors and the founders of cities and towns were to be considered as *hijosadalgo* (men of noble descent), with all the privileges of nobles of a similar class in Spain. As a result there was a tendency to consider the descendants of Spaniards as entitled to special privileges with regard to the learned professions. For example, a royal *cédula* (decree) sent to the Viceroy of Peru on July 14, 1758 prohibited "sambos [of black-Amerind admixture], mulattoes and other low castes" from practicing the legal profession. This New World aristocracy resided primarily in the various capitals of Viceroyalties and captaincies-general and was composed largely of the lower clergy, landowners, merchants, and local officeholders. From this creole aristocracy came

Palace of the captain-general, Antigua, Guatemala.

the leaders and partisans of the various Spanish-American revolutions. Francisco de Miranda, martyr of Venezuelan Independence, was a creole aristocrat; other members of this aristocracy include Miguel Hidalgo y Costilla and Augustín de Iturbide of the Mexican fight for independence; Mariano Moreno, who struggled to free the Río de la Plata area from Spanish domination; and José de San Martín and Simón de Bolívar, who led the struggle for independence in a number of areas throughout South America (Robertson 1961:28–29).

A major reason for the revolts of the creole was the Crown's tight control of the New World economy. Latin America had been organized to meet the requirements of the mother country. Each area was one component part of the larger empire. The Crown controlled what could be produced, where it could be exported to, and what and from where imports might come. The Crown discouraged the production of any goods in Latin America that could compete with the products of the mother country. Generally the production of olive oil, wine, silken goods, and textiles was prohibited in the New World as these were major products of Spain. Single colonies often received exclusive rights to the production of particular crops; however, these rights were frequently reallocated. For example, cacao production in New Spain was halted in the sixteenth century, and the exclusive right to grow cacao was transferred to Venezuela in order to underwrite the economic development of Caracas (Wolf 1959:188).

In Europe the Spanish fought an unending succession of wars under the Hapsburgs. This brought Spanish industry and agriculture into complete decay, which resulted in the higher taxation of the New World colonies. At the same time, Spain was unable to export the products of her own manufacturing to Latin America when her declining industries were unable to supply her own needs (Haring 1963:294).

When the Bourbons succeeded to the throne in the eighteenth century, Spain was economically bankrupt. Reforms were initiated in Latin America in order "to augment revenue by means of better administration, to promote commercial prosperity and to strengthen the defenses of the colonies against penetration by England and Portugal" (Pendle 1963:66–67).

First the Bourbons introduced a new type of organization, the intendant system, based upon the French model. Spain's New World Empire was divided into provinces, each of which was placed under the direction of a peninsular-born *intendente* (intendant), beginning with Cuba in 1764. The intendente was given considerable power, thus further aggravating the long-standing animosity between the creoles and the peninsular-born Spaniards. Second, the Crown also opened up trading, allowing greater freedom for the colonies to trade with one another and directly with Spain. Between 1778 and 1788 Spain's trade with America expanded as much as 700 percent. This economic activity bred greater regional self-consciousness, facilitated the influx of liberal ideas from Europe, and made even more glaring the anomalies of the imperial structure. A third change was an attempt to defend better the eastern shore of South America. Spain feared England might inspire a revolt for independence which, in turn, would help to develop English trade in South America. The Crown separated Buenos Aires from the control of the unwieldy Viceroyalty of Peru and created an eastern Viceroyalty, La Plata, and Buenos Aires entered a new era of prosperity as a result of greater freedom of shipping. But in 1796 Spain entered into war with England. Once again there was a scarcity of imported goods. The want accretion that had developed during the era of trade freedom had been great. The discontent of the creoles was greater than ever before. They had developed a higher standard of living as a result of the reforms, but now all of the imported goods they had become accustomed to were no longer available (Pendle 1963:67–68).

The Church The Church became the largest and wealthiest land-holding unit in Latin America during the Colonial period. As such it became a threat to the power of New World settlers (the encomenderos) and to the Crown.

Following Columbus's discovery of the New World, Ferdinand took steps to guarantee and to legalize his authority over the Church. By papal bulls of 1501 and 1508, under the title *Patronato Real* (Royal Patronage), Ferdinand secured a wide range of controls such as appointing clergy to the colonies, control over revenues, and the right to veto papal bulls (Gibson 1966:76).

In the New World there were conflicts between various religious groups. The conflict between peninsular Spanish and the creoles extended to the Church. The *peninsulares* held the most important appointments. The creoles and mestizos, while numerically more important, filled only the lesser offices. Another important division in the Catholic Church was between the "regulars" and the "seculars." The Missionary friars—especially the Franciscans, Dominicans, and Augustinians, plus other orders—were considered "regulars" because they lived by *regular* (vows or rules). The "seculars," on the other hand, were the parish priests who were not bound by vows or rules. They were called "seculars" because they lived in the world (*saeculum*) rather than in monasteries. Yet in the New World the regulars also lived in the world, as missionaries to Indians. The seculars were limited to serving the white society. As more and more Indians became Christianized the regulars began to lose their importance, and by the second half of the sixteenth century the Crown came to favor the seculars against the regulars because the latter had generally accomplished their purpose. Nevertheless, the regular orders continued to compete with the seculars, as well as among themselves. As Gibson (1966:78) has commented, "The familiar notion of a controlled, monolithic Spanish colonial church is inaccurate. Church history in colonial Spanish America is a history of constant internal squabbles."

Throughout Latin America the Church gained great wealth. Roughly one-half of the land of Latin American was controlled by the Church. In seventeenth-century New Spain:

> The religious orders had several important advantages over the hacendados [owners of haciendas]. The most obvious was tenure: hacendados died; the orders lived on. Besides, they were not interested in holding vast tracts of idle land merely to tickle their vanity, but put it to work raising crops for the market. They made it pay. Their estates were not plastered with mortgages, nor did they have to support the sumptuous town houses that advertised to the world the social prestige of the great families. On the contrary, the orders were soon in a position to lend money, and they made no small part of their income later on by operating the bankrupt haciendas of their rivals. They were not plagued with labor shortages, for the religious, living on the premises, were under no such pressure to sweat their labor as were the hired managers of the haciendas. They were, in short, scientific farmers (Simpson 1963:ix).

Organized banks did not begin operating until near the close of the Colonial era. Consequently, when a landowner needed to borrow money, he applied to the monasteries, for they alone had an accumulated surplus to invest. They were therefore really the bank of the Colonial era (Haring 1963:178).

Sometimes the consequence of this church wealth was ostentation. There were religious as well as military adventurers who flocked to the New World. Often priests and friars, who saw little hope of distinguishing themselves in Spain, came to the New World to seek their fortunes. Most of the clergy congregated in the larger cities. Mexico City, for example, had over eight thousand ecclesiastics in a total white population of sixty thousand in the late 1700s. In Lima a 1611 census revealed that 10 percent of the population were priests, canons, friars, or nuns. The historical records tell of ecclesiastics who abused their parishioners, kept mistresses, conducted orgies, exploited the confessionals, profiteered in business negotiations, and behaved in other ways unbecoming to their calling (Gibson 1966:84–85; Haring 1963:191–192). The Englishman Thomas Gage, who came to the New World as a member of the Catholic clergy, was amazed at the clerical life he observed. Entering the town of Jalapa de la Vera Cruz in 1625, a community of about two thousand Spanish and Indian inhabitants, Gage (1929:41) observed of the Franciscan friars:

> ... those wretched imps live in those parts as though they had never vowed unto the Lord, shewing in their lives that they have vowed what they are not able to perform. It was to us a strange and scandalous sight

to see here in Jalapa a friar of the cloister riding in with his lackey boy by his side, upon a goodly gelding (having gone but to the town's end, as we were informed, to hear a dying man's confession), with his long habit tucked up to his girdle, making shew of a fine silk orange-colour stocking upon his legs, and a neat Cordovan shoe upon his foot, with a fine holland pair of drawers, with a lace three inches broad at knee. This sight made us willing to pry further into this and the other friars' carriages, under whose broad sleeves we could perceive their doublets quilted with silk, and at their wrists the laces of their holland shirts. In their talk we could discern no mortification, but mere vanity and worldliness.

Yet there were other clergy who devoted themselves to helping others. Antonio de Montesinos, a member of the first Dominican group in Hispaniola, began speaking out against the conquistadors' abuses toward the Amerinds as early as 1511. Bartolomé de las Casas began as a soldier of fortune but at the age of forty, in 1514, saw the inequity of the system and spent the rest of his life as a defender of the Indians. His most famous writing, *Brevíssima relación de la destruyción de las Indias,* published in 1552, was a bitter indictment of the cruelties to the aborigines. He claimed that fifteen to twenty million Indians had been killed by the Spanish. The book became popular throughout Europe and was translated into six languages. It furnished fuel to Spain's enemies who made capital of Spain's inequities for their own ends and laid the foundation for the "Black Legend."[2] An English edition of Las Casas, published in 1689, for example, carries the title, *Popery truly Display'd in its Bloody Colours: Or a Faithful Narrative of the Horrid and Unexampled Massacres, Butcheries, and all manner of Cruelties, that Hell and Malice could invent, committed by the Popish Spanish Party on the Inhabitants of West-India....* The Franciscan Juan de Zumárrago, the first Bishop of Mexico, was also a defender of the Indians. He was instrumental in having Nuño de Guzmán removed as president of the audiencia (court) because of the cruelties he had allowed toward the Indians. Zumárraga also argued against the practice of branding Indians and opposed their being used as beasts of burden (Greenleaf 1961). Pedro de Gante, a Flemish Franciscan, founded a school for Indian boys on the outskirts of Mexico City in 1523 (Steck 1944). Toribio de Motolinía sought to reform the encomienda system in New Spain. Vasco de Quiroga, Bishop of Michoacán, inspired by Sir Thomas More's *Utopia,* attempted to set up utopian Amerind villages sheltered from the outside world (Warren 1963; Zavala 1937).

The Jesuits represented at least one order that attempted to uphold their vows. The Jesuits were defenders of the Indians. They established

---

[2] This was the belief that the Spanish, throughout their colonial history, were a lazy, cruel, and bigoted people. See Gibson (1971) for a review of the controversy.

numerous villages throughout Latin America, and by 1750 their villages harbored over seven hundred thousand Indians. By foregoing the extravagant luxuries of the other clergy, and through rigid discipline, they were able to acquire considerable wealth. Many of the wealthy Spanish preferred to endow the Jesuits rather than the other orders. They accumulated extensive land holdings and made the land productive through scientific farming. They made use of Indian labor and Negro slaves. The Jesuits organized industries such as flour mills, bakeries, lime manufacturing, rope, pottery, textiles, tanned leather, and ships, and they held a monopoly on drugs and medicines. In short, they became the dominant economic power in all Spanish America. Their wealth and power on the one hand and their defense of the Indians against the civil authorities on the other aroused the jealousy of their rivals. In 1767 they were expelled from the colonies. The Jesuits had been especially dedicated to missionary work in the frontier areas of northern Mexico and Paraguay. In these areas inhabited by the so-called "wild" Indians, secularization was postponed for many years, and this is the reason the Jesuits were able to prosper to such a large extent. Indians were rounded up and placed in "reductions"—communities of Indians under the control of the Jesuits.

In Paraguay, if not in other areas as well, the reductions served to isolate the Christianized Indians from other Indians, but it did not really integrate them into Spanish society. The Paraguayan communities were allowed to continue because they formed a buffer against the expanding Portuguese Empire in Brazil. Once the Jesuits were expelled from Latin America, these missions began to deteriorate. The demoralized Indians abandoned the missions and either retreated into the forest to survive on a marginal existence or were forced to work on the encomiendas (Service 1954:9–10).

Following the Conquest there had been a flurry of conversion. Motolinía (Steck 1951:245, 183) writes that as many as fifteen hundred Indians were baptized in Xochimilco in a single day. He claims that four million Indians were baptized during the first fifteen years following the conquest of New Spain. Zumárraga wrote in 1531 that the Franciscans had baptized more than one million Indians in the seven years since 1524 (Ricard 1933:112). The conversion of the Amerinds, however, required both the introduction of Christian doctrine as well as the extirpation of native religious belief. Mass conversion through simple baptism was easiest. While the teaching of Christian doctrine was harder, the eradication of pagan beliefs was the most difficult task the missionaries faced. The native religions, especially those of the native states, contained certain similarities to Catholicism: many recognized a supreme deity, the saints could easily be identified with lesser deities; there were beliefs similar to heaven and hell and reward and punishment in the afterlife; the Aztecs and Incas had converts and a hierarchy of priests; the cross was a symbol used in some areas (especially the Mayan); there were native feast and fast days; and there were also rites of confession followed by penance. Yet there were other practices that horrified the missionaries: cannibalism, human sacrifice, and attributions of divinity to material objects. In the early seventeenth century, in the Archbishopric of Lima, the priest confiscated 603 chief *huacas* (venerated objects), 3,418 *conopas* (talismans), and 617 mummies (one type of object venerated as huacas) in thirty-one settlements (Arriaga 1920:13–16).

The Catholicism that the Indian accepted was really a syncretism. Native beliefs and practices fused with a veneer of Spanish-Catholic beliefs and practices. For example, in many areas of native America the Indians had worshiped a pantheon of gods and found it difficult to accept the monotheism of Christianity. Even before the arrival of the Spanish, Nezahualcoyotl, King of Texcoco, attempted to spread a religious concept that approached monotheism. He believed that Tloque Nahauque was an invisible god who created the world and upon whom all things depended. While Indians of central Mexico accepted the Christian God as the creator, the Catholic saints were equated with Aztec deities. Even the attributes of the saints were changed to make them more human, the same as their Aztec predecessors; for instance, they were made able to lie, lose their tempers, and indulge in love affairs (Madsen 1957). Before the Conquest, Aztec villages each had an idol of a patron god who they believed protected the village. The Aztec ceremonies included adorning the village idol with robes and jewels and making offerings. With the introduction of Catholicism, each town adopted a patron saint, who, like the Aztec patron god, received clothing and offerings from the villagers in return for providing them with the necessities of life. Some Catholic feast days coincided with Aztec fiestas and on those days Indians made offerings to images of Catholic saints and pagan deities placed side by side on home altars (Madsen 1960:29).

Almost every anthropological study of Latin American peasants or Amerinds shows the influence of native tradition underlying the veneer of orthodox Catholicism.

The Mestizos Like the creoles, the *mestizo* (a person of white-Amerind admixture) formed another threat to the authority of the Crown. The mating of the Spaniards and Amerinds produced a variety of mixed types who were generally given only a limited place in the New World society. Throughout the Conquest and the Colonial period, the Crown dealt with mestizos primarily by acting as if they did not exist.

As early as the sixteenth century, vagrancy had become a major problem of the colonies, with the vagabonds coming primarily from the mestizo and mulatto populations. The mestizo was allocated a place neither in the economic structure nor in the social structure because he was neither Negro nor Indian and tried to be white without success (Bagú 1952:113). While the creoles provided most of the leadership in the revolts against Spain, the mestizo, having no loyalties at all to the European rulers, often provided the manpower.

Other Foreign Powers　The other foreign powers that attempted to take over parts of Latin America were a final element in the New World arena that had an effect on the Crown policies during the Colonial period. Although Spain and Portugal had divided the territory of the entire New World between themselves, the French, English, and Dutch refused to accept this division as final, and each attempted to carve her own niche in the New World. The following discussion will be limited to the attempts of these powers in Latin America.

Probably the French were the first to contest the Spanish claims, seizing some of Cortes's ships as early as 1523 (Pendle 1963:76). The French attempted to establish a colony at Maranhão, in Brazil, but were frustrated by the Portuguese. In 1633 an expedition was sent to Guiana but failed. Other expeditions to Guiana followed, some of which were successful, and from 1651 onward the French Cayenne Company succeeded in establishing the colony of French Guiana on a permanent basis. The French colonized part of St. Christopher Island in 1627, sharing it with English colonists already there. Later the French occupied other Caribbean islands, including Martinique and Guadeloupe, and by the end of the seventeenth century had firmly occupied a part of Santo Domingo. French colonial expansion was initiated by private enterprises. Under Louis XIV, however, several powerful colonizing companies were created with state support, most important of which was the Company of the West Indies. In 1676 its territorial holding reverted to the French Crown (Zavala 1962:56–57).

The Dutch were primarily interested in Brazil. In 1621 the Dutch West India Company was chartered with the specific purpose of supplanting the Portuguese in Brazil. The Dutch seized Recife and Olinda in the state of Pernambuco in 1630. They then expanded their holdings until they controlled a territory of some twelve hundred miles in northeastern Brazil (Herring 1968:218–219). The Dutch eventually were expelled from Brazil as the fortunes of European wars changed, and they withdrew completely in 1654. They were able to hold only a small section of the northeast mainland—the colony of Surinam. The Dutch relocated in the Caribbean and centered their operations on Curaçao, which they had successfully captured in 1634. They transferred their knowledge and technology of plantation economy based on slave labor, which they learned in Brazil, to their other American possessions.

Possibly the greatest threat to Spain's New World possessions came

from England. The French and, particularly, the English made use of buccaneers in their battles with Spain. The buccaneers were centered on the
island of Tortuga, north of Hispaniola. The English government sponsored
the buccaneers, at least unofficially. At first the English were content with
the riches the pirates gained from capturing the Spanish treasure ships.
Eventually, however, the buccaneers became an anachronism—and sometimes even an embarrassment—as the English Crown began to support
different policies toward Spain. England attempted to gain a foothold along
the east coast of Central America and the north coast of South America.
Her success on the mainland was permanent only in the case of British
Honduras and British Guiana. On the islands of the Caribbean she was more
successful, and Jamaica became the English stronghold in the Caribbean.
The buccaneers continued harassing Spanish ships and periodically made
forays among coastal towns, carrying off everything in sight, often including
some of the inhabitants.

Illicit trade that was sponsored by the English, while less glamorous
than the bold exploits of the buccaneers, had the farthest reaching effect on
the Spanish Crown. While the buccaneers were an annoyance, the illicit
trade affected the basic structure of Spanish colonial administration. Spain's
control over her New World possessions was based on a monopoly over
trade. Success was possible only if she could govern who traded what with
whom. The New World population was none too happy with Spain's repres-
sive controls over trade, and English trading ships offered an alternative for
these settlers. England, which was in the midst of the Industrial Revolution,
was looking for new markets for manufactured goods. The coasts of Latin
America, especially the east coast of Central America, proved a ripe market.
Here the settlers could buy products unavailable to them through Spain and
other products that could be purchased more cheaply than from Spain.
Local officials were only too willing to turn their backs on the whole affair.
The illegal English trade was often one of the few occasions that these
officials had to receive bribes.

The trade in eastern Central America meant that the Spanish had to
restore control over the coastal area or lose it to the English. The eastern
coast had generally been ignored by the Spanish because it was still a
frontier area with unconquered Indians and hot, humid lowlands. To com-
bat the English threat, the Spanish were forced to build a number of forts
and maintain armed forces along the coast at considerable expense. For
example in 1781, more than half of Costa Rica's governmental expenditures
were for the protection of the lowlands (Fernández 1889:417).

Like the Indians, the creoles, the mestizos, and the Church, the northern European powers formed part of the arena of confrontation to which
the Spanish Crown was forced to adapt during the Colonial period through
continual changes in its policies. Although possibly of less significance than

either Spain or Portugal, the northern Europeans, by participating in the Colonial interaction sphere, have left their own unique mark on the syncretism we now call "modern Latin American culture."

THE AFRICAN INTERACTION SPHERE

The third major component in the Latin American cultural tradition derives from cultures of the various African peoples brought to the New World as slave laborers. It will never be possible to determine exactly how many Africans were brought to the New World. The records of the Brazilian slave trade were burned once abolition was declared. At the same time many Spanish records were lost, and records are generally lacking from the time slavery became illegal and illicit trade began. An educated guess puts the number of slaves reaching the New World at about fifteen million (R. R. Kuczynski 1936, used by Mintz 1961:580 and Zelinsky 1949:159; Davidson 1961:79), however, others have suggested figures as high as fifty million. Certainly the number fifty million might well be the figure of lives lost to the African continent as a result of slavery. Many individuals died on the African continent at the hands of slavers who sometimes forced their captives to march as far as a thousand miles to trading posts; others died as a result of raids and wars. Slave ships counted on losing as much as 15 to 20 percent of their human cargo in transit from Africa to the Americas. The blacks suffered from inhuman treatment, malnutrition, disease, and unfit living conditions. Sometimes blacks were kept in the holds of ships on the African coast for as long as six months waiting until the captain was able to fill his ship. Once at sea, most of the hours of the day were spent in the hold—even on good days. When the weather was bad, the captives were not allowed on deck. In the hold they were chained together, cramped into quarters about the size of a coffin—so small that a slave could not sit upright. A white eyewitness observer on one of the ships traveling to Brazil noted the following while standing on deck (quoted by Lawrence F. Hill 1932:133):

> The stench below was so great that it was impossible to stand more than a few minutes near the hatchways. Our men who went below from curiosity, were forced up sick in a few minutes; then all the hatches were off. What must have been the sufferings of those poor wretches, when the hatches were closed! I am informed that very often in these cases, the stronger will strangle the weaker; and this was probably the reason why so many died, or rather were found dead the morning after the capture. None but an eye witness can form a conception of the horrors these poor creatures must endure in their transit across the ocean.

A selective process operated on the slave population so that only the physically strongest reached the New World. The weak, elderly, and sick either were not shipped or died en route.

A slaving mythology developed in the New World that provided a social charter for the actions and attitudes of the slavers toward their slaves. Although not everywhere the same, the mythology that was held in most places included at least some of the following ingrediences—some of which continue to be perpetuated even today. If the Negro could somehow be considered inferior to the European, the slave would not have to receive the same humane treatment a European might expect. Thus the Negro slave came to be considered something mentally, morally, and culturally less than his European owner. The earliest prejudices against the Negroes center on their supposed cultural and moral inferiority. For example, Cavazzi (1687; quoted in Davidson 1961:100–101) described the Angolans as, "People more animal-like than reasonable," or, "Dancing among these barbarians having no motive in the virtuous talent of displaying the movement of the body, or the agility of the feet, aims only at the vicious satisfaction of a libidinous appetite." These same kinds of ideas were still so prevalent in 1941 that anthropologist Melville Herskovits found it necessary to present data to disprove the popular notion that "Negroes are naturally of a child-like character, and adjust easily to the most unsatisfactory social situation which they accept readily and even happily in contrast to the American Indians, who preferred extinction to slavery" (Herskovits 1958:1). The truth of the matter is that the African continent was populated by societies on a wide range of levels of sociopolitical integration. The Bushmen, who by then held only the Kalahari Desert region of southwest Africa as their area, were people on a low level of technological development. In socio-political terms, they were organized on a band level in which small family units were engaged in hunting and gathering. South Africa was not, how-ever, a major source area for slaves, nor were most of the Africans organ-ized on the band level. Instead, in both East and West Africa, peoples were organized into more complex political units: tribes, chiefdoms, and states. In east Africa, primarily the Sudan, Ethiopia, and Nubia, the effects of civilization brought to Egypt from the Near East had a strong influence. Later this area was also influenced by contact with India and Malaysia. The period from 1 to 500 A.D. saw the rise of the early empire of Ghana in the western Sudan (Murdock 1959: 45). Throughout the continent, agri-culture and animal husbandry replaced hunting and gathering. North Africa was especially influenced by the great powers of the Mediterranean—the Phoenicians, the Greeks, the Romans, and the Macedonians. In 639 A.D. the Moslem Arabs began the conquest of North Africa, converting the pop-ulation to Islam. Overwhelming evidence clearly suggests that many African peoples were living in organized and complex political systems at the time of slave raiding. In the concern for demonstrating Negro inferiority, those who admitted to the existence of kingdoms in Africa still found it a difficult fact to accept. As the African historian Robert O. Collins (1968:211–212) remarked,

> If, however, the existence of African States could not be denied many refused to attribute the origins and evolution of African States to the Africans themselves. Those who accepted African inferiority could hardly admit that sophisticated and complex state systems could be developed by these same inferior people. Thus, they insisted that such institutions of central government must have been borrowed or derived from politically superior peoples. Although incapable of proof such ideas persist to this day . . . possessed by certain authorities who argue that centralized political organizations in Africa are the result of Hamitic peoples transmitting their knowledge of government to politically inferior peoples. The myth has not easily succumbed to reality.

In the New World, as the Negroes adopted more and more of the cultural traits of the Europeans, it became difficult to defend Negro inferiority on the basis of "cultural inferiority." The discrimination against the Negro shifted gradually to greater emphasis on the supposed "biological inferiority" of the slaves as a charter for action. For some, "Negro" became synonymous with "disease carrier." Sir Harry Hamilton Johnston (1969: 14–15) observed:

> Africa is the chief stronghold of the real Devil—the reactionary forces of Nature hostile to the uprise of Humanity. Here Beelzebub, King of the Flies, marshals his vermiform and arthropod hosts—insects, ticks, and nematode worms—which more than in any other continent (excepting negroid Asia) convey to the skin, veins, intestines, or spinal marrow of men and other vertebrates the micro-organisms which cause deadly, disfiguring, or debilitating diseases, or themselves create the morbid condition of the persecuted human being, beast, bird, reptile, frog, or fish.
>
> Africa and negroid Asia—India to the Philippines—seem to have been the great centres for originating and maturing the worst maladies which have afflicted, arrested, or exterminated mankind and his domestic animals.

The belief in the Negro being a bearer of deadly diseases provided a rationale in some areas for the segregation of the Negro slaves from other populations. In other cases the Negro was said to be biologically inferior in terms of limited mental capabilities.[3]

Most of the slaves were taken from the immediate hinterland behind the coast of West Africa. A secondary source of slaves was the East African

---

[3] See, for example, *The Biology of the Race Problem*, by Wesley C. George, 1963, prepared by the Commission of the Governor of Alabama, which is a racist argument against the integration of public schools.

coast (Curtin and Vasina 1964). Zelinsky (1949:159) suggests the following numbers of slaves brought to the New World: nearly nine hundred thousand in the sixteenth century; two million seven hundred and fifty thousand in the seventeenth century; and rising to the height of seven million during the eighteenth century; with a drop to somewhat more than four million in the nineteenth century as abolition began to spread.

Generally, Negro males were preferred to females so that about three men were imported for every woman. On some plantations the ratio was as high as seventeen to one. Slave trading was perpetuated because the life span of the plantation laborer in the New World was only about seven years. Approximately one-seventh of the entire labor force had to be replaced every year (Tannenbaum 1963:35–36). Importation of these new slaves was necessary because the Negro woman tended to be barren under slave conditions. As a West Indian proprietor observed:

This morning (without either fault or accident) a young, strong healthy woman miscarried of an eight months' child; and this is the third time that she has met with a similar misfortune. No other symptom of childbearing has been given in the course of this year, nor are there above eight women upon the breeding list out of more than one hundred and fifty females. Yet they are all well clothed and well fed, contented in mind, even by their own account, overworked at no time, and when upon the breeding list are exempted from labor of every kind. In spite of all this, and their being treated with all possible care and indulgence, rewarded for bearing children, and therefore anxious themselves to have them, how they manage it so ill I know not, but somehow or other certainly the children do not come (M. G. Lewis 1929:314–315).

Thus during the Colonial period, Latin America became an interaction sphere between three basic components, the Amerinds, the Iberians, and the Negroes, each contributing genetically and culturally to the formation of the modern Latin American population.

THE COLONIZATION OF THE LOWLANDS

In the highlands a labor supply was available because of the large native population already in existence before the arrival of the Spanish. The lowlands underwent a different type of conquest and colonization. In the Caribbean, the natives were exterminated very early following Contact. On the mainland, the area was one of lower Indian organization than Nuclear America prior to the Conquest. This area was inhabited by lowland tropical forest tribes and chiefdoms. The Iberian settlers were unable to find a suitable labor supply amongst the lowland Amerinds except through enslavement, which was discouraged by the Crown. In the lowlands, the

Africans became the work force and the plantation became the primary economic and social institution of the Colonial period.

Brazil   The Portuguese began serious colonization of Brazil in the 1530s under King João III. He divided the Brazilian coast into twelve political units known as *capitânias,* each enormous in size, and he granted these political units to *donatarios* (concessionaires). The donatarios were given considerable control in such matters as financing of settlement, development, and defense. As a result, some capitanias remained unsettled. The King eventually decided that more central authority was necessary and established a government at Bahía (present-day Salvador) in 1549 under a captain-general. Most of the colonists settled along the coast, especially in northeastern Brazil.

At first the only commercial crop produced in Brazil was dyewood. However, sugar rapidly changed from a luxury in Europe to a necessity. The Northeast became a sugar producing area with the introduction of sugar cane in 1532. In 1538 Africans were imported as a work force. In the beginning, these sugar plantations were small operations; however by the second half of the sixteenth century, wealthier persons from Portugal who had experience in managing large estates and could afford to build sugar refineries and acquire sufficient labor were attracted to Brazil. During most of the seventeenth century, northeastern Brazil was the world's chief source of sugar (Pendle 1963:70; James 1959:398–401).

Whereas the New World Spanish settlers seemed to congregate in the cities, the Portuguese population of northeastern Brazil was primarily a rural population. The basic settlement was that of plantations grouped around sugar mills (*engenhos*) which, in turn, were situated near rivers. "The landowners' country mansions were of simple architecture, in a style that owed something to the Franciscan monasteries. They had thick walls, and a wide veranda in front and at the sides, with sloping roofs of tiles or straw as protection against the tropical sun and rain. Adjoining the main house were a chapel (beneath whose floors the family buried their dead) and the slaves' quarters, made of mud and thatch" (Pendle 1963:71).

The Brazilian historian-sociologist, Gilberto Freyre (1964:380), describes the plantation owner's life as "hammock-oriented," with everything done for him by his slaves:

> Slothful but filled to overflowing with sexual concerns, the life of the sugar-planter tended to become a life that was lived in a hammock. A stationary hammock, with the master taking his ease, sleeping, dozing. Or a hammock on the move, with the master on a journey or a promenade beneath the heavy draperies or curtains. Or again, a squeaking hammock, with the master copulating in it. The slave-holder did not have to leave his hammock to give orders to his Negroes, to have letters

written by his plantation clerk or chaplain, or to play a game of back-gammon with some relative or friend. Nearly all of them traveled by hammock, having no desire to go by horse; and within the house they permitted themselves to be jolted about like jelly in a spoon. It was in the hammock that, after breakfast or dinner, they let their food settle, as they lay there picking their teeth, smoking a cigar, belching loudly, emitting wind, and allowing themselves to be fanned or searched for lice by the pickaninnies, as they scratched their feet or genitals—some of them out of vicious habit, others because of a venereal or skin disease.

The estimates of numbers of African blacks brought to Brazil from the middle of the sixteenth to the middle of the nineteenth century generally range from four million to eighteen million, while T. L. Smith (1954:141–142), an authority on Brazil, suggests that even the more conservative figure is an exaggeration. In any event, the Africans became the largest population component of Brazil by the end of the eighteenth century.

It has been argued by Gilberto Freyre (1964), Frank Tannenbaum (1963), and others, that slavery under the Portuguese and Spanish was less harsh than under the English. Marvin Harris (1964) has argued against this distinction. Whichever point of view one accepts, it is clear the planters of northeastern Brazil were not lacking in cruelty toward their slaves. Freyre (1964: 305, 307) himself gives numerous examples, for instance, the tale of the planter's wife who, being jealous of her husband's interest in a female slave, had the suspected girl's breasts cut off and nails drawn; in at least one instance, a planter's wife had a girl's eyes gouged out and served to her husband for dessert in a jelly dish floating in fresh blood. Worse fate was bestowed upon the Negro or mulatto male guilty of having intercourse with a white female of the planter's family—he was castrated with a dull knife, the wound was sprinkled with salt, and then he was buried alive.

Some slaves committed suicide, others revolted, and still others escaped from the plantations and took to the jungle where they established fugitive slave settlements called *quilombos*. Probably the most famous of these was the "Negro Republic" of Palmares in Pernambuco. It spanned almost the entire seventeenth century and came to contain thousands of fugitives who formed a society modeled after the West African kingdoms (Kent 1965).

Under the pressure of competition from the rapidly expanding English and French plantations in the West Indies, the fortunes of the northeastern sugar plantations began to wane. In the south of Brazil, in São Paulo, a new style of life no longer dependent upon the plantation was developing, that of the *bandeirante*. Semimilitary expeditions called *bandeiras* were being sent into the southern interior. Their main objective was to search for gold; instead they found Amerinds and took them as slaves. The Jesuits claimed that some three hundred thousand natives were enslaved by the bandeirantes between 1614 and 1639. Intermarriage between the explorers and the

Amerind women was so common that a large mestizo population, known in Brazil as *mamelucos,* was produced.

The Brazilian Jesuits learned Tupí-Guaraní, the language of some of the coastal natives. They adopted this as the contact language of their missions—just as missionaries had learned and spread Nahuatl in Mexico and Quechua in Peru. An intertribal jargon, *lingua geral,* developed based on Tupí-Guaraní languages and was used to teach Christianity to the Amerinds. It became the dominant language of the mamelucos and eventually the language of the common people, even the Negro slaves and the European colonists (Wagley 1963:15–16).

In 1695 gold was discovered in the state of Minas Gerais; in 1719 it was discovered in Mato Grosso; and finally in Goyaz in 1725. Diamonds were discovered in 1729 along some of the tributaries of the São Francisco River (Munro 1950:265). A gold rush atmosphere developed that attracted not only new Portuguese settlers but many of the sugar cane planters who came with their slaves. In fact, the Negroes provided a great deal of the labor, as well as the technical know-how, in the mining area. Those planters who remained in the Northeast began to switch from sugar to cotton.

The Caribbean   While the focus of sugar production lay in the northern coastal area of Brazil at the beginning of the seventeenth century, the Caribbean islands became important producers during the eighteenth century. Prior to the development of sugar plantations, the Caribbean had been populated primarily by whites. In the northern European territories the white settlers, functioning as small landholders, logwood cutters, and pirateers, formed the matrix of the population. Exquemelin (1969:64–65), a surgeon who traveled with the buccaneers, recounts the plight of many European whites who were shipped to the Caribbean as bond slaves (individuals who worked to free themselves from slavery and who were sold from one master to another just as slaves). He described one planter on St. Kitts who had beaten to death more than a hundred servants.

> The English treat their servants no better but with greater cunning. The lads are usually indentured for seven years, and when they have served for six they are ill-treated beyond endurance, so that they are driven to beg their master to sell them to someone else. This request is not refused, which means they are sold for another seven years, or for three at the least. I have seen men who have been enslaved in this manner for fifteen, twenty and twenty-eight years. Often these fellows are so simple they will sell themselves for a whole year for the sake of a good meal (Exquemelin 1969:66).

Henry Morgan and many other buccaneers came from the ranks of these white indentured servants. In fact, it was the pressure from the planters who were losing their white bond slaves to piracy that was in part responsible for the demise of the buccaneers.

The colonial plantation in the Caribbean was

Initially conceived as an instrument for organizing the commercial possibilities of tropical land and labor. . . . It served as the vehicle for importing large numbers of Negro slaves and became a major determinant of racial composition and population patterns; it mined the soil and created a temporary but spectacular wealth over which European nations fought numerous wars; it made impossible the development of a European population composed of independent farmers and tradesmen, and gave rise to a two-class society divided, by racial and economic gulfs. No institution is so vital to the understanding of past and present in the West Indies as the colonial plantation, for none has so deeply affected the patterns of land and people (West and Augelli 1966:82).

In the English and French West Indies, the sugar plantation dominated the countryside during the eighteenth century. (The Spanish Caribbean holdings did not convert to sugar production until almost the nineteenth century, then filling the void left by the declining fortunes of the English and French estates.) The growth of sugar cane production, beginning in Barbados in 1640, transformed island landscapes from heavy forests to cane fields in a matter of a few generations, and reached its climax in Jamaica and St. Dominque in the eighteenth century. Much of the growth of the industry can be attributed to the Dutch who had been expelled from Brazil. They brought the technical skills for sugar production to the Caribbean and supplied credit and shipping to the English and French planters. As elsewhere in the lowlands, Negro slaves rapidly replaced earlier types of labor.

Because of the high operating costs of sugar production for machinery and slaves, the large plantations spread at the expense of the small farms. However, the size of farms also varied according to the size of the island. For example, on the small Leeward Island, the plantations averaged about one hundred acres, whereas those of Jamaica averaged about ten times that. The English islands tended toward a monocrop and were dependent upon imports from the North American colonies to feed the populations. The French planters tended to be more diversified, producing not only sugar, but also cacao, cotton, and food crops.

The sugar plantation not only changed the landscape but also drastically reversed the ratio of whites to Negroes. At the end of the seventeenth century the whites on most islands outnumbered the Negroes; by the end of the eighteenth century the pattern was reversed and the islands had many more Negroes than whites. On the one hand, the numbers of Negroes grew due to the increased slave trading necessary to meet the manpower demands of the plantations. On the other, the number of whites decreased due to the departure of the small farmers who could compete neither with the large estates for land nor with the Negro slaves in the labor market.

Miscegenation between the white planters and the Negro slaves produced an intermediate group, the mulattoes. The mulattoes formed 3 to 10 percent of the population. They were accorded higher status than the Negroes by virtue of their lighter skin color. Many, in fact, were given their freedom. Those who remained slaves were generally given easier jobs around the planter's house, rather than in the fields. The mulattoes were important as an intermediate free group because there were certain essential economic and military functions for which slave labor was useless and for which no whites were available (Harris 1964:86–87).

The planters generally established close credit ties with a merchant in Europe who acted as the agent for the sale of sugar and through whom needed supplies were purchased. The merchants were willing to extend easy credit to the planter. These advances led to gross extravagance by the planters who, although giving an outward air of opulence, were in heavy debt to the agents. A debt of £150,000 was not unusual. Because of the unhealthy tropical climate and the lack of educational and other facilities, many of the planters were really absentee landlords. Many lived in Europe, visiting their plantations infrequently and leaving the actual management of the plantation to an assistant. The French plantations were generally smaller than those of the English and absenteeism was less prevalent among the French planters than the British (West and Augelli 1966:82–99).

THE CONQUEST OF SOUTHERN SOUTH AMERICA

The Nomads and the Gauchos   At the time of the Spanish Conquest, most of southern South America was inhabited by nomadic hunters, fishers, and gatherers. They followed one of the three basic subsistence patterns: in southern Chile the Amerind practiced archipelagic shellfish gathering, those in Argentina and Uruguay practiced plains hunting and gathering, and in Paraguay they adapted to the environment of Chaco.

The nomads of southern Chile—the Chono, Alacaluf, and Yahgan—occupied the Chilean archipelago, a rugged, wind-swept, cold, and mountainous region with hundreds of islands, fiords, and channels. They traveled by canoe in small bands, subsisting on shellfish collected by the women who dove into the icy waters, as well as on sea mammals and birds hunted by the men. Another group living in Tierra del Fuego, the Ona, subsisted by hunting guanaco (an animal related to the camel) and tuco tuco (a small rodent). Those living on the coast collected and hunted the same animals as the Yahgan. All of these groups have become virtually extinct (Steward and Faron 1959:397–408).

Throughout Patagonia and the Pampas of Argentina lived hunters and gatherers similar to the Ona; the historically best known were the Tehuelche, Puelche, Querandi, and Charrua. In the Gran Chaco were other hunters, fishers, and gatherers. The Amerinds of Patagonia, the Pampas, and the Chaco were all more successful than the Chilean nomads in adapting to the Spanish expansion into their native territory. In the plains and the Chaco there quickly developed equestrian societies based on Spanish-introduced horses which were used for hunting, stealing Spanish cattle, and raiding Spanish villages (Steward and Faron 1959:408–424).

During most of the Colonial period, southern South America developed in the shadow of Peru. At first Argentina was merely a stopping place for those searching for a route to the Andes that would lead them to the precious metals. The Río de la Plata (the River of Silver) was the main route. The Indians living in the area that eventually became Buenos Aires were especially hostile. As a result, the early settlers moved to Asunción, Paraguay where the Indians were less hostile. In 1580 the Spaniards again settled at Buenos Aires with ten Spaniards and fifty creoles.

Southern South America was under the jurisdiction of the Viceroyalty of Peru through most of the Colonial period. Buenos Aires was located three thousand miles from the Viceregal city of Lima. As a part of Spanish control over trade, direct commerce between Buenos Aires and the outside world was prohibited. While Buenos Aires had an easily accessible port, the Crown insisted that all imports come by way of Peru, usually at prohibitive costs.[4] Buenos Aires thus became a center for contraband. In 1776 Spain reorganized her New World Empire and established a separate Viceroyalty of La Plata with Buenos Aires as the administrative center. As was the case elsewhere, the Crown attempted control of the new Viceroyalty by appointing only peninsular-born Spanish to important offices. While Buenos Aires became an important settlement, the conquest of the rest of Argentina moved at a slower pace. The settlers who moved into the pampas of hinterland Argentina and Uruguay adapted their way of life to that of the Amerinds. The Amerinds, in turn, adopted the Spanish horse and became highly mobile cattle raiders, even as late as 1876. Out of this syncretism of two traditions came the South American cowboy, the *gaucho*. Also in the backlands miscegenation took place between the Spanish and Amerind, producing a mestizo population that contrasted physically and culturally with the Spanish of Buenos Aires.

The one sizable aboriginal group in southern South America was the Araucanians of Chile. Unlike the shellfishers of the extreme South, the Araucanians were agriculturalists and herders. The aboriginal population numbered between five hundred thousand and one and one-half million. Those living north of the Bío-Bío River, known as the Picunche, were absorbed by the Spanish during the first century of the Colonial era and controlled through encomiendas. Those living south of the river, Mapuche and Huilliche, remained outside of the influence of the Spanish institutions during the Colonial period.

---

[4] Goods from Spain bound for Buenos Aires were sent to Porto Bello, carried across the Isthmus of Panama, put back on ship and carried down the Pacific coast to Callao and then carried mule-back across the Continent.

Gauchos of southern Argentina. (Courtesy of Scott Whiteford.)

Throughout the Colonial era, southern South America was marginal to Spanish development. Lacking gold, silver, and native labor, it was amenable only to European mixed farming. The immigrants gradually pushed out the small native population, with the exception of the Mapuche, who were finally pacified in 1884 when they were put on reservations (Faron 1968:12). It is really not until the nineteenth century, with the advent of numerous European immigrants, that southern South America became of major importance in the affairs of Latin America.

RACE RELATIONS DURING THE COLONIAL PERIOD

While the Spanish Crown legally recognized the three major New World population components of the Colonial period—the Amerind, the Negro, and the Spaniard—it tended to ignore the new population that began to develop in Latin America as a result of miscegenation.

"In a way, the Spanish Conquest of the Americas was a conquest of women. The Spaniards obtained the Indian girls both by force and by peaceful means. The seizure of women was simply one element in the general enslavement of Indians that took place in the New World during the first decades of the sixteenth century" (Mörner 1967:22). Racially mixed offspring were produced as a result of marriage, casual intercourse, and concubinage between Spaniards and Amerinds. The resulting offspring was the mestizo—generally the child of a Spanish father and an Amerind mother. Later, as white women migrated to the New World, there were also instances of offspring produced by Spanish mothers and Amerind fathers.

Initially the Amerinds formed the only available labor source for the Spanish in the New World. Each Spaniard considered himself a "gentleman" in the New World: this was his reward for participating in the Conquest. It made no difference if in Spain he had been a beggar, a thief, or an artisan. In the New World he was the conqueror who would not labor with his hands. He emulated the life styles of the nobility of Spain. To the Amerind of the highlands, as the vanquished, fell the lot of farm and mine labor.

The lowlands gained importance to the Crown only after new export crops were introduced. The development of cash crops, in turn, created a situation of potential conflict between the highland and lowland Spanish settlers over Amerind labor. The conflict was avoided, however, through the introduction of Negro slaves into the lowlands.

In the lowlands, the counterpart of the mestizo, the mulatto, resulted from Spanish and Negro mating. The mulatto's father was white and the mother was Negro. Two other fairly common admixtures of the Colonial period were the *zambos* (Negro-Indian admixture) and the *pardos* (Negro-Indian-Spanish admixtures). Through time, as pardos bred with mulattoes and mestizos with zamboes, and so on, a complex variety of "racial" types were identified in Latin America, varying considerably from one locale to another. In Colonial Mexico, for example, the following terminology was used (Leon 1924:41–47; reproduced in Rosenblat 1954, vol. 2:169):

TABLE 3.1

Español (Spaniard) male mates with an *India* (Amerind) woman and produces a *mestizo*
Mestizo male mates with an *Española* woman and produces a *castizo*
Castizo male mates with an *Española* woman and produces an *español*
Español male mates with a *Negra* woman and produces a *mulato*
Mulato male mates with an *Española* woman and produces a *morisco*
Morisco male mates with an *Española* woman and produces a *chino*
Chino male mates with an *India* woman and produces a *salta atrás*
Salta atrás male mates with a *Mulata* woman and produces a *lobo*
Lobo male mates with a *China* woman and produces a *jíbaro*
Jíbaro male mates with a *Mulata* woman and produces an *albarazado*
Albarazado male mates with a *Negra* woman and produces a *cambujo*
Cambujo male mates with an *India* woman and produces a *sambaigo*
Sambaigo male mates with a *Loba* woman and produces a *calpamulato*
Calpamulato male mates with a *Cambuja* woman and produces a *tente en el aire*
Tente en el aire male mates with a *Mulata* woman and produces a *no te entiendo*
No te entiendo male mates with an *India* woman and produces a *torna atrás*

For Colonial Peru, Blanchard (1910:58–59; cited in Rosenblat 1954, vol. 2:171–172) gives the following terminology:

TABLE 3.2

Español male mates with an *India* woman and produces a *mestizo*
Mestizo male mates with a *Mestiza* woman and produces a *mestiza*
Español male mates with a *Mestiza* woman and produces a *cuarterona de mestizo*
Español male mates with a *Cuarterona de Mestizo* and produces a *quinterona de mestizo*
Español male mates with a *Quinterona de Mestizo* and produces an *español* or a *requinteron de mestizo*
Español male mates with a *Negra* woman and produces a *mulato*
Mulato male mates with a *Mulata* woman and produces a *mulata*
Español male mates with a *Mulata* woman and produces a *cuateron de mulato*
Español male mates with a *Cuateron de Mulato* woman and produces a *quinterona de mulato*
Español male mates with a *Quinterona de Mulato* woman and produces a *requinterona de mulato*
Español male mates with a *Requinterona de Mulato* woman and produces a *gente blanca*
Español male mates with a *Gente Blanca* woman and produces a *casi limpios de su origen*
Mestizo male mates with an *India* woman and produces a *cholo*
Mulato male mates with an *India* woman and produces a *chino*
Español male mates with a *China* woman and produces a *cuateron de chino*
Negro male mates with an *India* woman and produces a *sambo de indio*
Negro male mates with a *Mulata* woman and produces a *zambo*

Although the intellectuals of the Colonial period who were concerned with genealogy could produce almost an infinite series of possible "race" mixtures, the actual resulting phenotypes (the genetic characteristics which are manifest in individuals) were classified under only a few terms in everyday life. A person was a "pure" Spaniard, Negro, or Amerind, or else he was an admixture, in which case his skin color was the primary element used by others to classify him. Lighter admixtures considered themselves Spanish wherever it was socially and legally possible. Just as in the United States where many people classified anyone with even a "drop of Negro blood" as being Negro, in Latin America the logic was reversed. Anyone with a "drop of white blood" stood a chance of being considered white. The race relations of Colonial Latin America, therefore, were not based on the strict Negro-white dichotomy of the United States. In Latin America, Amerinds as well as in-between mixtures, such as mulatto and mestizo, were also recognized.

In some ways the various phenotypical classifications played less of a role in intergroup relations than did the discrepancy in the Spanish New World between legal status and social status. Legally all Spaniards were treated equally; socially the peninsular Spanish received greater privileges than did the creoles. Legally the Amerinds ranked second only to the Spanish; socially the Amerinds ranked at the very bottom of the hierarchy. Mörner (1967:60) suggests that the various ethnic groups were distinguished by law and social status in the following manner:

TABLE 3.3

A. Legal condition:	B. Social Status:
1. "Spaniards"	1. Peninsular Spaniards
2. Amerinds	2. Creoles (New World Spaniards)
3. Mestizos	3. Mestizos
4. Free Negroes, Mulattoes, Zamboes	4. Mulattoes, Zamboes, Free Negroes
5. Slaves	5. Slaves
	6. Amerinds

Since the mestizo was initially the illegitimate offspring of a Spaniard and an Amerind woman, the term mestizo became synonymous with illegitimate and new terms such as *montaneses* were substituted for mestizo. Negroes found themselves in different social and legal situations in the United States than in Latin America. In the United States the only slaves were Negroes. In Latin America, although most Negroes were slaves, not all slaves were Negro. Whites, especially Jews and Moors, were deported to Latin America as slaves. Also, enslavement of the Amerinds was used as a mechanism of control in those areas which were sparsely populated by Amerinds. "In the countries of Latin America the institution of slavery was certainly as cruel as it was in the United States, but perhaps with the subtle difference: while the Spaniard or the Portuguese was cruel to the *slave,* the North American was cruel to the *Negro.* And this may account in part for the somewhat more ready acceptance of the free Negro into the society of Spanish and Portuguese America" (Herring 1968:94).

During the Colonial period in Latin America, the aboriginal population was the focal point of a conflict of interests involving the Church, the Crown, and the New World colonists. All three interest groups sought to maximize their respective control over the aboriginal population. Outright enslavement of the Amerinds was the method preferred by the colonists. However, neither the Crown nor the Church could permit this to happen without surrendering their own vested and potential interests in the New World manpower resource (Harris 1964:17). Therefore, laws were passed by the Crown, and encouraged by the Church, that prohibited the exploitation of the Amerind by the colonists.

Few churchmen, however, expressed any moral reservations about the slave trade with Africa. On the contrary, the enslavement of the Negroes was frequently viewed as a religious duty in accord with the highest moral principles. In some instances the clergy had slaves themselves!

The reason for permitting and even encouraging the enslavement of Africans lies in the fact that all three interest groups, the Church, the Crown, and the colonists, stood to gain from the enslavement of the African Negro. Africans who remained in Africa were thought of as being of no use to the whites, since effective military and political domination of that continent by Europeans was not achieved until the middle of the nineteenth century. To make use of African manpower, the Africans had to be removed from their homeland. The only way this could be accomplished was to purchase them as slaves from dealers on the coast of Africa. For both the Crown and the Church, it was better to have Africans under the control of the New World colonists than to have Africans under the control of Africans. This was especially true since the Negro slaves were destined primarily for work in the lowlands. The importation of the slaves from Africa would not interfere with the interests of the Church, State, or the colonists of the highlands (Harris 1964:17).

Throughout the Colonial period there was growing resentment toward slavery, with the abolitionists eventually winning. The abolition of slavery during the nineteenth century brought about the collapse of the plantation system in many of the lowland areas. Negroes refused to work on plantations because of the stigma of slavery so long attached to plantation labor. Many became small independent rural farmers, often growing subsistence crops. The plantation owners began to look elsewhere for laborers. Beginning about 1820, a number of new cultural groups were introduced into the plantation area of Latin America. Of special importance were the Chinese and East Indians, but Javanese, Portuguese, and others were also imported.

A new period of foreign settlement was beginning. The European nations, especially Germany and Italy, sent colonists to the New World. Most of them settled in Chile, Argentina, Uruguay, and southern Brazil. Their descendants form a sizable part of the population today in these countries.

While the interaction spheres of the pre-Contact period represented a diversity of beliefs and traditions, these were brought together into a single Colonial interaction sphere dominated by Spanish institutions. Yet these institutions were not the same in the New World as they were in Spain. In Latin America the institutions were adapted to the unique New World situation.

RECOMMENDED READING

Bishro, Charles J., 1956, The Iberian Background of Latin American History: Recent Progress and Continuity Problems. *Hispanic American Historical Review* 36:50–90.
   An excellent summary of what has been learned and what has not yet been learned about the Spanish settlers of the New World.
Boxer, C. R., 1962, *The Golden Age of Brazil, 1695–1750: Growing Pains of a Colonial Society.* Berkeley, Calif.: University of California Press.
   The best discussion of the colonial development of Brazil.
Chevalier, François, 1963, *Land and Society in Colonial Mexico: the Great Hacienda.* Berkeley, Calif.: University of California Press.
   One of the very few discussions of seventeenth-century Mexico.
Foster, George M., 1960, *Culture and Conquest: America's Spanish Heritage.* Chicago: Quadrangle Books, Inc.
   An important attempt to trace the Spanish traits that diffused to the New World and the regions of Spain they represented, as well as the syncretisms that occurred.
Gibson, Charles, 1964, *The Aztecs Under Spanish Rule: A History of the Indians of the Valley of Mexico, 1519–1810.* Stanford, Calif.: Stanford University Press.
   A monumental work dealing with the post-Contact situation among the Aztecs and their descendants.
————, 1966, *Spain in America.* New York: Harper and Row, Publishers.
   A highly recommended introduction to Latin American history.
Harris, Marvin, 1964, *Patterns of Race in the Americas.* New York: Walker and Company.
   This book should be read in conjunction with Tannenbaum for differing interpretations of Spanish-black relations.

Johnston, Sir Harry, 1910, *The Negro in the New World*. London: Methuen & Co., Ltd.
Remains one of the most comprehensive studies of the diversity of Negro populations in the New World.

Kubler, George, 1946, The Quechua in the Colonial World. In Julian Steward (ed.), *Handbook of South American Indians*. Washington, D.C.: Smithsonian Institution, Bureau of American Ethnology, Bulletin 143, vol. 2, pp. 331–410.
The study remains the best review of the descendants of the Inca during the Colonial period.

Mörner, Magnus, 1967, *Race Mixture in the History of Latin America*. Boston: Little, Brown and Company.
The best short summary of race relations during the Colonial period. It includes an extensive bibliography.

Sauer, Carl O., 1966, *The Early Spanish Main*. Berkeley, Calif.: University of California Press.
This work describes the initial attempts by the Spanish at establishing a New World Empire.

Service, Elman R., 1955, Indian-European Relations in Colonial Latin America. *American Anthropologist* 57:411–425.
Describes how the native levels of development affected the nature of Spanish control in various areas of Latin America.

Simpson, Lesley B., 1950, *The Encomienda in New Spain*. Berkeley, Calif.: University of California Press.
The standard work on an important colonial institution.

Tannenbaum, Frank, 1947, *Slave and Citizen: the Negro in the Americas*. New York: Alfred A. Knopf.
An early attempt to describe the relations of blacks with the Europeans during the Colonial period.

CHAPTER 4

The modern Latin American interaction spheres

▣▣▣▣▣▣▣▣▣▣▣▣▣▣▣▣▣▣▣▣▣▣▣▣▣▣

FOLLOWING INDEPENDENCE

Having successfully led wars of independence against the Spanish, the creoles took control of the newly established Latin American republics but maintained a way of life and economic organization modeled after the Spanish they had grown to hate.

The Highlands   In the highland areas, the encomienda, the corregimiento, and the mita of the Spanish Colonial period gave rise to the *hacienda,* beginning in some areas as early as the end of the sixteenth century and dominating the highland landscape by the nineteenth century. The *reducción* was another institution also directly related to the other Spanish institutions. Throughout the Colonial period the Crown collected Indians into nucleated villages that were known as *reducciones* or *congregaciones.* By clustering the Indians in one location, better use could be made of their labor. While the colonists favored the collection of Indians, especially in areas where they normally were dispersed, they were unhappy with the land tenure system devised by the Crown for these Indian villages. Land was given to the Amerind villages under communal tenure. Further, it could neither be sold nor pawned. As a result, some of the coveted lands remained in the hands of the Indians until Independence. The Republican period saw the expansion of private landholdings at the expense of these communal lands.

Hacienda fortification.

The hacienda was a state within a state, a power domain unto itself.
The hacienda was the privately owned landed estate. If a colonist had been
fortunate enough to obtain ownership of land, he still had problems of
obtaining labor. The *hacendado* enticed Indians to settle on or near his
land. He agreed to pay their tribute or taxes and to give them wages. He also
allowed the worker to purchase goods on credit from the hacienda store
(*tienda de raya*) and to borrow small sums of money. In return the Indian
promised to repay the debt through labor. (The workers were known as
gananes or *peones*.) In this way the haciendas were able to maintain a
permanent work force through debt peonage. As Eric Wolf (1959:204) has
described the hacienda:

Organized for commercial ends, the hacienda proved strangely hybrid
in its characteristics. It combined in practice features which seem oddly
contradictory in theory. Geared to sell products in a market, it yet aimed
at having little to sell. Voracious for land, it deliberately made inefficient
use of it. Operating with large numbers of workers, it nevertheless per-
sonalized the relation between worker and owner. Created to produce
a profit, it consumed a large part of its substance in conspicuous and
unproductive displays of wealth. Some writers have called the institution "feudal," because it involved the rule of a dominant landowner
over his dependent laborers. But it lacked the legal guaranties of security which compensated the feudal serf for his lack of liberty and self-
determination. Others have called it "capitalist," and so it was, but
strangely different from the commercial establishments in agriculture
with which we are familiar in the modern commercial and industrial
world.

The hacienda generally consisted of a big house (the house of the hacendado), with fortress-like high walls, parapets, and turrets used as defense against raids, a chapel, store, outbuilding, and jail, plus houses for the permanent resident workers. Other laborers worked on the hacienda while continuing to live in their native villages and maintaining their own plots.

The hacendado ruled the hacienda as a Spanish father ruled his family. The workers were his "children" and he was their "father." "Children" who obeyed and were faithful to their *patrón* were rewarded with small favors. Those who disobeyed were whipped, tortured, or even killed. On the hacienda, the relationship between patron and peon was based on direct, face-to-face interaction.

The hacienda seems to have developed as an adaptive institution during the seventeenth century, the century of Depression. While tied to cash cropping, the hacienda tended to be fairly diverse and fairly self-sufficient. In times of recessions in the market, it was able to survive due to its diversity.

The haciendas were tied together by communication networks. Interspersed through the areas dominated by the haciendas were the Indian villages. Unlike the haciendas, the Indian villages were separated from one another by different languages and customs. Especially following Independence, the haciendas encroached more and more on the communally held village lands.

Governments from time to time enacted laws which put an end to communal land. These laws generally made it easier for the hacendado to acquire more land. As great numbers of Indians were removed from their landholdings, they became increasingly dependent on the haciendas for their survival. In Mexico, for example, by 1910 some 8,245 haciendas controlled 40 percent of the nation's land. Ninety-six percent of the families living in rural areas owned no land whatsoever; the majority worked as peons on the hacienda (West and Augelli 1966:319).

The Amerind villages did not completely disappear, however. In some cases they represented an advantage for the hacendado. Labor could be drawn from these villages during peak seasons, but the inhabitants would not have to be cared for the rest of the year. For the most part, the traditional hacienda farming cycle did not conflict with the native farming cycle.

The mestizos were neither a part of the communal village nor a part of the hacienda. While the Amerind remained group oriented, the mestizo learned to act as an individual. While the hacendado was concerned with local power, it was the mestizo who learned to operate at the national level and fill the power vacuum left by the Spanish. The hacienda and the Indian villages represented forces of regionalism; the mestizo, forces of centralism and nationalism. While the haciendas and Indian villages were committed to agricultural development, it was the mestizo, often through the backing of foreign investment, who was committed to more industrialized development, the extraction of raw minerals, petroleum exploitation, textile production, and railroad construction (Wolf 1959:233–256).

The Lowlands   In the lowlands, Independence (some areas have yet to gain their independence) brought about less of a dramatic change than did the emancipation of the slaves.

Once freed from slavery the Negroes were reluctant to continue working on the plantations. Plantation work to this day carries the stigma of slavery. The blacks became a freed peasantry. Many took to the hill lands and other areas not used by the coastal plantation. In their new surroundings they practiced subsistence farming and in some areas established communal villages. Others moved to the cities to become shopkeepers and manual laborers.

The plantations were in dire need of labor and began to look to other countries for surplus labor. The East Indians were imported in large numbers and proved to be the most satisfactory workers, although many other foreigners were brought to the lowlands. The early foreigners came as indentured servants, but later the workers became wage laborers.

The plantations changed in their organization. Out of the family-owned colonial plantation grew the modern factory-in-the-field type of plantation. The modern plantations are huge land holdings generally devoted to a single crop such as sugar cane. The fortunes of the entire plantation depend upon the success of the single crop. These plantations are tied to international markets and are often controlled by international corporations. The international corporations, like the United Fruit Company, hold plantation operations in more than one country. By threatening to move out of a country, the large corporations have been able to influence government decision making in the form of reduced tariffs and maintain a certain freedom of control over the employees. Labor unions developed to promote worker rights, but in some areas the union remained weak due to the companies' ability to group individuals against each other. The face-to-face relations of the hacienda are not found on the modern plantation. The managers often do not even know the names of their workers. Anyone doing a specific task receives a specific pay; to the manager, one man is then interchangeable for another.

The hacienda retarded nationalism because of its control over local power, though the hacienda did act as an acculturating agent in that the Indians who became tied to the hacienda through debt peonage lost most of their Indian heritage and incorporated the elements of modern Latin America into their way of life. The modern plantation, on the other hand, through foreign investment and often foreign control, retarded nationalism by dominating the effective control over territory at the expense of the government. It also introduced culturally distinct populations that did not accept the values of the state. As overpopulation has increased in the lowlands in recent years, the foreign laborers have been competing with nationals for work.

MODERN LATIN AMERICAN SOCIETY

Modern Latin American Society   The nature of modern Latin American society is difficult to discern. Often it is a paradox: revolution and stability; nationalism and regionalism; a growing middle class in a dual sector society.

Despite recent industrialization, frequent revolutions, and increasing nationalization, the structure of Latin American societies has remained surprisingly stable. This stability is seen by many as excessive stability retarding development. According to Claudio Véliz (1965:1):

In spite of its reputation for frequent and violent political upheaval, perhaps the principal contemporary problem of Latin America is excessive stability. There exists in the region a resilient traditional structure of institutions, hierarchical arrangements, and attitudes which conditions every aspect of political behavior and which has survived centuries of colonial government, movements for independence, foreign wars and invasions, domestic revolutions, and a confusingly large number of lesser palace revolts. More recently it has not only successfully resisted the impact of technological innovation and industrialization, but appears to have been strengthened by it.

A similar point of view is expressed by Osvaldo Sunkel, the Chilean economist, in an analysis of change in Chile. He suggests that although there has been rapid and intense change within Chilean society during the past thirty or forty years, there is a persistence of the basic institutional structure which, he suggests, "exerts a limiting and controlling influence over the process of social change" (Sunkel 1965:116).

Groups most commonly identified within Latin American society as agents of reform are often less concerned with reform than with greater access to power within the society and greater participation in the already well-established institutional structures (Véliz 1967:3–4). These groups include the military (cf. Nun 1967), the peasant (cf. Hobsbawm 1967), the progressive clergy (cf. de Kadt 1967), and the middle class. Each of these groups claims that it speaks for an emerging national consensus and that its interests are the authentic interests of the future nation.

Very often these groups, in their efforts to establish the nation and to support their claim to be the genuine representative of this nation, seek to gain control of the state. The group that controls the state cannot represent the nation if the nation does not exist, but control of the state very often gives this group distinct advantages over its competitors: money, police and military support, direct access to the communications media, and a chance to win broader support by performing services for the population (Baily 1971:7).

A nation exists because it commands men's loyalties through a broad census on fundamental values and procedures. Such a consensus has yet to emerge in most Latin American countries. Nationalism in Latin America has often developed to provide a legitimacy to those in power.

Following Independence there was considerable reliance on foreign powers. According to Whitaker and Jordan (1966:14), the new ruling elites believed they could best develop the new nation by drawing as fully as possible on foreign investments, foreign enterprise, and foreign culture. They increasingly looked to England, France, and the United States for models.

Samuel L. Baily (1971:13–16) suggests that there were a number of obstacles as well as favorable factors affecting the development of nationalism in the nineteenth century. Localism or regionalism, personalist politics, rigid class distinctions, a foreign controlled Church, and the rejection of the past as a basis for unity all provided barriers to nationalism. On the other hand, wars and territorial struggles, a developing sense of distinct identity, a drive to modernize which improved communication networks allowing greater centralized governmental control, and the process of miscegenation helped to stimulate the development of nationalism.

During the early twentieth century the United States expanded its political influence and economic interests in Latin America. This, in turn, provoked strong feelings of anti-North Americanism. The Latin American countries became interested in industrializing and modernizing but felt that many of the North American companies were challenging the sovereignty of the nations by their attempts to influence government decision making. In some cases the anti-North American sentiment became so strong that it resulted in the expropriation of the Latin American holdings of various United States companies such as oil holdings in Bolivia in 1937 and in Mexico in 1938. In general the feelings of nationalism that developed during the nineteenth century were limited to the ruling elites. In more recent years these feelings became more widely diffused, pronounced, and varied. The content of the nationalism of various Latin American countries has become somewhat more clearly defined, and the idea of nationalism has spread to many more sectors of the society.

AMERIND-AMERICA
AFRO-AMERICA
EURO-AMERICA
MESTIZO-AMERICA

MAP 4.1   Modern interaction spheres.

MODERN INTERACTION SPHERES

Nationalism, whatever its form, has become a part of the ideology of many contemporary Latin Americans. Some have placed such great emphasis on national differences that they deny there is a "Latin America." The only reality is said to be nations themselves. If we consider cultural traditions, however, there is still a Latin American tradition shared by millions. Within this tradition, four divergent life styles have emerged. In part they are similar because they share the same basic heritage; yet they differ because of a number of historical and ecological factors. These four life styles cross-cut national boundaries and reflect modern interaction spheres. These will be referred to as Amerind-America in highland Mexico, Guatemala, and the Andes; Afro-America in the Caribbean and the coastal areas of northern South America and eastern Central America; Euro-America in Argentina, Chile, Uruguay, and southern Brazil; and Mestizo-America throughout the remainder of Latin America.

There have been several previous attempts to delineate cultural or ethnic subdivisions for the Latin American culture area from which the present typology is derived. Elman R. Service (1955) divided Latin America into the following types: Euro-America, Mestizo-America, and Indo-America. Because the concern of his article was with Amerind-European relations during the Colonial period, the African element was not considered. Charles Wagley (1957), focusing on the Latin American Negro, devised a typology of Euro-America, Indo-America, and Plantation-America.[1] In order to focus on the black heritage of Latin America, Wagley included both the Indo-America and Mestizo-America of Service in his Indo-America. Another approach has been that of Marvin Harris and the geographer John Augelli, who have emphasized the highland-lowland contrasts of Latin America. Harris (1964) distinguished the "highland heritage" from the "plantation heritage." Augelli (1962), emphasizing ecological and cultural differences in Middle America, distinguished the mainland (highlands) from the rim-land (lowlands). He later changed the terminology to Euro-Indian-Main-land and Euro-African-Rimland (West and Augelli 1966:11), each with a number of subdivisions.

THE AMERIND-AMERICAN INTERACTION SPHERE

This area includes southern Mexico and Guatemala in Mesoamerica and highland Ecuador, highland Peru, and Bolivia in South America. Most

[1] Later Wagley (1968) used the terms Ibero-America, Indo-America and Afro-America to designate the same spheres.

Lacandon Indians from eastern Chiapas, Mexico. The most remote of the Mayan Indians today. (Courtesy of Jaroslaw T. Petryshyn.)

modern Amerind communities are found in areas of former pre-Columbian native empires. Other Amerind communities are found scattered throughout Latin America. In areas not inhabited by the Amerind, the mestizo, white, or Negro predominate as the cultural type. Ángel Rosenblat (1945) esti-

Uru Indian of the Lake Titicaca region. Uru live on "floating islands." Their language is related to the Mayan languages. (Courtesy of Jaroslaw T. Petryshyn.)

mated that there was an indigenous population of thirteen million three hundred eighty-five thousand in the New World at the time of contact with the Europeans. Later Woodrow Borah (1962:179), using a different method of analysis, estimated a New World population of one hundred million. The anthropologist Henry F. Dobyns (1966) has presented further evidence that tends to support the conclusions of Borah. Dobyns sees

Chipaya Indian of Bolivia. The Chipaya, as well as the Uru, language is related to the Mayan languages. (Courtesy of Jaroslaw T. Petryshyn.)

an aboriginal population of about ninety million. An intermediate estimate of forty to fifty million was accepted by Karl Sapper (1924) and Herbert Spinden (1928) in the 1920s, and more recently by Magnus Mörner (1967:12). Whatever the exact figures might be, it is clear that the bulk of the New World Amerind population was clustered around two centers: central Mexico and the central Andean area.

Following contact with the Europeans, and later with the Africans in some areas, the Amerind population declined with remarkable rapidity not as a result of death from war but from disease. In the New World, the Amerinds had lost whatever immunity to diseases they once may have had. Smallpox, typhus, measles, influenza, and syphilis were as effective in eliminating the indigenous population as a nuclear holocaust might have been. Borah and his colleagues, who estimate twenty-five million two hundred thousand as the population of central Mexico in 1519, show a dramatic drop to six million three hundred thousand in 1548 and only one million seventy-five thousand by 1605. Following 1605 the populations began to increase. Similar dramatic reductions of the native population occurred in the Andes. Between 1524 and 1720 the Andean area was decimated by a number of epidemics including measles, influenza, smallpox, and diphtheria (Dobyns 1963). The pre-Contact Andean population that may have numbered as many as thirty million declined to one and one-half million by 1650 (Dobyns 1966:415). C. T. Smith (1970:460) argues for a smaller population of the pre-Columbian Andes based on an analysis of the Lake Titicaca region. He also suggests that population decline may have begun before the arrival of the Spanish.

Because central Mexico and the central Andes had large populations before the arrival of the Spanish, the decimation by disease still left a sizable native population—probably at least one million Amerinds in each area. In areas where the native population had been small to begin with, disease, coupled with war and enslavement, reduced many groups to the point of extinction. In these other areas, the Europeans and the Negroes replaced or interbred with the native population forming a mestizo or mulatto population.

There are still many Amerinds whose primary identification is with a native group (e.g., Aymara) or a native community (such as Zinacantan), rather than with a nation such as Peru or Guatemala. In such areas Indian languages are still used, often as frequently as, or even more frequently than, Spanish. Several million in Peru speak Quechua; at least one and one-half million speak Mayan languages in Guatemala and Mexico. Aymara and Quechua are spoken by more people in Bolivia than Spanish (Wagley 1968:31).

Even though the indigenous peoples of these areas speak native languages and wear native costumes, this does not mean that their way of life exactly duplicates that of their aboriginal ancestors. During their four hundred years of subjugation, first by the Spanish and later by the nationals of the country, the Amerind cultures have become greatly hispanized. Many of the so-called native costumes actually derive from seventeenth-century Spanish footmen uniforms. Almost all of these Amerind groups are at least nominally Catholic, although their religion is a syncretism of Catholicism and aboriginal beliefs and rituals. Their crops are still basically pre-Columbian varieties; however, they have added Old World crops and adopted European domestic animals. Their village administration is derived from the Spanish forms impressed on them during the Colonial period. European ritual kinship (compadrazgo) and numerous other customs of European origin are important elements in their culture today (Wagley 1968:31–32). Wagley and Harris (1965:45) use the term "Modern Indian" to distinguish the Amerinds of Amerind-America from those small groups of dispersed aborigines who inhabit the Chaco of Bolivia and Paraguay, such as the

Mbaya and Abipon; or the headwaters of the Amazon tributaries, such as the Yąnomamö and the Shavante; or who live on isolated reservations, such as the Talamanca of Costa Rica and the Araucanians of Chile. These isolated groups, decimated by warfare and disease, constitute an insignificant segment of the contemporary Latin American population, "and as long as they retain their aboriginal cultures and their identity as tribesmen they are in reality carriers of distinct cultures within the geographic boundaries of Latin America and not subcultures of modern Latin America" (Wagley and Harris 1965:44).

Amerind-America is comprised primarily of acculturated Amerinds of the highlands whose main difference from the mestizo is that they continue to maintain an Amerind identity in spite of considerable changes in their cultural content. For example, the inhabitants of the Verapaz region of the northern part of Guatemala have been subjected to repeated foreign cultural dominance since about 400 A.D. when they came under the control of people from central Mexico. In post-Contact times they were ruled by the Spanish, especially the Dominicans. After Independence the area was developed for coffee production by the Germans and English. The natives were incorporated into a world economy, yet they managed to retain their language and much of their own culture. Most important, they consider themselves "Verapazeños," not "Guatemalans" (King 1967).

The modern highland Amerind community is the present point in an ongoing process of adaptive changes to colonial and republican institutions. It has been the Amerinds' very ability to change that has given the appearance of stability to their communities. In the Andean highlands during the Colonial period, considerable change took place in the native culture. Primarily the ethnic identity of the Amerind has kept him from being assimilated into larger societies. Although the present culture content of Amerinds may differ from that of the mestizos, it also differs from the Amerind culture of pre-Contact times.

South American Amerind-America is made up of those countries in which the Amerinds form a large *percentage* of the population. It is difficult to ascertain the exact number of Amerinds in each country. Estimates vary considerably due to poor census data and the problem of determining who is an Amerind. In Peru and Boliva, the Amerind population numbers somewhere from four and one-half to seven million, which is 37 to 62 percent of the total population. Ecuador has only nine hundred sixty thousand to one million nine hundred sixty thousand Amerinds, but they form 27 to 60 percent of the entire population. On the other hand, Brazil, with an Amerind population somewhere between one-half million and over one million, is not considered a part of Amerind-America because the Amerind population accounts for only 1 or 2 percent of the total population (Steward and Faron 1959:457).

The assimilation of the Amerind was most rapid along the coastal areas of South America. However, it was accelerated everywhere after the early nineteenth century revolutions launched the American republics on independent courses and allowed modernization to undermine the feudal colonial institutions. Despite these trends nearly 50 percent of the population of the central Andes is classified as "Indian" today, and most of these individuals inhabit the highland (Steward and Faron 1959:144).

In contrast to the United States where blacks and even orientals have been physically segregated while practicing essentially the same culture as whites, the situation in Amerind-America is one in which the physical segregation of Amerinds and mestizos has been much less marked, yet one in which cultural segregation has been important. This in turn has had three effects.

First, since the Amerinds pursue goals, many of which are distinct from those of mestizo culture, competition between the two groups is somewhat mitigated. Second, because of the frequent interaction and contacts between Amerinds and mestizos and because of the frequency of "passing" from Amerind status to the higher mestizo status, the mestizo culture absorbs a good many Amerind elements, at least in modified form. The mestizo culture is not, therefore, a purely European mode of life and thought.

Third, because Indians follow their own cultural patterns they do not participate in many aspects of national life. From the economic point of view, they are regarded in most regions as "dead" because their consumption of the products of modern commerce and industry is relatively insignificant; under the colonial economic system their function was the bearing of burdens and the performance of manual labor on the farms and in the mines, and as a matter of policy their rewards were kept barely above the subsistence level. In a modern economy this runs counter to the needs for an internal market (Gillin 1949:164).

THE MESTIZO-AMERICAN INTERACTION SPHERE

In many of the Latin American countries the mestizo either has become a symbol of nationalism or embodies the ideal of future integration. In Peru, the terms *criollo* and *cholo* are used for mestizo; in Brazil, *caboclo*; and in Guatemala, *ladino*. Sometimes the difference between an Amerind and a mestizo is little more than a pair of shoes—the Amerind goes barefoot while the mestizo wears shoes. Again, it is a question of cultural identity. In many cases the Amerind and mestizo are biologically indistiguishable. In most of Latin America, "races" are conceived as being primarily genetically distinguishable groups, but the salient distinguishing characteristics are often social or cultural. As a result, Latin America is characterized by frequent mobility of individuals from one "racial group" to another, as when an

Amerind learns to speak Spanish, adopts more modern Western dress, moves to town, and "becomes" a mestizo, although townspeople maintain their view that Amerinds are inherently inferior because of biological differences.

The mestizos have become important as holders of political office, as intellectuals, and as businessmen throughout Mestizo-America. Although the difference between the Amerind and the mestizo is more frequently cultural rather than biological, the mestizo is often indifferent or hostile to the Amerind and his culture and frequently behaves as if the Amerind did not matter or did not exist. For example, General Jorge Ubico, dictator of Guatemala for many years, attempted to deny the presence of Amerinds in Guatemala to the outside world. In a motion picture made to show Ubico's accomplishments, shots of Amerinds were edited from the film whenever possible. Wherever Ubico was shown, he managed to be surrounded solely by mestizos. This propaganda film attempted to show Guatemala as a mestizo nation although more than half of the population is Amerind (Tannenbaum 1962:115).

In Mestizo-America the inhabitants have lost their identity with specific Amerind groups and instead identify themselves as "Mexicans," "Peruvians," and so on. Mestizo-America includes central and northern Mexico, Colombia, Honduras, Nicaragua, El Salvador, Costa Rica, Panama, Paraguay, parts of Brazil, and lowland Ecuador and Peru. The traditions of Mestizo-America form the basis of modern Latin American culture. It is a blend of medieval Spanish elements such as Catholicism, nontechnological materialism, and family forms, as well as Amerind elements such as the *tortilla* of Mesoamerica and *chuño* (paste made from frozen potatoes) of the Andean region, and more recent technological innovations from western Europe and the United States.

The following widespread traits help to characterize mestizo culture (Gillin 1949:170–173). Ideologically the culture is humanistic, rather than puritanical. In other words there is more concern with logic and dialectics than with empiricism and pragmatics. Although conspicuous consumption has begun to increase in recent years, great value is still placed upon the manipulation of words and other symbols rather than upon the possession of things.

Second, family organization is more important socially in Mestizo-America than in the United States, regardless of social class. Because of Catholicism, marriages are monogamous and indissoluble. The extended family is of much greater functional importance than in the United States. These extended groups function as units in political, business, and social affairs. One can always turn to brothers, uncles, and cousins in time of need.

A third feature is the institution of ritual kinship (compadrazgo). A person has, in addition to his consanguineal and affinal kin, a group of fictive kin to which he is bound by various rights and obligations. The fictive ties derive from the institution of godparenthood. *Compadres* (male fictive kin) and *comadres* (female fictive kin) are generally persons of the same generation. A compadre serves as godparent to one's godchild, but the relationship between parent and compadre is of greater importance than that between godparent and godchild (see Chapter 6).

Fourth, although romantic love plays a role in the mestizo pattern of marriage, all the blood relatives take an active interest in the choosing of a marriage partner. Marriage is thought of as an alliance between two extended families.

Fifth, in general, women have less individual freedom than do men in interpersonal relations. The man ideally dominates the family and the place of married or marriageable women is in the home. The only friends the females have are other female kin. Young girls are still chaperoned.

Sixth, there is a strong double sex standard. A man, even one who maintains a high social position, does not lose his standing by visiting a brothel or supporting a mistress provided he does not neglect his obligations to his family. Yet women must remain virgins until marriage and must remain faithful afterwards.

Finally, consistent with the structure and function of the familial institutions, it is not customary to introduce outsiders into the family circle as guests until they are very well known and highly trusted. Social interaction between men is carried out in bars, clubs, and the like but generally not in the home.

At one time the creole (criollo) culture of Peru represented an upper class way of life derived from eighteenth and nineteenth century Spanish culture, tinged with strong French influences (Tschopik 1948:255–256). Today in coastal Peru the term criollo is used to designate a set pattern that represents an integral part of mestizo culture. In Lima the majority of those oriented to the criollo outlook are now found in the lower and middle classes (Simmons 1965:519–520).

Criollo symbols include various spicy dishes that are prepared differently from other Peruvian foods; stylized songs and dances such as the *marinera* and *vals criollo*; a type of fiesta (*jarana*) in which there is considerable drinking and dancing and which lasts long into the night or even several days; and a belief in a stereotype that depicts the criollo as possessing exceptional cleverness in turning a situation to his own advantage. The ideal criollo is a rogue, someone who "gets away" with something. He eats without paying, smokes without buying cigarettes; he is a gate-crasher.

While the criollo believes he is acting as the upper class of Lima acts, he has actually developed a unique way of life that is associated with lower and middle-class status in Lima. Only in rural mestizo communities is the criollo way of life a mark of the local upper class (Simmons 1965).

Whereas the Amerind has maintained primary identity with his cultural heritage, the mestizo has been in the forefront of nationalism. During the Colonial period the mestizo was both socially and culturally disinherited. His chances of survival lay neither in accumulating cultural goods nor in clinging to cultural norms but in an ability to change, to adapt, to improvise. Eric Wolf (1959:238–239), in describing Mesoamerica, writes that the mestizo came to be the very antithesis of the Amerind:

The Indian could turn a face to the outside world that yielded no knowledge and accepted no premise of the larger society; but the mestizo would have to operate with its premises and logic, so as to be counted among "men of reason" (*gente de razón*), as non-Indians are called in Middle America. Where the Indian valued access to land, land to work by the sweat of his brow, the mestizo would value manipulation of people and situations. Above all, he would value power, the instrument that would make people listen where society granted him no voice and obey where the law yielded him no authority. Where the Indian saw power as an attribute of office and redistributed it with care lest it attach itself to persons, the mestizo would value power as an attribute of the self, as personal energy that could subjugate and subject people.

THE AFRO-AMERICAN INTERACTION SPHERE

The third area has been termed both "Plantation-America" and "Afro-America" by Charles Wagley (1957, 1968). The area includes northeast Brazil, French Guiana, Surinam, Guyana, the Caribbean coast of Central America, and the Caribbean. This region lacked both the human and mineral resources of Amerind-America at the time of Contact.

The Amerinds who did inhabit this area were killed off at a very early period in colonial history by disease or warfare, enslaved, or driven into more inaccessible areas. Commercial agriculture became the economic base of Afro-America, with the plantation as the primary institution. Sugar cane was the main crop, although in some areas cacao, cotton, and tobacco were important. African slaves provided a labor force on the plantation in the absence of a ready supply of Amerind laborers.

Charles Wagley (1957:9) has summarized the basic common features of this region as follows: ". . . monocrop cultivation under the plantation system, rigid class lines, multiracial societies, weak community cohesion, small peasant proprietors involved in subsistence and cash crop production, and a matrifocal [mother-oriented] type family form." Other shared features include such things as similarity of local food crops, especially manioc, yams, okra, rice, chick peas, papaya, bananas, and plantains. Women do most of the selling at local markets. African elements still influence folklore and religious beliefs.

Although there are some characteristics which are common to all of Afro-America, there is considerable diversity between the various Negro and part-Negro populations of Afro-America, more so than in the other three interaction spheres of Latin America. Seven major subgroups can be identified in Afro-America. Certainly the differences in the African heritage brought to the New World must account for some of the diversity, but as Herskovits (1958) and others have noted, the bulk of the slaves were brought to the New World from West Africa and in many ways shared a similar culture. In understanding the New World situation, it is more fruitful to examine the nature of the institutions to which the various Negro populations were, and are, adjusting than merely to study "Africanisms." The Negroes were brought into a New World situation where there was considerable cultural diversity.

Before discussing the areas in which black populations are found today, it may be worthwhile to examine briefly the Latin American countries without Negroes and determine the reasons for the absence of them. Only seven Latin American countries have a limited Negro population today: Argentina, Bolivia, Chile, El Salvador, Paraguay, Peru, and Uruguay. Some African slaves were imported during the Colonial period in all of these countries and for the most part have either become extinct, migrated, or been absorbed into the population through miscegenation.

Peru, Bolivia, and to a certain extent El Salvador, were highland areas in which pre-Columbian natives were organized on a state level of sociopolitical integration. In these areas the Spanish settlers found ample Amerind labor for their agricultural and mining labor forces (Service 1955). Other areas in which few Negroes are found, such as Argentina, Chile, and Uruguay, were marginal areas prior to Contact. Europeans later introduced new means of exploiting the environment and they themselves constituted the labor force. Paraguay developed under the shadow of Argentina even though the Amerind influence has been somewhat greater.

Today one finds Negro populations in all other areas of Latin America. However, there is considerable variation in cultural types. As Whitten and Szwed (1970:17) have pointed out:

In various ways, and by various mechanisms, populations of Afro-Americans have been excluded from full participation in the nations, states, and territories to which they were brought. Subject to English, French, Dutch, Spanish, Portuguese, and a bevy of "Creole" colonial policies, by a number of methods and through various ideologies, Negroes in the New World have diversified and endured until the picture today is one of multiple cultures and subcultures existing in various environments and participating in multiple ways in the socio-economic lives of their respective societies.

For the purpose of this discussion, seven Latin American Negro cultural types will be distinguished: (1) the Afro-American Negro, (2) the Amerind Negro, (3) the Ibero-American Negro, (4) the French-American Negro, (5) the Dutch-American Negro, (6) the Anglo-American Negro, and (7) the Hispanic West Indian Negro.[2]

The Afro-American Negro   One of the "Afro-American Negro" groups is the Bush Negro found in the interiors of Surinam and French Guiana.[3] These Negroes escaped from the plantations and their adaptation to the New World setting was one of isolation from the institutions of the dominant cultures. They continue to survive today in some of the most marginal areas of Surinam and French Guiana. More than any other New World Negro population, the Bush Negroes have attempted to retain African features in both their material culture and their institutions to emphasize their African heritage. Within the past few years greater contact with the outside world has occurred with the introduction of radios and the movement of some of the young people to the city (Price 1970:65).

A second Afro-American Negro group is the Maroons of the interior of Jamaica. They were former Spanish-owned African slaves who escaped from coastal plantations and settled in the remote highlands of the island. According to Maroon tradition, they are descendants of the Ashanti people of Africa. The French scholar Roger Bastide (1971:65) suggests that the Maroons have preserved a large proportion of Ashanti and Fanti heritage.

The Amerind Negro   The "Amerind Negro" is found in British Honduras, Mexico, Guatemala, Honduras, Nicaragua, and on the island of

---

[2] The term "type" will be used here only in a very general sense because of the exploratory nature of this classification. Types in the present analysis should not be thought of as formal types. It is not the purpose of this "typology" to establish abstract types and/or types that are defined by a few criteria that can be uniformly applied to all types. Instead I wish to point out some historically real types, each of which can be distinguished by at least one criterion of relative importance. The problems involved in attempting to stress historical considerations in a meaningful treatment of the Negro in Latin America have pointed out some of the difficulties of comparative studies and of making broader and more abstract types that may help to explain the situation. The more abstract the category, the more it ignores differences within the type.

It should be pointed out before presenting a description of the types that a problem arises in assigning titles to these types. This problem has not been resolved. Language is not a major criterion of the classification, although the names of some of the types might suggest this. The correspondence of language is primarily a result of indirect, historical reasons. The same holds true for nationality. Each of the categories or types is comprised of subtypes that vary from the general characteristics of the general types in some of their traits. Some of the more obvious subtypes will be discussed briefly, but further refinements of the classification await future research.

[3] The Bush Negroes are divided into several tribal groupings known as the Djuka, the Saramaca, the Matawey, the Paramaka, and the Boni.

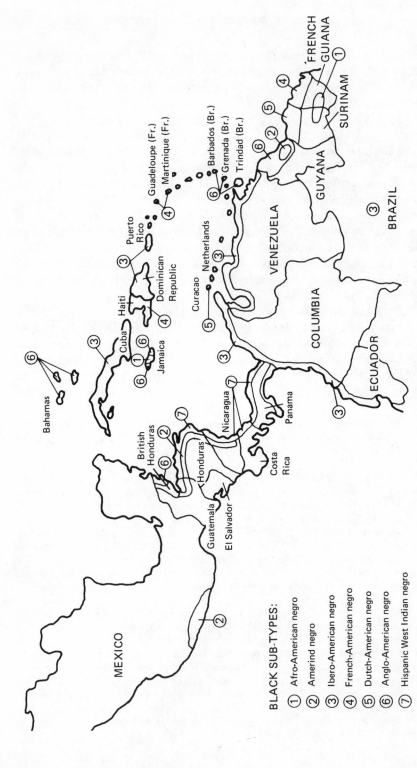

BLACK SUB-TYPES:

① Afro-American negro
② Amerind negro
③ Ibero-American negro
④ French-American negro
⑤ Dutch-American negro
⑥ Anglo-American negro
⑦ Hispanic West Indian negro

MAP 4.2   The Afro-American interaction sphere.

St. Vincent. The Amerind Negroes represent the remnants of the escaped colonial Negro slaves who also adapted, through isolation from the institutions of the dominant culture, by intermixing with Amerind groups and adopting many of their cultural traits. The Amerind Negroes continue to exist in areas that have never been successfully exploited by means other than subsistence agriculture. Only the Black Caribs of British Honduras have been at all integrated into the national culture. They have developed an economic specialization within the national economic system as sailors.

The Amerind Negro groups can be further divided, according to the cultural tradition they manifest, as a result of their particular adaptation in each area. The Black Caribs are found on St. Vincent Island (in the Lesser Antilles), the original homeland of this group, on the Caribbean Coast of British Honduras, Guatemala, Honduras, and the Bay Islands. Most Black Caribs were deported from St. Vincent to the coastal region of Central America at the end of the eighteenth century. The Miskito are found on the Caribbean coasts of Honduras and Nicaragua. They represent a group that developed after Contact through the admixture of an indigenous coastal population with Negroes and buccaneers (Helms 1971b:18). The Miskito were considered *Zamboes* (of Negro-Indian admixture) during the Colonial

Amerind Negro village on the coast of Nicaragua. (Courtesy of Mary W. Helms.)

Miskito man at dry season fishing camp, Nicaraguan coast. (Courtesy of Mary W. Helms.)

period, but in more recent years they have begun to be identified as *Indios* (Indians) in order to be distinguished from the Hispanic West Indians who have settled on the coast (Helms 1971a). Finally, there are the Mexican Negroes found on the west coast of Mexico in the state of Guerrero where they have adopted many Amerind traits and live as subsistence agriculturalists somewhat isolated from the rest of the nation.

The Ibero-American Negro   A third major Negro type is the "Ibero-American Negro" found primarily in countries where sugar plantations were established by the Spanish or the Portuguese during the Colonial period. With the exception of Colombia and Ecuador, there has been considerable racial intermixing so that the dominant physical type in many of these countries is a mulatto, pardo, or zambo type. The Ibero-American Negro represents a cultural type that is widely spread throughout the countries of Cuba, Venezuela, and Panama. The Ibero-American Negroes in Colombia and in Ecuador are localized in the lowland coastal areas. They are descendants of colonial plantation slaves who escaped from the plantation system in other regions but did not adopt Amerind cultural traits to the same extent as did the Amerind Negroes. The Ibero-American Negroes of Colombia and Ecuador are, in part, dependent upon the coastal lumber industry for wage labor which, in turn, ties them to the national economy (Whitten 1965:51). The Ibero-American Negro has adopted Spanish (or in the Brazilian subtype, Portuguese) as his language and Catholicism as his

120

religion. His adaptation has generally been to New World Ibero-American values and institutions.

A subtype of the Ibero-American Negro is the Brazilian Negro who differs from the other blacks of this type as a result of Portuguese influence. The Brazilian Negro is found throughout many areas of Brazil, although primarily in the Northeast, which was the colonial sugar producing area. In this population there is a considerable range of integration with the national culture from isolation to assimilation.

The French-American Negro   A fourth major Negro type is the "French-American Negro." This cultural type is found in Haiti and the two remaining French possessions in the Caribbean, French Guiana and the islands of Guadeloupe and Martinique. Like the Ibero-American Negroes, the French-American Negroes were brought to the islands as slave laborers on the sugar plantations. A distinction must be made between the blacks of this type living in Haiti, which has been independent since 1804, and those inhabiting the two French dependencies.

In Haiti the African influence has remained strong, although it has been tempered by European elements (Herskovits 1971:30). As much as 90 percent of the population is classified as black and the remaining 10

Ibero-American Negroes on way to cemetery following funeral for deceased child. Women are dancing with the coffin just as people did in sixteenth century Spain. Lowland Ecuador. (Courtesy of Norman E. Whitten, Jr.)

Ibero-American Negro woman vendor from all black community in the northern highlands of Ecuador. (Courtesy of Norman E. Whitten, Jr.)

percent as mixed black and European. The mulattoes of Haiti may constitute yet another subtype of French-American Negro in that they have identified more strongly with French traditions than have the Negroes. Throughout their many years of independence the Haitians have developed their own unique Caribbean culture. However, for the purposes of an exploratory typology it seems valid to include the Haitian Negro in the category of French-American Negro.

On the two remaining French possessions in the Caribbean, French Guiana and the islands of Martinique and Guadeloupe, the population is primarily mixed black and European. The French-American Negro of these areas practices subsistence agriculture; however, bananas, sugar, and coffee are grown for export on a small scale. The legal position of this group is different from that of other Caribbean blacks. Since 1946 French Guiana and the two islands have been overseas *départments* of metropolitan France, with direct representation in the French parliament. The French-American Negroes differ from the other Negro types in that they have been somewhat influenced by French institutions, although to a lesser degree than have the Ibero-American Negroes been influenced by Iberian institutions.

The Dutch-American Negro   The fifth major Negro type is the "Dutch-American Negro" found in Surinam and the Netherlands Antilles (Aruba, Bonaire, Curaçao, and the Leeward Islands of St. Eustatius, Saba, and the southern portion of St. Maarten). The economy of the Netherlands Antilles is based on the oil of Curaçao and Aruba. The islands never developed as important plantation areas. A great deal of miscegenation has occurred, so that the mixed population forms two-thirds of the inhabitants. In Surinam the Dutch-American Negro is found along the coast and is much more acculturated than the Bush Negro of the interior. The Dutch-American Negro population of Surinam is also mixed. The blacks of this country were originally imported to serve on plantations.

In general the Dutch have not been successful in establishing the Dutch way of life as the dominant cultural type of the area. Instead there are a wide variety of different cultural elements: Spanish, English, Javanese, East Indian, and others, all contributing to the creation of a very cosmopolitan culture for the Dutch-American Negro. The islands are quite different from each other in cultural and ecological aspects. The blacks of Curaçao, Aruba, and Saba speak *Papiamento*, a mixture of Spanish and Portuguese plus elements of African languages, English, and other influences. The blacks of the northern islands speak a dialect of English. However, it is primarily Dutch administration that holds the islands together as an entity.

The Anglo-American Negro   The sixth major type of Latin American Negro is the "Anglo-American Negro" found in those areas where the English developed sugar plantations during the Colonial period. This Negro type is found on the present and former British-controlled islands and in Guyana (British Guiana) and British Honduras, as well as the North

Dutch-American Negro woman preparing food for a wedding, Paramaribo, Surinam. (Courtesy of B. E. Pierce.)

American and British controlled Virgin Islands. Some of the blacks have remained plantation workers; others have become peasant agriculturalists. In these British areas, the blacks speak dialects of English and most are Protestant.

In British Honduras the Anglo-American Negroes, called "creoles," are

Anglo-American Negro turtle fisher. San Andrés Island. (Courtesy of Jay D. Edwards.)

the ruling majority. The economy of this country is based upon the lumber industry. The Anglo-American Negroes live along the north coast, in and around the capital, Belize, whereas the Black Caribs (the Amerind Negro component of British Honduras) occupy the south coast.

In Guyana the Anglo-American Negroes are found along the coastal region; some work on sugar plantations whereas others are peasants. About 35 percent of the population of Guyana are Anglo-American Negroes.

On the larger islands of the Caribbean, such as Barbados, Jamaica, and Trinidad-Tobago, the black population constitutes a majority and forms both a labor force on sugar, cacao, or banana plantations, and a peasantry.

On the smaller islands of the British Leeward and Windward Islands, the economies are mixed. Sugar cane plantations are important where ever the ecology permits. Peasant farming is basic to all of the economies. The Anglo-American Negroes, as pure bloods or mixed, also form a majority of the population on these smaller islands.

August 7 holiday race, Providencia Island. (Courtesy of Jay D. Edwards.)

The Cayman, Turks, and Caicos Islands were populated in the eighteenth century by settlers from Jamaica. The population of these islands is about 50 percent mulatto and 20 percent Negro—with an economy based on fishing.

The blacks of two other island groups may form a subtype of the Anglo-American Negro. The blacks of the Virgin Islands and the Bahamas have been under the influence of the United States, as well as the British. The Virgin Islands are governed by the United States and Britain. The vast majority of the islanders are Negro. In the American area there are some sugar plantations and small industries, as well as subsistence farming. In the British area semisubsistence peasant farming is still the characteristic economy, supplemented with fishing.

The people of the Bahamas have been more closely linked with the continental United States in the last two centuries than with the islands of the Antilles. The plantation has never been important on these islands due to the ecology. Less than 2 percent of the archipelago's land is suitable for cultivation. The population is made up primarily of fishermen, with crayfish being a major export. The black population of these islands exhibits less continuity with the Colonial period than that of other Anglo-American Negro groups. A major influx of settlers took place from the Carolinas following the American Revolution. These settlers, who were loyalists, established cotton plantations on the islands. However, the plantations were

126

destroyed in 1834, when slavery was ended. A large number of people moved to the islands following World War II.

A rather unique situation exists on the islands of Providencia and San Andrés. These islands are owned by Colombia. However, the Colombian government has left the population isolated from Iberian institutions. As a result the black population is best considered a subtype of the Anglo-American Negro type rather than part of the Ibero-American Negro type. The Negroes of Providencia and San Andrés are English-speaking Protestants who migrate to other Caribbean islands as temporary laborers.

The Hispanic West Indian Negro   The seventh major Negro culture type of Latin American Negroes is the "Hispanic West Indian Negro," or in Richard Adams's (1956:901) terminology, "the Africo-Euro-American

Hispanic West Indians, Puerto Limón, Costa Rica.

cultural tradition." In terms of continuity with the Colonial period, this type of black lacks the continued adaptation to a single set of cultural traditions manifested in the other six major Negro types. The Hispanic West Indian Negroes are found primarily along the Caribbean coast of Central America. They are Anglo-American Negroes who have migrated to Central America originally to work on the Panama Canal or for the United Fruit Company on its banana plantations. The Hispanic West Indian Negroes are found in the Limón region of Costa Rica, the Canal Zone and the Bocas del Toro regions of Panama, in the areas surrounding Bluefields and Puerto Cabezas in Nicaragua, in the Ulua Valley, on the Bay Islands of Honduras, and in the area surrounding Puerto Barrios in Guatemala. A few Hispanic West Indian Negroes are employed on the Pacific coast of Central America, in Puntarenas and Golfito in Costa Rica, having migrated from Panama, and in the Puerto Armuelles banana producing region of Panama.

Only in Panama do these Negroes form a large segment of the population. In the other Central American countries, these Hispanic West Indian Negroes represent less than 5 percent of the total population. Their culture involves a combination of some African survivals, a very strong West Indian, or Anglo, background, and, depending upon the length of residence in Central America, some adoption of Spanish-American traits. This population is usually English-speaking, with some ability to speak Spanish.

In summary, six of the seven Negro "types" in Latin America represent a continuity from the colonial Negro slave to the present Negro type. Only the Hispanic West Indian Negro is a recent immigrant in the areas in which he is found.

The Amerind, Ibero-American, and Anglo-American Negro "types" show the greatest amount of acculturation and integration. Among the Ibero-American and Anglo-American types, the acculturation and integration has been on a national level. The Amerind Negro, on the other hand, has become acculturated and integrated to regional Amerind subcultures and generally remains isolated from institutions on the national level.

The Haitian French-American Negro has developed his own unique cultural tradition that serves as a model on the national level. The French-American Negro of the French Antilles, the Dutch-American Negro, the Afro-American Negro, and the Hispanic West Indian Negro are much less acculturated and assimilated to the dominant national institutions of the countries in which they are found.

In the French and Dutch administered areas, the ruling colonial power constitutes a small minority, while the blacks form a large majority, a situation characteristic of M. G. Smith's (1965:234–235) description of a plural society. These blacks have maintained many institutions separate from the ruling minority since the period of slavery.

The Hispanic West Indian Negroes, on the other hand, constitute a minority group in the Central American republics in which they are found. While the United Fruit Company maintained a monopoly of power over the Central American lowlands, the blacks of the lowlands maintained institutions separate from the ruling Spanish-speaking highland populations. The Hispanic West Indian Negroes were really never acculturated or assimilated into the dominant culture or society to any great extent. Many of them were migrant laborers. In recent years, however, with the United Fruit Company losing its monopoly over the eastern lowlands, many of these Negroes have begun to make their permanent home in Central America. In so doing they have begun to adopt the institutions of the dominant Spanish-speaking peoples and are beginning to become acculturated and assimilated.

The context to which Latin American Negroes adapted, and are adapting, seems to be of considerable importance in any attempt to classify Latin American Negro groups. Although most classifications have tended to emphasize differences in African heritage in order to explain differences among contemporary groups, the significance of the New World historical context cannot be overlooked.

THE EURO-AMERICAN INTERACTION SPHERE

The Euro-American interaction sphere of Latin America includes the southern part of South America: Argentina, Chile, Uruguay, and southern Brazil. These areas are generally temperate, rather than tropical, resembling the United States more closely than any of the other cultural spheres. Like Afro-America, Euro-America lacked gold and silver and a native labor supply. The area did, however, lend itself to European mixed farming. The Europeans introduced cattle and horses into the region known as the *pampas* (plains), and here the South American version of the cowboy, the gaucho, flourished.

Following Independence, non-Spanish populations were no longer forbidden immigration to Latin America. The first half of the nineteenth century saw many attempts by Germans, English, Italians, Scottish, Irish, and others to establish rural agricultural colonies in Latin America.

It was early in the second half of the nineteenth century, however, that Euro-America received a significant influx of immigrants from Europe. Between 1857 and 1930, Argentina, for example, received more than six million European immigrants, of which approximately one-half settled permanently. Almost half of these Argentine immigrants were Italians. Between 1820 and 1930 Brazil admitted four and one-half million Italians (Humphreys 1946:51).

The Italian immigration into Argentina occurred during an era of

Gauchos of northwest Argentina. (Courtesy of Scott Whiteford.)

dramatic change within the country. The railway began to penetrate many areas never before linked with Buenos Aires; barbed wire made possible an effective cattle industry, as did refrigerator ships; and Argentina changed from a wheat importing to a wheat exporting country. While one-half of the immigrants came from Italy, another one-third came from Spain. The bulk of the Italians settled in Buenos Aires. In fact, only about one-sixth of all immigrants settled in the rural area. Many of the Italians still had not assimilated by World War I, and many younger men returned to Italy to fight for the Fascist regime. France, England, and Germany also sent sizable numbers of immigrants to Argentina. The citizens of Buenos Aires have a dialect of Spanish that is heavily Italianized and easily distinguished from the dialect of Spanish spoken in the interior. A subdialect of Buenos Aires, *lunfardo,* the speech of the slums and waterfront districts, is also heavily influenced by Italian and almost incomprehensible to the uninitiated (Scobie 1964:193). Italian influence also prevails in the cuisine favored by the *porteños* (the people of Buenos Aires). Cochran and Reina (1962:30) estimate that, "probably 90 per cent of the Argentine population traces its descent from immigrants who arrived in the country after 1860." Argentina also became the home of some one hundred seventy-five thousand European Jews, making the Jewish community of Argentina the fifth largest in the world. Most became businessmen and professionals, although there were attempts to establish Jewish agricultural colonies (Winsberg 1964).

In Brazil, German-speaking immigrants (German and Swiss) began arriving in the 1820s. With the growth of the coffee industry around São Paulo, Mediterranean Europe provided the bulk of newcomers, the majority migrating from Italy, Spain, and Portugal. While the Mediterraneans have intermarried with the Brazilians, Germans have tended to remain apart. Between 1884 and 1963 the Portuguese and Italian immigrants numbered one and one-half million each, the Spanish numbered almost seven hundred thousand, the Germans about two hundred thousand, and the Russians about one hundred thousand (Poppino 1968:157–199).

In the extreme south of Brazil (the states of Paraná, Santa Catarina, and Rio Grande do Sul) there is a major concentration of European immigrants. The European settlers have multiplied very rapidly, more so than the Brazilian population of Portuguese descent. Before World War II it was estimated that about one million people in the extreme South were of German descent. In Paraná today there are also a quarter of a million persons of Polish descent (Wagley 1963:85). In these southern states, the Europeans have developed a mixed farming system of small farms that are worked by the family and produce a variety of crops, livestock, and dairy products. Until 1938, the Germans resisted assimilation. In that year, the government passed a law requiring all school instruction to be in Portuguese. This law was especially aimed at the German schools where children were taught in German. Since that time, assimilation has increased, even though some German schools continued illegally in Paraná as late as 1956. While many Europeans continue as farmers, others have moved to urban centers where they have taken bureaucratic and administrative posts. The Brazilian Europeans form the basis of a regional middle class.

Chile has had fewer immigrants than either Brazil or Argentina. Major immigration has taken place in the south central region of the country. In the last half of the nineteenth century the frontier area surrounding Valdivia was the scene of colonization by some thirty-six thousand immigrants: Germans, Swiss, English, French, Spanish, and Chileans. By 1946 Humphreys estimated the German element in Chile at about thirty thousand (Humphreys 1946:61). Around the time of Independence, Basques from northern Spain migrated to Chile, adding an important element to the Chilean upper classes. Also, a small number of Irishmen, Frenchmen, and others have played important roles in the nation's history (Silvert 1965:18). The total immigration of English, Germans, Irish, French, Italians, Yugoslavs, and Arabs to Chile has probably not totaled more than one hundred thousand (Herring 1968:642).

In Uruguay nine out of every ten individuals were either born in Europe or have parents or grandparents who were born in Europe. Most are of Italian or Spanish extraction (including Basques), and there are lesser numbers of German, French and English. Some four hundred thousand immigrants migrated to Uruguay in the period following Independence. Like the immigrants of Argentina, they formed an urban middle class (Herring 1968:786, 791) in Montevideo, the capital, and in Salto, Uruguay's second largest city. The few Amerinds who had inhabited the area were killed off or driven into Paraguay during the sixteenth century. Almost one-fourth of Uruguayan surnames are Italian or Hispanicized Italian. Less than 1 percent of the population are descendants of blacks who migrated from Brazil.

In the area denoted as Euro-America, the Amerind population was small at the time of the Conquest and/or killed off during European expansion. The population of the area was formed by the Iberian colonists. Following Independence, other Europeans added an important element to the national character of most of the countries. The Italians and the Germans, as well as the continued immigration from Spain, have played the most important immigrant roles.

MAJOR GROUPS OF OTHER IMMIGRANTS

Besides the European immigration into the Euro-American countries of Latin America, there have been other immigrants who form important minority groups throughout Latin America.

The Portuguese of Guyana began with a lower status than was the case of most European immigrants because they were brought to the country to do the work of slaves. Most arrived before 1860 following the freeing of plantation slaves. They remained as plantation workers for a very short period and then became peddlers, hawkers, pawnbrokers, and small shopkeepers (Despres 1967:62–63).

Scattered throughout Latin America are small populations from the Middle East that are generally grouped under the Spanish term *Turco* (Turk), regardless of their nationality. This population has received little or no attention from social scientists. The scanty data available suggest that they have generally entered into some facet of retail trade where ever they are found.

Besides extensive German migration to southern South America, there have been smaller groups of Germans who have become influential throughout Central America. The Germans played a major role in the development of the coffee industry in the Alta Verapaz region of Guatemala (King 1965).

Throughout the British-dominated Caribbean, descendants of the English continue as an elite upper class who have set the standards of culture for centuries. Today, however, their numbers are small and their political power is considerably less than even fifty years ago.

There are also small groups of people from the United States scattered throughout Latin America. Most are only temporary inhabitants of the countries and are in Latin America only because of their jobs. Possibly the largest permanent migration to Latin America from the United States took place following the Civil War. Some of the Southerners who refused to accept the abolition of slavery in the United States moved to Latin America —some to the British colonies, British Honduras, and the Bahamas, others to Brazil where they were able to continue a plantation system based upon slavery for a few more years until slavery was abolished in Latin America. Two thousand migrated to Brazil between 1866 and 1867 and settled in the Amazon jungle of Paraná, founding Vila Americana, whose cemetery still flies the Confederate flag. Many of the descendants have been assimilated into the national culture. However, they still maintain some symbolic ties with the Old South through memberships in the American Descendancy Fraternity.

It is possible only to present the major European immigrant groups in an introduction to Latin America. If one were to look at any Latin American country in detail, he would find a history of numerous other immigrant groups, many of whom came to Latin America to organize farming colonies. Most of the colonies proved unsuccessful. For example, in Costa Rica one of the first attempts at colonization was undertaken in 1830 by a group of Americans. They settled in northwest Costa Rica, establishing the settlement of Filadelfia. The colony lasted only a few years. In 1852 and 1861 the government of Costa Rica negotiated with the Sociedad de Berlin and the Sociedad Itineraria del Norte for the establishment of farming colonies, neither of which materialized. In 1890 a colony of Cuban political refugees began settlement in northwest Costa Rica at La Mansión with one hundred families. They returned to Cuba following the Spanish-American War. The Costa Rican government signed a contract in 1891 for the establishment of an American colony in the eastern lowlands. The project failed. In 1892 a contract was signed to bring Swedish families into northeastern Costa Rica. This colonization attempt also failed. At about the same time an experiment to settle Irish families in the eastern lowlands also failed. A second attempt to settle the lowlands brought 535 Spanish families beginning in 1893. Most returned home and the rest migrated to the urban centers and entered into the commerce trade. In 1894 unsuccessful attempts were made to bring immigrants from Japan. At present there are only two immigrant colonies in Costa Rica, both of which began in the 1950s—an Italian colony at San Vito de Java in extreme southern Costa Rica and a Quaker colony in northwest Costa Rica. Both are agricultural colonies (Masing 1965:19–26).

The Chinese   A decline of the plantation system followed the emancipation of the blacks. Many of the freed Negroes refused to continue working on the plantation and became peasant subsistence farmers instead. Lacking a slave work force made up of Africans and their descendants, the planters had to turn elsewhere for laborers. India and China, with a surplus of people, were important population pools from which the planters recruited their laborers. These new workers came to the New World as indentured laborers, not as slaves. Ideally an indentured laborer agreed to work in the New World for a specific period of time in return for a set sum of money, as well as transportation to his native land following completion of his contract. In reality, the contract laborer was often treated no better than a slave and, like the hacienda peon, was tied to his employer through bonds of perpetual indebtedness. The Chinese were imported as laborers mainly in Peru and Cuba. Between 1847 and 1874 more than seventy-four thousand Chinese "coolies" were brought to Peru. Many were sold as slaves; many others were used as laborers on the Guano Islands. Between 1847 and 1867, more than one hundred fourteen thousand Chinese were brought to Cuba; another one hundred fifty thousand were admitted during the first half of the twentieth century (Humphreys 1946:63). Today Cuba has the largest Chinese population, with Peru and Mexico tied for second (Kwong 1958:41). Morton Fried (1958) found the largest Chinese populations of the British Caribbean on Jamaica (6,879), Trinidad (5,599) and British Guiana (3,567).

The lot of the early Chinese immigrant was incredibly hard. In China he was often tricked into signing a contract or "shanghaied." Conditions on the coolie ships were often worse than those aboard the ships from Africa during the slaving days. Like the Africans, many Chinese died aboard ship due to disease and overcrowding. For example, a Peruvian ship, the *Luisa Canevaro,* lost 26 percent of its Chinese cargo during one stormy voyage in which the hatches had to be battened down for at least a month, during which time the "coolies" were not allowed on deck, nor could they wash their bedding or clothing, nor could they breathe any fresh air. Many died of dysentery and suffocation (W. Stewart 1951:61).

Those who worked on the islands of Peru had a high death rate often brought about by suicide. Their hard life was described by D. J. Williamson, United States consul to Peru in 1870 (quoted in W. Stewart 1951:97–98):

> Those employed on the Guano Islands have a daily task to perform of 100 wheelbarrow loads of Guano, should they fail to get that amount to the shute [by which it was conveyed to the boat], their task has to be completed on Sunday. They are indifferently fed and clothed, and as a consequence one fourth of their number, become sick, but are not admitted to the Hospital while they retain strength enough to stand. I have been informed by American Captains, trading at the Chincha and Guañape Islands that many of them too weak to stand up are compelled to work on their knees picking the small stone out of the

Guano, and when their hands become sore from constant use of the wheelbarrow it is strapped upon their shoulders, and in that way they are compelled to fulfill their daily task. . . . Life to the Chinaman under such circumstances possesses no attractive features, and death (at all times and in its worst phases a matter of indifference, supposing as the Coolie does, that it is the mere transition from an unhappy state to the enjoyment of all the glories of his celestial fancy) is welcomed by him as his deliverance from the miseries of his lot in life. This feeling necessitates the constant employment of a guard around the shores of the Guano Islands, where they are employed, to prevent them from committing suicide by drowning, to which end the Coolie rushes in his moments of despair.

Lucy M. Cohen (1971) has also found a high incidence of suicide among the Chinese who were imported to work on the Panama Railroad in the mid-nineteenth century. Bodies that had washed ashore gave evidence of death by self-inflicted drowning. Corpses were found hanging from trees as a result of suicide. Also, the Chinese tried to impale themselves upon machetes or other sharp instruments used in their work or to die by self-inflicted starvation. Cohen suggests that although some suicides have been reported from haciendas or plantations with "coolie" laborers, suicide appears to have been much more extensive in the guano beds of Peru and on the Isthmus, where the combination of a harsh environment and wretched labor conditions imposed greater adaptational challenges than on the plantations. For the Chinese on the Cuban and Peruvian plantations, escape offered the potential promise of relief. If successful, they could find new work modes such as positions as house servants. Such alternatives never existed for the guano worker or the Isthmian Chinese during the early period of migration to these areas.

By the early twentieth century, those who survived had moved from manual labor into positions of commerce. Although the Chinese represent a very small percentage of the total population in the countries in which they are found, their economic importance is generally far beyond their numerical importance. They have especially established roles as middlemen. Often they offer services not available from other sources. They are characterized by other Latin Americans as operating under different economic strategies than the Iberian-influenced Latin American. Whereas the other Latin Americans operate on the basis of the "big kill" where profits come from high prices even though the merchandise may move very slowly, the Chinese operate on the basis of small profits with a large turnover of merchandise.

Unlike the African slave population, the Chinese coolie immigration was exclusively male. Many Chinese married members of other Latin American populations, white, Amerind, Negro, and mixed. Many became partially acculturated—taking Spanish and Portuguese first names such as "José

Chinese settler in eastern lowlands of Costa Rica.

King Hong" or "Joaquim Fung." They have also adopted Latin American clothing, Catholicism (at least superficially), and the Spanish or Portuguese language. However, the Chinese have consciously maintained some of their native traditions. Although no study has been carried out, it would appear that most, if not all, Chinese are bilingual, retaining some dialect of Chinese. In lowland Costa Rica, for example, the Chinese speak Spanish, a dialect of Chinese, and "banana English" (a West Indian dialect of English). In some areas of Latin America, Chinese clubs and family associations are maintained.

By the twentieth century, Chinese males were able to bring their wives with them as they migrated to Latin America, or to send for them once they were established. This resulted in changed family forms, at least in those areas where there is a sizable Chinese population, as there had previously been a tendency for the members of Chinese populations to intermarry.

Fried (1956) and others have noted a double loyalty among the Chinese. Many maintain citizenship in China (or Taiwan), as well as citizenship in the country in which they have settled. In some areas considerable sums of money are sent back to Nationalist and/or Communist China.

Other Asiatic Immigrants A second group imported to serve as a working force following the abolition of slavery was the "coolie" of India (called "East" Indian in contrast to the "American" Indian and "West" Indian) who also came as an indentured laborer to work on the Latin American plantations. East Indian settlement has been most extensive in

136

Trinidad where these workers form 40 percent of the total population and in Guyana where they form approximately 50 percent of the population. About twenty thousand East Indians remain in Jamaica and smaller groups are found scattered throughout the Caribbean and along the Caribbean coast of Central America.

At the time that slavery was abolished in the 1830s, both British Guiana and Trinidad were sparsely populated areas. As a result, it was possible for former slaves to find land of their own to farm as free men. In these two countries the East Indians were imported as the new plantation laborers. The East Indian "coolie" system was maintained from 1845 to 1916. Unlike Chinese migration, the East Indian migration was not restricted to men. Also, by law, families were not allowed to be separated. While most of the immigrants were from agricultural and artisan castes, a surprising number were also from the highest castes, the Brahmans and the Kahattryas. Most were Hindus from the United Provinces. During the period of indentured labor, 238,960 East Indians migrated to British Guiana (Despres 1967:56) and 143,900 migrated to Trinidad (Klass 1961:9).

In Trinidad and Guyana the importance of the caste system has declined, although some social, marital, and religious implications of caste persist. In both areas the East Indians continue to form an important rural segment, both as plantation workers and agriculturalists. Their movement into other occupations has been rather slow. Although they have lost many important caste distinctions, they have, more than other immigrants, resisted acculturation. Hence the East Indians still remain as distinguishable ethnic groups. Besides Trinidad and Guyana, much smaller populations of East Indians are still found in other areas of Latin America, e.g., British Honduras and Surinam.

In Surinam, East Indians were imported between 1873 and 1918. Today they number some ninety-three thousand, one-quarter of whom live in the capital, Paramaribo. Many have become successful in Surinam. After fulfilling their contracts they became independent farmers. Many were able to send their children to the Netherlands in order to obtain a higher education. Quite a few have become professional people (de Waal Malefijt 1963:21–22).

As the sources for indentured labor began to close in India, the Dutch began looking elsewhere for manpower for the Surinam plantations, recruiting laborers from Java between 1891 and 1939. Today the total Javanese population of Surinam is about forty-three thousand. The bulk of this population is rural. Their villages generally contain not only Javanese, but East Indians and creoles as well. Within a village, each ethnic group has its own appointed leader. The most typical Javanese settlements are devoted to rice farming, supplemented by manioc, bananas, vegetables, coconuts, and fishing. In some villages the people work part-time on plantations and maintain crops of their own. Some Javanese still work on the plantations or in the bauxite industry. About fifty-five thousand live in Paramaribo where they run small shops, work in factories, or are hired as house servants. The few intellectuals and white collar Javanese also reside in Paramaribo (de Waal Malefijt 1963:22, 33–36). In general, Javanese culture in Surinam possesses a marked degree of internal cohesion.

Another oriental group, the Japanese, began extensive migration to Latin America somewhat later than the other Asiatic groups. The first laborers to Peru arrived in 1898; the first Japanese settlement in Brazil began in 1908. The Japanese population in Peru has become primarily an urban one. The twenty to thirty thousand Japanese, most of whom live in Lima or Callao, are engaged in retail trade, small crafts, or in the barber shop business. A much smaller number live in agricultural colonies growing cotton in the Chancay Valley.

In Brazil, the Japanese immigrants have been primarily agriculturalists. There are approximately one-quarter of a million Japanese who have settled in Brazil. They have established themselves as hard-working cultivators of pepper, cotton, sugar, rice, tea, and silk.

Japanese agricultural colonies have also been established in Colombia and Paraguay. When in 1934 Brazil set strict quotas on oriental immigration, Japan was forced to look elsewhere for outlets for her surplus population. By 1958, 4,660 Japanese had entered Paraguay. The Japanese migrated as families and established agricultural colonies where they are still found today (N. Stewart 1967:79).

One other oriental group, the Koreans, also migrated to Brazil as agriculturalists. They have been less successful than the Japanese due to the fact that the Korean migrants were recruited from all walks of life; many had no prior farming experience and moved to the cities after unsuccessful attempts at agriculture.

The Religious Immigrants   The immigrants who have been described thus far came to Latin America in search of economic opportunities. There have been others who have migrated to Latin America to escape religious persecution, in particular the Jews and the Mennonites.

The largest Jewish colonies are found in Euro-America. These groups have already been described. Others are found scattered throughout Latin America. The Jews have inhabited the Mexico-Central America area since 1521, but there has been no continuity of any one community. Immigration has been episodic rather than continuous. During the Colonial period their presence in New Spain was illegal. Most Jews of this period were Sephardim (Mediterranean). From 1821 to 1875 the principal immigration came from north of the Pyrennes. Between 1870 and 1915 there was an influx of Jewish immigrants from the eastern Mediterranean, the Middle East, the

Ottoman Empire, and North Africa. Since 1917 the Jews have been Ashkenazim (East European) from Poland, Russia, Latvia, Estonia, Germany, Austria and France (Liebman 1970:16–17).

Many of the descendants of Jewish immigrants who migrated before World War I have converted to Catholicism. Those who maintain Judaism still recognize the distinction between Sephardim and Ashkenazim. Each has its separate community. The Arab or Oriental Jews are divided into the Aleppo and the Damascus congregations (Liebman 1970:17–18).

Another major group of religious immigrants are the Mennonites found in Paraguay, Mexico, and British Honduras. They have attempted to remain a separate ethnic group and have consciously resisted attempts at assimilation. They have organized farming colonies in the countries in which they have settled.

The Mennonites of British Honduras arrived in 1958 from northern Mexico. They are of European stock, speak German, and maintain their own form of Protestantism. The immigrants are from two churches, the Rheinland and the Klein Gemeinde, and form two closed communities, one on the upper Belize River, and the other at Blue Creek on the Mexican border. They have the reputation of being excellent farmers. In general, they refrain from accepting public office or voting (Waddell 1961:74–75).

Menno was the first Mennonite colony in South America. It is the largest colony in the Chaco of Paraguay with a population of over four thousand. Several other Mennonite colonies have been established in the Chaco region. More recently other sections of Paraguay have been colonized. Some of the colonists have come from Canada, others from Europe. For all the immigrant Mennonite groups, religion has an all-pervading effect on colony life (Fretz 1962:49–106).

The Old Colony, an offshoot of the Mennonite Church in Mexico, had traditionally been left alone by the government. In recent years, however, the government has put greater pressures on the colony to assimilate. The colonists are now learning Spanish, but there is considerable conflict over the nature of education for the colony's children. The Mexican government insists on teaching the children, while the colonists insist on maintaining their own form of schooling (Redekop and Loomis 1968).

There are other religious colonies throughout Latin America such as the Quakers of Costa Rica, but generally their effect on the modern Latin American tradition has been minimal.

THE EMIGRANTS

In considering a culture area such as Latin America it is important to recognize not only those who have immigrated into the culture area but also the people who have moved from Latin America, transplanting Latin American culture to other areas of the world.

A considerable part of Latin American emigration has been to the United States. Today there are sizable groups with a Spanish heritage, as well as a number of black West Indians. There are approximately five million persons of Mexican ancestry residing in the United States. Most are found in California, Arizona, New Mexico, Texas, and Colorado, but significant numbers are also found in Chicago and other industrial centers (Forbes 1970:7). Some of these people trace their ancestry in the United States back three hundred years, reckoning as ancestors individuals who were living in the Southwest before it was annexed to the United States. Most, however, came to the United States at a later date, especially during the First and Second World Wars when manpower needs for cheap labor were great. While the Mexican-Americans have been frequently discriminated against, at least in the Southwest, they have managed to retain a great deal of their traditional culture.

During most of the history of Spanish-speaking people in the United States, they have been a politically impotent group. According to Burma (1970:xviii), factors contributing to this condition include a high proportion of the population ranked at the bottom of the socioeconomic scale, an expectation of someday returning to Mexico, a feeling of fatalism, discrimination and violation of civil rights, numerically insignificant populations except in a few localities, inability to cooperate with non-kin, and a distrust of government as a solution for problems. Consequently, outside of New Mexico, few Spanish-speaking people have been able to achieve positions of leadership or have even sought them. It was only following World War II, with the return of Spanish-speaking veterans who asserted new values and attitudes, that Mexican-American political organizations began to elect a few Spanish-speaking officials. At the same time, the League of United Latin American Citizens, the G.I. Forum, and other groups were organized.

During the 1960s, the rise of nationalistic attitudes among blacks was paralleled, to a certain degree, by the rise of nationalistic attitudes among urban Mexican-Americans. Like the blacks, the Mexican-Americans developed militants, semimilitants and ethnically oriented liberals. Boycotts, strikes, marches, sit-ins, and riots have occurred, but with far less frequency, far less effect, and involving a lower proportion of the Mexican-Americans than is the case with the black populations. A resurgence of pride in *la raza* (the race) and in things Mexican, coupled with a general decline in a positive attitude toward assimilation and a desire for cultural pluralism, is resulting in a new force, a new strength, and a new unity among the Mexican-Americans (Burma 1970:xviii).

Puerto Ricans became citizens of the United States in 1917. Of three and one-half million Puerto Ricans, one million live in the United States—

with over six hundred thousand living in New York City where most exist in poverty. Economic factors certainly contribute to emigration from Puerto Rico; however, in his study of Puerto Rican families in New York, Oscar Lewis found that personal social-psychological crises, such as a husband's death, were more important factors (Lewis 1965: xxxvii–xxxviii).

The first Puerto Rican migrants were cigar makers who settled on the lower east side of New York. They were followed by merchant seamen, women garment workers, and then almost every labor category from rural farm worker to street vendor. The 1950s was a period of heavy migration, when forty-one thousand made the trip to the United States annually. Like the Mexican-Americans, the Puerto Rican has generally been hired in unskilled or semiskilled, low paying, occupations.

Other Puerto Ricans have migrated to Hawaii. They came during the first half of the twentieth century as laborers on the sugar plantations. There are about thirteen thousand in Hawaii today.

A third Spanish-speaking group in the United States are the Cubans. The majority are centered in Miami. Most came to the United States following Castro's revolution. Unlike other Spanish-speaking groups, many Cubans are of middle-class professional origin. They offer considerable competition to other minority groups because of their training. However, even when they have been able to find work comparable to their training, they generally receive low wages. It is not uncommon to find well-educated Cubans work-

Cuban settlement, Miami.

Cuban settlement, Miami. Supermarket with bilingual signs.

ing as menial laborers. Because of the large influx of Cubans over a short period of time, they have had to compete with each other on the labor market.

West Indian blacks have also been migrating from Latin America. Some have come to the United States where they are discriminated against as "Negroes." This group has received only limited study by social scientists.[4] Today many are recruited by agencies in Central America and the Caribbean to work as domestics in the larger east coast cities of the United States.

Between 1952 and 1962 some three hundred thousand West Indians migrated to Great Britain (Hill 1963:3), a period during which there was a scarcity of labor in some areas. The majority settled in London. In general they settled in communities that were losing white workers. Most were from Jamaica, an island suffering from overpopulation.

The major groups that came to settle in Latin America differed in the opportunities available to them and the adaptive strategies utilized in dealing with the opportunities. The Africans, migrating as slaves, were the only group without an opportunity to return to their native lands. Although men, women, and children were captured by slave traders, family groups were frequently broken up. They were introduced into ecological niches previously unexploited by the Europeans.

Early Spanish settlement was almost exclusively male. They took

[4] See, for example, A. E. Smith 1933 and Reid 1937–1938.

142

Amerind or black women as mates thus creating the mestizo and mulatto groups. Later the Europeans settled as families. Many of the post-Colonial European immigrants settled in unexploited ecological areas, introducing new farming technology.

The East Indians came in family groups as a substitute for black slave labor. As the blacks settled elsewhere, the East Indians became the main plantation workers, resisting acculturation.

The Chinese, on the other hand, were a male labor force. Those working in newly exploited ecological zones committed suicide in large numbers; those brought to work on plantations were assimilated because of the chances they had available to escape to the city.

RECOMMENDED READING

Adams, Richard N., 1967, *The Second Sowing: Power and Secondary Development in Latin America*. San Francisco: Chandler Publishing Company.
An important work dealing with some of the major processes operating in Latin American societies. Especially interesting for its treatment of power and of the middle class.
Bastide, Roger, 1972, *African Civilisations in the New World*. New York: Harper Torchbooks.
Considers the African influences in colonial and contemporary black populations in the New World.
Gillin, John, 1949, Mestizo America. In Ralph Linton (ed.), *Most of the World*. New York: Columbia University Press, pp. 156–211.
Although somewhat dated, this discussion of Mestizo-America is the only extensive treatment available.
Gonzalez, Nancie L., 1969, *The Spanish-Americans of New Mexico: a Heritage of Pride*. Albuquerque, N.M.: University of New Mexico Press.
An anthropologist's view of the Latin American tradition in the United States.
Klass, Morton, 1961, *East Indians in Trinidad*. New York: Columbia University Press.
A study of village life in an East Indian settlement.
Steward, Julian, and Louis Faron, 1959, *Native Peoples of South America*. New York: McGraw-Hill, Inc.
Still the best one-volume summary of South American Indians. It is strong in its discussion of various groups at the time of Conquest but weak on the study of contemporary Amerind groups.
Stewart, Watt, 1951, *Chinese Bondage in Peru: a History of the Chinese Coolie in Peru. 1849–1874*. Durham, N.C.: Duke University Press.
A readable account of the plight of the early Chinese in Peru.
Whitaker, Arthur P., and David C. Jordan, 1966, *Nationalism in Contemporary Latin America*. New York: The Free Press.
One of the important syntheses on the problem of nationalism.

Whitten, Norman E., Jr., and John Szwed (eds.), 1970, *Afro-American Anthro-pology: Contemporary Perspectives.* New York: The Macmillan Company.
A modern introduction to contemporary problems of interpreting Afro-American culture. Includes important articles on a variety of Afro-American subcultures.
Wolf, Eric R., 1959, *Sons of the Shaking Earth.* Chicago: University of Chicago Press.
Although the account of prehistory is now out of date, the discussion of the Colonial period is excellent, as is the section on the mestizo.

RECOMMENDED CASE STUDIES
IN CULTURAL ANTHROPOLOGY

Buechler, Hans C., and Judith-Maria Buechler, 1971, *The Bolivian Aymara.* New York: Holt, Rinehart and Winston, Inc.
An example of an Amerind-America population caught up in the process of national reform.
Horowitz, Michael M., 1967, *Morne-Paysan: Peasant Village in Martinique.* New York: Holt, Rinehart and Winston, Inc.
A study of village life in a French-American Negro community.
Madsen, William, 1964, *The Mexican-Americans of South Texas.* New York: Holt, Rinehart and Winston, Inc.
Description of an emigrant group which has carried the Latin American tradi-tion to the United States.
Richardson, Miles, 1970, *San Pedro, Colombia: Small Town in a Developing Society.* New York: Holt, Rinehart and Winston, Inc.
San Pedro is a town in Mestizo-America which is considered backward by other Colombians.
Vogt, Evon Z., 1970, *The Zinacantecos of Mexico: A Modern Maya Way of Life.* New York: Holt, Rinehart and Winston, Inc.
Another example of life in an Amerind-American village, with emphasis on ceremonial aspects.

CHAPTER 5

The study of Latin Americans

The year 1492 marks the date of European recognition of the Latin American Indian as a result of the discovery of the island of San Salvador,[1] in the Bahamas, by Christopher Columbus. It seems possible that other Europeans may have reached the New World prior to Columbus; however it was the Columbus expeditions of 1492–1493, 1493–1496, 1498–1500 and 1502–1504 that awakened Europe to a new world. Rowe (1965) suggests that Europe had not really been interested in other lands and other ways of life until the Renaissance. Most accounts of travel during the Middle Ages in Europe were met with disbelief. The Renaissance ushered in a new intellectual climate for Europe, and scholars became interested in cultures other than their own. There was an awakening of interest in the writings and monuments of the classical cultures of Greece and Italy. In this new era of growing curiosity about the world and man's diversity, Columbus sailed to the west to find a new passage to the Indies. His discoveries met acceptance because of the changing European outlook. If there were earlier contacts with the New World, they were met with disbelief and disinterest.

SPECULATION ABOUT THE AMERINDS

It was accepted without question that Columbus had succeeded in finding a new route to the Indies. The inhabitants he found were, therefore, referred

[1] This tiny island was later named Watlings Island by the English.

to as "Indios" (inhabitants of the Indies). For almost seventy-five years, no one really questioned who these peoples were. However, once it was realized that Columbus had discovered some new and unknown world, interest in the origin of these "Indians" began to grow. Lee Huddleston (1967) has compiled the major theories which attempted to explain the presence of people in the New World. The theories generally fell into two types: (1) the more cautious scientific approach which hypothesized an Asiatic origin for the Indians who then came to the New World by way of a land bridge somewhere in the northwestern part of the New World, an area still unexplored in the sixteenth century, and (2) a more speculative approach stressing a multiplicity of explanations. The first point of view was most clearly stated in the writings of José de Acosta (1590), but his theory found greater acceptance in northern Europe than it did in Spain. It is the Acostan point of view that has been substantiated by the modern sciences of archaeology, physical anthropology, and linguistics. The other major literary tradition, exemplified by Gregorio García in his book, *Origen de los indios de el nuevo mundo, e Indias occidentales . . . ,* first published in 1607 and later republished in 1729 with considerable additions by the editor, Andrés González de Barcia Carballido y Zúñiga, stressed a multiplicity of explanations for the origin of the Amerinds. The settlement of the New World from Atlantis (a continent which was supposed to have existed in the Atlantic inhabited by a highly developed civilization and destroyed when the landmass sank into the ocean), settlement by the Carthaginians, settlement by the Hebrews of the Ten Lost Tribes, or settlement by early Spaniards many years before Columbus were some of the theories given. None of these explanations have ever received scientific support, but unfortunatly it was the theories described by García that gained the greatest support from the Spanish writers, especially following the republication of his book in 1729. Theories about the origin of New World Indians multiplied as each new century brought with it new generations of writers, each with his own new speculation about the origin of the Amerind: they were Egyptians, inhabitants of the lost continent of Lemuria (later called Mu), the early Welsh, the early Irish, the crew of Alexander the Great, and so on. Some of these theories continue even today with new twists added, such as the development of the New World high civilizations by the inhabitants of another planet who arrived and left in flying saucers.

Why were many of the early writers unwilling to accept Acosta's theory? And why do people feel the need to speculate on Indian origins even today? The early writers were greatly influenced by the Bible. Every theory had to take into account the belief that all mankind derived from Adam and Eve and then again from Noah following the Flood. The Bible was scoured for passages which gave some explanation of the New World. For example, the name Peru was thought to be a corruption of Ophir, a great-great-great grandson of Noah, while Yucatán was thought to be derived from Iectan, the name of Ophir's father (Huddleston 1967:42).

Also, there was considerable faith put in the writings of the classical authors by some of the writers interested in the origin of the Amerinds. For example, Gonzalo Fernández de Oviedo y Valdes (1944) accepted Aristotle's story of Carthaginian merchants who, in ancient times, discovered an island in the Atlantic as a description of America; Augustín de Zárate (1933) considered Plato's description of life on the lost continent of Atlantis to be an accurate description of customs still preserved by the Amerinds of Peru. The followers of the "Acostan tradition," on the other hand, generally maintained that the classical writers had not known of the New World and, hence, their descriptions of lost islands and continents could not have applied to the New World.

Finally, there was disagreement over the methodology of cross-cultural comparison. Many of the early writers took as conclusive proof of a historical tie the fact that there were one or two cultural traits that appeared to be similar in the New World and in whatever area they hypothesized the Amerinds had originated. Circumcision amongst the Amerinds of Yucatán suggested a Jewish origin to some writers. Others emphasized physical characteristics, for example, the fact that both the Chinese and the Amerinds had small eyes and flat noses. Special importance was attached to linguistic evidence. Generally only a very small corpus of words was analyzed, through questionable techniques, to establish a genetic relationship between the Amerinds and other peoples. The Indians of Yucatán supposedly referred to God by the Greek word *Teos,* therefore some writers concluded the Indians were ancient Greeks. The Peruvian Indian language, Quechua, used the word *muchar* (·ceremonial kiss), and the ancient Basque language, Viscaine, utilized a similar word, *mucho,* to mean ceremonial kiss, and, therefore, the Indians were thought by other authors to be Basques. In 1681 Diego Andrés Rocha used as evidence to support his belief that the Indians had descended from the Jews the fact that if the "n" in the word "Indio" were inverted, it would read "Iudio," which was one of the Spanish spellings of "Jew" (Huddleston 1967:93).

The influence of Biblical traditions, an acceptance of the statements of classical writers, and questionable methods of cross-cultural comparison still account for some of the erroneous explanations of the origin of the Amerind held in some quarters even today, as well, possibly, as the appeal of the exotic and the mystical. The scientific community has based the support of its theory that the Amerinds originated in Asia and migrated to the New World across a land bridge, the Bering Straits, on a rigorous use of linguistic, biological, and cultural evidence. Linguistic comparisons are not made on the basis of a few selected words, but rather on the comparison of hundreds and sometimes thousands of words. Comparisons are made of isolated languages, as well as language families. Biological comparisons are no longer based on the similarities of the phenotype but rather primarily on genetic features through serology, the study of blood type grouping.

Finally, the comparison of cultural traits, both archaeological and ethnological, has been made more rigorous due to the influence of migrational theory devised by the German Kulturkreislehre. Wilhelm Schmidt (1939:138–173) and others of the Kulturkreis school established two criteria, quality and quantity, which must be met before a strong case of contact between two areas can be made. To meet the criterion of quality, two traits found in different areas can be thought of as historically linked only if they are the same in form and function. To meet the criterion of quantity, there must be a number of traits which are the same in form and function. More recently, anthropologists have further stipulated that in both areas being compared for historical ties, the traits considered as demonstrating historical links should be found over a restricted area at roughly the same time period.

In order to discuss the study of Latin America by various scholars, it will be helpful to divide the work into four major time periods: 1500–1800, 1800–1900, 1900–1940, and 1940 to the present.

1500–1800: PRE-CONQUEST, CONQUEST, AND COLONIAL STUDIES

Mesoamerica   Prior to the conquest of Latin America by the Spanish and Portuguese, there had been a literary tradition of hieroglyphic writing in highland Mexico and in the Maya area. Some of these written texts, called codices, have survived to the present. Various writing surfaces were utilized, most commonly deerskin, fiber paper, and woven cotton cloth. A thin layer of chalk was spread over the material to provide a smooth, white surface. Most frequently the codex was in the form of a strip about twelve inches wide and several feet long and was folded accordion style (Dibble 1966:270–271).

In Mesoamerica, there seems to have been at least two systems of writing, neither of them based on a phonetic alphabet. The simplest, used by the Mixtec and Aztec, was a form of picture writing called rebus or puzzle writing. In this system of writing, pictures or ideographs were used which represented sound values. For example, in English, the pronoun "I" would be represented by a picture of an eye. A more complex writing system was used by the Maya. It was a logographic system that combined certain aspects of the rebus system with phonetic and semantic elements (Coe 1966:163–166).

Most of these codices have been lost forever. Although the writing tradition probably extends back to a thousand years before the Spanish Conquest, the surviving codices of the Aztecs, Mixtec, and Maya are few in number, and only a few have any great antiquity. The scarcity of these codices is, in many cases, a result of purposeful destruction. Approximately fifty codices have survived from the pre-Contact period; three are Mayan and seven are Mixtec.

Aztec tradition tells us that in the early 1400s the Aztec King, Itzcoatl, collected Mexican histories and burned them and then wrote an official history which emphasized the importance of the Aztecs. More codices were destroyed by the Spanish missionaries. In both the Aztec and Maya areas, the early Spanish missionaries deliberately burned indigenous documents because they were considered "pagan." Hence in a few short years following the Conquest, most of the remaining pre-Contact literature of the New World was destroyed, an invaluable loss to future scholars. The Maya codices have been only partially translated, as the natives quickly forgot their system of writing. Probably the Mayan literati were composed of a small number of persons; once they died, the Maya system of writing quickly died with them. Besides the pre-Contact codices, there are others—as many as three hundred fifty according to Morley (1956:249–255)—from the Central Mexican highlands written by natives shortly after the Conquest. Ten or twelve post-Conquest native documents have survived from the Maya area. The Spanish priests themselves provided the world with some of the best descriptions of the early post-Contact New World, in particular, Fray Bernardino de Sahagún's (1950–1963) collection of Aztec material, *Historia general de las cosas de Nueva España*, written in the mid-sixteenth century, yet virtually unknown to European writers for three hundred years, and Bishop Diego de Landa's *Relación de las cosas de Yucatán* (Tozzer 1941) which was begun about 1566.

In Spain, during the early part of the Conquest, Peter Martyr d'Anghera (1912) was another figure of extreme importance in recording information about the New World. Although he never traveled to the New World himself, he was the first systematic reporter of the New World. He collected information from returning explorers and inspired the explorers to make notes about native customs.

In the Middle American area, the most important early works are those by Bernal Díaz, Hernán Cortés, Bernardino de Sahagún, Diego Durán, Diego de Landa, and several native accounts. Bernal Díaz del Castillo, born in 1492, the same year in which Columbus discovered the New World, participated in the first three main discoveries and conquests of Middle America. He accompanied Francisco Fernández de Cordova in 1517 on his exploration of coastal Yucatán. Díaz returned with Juan de Grijalva in 1518 for further exploration of what is now the state of Tabasco. In 1519 he accompanied Cortés on his conquest of New Spain. At the age of sixty-eight he wrote an account of these adventures, *Historia verdadera de la conquista de la Nueva España* (Díaz 1956), which was first published in 1632, many years after it had been written. This book is an invaluable document of an eyewitness account of Indian life at the time of the Conquest. Also important are the five letters written by Hernán Cortés to the King of Spain between 1519 and 1526 (MacNutt 1908). A third account of the Conquest and the Indians of Mexico comes from an anonymous conqueror who accompanied Cortés (Anonymous Conqueror 1917). The original Spanish text has been lost but an Italian translation was published in 1556.[2]

Two native accounts of the period of Conquest have also survived. *Cedula de Cuauhtemoc* is the oldest known source of the Nahuatl language written in European script. This account was issued in 1523 and in part describes the founding of the Aztec capital, Tenochtitlán. The second native document, *Anales de Tlatelolco,* written between 1524 and 1528, describes the history of Tenochtitlán from 1152 to 1528 (Vogt 1969:5).

A major contribution to the ethnography of post-Conquest Mexico was Bernardino de Sahagún's *Historia general de las cosas de Nueva España* (1950–1963), which was written in the sixteenth century. Sahagún learned the Aztec language, Nahuatl, and interviewed many of the natives in their own language. His work is an extensive compendium of information covering a wide variety of Indian life.

Fray Diego Durán moved to the New World when he was a young boy. He grew up in Mexico City and became a Dominican. He was interested in recording Aztec traditions, as he felt the missionaries had little idea of how many Aztec religious beliefs and practices had survived the Conquest. His *Book of the Gods and Rites* (Durán 1971) was written between 1576 and 1579; *The Ancient Calendar* (Durán 1971) was written in 1579; and *The History of the Indies* (Durán 1964) was written about 1580 or 1581. Much of his ethnographic material is excellent and has been confirmed by modern archaeological research.

Besides Durán's *History,* there are a number of works from the second half of the sixteenth century that are similar, or even identical. These include the *Crónica Mexicáyotl* attributed to Fernando Alvarado Tezozómoc (1949), the *Codice Ramírez* (Anonymous 1944), the *Historia de los Yndios Mexicanos,* by Juan de Tovar (1860) and Chapter VII of Acosta's *Historia natural y moral de las Indias* (1590). While some of these writers apparently copied Durán, he in turn acknowledges the use of an earlier source, which since has been lost. Bernal (1964:xxix) believes this early source was a col-

---

[2] Recent research (Gómez de Orozco 1961:23–33) has suggested the writer may never have been to the New World. Three other eyewitness accounts known as *Relaciones,* by Francisco de Aguilar (1963), Andrés de Tapia (1950) and Bernardino Vásquez de Tapia are concerned almost exclusively with military matters.

lection of native material by a Franciscan missionary, Olmos, who began collecting information on Aztec history as early as 1533. His precise research methods set the standards for later researchers, including Sahagún.

Bishop Diego Landa's *Relación de las cosas de Yucatán* (Tozzer 1941) remains the basic source on the lowland Maya written by a Spaniard. Because the Maya were still secretly worshiping traditional deities and maintaining many pre-Columbian customs when Landa arrived in Yucatán in 1549, he decided to teach the natives a lesson by burning all of their books of knowledge, the codices. Later, however, Landa became interested in the culture of the Maya. He learned their language and collected information on a variety of subjects upon which his book was written in 1566. Landa's work was not published until 1864, by which time part of the original manuscript had been lost.

Three important post-Conquest documents have survived from the Maya area which were recorded by native chroniclers, the *Popul Vuh* (Recinos 1950), a sacred book of the Quiché Mayas of highland Guatemala which deals with myths, cosmology, and religion; the *Annals of the Cakchiquels* (Recinos and Goetz 1953), also from the Guatemalan highlands and similar to the *Popul Vuh*; and the *Book of the Chilam Balam of Chumayel* (Roys 1933), which contains an important history of northern Yucatán.

South America   The most important early studies in South America come from Peru. An anonymous conquistador, who accompanied Pizarro on the Spanish Conquest of Peru in 1532, wrote an account of the Conquest which was published in 1534. Also important was the *Relation of the Discovery and Conquest of the Kingdoms of Peru,* by Pedro Pizarro (1921), a page who participated in the Conquest of Peru with his namesake. A very fine description from the post-Conquest period comes from Pedro de Cieza de León (1943–1945). He arrived in Peru in 1548, having traveled the full length of the Inca Highway from Colombia to Peru. His account, *La Crónica del Peru,* was first published in 1553. *Nueva crónica y buen gobiernor,* by Felipe Guaman Poma de Ayala (1936), published in 1613, is the only illustrated Peruvian codex. Its drawings of Andean life include depictions of Inca customs which are not known from other sources. Another important early chronicle is *Suma y narración de los Incas,* by Juan de Betanzos (1880), written in 1551.

John Murra (1970) has suggested several other important early Andean sources: Domingo de Santo Tomas, Juan Polo de Ondegardo, and Francisco de Ávila. Santo Tomas (1951a and 1951b) produced the first grammar and dictionary of an Andean language. Polo (1873 and 1916) served as a corregidor in the southern highlands for several decades, beginning in the 1540s. His memoranda and letters were a major source of information on the Inca for the colonial Spanish elite. Between 1598 and 1607, thirty tales and legends were collected in Huarochirí, in the highlands above Lima, and were saved by a Cuzco-born priest, Francisco de Ávila (1967). This collection is important because it is not a chronicle; instead it presents the natives' own outlook.

Finally, of extreme interest is the work of Garcilaso de la Vega, surnamed "El Inca." He was born in Cuzco in 1539, the son of a Spanish conquistador and an Inca princess. The knowledge gained from Inca relatives during childhood enabled him to write of the history of the Inca in his *Royal Commentaries of the Incas* (1966).

1800–1900: REDISCOVERY

A great deal of the early material collected in Latin America about the Amerinds eventually made its way to the archives of Spain and in many cases was forgotten or lost for centuries. Finally in the nineteenth century there developed a renewed interest in the ancient civilizations of Latin America. A new breed of historical scholars, such as William Prescott, searched the archives of Europe for primary source material. At the same time, new exploration was undertaken in search of the remains of past civilizations in the New World.

Mesoamerica   Alexander von Humboldt, who traveled extensively in the New World, published the first systematic treatise on American antiquities in 1814 (Humboldt 1814). His observations did little to stir the imaginations of the Europeans. In 1785, Antonio del Río, an artillery captain in the Spanish army, reported to Carlos III, King of Spain, that he had discovered a large, ruined city (Palenque) in the jungles of southern Mexico. Although little attention was given the report at the time, a copy made its way to London where it was published in 1822 (del Río 1822). It was this English publication that reawakened an interest in the pre-Columbian development of Latin America.

The description of a lost city (Palenque) in the jungles of Mexico excited the eccentric adventurer Jean-Frédéric-Maximilien, Baron de Waldeck. He arrived in Central America in 1832 and visited Palenque, staying for two years. He made a number of drawings, but few were made with any accuracy. For example, he depicted one Mayan figure with a French "liberté" hat; and he drew the stylized parrots of the Maya as elephants. Waldeck's drawings were used as evidence by writers who believed that the builders of Palenque had a transoceanic origin (Waldeck 1838; Waldeck and Brasseur de Bourbourg, 1866a, 1866b).

At about the same time that Baron Waldeck began his work in the jungles of southern Mexico, an Englishman, Edward King, later Lord Kingsborough, was publishing a compilation of many primary sources on the New World Indians that had been buried in archives and museums for centuries. Lord Kingsborough had collected everything known about pre-Columbian civilizations available in Europe to support his belief that the Indians were the Lost Tribes of Israel. The collection was published in nine lavish volumes as *Antiquities of Mexico* (1830–1848). Although the evidence he published did not support his theory, the volumes were of extreme importance, because they brought into print so many previously unknown and unavailable primary sources.

The books by Baron Waldeck and Lord Kingsborough stirred the imaginations of Europeans and North Americans alike, especially since they so closely followed the report of the discovery of the lost city of Palenque by del Río. Who had built the city and who were the people described in the works of Kingsborough? These became vital questions. In 1839 two expeditions set out to explore the Maya area, in particular Palenque. One expedition, American-organized, was made up of the lawyer turned traveler-writer, John L. Stephens, and the architect, Frederick Catherwood. The other, organized by the British, was under the direction of John Caddy and Patrick Walker. Although the British expedition was the first to arrive at Palenque, it was ill-fated (Pendergast 1967), and it was the American expedition that left its mark in the annals of Latin American history.

Stephens, acting as United States Consul to the Republic of Central America, which was on the verge of collapse, traveled through Central America and Yucatán on two expeditions, giving the world the first popular descriptions of the Mayan cities (1841, 1843). Catherwood made excellent detailed drawings of the art and architecture. Those drawings not destroyed later in a fire were published in 1844, as *Views of Ancient Monuments* (Catherwood 1844). Both explorers had previously traveled in Egypt and were well equipped to compare the arts and architecture of the two areas. Stephens and Catherwood both felt that the area from Honduras to Yucatán had been inhabited by culturally similar groups of people and that their development had occurred in the New World without stimulus from Egypt or anywhere else in the Old World. In other words, they had discovered a lost civilization right on the doorsteps of the United States. The vivid descriptions by Stephens and the accurate drawings of Catherwood presented a convincing argument. Yet there were skeptics.

Many were still intrigued by what they considered to be similarities between the Old World and the New World. A few, such as Augustus Le Plongeon, thought the origin of the proposed similarities was to be found in the New World. He hypothesized that the Maya sailed to the Nile, the Euphrates, and the Indian Ocean area eleven thousand five hundred years ago, carrying civilization with them. Most of the writers, however, saw the origin occurring in the Old World. G. Elliott Smith (1916 and 1933) and

William J. Perry attempted to prove that the Egyptians had carried civilization to the Maya. Wild speculation over New World origins reached its peak with the publication, in 1882, of *Atlantis: the Antediluvian World,* by Ignatius Donnelly, whereby the old Platonic idea of a lost continent was reintroduced into the study of Latin America.

South America   While Mesoamerica was being rediscovered, the rediscovery of the South American pre-Columbian heritage lagged behind. Several historians, William H. Prescott and Sir Clements Markham, in particular, brought to light many of the old chronicles on Peru. The first "dirt" archaeologist was E. George Squier. He was sent to Peru in 1853 as Abraham Lincoln's representative and published his studies of Peru in 1877 as *Peru: Incidents of Travel . . .* (Squier 1877).

The nineteenth century was a period of renewed interest in Latin America for Americans and Europeans. Pre-Columbian accomplishments were rediscovered. Some of the archivists and travelers made outstanding contributions, but as the twentieth century appeared on the horizon, there were still many more questions than answers. Whereas the nineteenth century was generally one of speculation and armchair hypothesizing, twentieth century anthropology can be characterized as the era of data collecting.

1900–1940: THE ERA OF EXCAVATION AND OBSERVATION

At the turn of the century, the ethnographical, archaeological, biological, and linguistic study of the Latin Americans began with a new breed of scientist, the anthropologist, arriving in Latin America.

Mesoamerica   Between 1896 and 1901 Frederick Starr carried out biological and ethnological studies in southern Mexico (Starr 1899, 1900–1902). Of special importance was the extensive photographic collection he assembled on the physical (and cultural) variations of different Indian groups living in the area. Edward Herbert Thompson (1965), diving into the Sacred Cenote of the Maya at the Chichén Itzá, proved beyond a reasonable doubt that it had been used for human sacrifices as described by Bishop Landa many centuries earlier. Alfred Tozzer (1907) lived with the Lacondon Maya, the least acculturated of the Maya groups, between 1902 and 1904, collecting extensive ethnographic data.

In 1914 the Carnegie Institution of Washington began its field work in Middle America under the direction of Sylvanus G. Morley. Numerous studies resulted from this project on Mayan ethnology, archaeology, and ethnohistory.

Between 1917 and 1920, Manuel Gamio (1922), a student of the

American anthropologist Franz Boas, directed a multidisciplinary study of the Valley of Teotihuacán. This project was the first major research project dealing with a culture of Middle America through time (Vogt 1969:12).

South America Over a number of years, Max Uhle, a German, and Julio C. Tello, a Peruvian, collected vast quantities of pre-Columbian artifacts and discovered many new sites of Inca and pre-Inca times. The Shippee-Johnson expedition in 1931 used aerial photography to locate many new Andean sites.

During this era the jungle Indian of South America was also examined through field research. John Gillin compiled a holistic study of the Barama River Caribs (Gillin 1936), of what today is known as Guyana, in 1932 and 1933. Samuel A. Barrett (1925) examined the life of the Cayapa Indians of Ecuador with special attention given to their material culture. Curt Nimuendajú (1939, 1942, 1946) reported on the life of a number of groups in Brazil.

New Directions Two other studies are important because they are concerned with groups other than traditional Amerind populations. From November, 1926 to July, 1927 Robert Redfield studied the Mexican peasant village of Tepoztlán (Redfield 1930). This study served as a catalyst for a great deal of the research that followed relating to peasants or communities. Another new direction of research was undertaken by Melville J. Herskovits and his wife Frances in the Caribbean. Anthropologists had ignored the Caribbean because the Indian had been exterminated during the early post-Contact period. Herskovits directed his attention to the culture of the Negroes who had been brought to the Caribbean from Africa during the Colonial period. His studies of Bush Negroes (Herskovits and Herskovits 1934), a Haitian valley (Herskovits 1937) and a Trinidad village (Herskovits and Herskovits 1947) dominated Caribbean studies for a number of years.

The period of 1900 to 1940 was one of considerable active field research. Only a few of the major figures of the period have been mentioned in order to indicate the nature of anthropological investigation during this time. Certainly many others are worthy of inclusion but were omitted in order to keep this historical survey brief.

1940 TO THE PRESENT: A PERIOD OF SYNTHESIS

The recent anthropological study of Latin Americans has been extensive. Many new avenues of research have been explored. In this section the summary will actually take into consideration only a small portion of the research that has been undertaken.[3]

Recent research has witnessed a marked increase in the use of large-scale projects to implement the collection of new data. A second important trend of this period has been greater concern with synthesizing data that has already been collected.

Mesoamerica There have been large-scale studies of archaeology, ethnology, and culture change in Mesoamerica. The Tehuacán Valley Project is concerned with the origin of domesticated maize in the New World. The project has taken a multidisciplinary approach to the study of how man first learned to modify wild plants to improve their yield in the New World.

A second large-scale archaeological project is the Teotihuacán Valley Project. Teotihuacán was probably the largest New World urban center of pre-Columbian times. Early archaeological research focused on the large civic ceremonial structures of the area. Today the modern researcher is reconstructing a number of facets of life: trade relationships, political and social structure, crafts, religious life, settlement pattern, and ecological adaptations, among others. The work actually involves three independent but related projects. One project was a series of excavations and reconstructions undertaken by Mexico's National Institute of Anthropology under the direction of Eusebio Dávalos and by the Mexican National Museum of Anthropology, under Ignacio Bernal. A second group conducted studies of the ecology and settlement patterns under the direction of William T. Sanders of Pennsylvania State University. A third group, from the University of Rochester, engaged in a detailed program of mapping under the direction of René Millon (Millon 1967:39).

Two important lowland projects are the studies of San Lorenzo Tenochtitlán and Tikal. San Lorenzo Tenochtitlán, which is actually a complex of three sites, is the oldest major Olmec ceremonial center of the lowlands. Three years of field work have been carried out by Yale University under the direction of Michael Coe, and the Instituto Nacional de Antropología e Historia (Cobean, et al. 1971:666). Extensive field work has been undertaken by the University of Pennsylvania at Tikal, the largest of the Mayan sites. Edwin M. Shook served as field director of the project for a number of years. A series of research reports have been published, including a detailed map (Carr and Hazard 1961) covering a zone of three square kilometers at the center of the site.

The Instituto Nacional de Antropología e Historia (INAH) of Mexico,

---

[3] The reader who wishes to learn more about current research is referred to the latest volumes of *The Handbook of Latin American Studies* and *The Latin American Research Review.*

has undertaken the most extensive program of archaeological investigation in Middle America. It has also sponsored a number of studies in ethnography and ethnohistory by Mexican scholars such as Roberto J. Weitlaner, Fernando Cámara Barbachano, and Wigberto Jiménez Moreno, to name just a few.

Two other important contributions to large-scale research in Middle America come from the Instituto Nacional Indigenista and the Tzeltal-Tzotzil Project. Established in 1948, the Instituto Nacional Indigenista has specialized in applied anthropology.[4] It has field centers in Chiapas, Oaxaca, Chihuahua, Yucatán, and Jalisco. The work emphasizes education and community development (Vogt 1969:13). The Tzeltal-Tzotzil Project was initiated in 1957. It is a joint project sponsored by the University of Chicago, Harvard University, and Stanford University. The project has specialized in the collection of linguistic and ethnographic materials from the Tzeltal- and Tzotzil-speaking Maya of the southern highlands of Mexico. Several important monographs that have already been published are Frank Cancian's (1965, 1972), Evon Vogt's (1969, 1970), Sarah C. Blaffer's (1972), and June Collier's (1968) studies of Zinacantan, a Mayan community.

In 1943 the Smithsonian Institution established the Institute of Social Anthropology as part of the Good Neighbor Policy. Anthropologists, sociologists, cultural geographers, and linguists were assigned to Bolivia, Mexico, Peru, and Brazil as visiting professors to teach contemporary social science and to participate with nationals of those countries in making basic studies of rural communities of the type that might be expected to test the growing impact of modernization (Foster 1969:204). Although not all of the scholars followed the expressed aims of the program, very important studies resulted from this program and were published in Smithsonian Institution's Institute of Social Anthropology Series. Some of these studies have become classics of Latin American anthropology, especially John Gillin's study of Moche, Peru (1947), Allan R. Holmberg's study of the Sirionó of eastern Bolivia (1950), Ralph L. Beal's study of Cherán, Mexico (1946), and George M. Foster's study of Tzintzuntzan, Mexico (1948).

South America   The large-scale approach to anthropology has also been used in Peru. In 1946 plans were formulated to study the human history of a single valley. Virú Valley, in northern Peru, was chosen as the site. The project was designed to include archaeologists to study the human adaptation to the valley environment over a long period of time, ethnologists to investigate the life ways of the modern inhabitants of the Virú Valley, and

---

[4] See Juan Comas, *La antropología social aplicada en México*, 1964, for a more extensive discussion of applied work in Mexico, as well as Richard N. Adams, *Introducción a la antropología aplicada*, 1964, for a discussion of work in Guatemala.

geographers to study the natural valley and its environment (Willey 1953: xvii).

An important study of applied anthropology was also undertaken in Peru. In 1952 Cornell University began its Vicos Project under the direction of Allan R. Holmberg. In that year Holmberg rented a hacienda, called Vicos, for the purpose of teaching the Indians who worked the hacienda fields how to assume the responsibility of running the hacienda themselves. Cornell cooperated with the Peruvian Institute of Indian Affairs. The hacienda provided the focus for a number of studies of directed culture change by Cornell students and faculty.[5]

The Caribbean   The most important large-scale project in the Caribbean has been Julian H. Steward's (1956) study of Puerto Rico, initiated in 1947. It represented the first organized attempt to describe and analyze a whole complex cultural system in Latin America from an anthropological point of view. At the time of the study, Puerto Rico had a population of approximately two million.

The fieldworkers operated within a common theoretical system and collected comparable data. The communities chosen for study were seen as samples representing types of communities which were historically and ecologically significant in contemporary and historical Puerto Rico. These communities included small independent farmers, a modern privately owned sugar plantation, a government-owned sugar plantation, and a traditional type of plantation system. These communities were seen as emerging from the various political, economic, and ecological changes which Puerto Rico had undergone in the course of its history (Strickon 1964:140).

The projects reviewed here represent something of the range of field studies undertaken during the past thirty years. There are others of importance that are not covered here, but many of these projects will be discussed elsewhere in the book.

Possibly the most important aspect of research in recent years has been the attempts to synthesize vast quantities of data that were already collected about the Latin Americans. These syntheses have, basically, taken two different forms: handbooks and classifications. The handbooks that provide the most inclusive coverage of the indigenous peoples of Latin America are the *Handbook of South American Indians* (Steward 1946–1959) and the *Handbook of Middle American Indians* (Wauchope 1965–   ).

The *Handbook of South American Indians* was planned in 1932 at the suggestion of the Swedish ethnographer, Baron Erland Nordenskiöld. A committee of the National Research Council requested that the Bureau of Ameri-

---

[5] See Holmberg (1966) for a list of publications resulting from the Vicos Project.

can Ethnology of the Smithsonian Institution undertake the tasks of editing and preparing the work. More than ninety North and South American scholars participated in the project. Because so much of the data on the South American natives were scattered in obscure sources published in a dozen languages, the *Handbook* was an attempt to assemble all available information on South American physical anthropology, linguistics, archaeology, and ethnology (Steward and Faron 1959:v). The work was published in six volumes plus an index. Material from the *Handbook* was further synthesized and incorporated into a theoretical framework and published in one volume as *Native Peoples of South America* (Steward and Faron 1959).

The National Research Council sponsored a similar synthesis of material on the Middle American Indians. It was assembled and edited at the Middle American Research Institute of Tulane University, under the direction of Robert Wauchope. Following in the tradition of the *Handbook of South American Indians,* the *Handbook of Middle American Indians* is an encyclopedia providing a summary and interpretation of the Indian culture of Mexico and northern Central America from remote times to the present. More than three hundred scholars contributed material on archaeology, natural environment, ethnology and social anthropology, ethnohistory, linguistics, and physical anthropology.

There have been a number of other important summary studies which have not been as extensive in scope as the handbooks but which are invaluable contributions to more restricted geographical or topical areas. In the 1930s the Mexican government sponsored an in-depth study of its indigenous population. The results were published by Carlos Basauri (1940). Between 1939 and 1949, the Instituto de Investigaciones Sociales of the University of Mexico also collected information on the Indians of Mexico which was published in 1957 as *Etnografía de México.*

Two other studies are important because they include Latin American subcultures other than the Amerinds. From 1953 to 1955, Richard N. Adams collected field data on the Central American republics (with the exception of Costa Rica) as part of a study sponsored by the World Health Organization (Adams 1957). The survey covered all the major subcultures of each country and is still the basic source for research in Central America. For scholars working in Nicaragua, El Salvador, and Honduras, this study remains the only extensive coverage in English. Additional material was contributed to the research by Ofelia Hooper for Panama, Doris Stone for Nicaragua and Honduras, and Edwin James for El Salvador.

A second study, by sociologists and anthropologists, is the material published by the Pan American Union on the middle class in Latin America, *Materiales para el estudio de la clase media en la América Latina* (Crevenna 1950–1951). Influenced by the work of W. Lloyd Warner and August B. Hollingshead in the United States, North American and Latin American scholars undertook an analysis of the middle-class phenomenon in many of the Latin American countries.

In addition to these large-scale research projects, handbooks, and summaries, the modern era of the anthropological investigation of Latin Americans is especially characterized by many attempts to synthesize material in order to classify the Latin American population in various subtypes.

CLASSIFYING THE CONTEMPORARY LATIN AMERICANS

Redfield's Folk Urban Continuum   Probably the single most influential anthropological publication relating to Latin America in the twentieth century has been Robert Redfield's *The Folk Culture of Yucatán* published in 1941. This book marked a culmination of theories Redfield had been developing for ten years. In 1923, after practicing law for a brief period following graduation from the University of Chicago Law School, Redfield traveled to Mexico. His interest was so aroused by this country and its problems that he returned to the University of Chicago in 1924 to begin graduate work in anthropology. In 1926 he and his family returned to Mexico for eight months to study the peasant community of Tepoztlán. In 1930, Redfield became a Research Associate of the Carnegie Institution. He and his associates undertook ethnological and sociological investigations in Yucatán and Guatemala (Cole and Eggan 1959:653). The result of these investigations was a study of four communities on the Yucatán Peninsula and the development of an evolutionary scheme to explain their differences. Two North American anthropologists, Redfield and Asael Hansen, and a Mexican school teacher assigned to the village of Chan Kom, Alfonso Villa Rojas, were the principal investigators.

The four communities studied were Mérida, the capital of Yucatán, a city of 96,660; Dzitas, a town of 1,200; Chan Kom, a peasant village of 250; and Tusik, a tribal village of 106. Most of the information published from these studies focused on Chan Kom and Tusik. Hansen never published his full study of Mérida. The community was described only in a short article (Hansen 1934). Dzitas was reported in two long papers, one a study of disease (Redfield and Redfield 1940) and the other a study of folk literature (M. Redfield 1935). Tusik was described, along with other tribal Mayan groups, by Villa Rojas (1945). Chan Kom, the peasant village, received the fullest coverage through an ethnography by Redfield and Villa Rojas (1934) and a study of change by Redfield (1950). In 1941, Redfield published a synthesis of the work of the group, *The Folk Culture of Yucatán.*

In developing a conceptual framework for his data, Redfield seems to have been influenced by at least four sources. (1) Earlier anthropologists and sociologists who made use of polar types to distinguish between civilized and primitive aspects of society provided one of these sources—in particular, Sir Henry Maine's (1861 and 1887) distinction between status and contract; Lewis H. Morgan's (1877) opposition of societas and civitas; Ferdinand Tönnies's (1935) antithesis between *Gemeinschaft* and *Gesellschaft;* Émile Durkheim's (1932) contrasts between the social segment and the social organ and between the sacred and the profane; and Howard Becker's (1930) concept of the "sacred society." Other influences were (2) the concern with the distribution of cultural traits that was still prevalent in North American anthropology during the 1930s; (3) the focus on the community as a unit of analysis by the sociologists of the University of Chicago such as Ernest Burgess and Robert Park; and (4) sociologist Louis Wirth's (1938) characterization of urban life.

On the Yucatán Peninsula of Mexico, a cultural contrast existed between the Spanish-modern area of the heavily populated Northwest and the more Indian-rustic area of the sparsely populated Southeast. Redfield's four communities were chosen to represent points along the line of this contrast. He found that the four communities from Tusik to Mérida were progressively characterized by less organization of the customary ways of life, greater individualization of behavior, and greater secularization. These three characteristics—disorganization, individualization, and secularization—were found to be causally interrelated with mobility and heterogeneity and with one another.

Mérida was the only large city in Yucatán. As a primate city it served as a center of commercial activity and of political and social influences for the entire peninsula. The owners and managers of approximately 80 percent of the henequen (hemp used to make rope) haciendas lived in Mérida. The population of the city was heterogeneous, with over a hundred different occupations represented in the city directory. Many of the inhabitants had not been born in Mérida. Its population included mixed whites and Indians in varying proportions, some pure Indians, Syrians, Orientals, and a few West Indian Negroes. There was also considerable diversity in levels of education, literacy, and languages spoken.

To Redfield the town of Dzitas was a meeting place of both urban and rural ways of life. It was a center of trade situated on important lines of communication and included people of all degrees of Spanish and Indian admixture. Dzitas was a center of production and a shipping point of maize. Maize accounted for almost all of the exports of the community. Although most of the population farmed, as many as one-quarter of the men were not engaged in agriculture. These were the officials, teachers, shopkeepers, railroad employees, and others sent from Mérida who performed specialized services. This group, more than any other in Dzitas, maintained ties with the city.

The peasant village, Chan Kom, and tribal village, Tusik, were both composed of independent agriculturalists of Mayan descent. They differed in the fact that the people of Chan Kom accepted the government of Mexico and sought to follow city ways at least as far as they knew them; the people of Tusik were not only more independent of the city economically but also more hostile to the national government, and they sought to remain free of the city man and his ways. In other words, they wished to maintain their tribal identity. Describing Chan Kom, Redfield writes (1941:50) "So far as can be determined, no other village in the eastern part of the state has modified its ways so rapidly and consistently since the Revolution. It has a reputation in Yucatán for industry, determination and ambition." In contrast, Redfield (1941:51) found that, "Of all of the natives of Quintana Roo those of the X-Cacal subtribe are the most seclusive and the most resistant to modernizing ways. Tusik is one of the villages of this group." While the inhabitants of Chan Kom grew maize as a commercial crop to feed the henequen plantation employees, maize was strictly a subsistence crop for the people of Tusik. The main contact with the modern world for the X-Cacal Maya was through the sale of chicle.

According to Redfield, as one moved from the remote villages toward the city commercial dealings became more general, the role of wealth in determining status increased, there was an increasing degree of individual freedom over the control of wealth and in undertaking commercial ventures, individual ownership of land increased, the division of labor became more complex, the division of labor between sexes became somewhat less rigidly defined, collective effort became rare and individual effort occurred more frequently, and the discharge of special functions changed from predominantly sacred to secular. Family organization became progressively weaker as one went from village to city. The secularization of urban life occurred not only with the pagan elements of religion but in connection with Christian elements as well. In Mérida Catholicism emerged as a formal church that self-consciously organized and maintained itself in competition with other interest groups. The fiesta changed from a collective act of homage rendered by the community to its supernatural guardian to a commercial undertaking for the profit of individuals. In the villages, ideas about disease were closely interdependent with moral and religious conceptions; in the city they were less so. The secularization of folk medicine was associated with the transfer of the healing functions with the male shaman-priests to curers who were women (Redfield 1941).

While Dzitas and Chan Kom played a role in Redfield's continuum, it was the polar type to which he paid the greatest attention. Above all it was the folk pole that he described in greatest detail. In 1947 Redfield presented the following characteristics of the folk society (1947:297–299):

1.   The folk society is a small society.
2.   The folk society is an isolated society.

3. People who make up a folk society are much alike.
4. The members of the folk society have a strong sense of belonging together.
5. Secondary and tertiary tools (tools to make tools) are relatively few compared to primary tools.
6. The division of labor is limited.
7. The group is economically independent of all others.
8. The ways in which the members of the society meet the recurrent problems of life are conventionalized ways; they are the results of long communications within the group in the face of these problems; and these conventionalized ways have become interrelated within one another so that they constitute a *coherent and self-consistent system* (Redfield's definition of "culture").
9. A folk society is an organization of people doing many different things successfully as well as simultaneously.
10. The ends of the folk society are taken as given.
11. Behavior is personal, not impersonal.
12. Folk society is composed of families rather than individuals.
13. Folk society is a sacred society.
14. Folk society is characterized by much magic.
15. Folk society maintains a primitive world view, i.e., a disposition to treat nature personally, to regard attributes as entities, and to make symbolic rather than casual connections.
16. No place exists in the folk society for the motive of commercial gains.

Although Redfield never fully discussed the characteristics of the urban pole of his continuum, he did attempt to classify cities on the basis of their cultural role (Redfield and Singer 1954). A distinction was made between the carrying forward of an old culture, which he called the "orthogenetic" role, and the creating of new modes of thought that have authority beyond or are in conflict with old cultures and civilizations, which he called the "heterogenetic" cultural role of the city.

Although Beals (1961) suggests that the folk-urban continuum has generated more research than any other concept developed for Latin American field work, there has been considerable criticism of both Redfield's conceptualization and its factual base.

Sol Tax, working in highland Guatemala, found societies which represented neither the folk nor the urban but a combination of both. The Amerind communities that he studied were small and homogeneous as Redfield would have predicted; but the Indians were mobile, had impersonal relations, maintained formal institutions, and individuals acted primarily for economic reasons rather than for social good (Tax 1939:467). Tax's findings led Redfield to conclude, in his Yucatán study, that "there is no single necessary cause for secularization and individualization" (Redfield 1941:369). In a later article, Tax (1941:37) pointed out that there seemed to be two aspects of culture that cut across the dichotomy of the continuum. He found that the Guatemalan Indian "world view" or "mental apprehension of reality" was folk in character, but their social relations more closely resembled those of the urban type. Tax (1937) also found several types of communities—the nuclear town, conforming in its essential features to the basic Spanish colonial model, and a second type which did not fit well with the continuum model, the vacant town, characterized by the geographic duality of its partly resident Indian population. The Indians of these communities often had two houses, one in town and one near their fields. During the week they lived near the farmland and on weekends they came to town.

Although Redfield used communities as his basic unit, the type of community studied by John Gillin in Guatemala would be difficult to classify on the continuum. In San Luis Jilotepeque, two groups lived side by side in the same community without achieving cultural amalgamation. Although the customs of the two cultures dovetailed and overlapped at certain points with cooperative effect, the discreteness of the two configurations (Indian and Ladino) had been maintained (Gillin 1945).

Oscar Lewis (1952), in a study of families from Tepoztlán that had moved to Mexico City, found that the Tepoztecans living in Mexico City were able to adapt to city life with greater ease than American farm families who migrated to cities. There was little evidence of disorganization, of culture conflict, or of irreconcilable differences between generations. Therefore he concluded that urbanization is not a simple, unitary, universally similar process but assumes different forms and meanings depending upon the prevailing historic, economic, social, and cultural conditions. As possible reasons for the lack of disorganization or "breakdown," as he terms the process, Lewis gave the following (1952:41):

1. Mexico City has been an important political, economic, and religious center for Tepoztecans since pre-Hispanic times.
2. Mexico City is more homogeneous than cities in the United States.
3. Mexico City is conservative in tradition.
4. Mexico City is not as highly industrialized as many American cities and does not present the same conditions of life.
5. Mexican farmers live in well-organized villages that are more like cities and towns than like the "open-country" settlement pattern of North American farmers.
6. Tepoztlán is culturally similar to Mexico City. The similarities between the value systems of working-class and lower-middle-class families in Mexico City and those of Tepoztecans are probably much greater than those between families from the hill country of

Arkansas and working-class and middle-class families from St. Louis or Detroit.

Redfield has been criticized for focusing on only the community as a unit of analysis and ignoring the economic base of the Yucatán Peninsula as well as the national context in which the communities were found. Strickon (1965:36–37) and Mintz (1953:138) have both shown that the folk-urban continuum, for the most part, ignored the henequen plantations which were the most important economic aspect of the entire peninsula and upon which all four of his communities were economically dependent, directly or indirectly. Further, Redfield was not concerned with the relationship of the four communities to the Mexican nation. For example, the Revolution had played an important role in the development of the social, economic, and political characteristics of these communities, as had the earlier Caste War.

The Caste War, which began in 1847 as the peninsula's economy changed from dependence on maize and cattle haciendas to sugar plantations, was almost completely ignored in Redfield's analysis of Tusik, the tribal village, and Chan Kom, the peasant village. The parents of the inhabitants of both Chan Kom and Tusik were derived in part from the Maya who had been part-time laborers on maize and cattle haciendas and who had provided part of the manpower for the rebellion (Strickon 1965:48). Following the Caste War, Chan Kom was settled by former participants of the rebellion around 1880 (Redfield 1950:2). Chan Kom became a maize producing community providing food for the expanding henequen plantations. The village became tied to the regional economy.

Other participants of the Caste War migrated south into Quintana Roo. Some of the them founded the village of Tusik. Instead of forming a typical primitive society (one that had existed in isolation over a long period of time), Tusik was, in fact, a recently settled community made up of migrants from the North who had only a short time previously been exposed to creole culture. The only reason Tusik was isolated at the time Redfield's group studied it was as Strickon (1965:50) suggests:

> The interest of Mexico and the rest of the world in it was limited. The Santa Cruz Maya, the people of Tusik, were permitted to live relatively uninvolved with the larger economy and polity in an area that no one else wanted. These Maya raised maize for their own use and retained intact the military and religious structures they had developed in response to the pressures of the Caste War. They may have lost some of their pugnaciousness but very little of their suspicion of outsiders as they filled a niche, that of refugees, which had been an ongoing part of Yucatecan culture ever since Spain and the estate appeared on the peninsula.

Each of Redfield's communities played a specialized role in a larger encompassing system. The roles these communities played in the 1930s, during Redfield's studies, and the role they had played prior to the research, were determined by the larger system in which they all participated. The changes in Yucatecan communities, which Redfield saw as an evolutionary sequence, did not occur serially but rather as continual adjustments to the changing requirements of the more encompassing estate system and the ecological possibilities that their particular habitats offered to the needs of this larger system. The spatial distribution of communities, as seen by Redfield in the 1930s, was just one point in the ongoing adaptation of Yucatecan culture to the continually changing demands of the estate system. This system, in turn, linked Yucatán to the national and international economies (Strickon 1965:60–61).

Another problem with Redfield's analysis was his diachronic interpretation of synchronic material. J. Clyde Mitchell (1966:44) suggested that studies of urbanization in Africa have confused two different types of change. He distinguished between the overall changes in the social system, which he called processive change, and changes in behavior following participation in different social systems, which he called situational change. It would seem that Redfield confused situational change with processive change when he attempted a diachronic analysis from his synchronic data. In comparing urban life with its rural counterpart, Redfield was describing different situations, not a process. As each of Redfield's communities was an adaptation to a different type of environment, it is difficult to picture these communities as forming an evolutionary sequence. There is little reason to assume that Tusik will ever become another Mérida. What Redfield found was four different sets of social situations. In the city he found urban institutions, and in the rural area he found various rural institutions. These institutions existed contemporaneously with one another in Yucatán. Mitchell (1966:47–48) described the nature of situational change in modern Africa, and this seems also to be an appropriate description of the type of change Redfield actually was observing in Yucatán:

The individual does not bring his social institutions with him to town. The institutions are parts of different social systems and the individual moves f·om one into the other. It is fallacious, therefore, to think of rural in..itutions as changing into urban types of the same institutions. The fact is rather that urban dwellers develop institutions to meet their needs in towns and these, because of their different contexts, differ from rural institutions meeting the same need in the tribal social system. An urban social institution is not a changed rural institution; it is a separate social phenomenon existing as part of a separate social system so that the behavior in town of a migrant when it differs from that in his rural home is more than likely to be a manifestation of 'situational' rather than 'processive' change.

Victor Goldkind (1965, 1966, 1970) has presented another type of criticism of Redfield's work, i.e., his characterization of the peasant village, Chan Kom, as a homogeneous and classless community. Making use of Redfield's own data (Redfield and Villa Rojas 1934 and Redfield 1950), Goldkind found considerable evidence to the contrary. A limited-focus (Goldkind 1970) field study in Yucatán in 1964 provided further documentation of Redfield's misinterpretation of the empirical data. Redfield's tendency to overemphasize the homogeneity rather than the hetereogeneity of Chan Kom seems consistent with his view of the peasant village. Oscar Lewis (1951: 432) has criticized Redfield for the same tendency in his study of Tepoztlán.

Reinterpreting Redfield's data led Goldkind to the conclusion that Chan Kom was a socially stratified village during both of Redfield's visits to the community. Three extended families monopolized land holdings, commercial activities, political offices, and centrally located housing. These same families were the Spanish-speaking members of a basically Maya-speaking community who owned the statues of the community saints and influenced village decision making. The man who served as Redfield's primary informant was a member of one of these families and an important community leader. Following Redfield's studies, he eventually became so powerful that members of the other two influential families were forced to flee Chan Kom.

While Redfield's folk-urban continuum was an attempt to deal with some of the problems of societies more complex than had previously been studied by Latin American scholars, it suffered from an oversimplification of ethnographic data. Generally only three types of differences were recognized by Redfield—that associated with urban groups, that associated with peasants, and that associated with more primitive types of groups. As Oscar Lewis (1953:131) observed:

The typology involved in the folk-urban classification of societies tends to obscure one of the most significant findings of modern cultural anthropology, namely, the wide range in the ways of life and in the value systems among so-called primitive peoples. The "folk society," as used by Redfield, would group together food-gathering, hunting, pastoral and agricultural peoples without distinction. What has been said of the folk end of the folk-ridden formula applies also to the urban end. Focusing only on the formal aspects of urban society reduces all urban societies to a common denominator and treats them as if they all had the same culture. Thus, Greek, Egyptian, Roman, Medieval, and twentieth-century American and Russian cities would all be put into the same class.

In the 1950s there were a number of increasingly sophisticated attempts at classifying the diverse lifeways found in Latin America. The first of these was a study of the island of Puerto Rico.

Steward's Subcultures of Puerto Rico   A project that was to set an example of how a complex society could be studied was developed by Julian H. Steward. Beginning in 1947, a project under the sponsorship of the University of Puerto Rico was designed to study the social anthropology of the Puerto Rican people. Research was directed by Steward, with the assistance of Robert Manners, Sidney W. Mintz, Elena Padilla Seda, Eric Wolf, and Raymond Scheele (Steward 1956). Steward conceived of the island as a sociocultural system. As a structural entity it consisted of many kinds of sociocultural segments or subgroups and of institutions which were in a functional relationship to one another and to the whole.

According to Steward (1956:47), a total national culture is divisible into two general kinds of features—those that function and must be studied on a national level, and those that pertain to sociocultural segments or subgroups of the population. The former include features such as the form of government, legal system, economic institutions, religious organizations, educational systems, law enforcement, military organization, and others. These institutions have aspects which are national and sometimes international in scope and which must be understood apart from the behavior of the individuals connected with them.

The sociocultural segments or subcultural groups of individuals are amenable to the methods of direct observation used by ethnology. There are several categories of such groups in modern states and nations. First there are the localized groups which may result from differentiation that has occurred during national development—for example, subcultures arising from local specialization in production or cultural ecological adaptations. These may also consist of ethnic minorities. The latter may be native inhabitants who have survived from a prenational period or immigrants who brought a distinctive culture into the nation. Second there are "horizontal" groups such as castes, classes, occupational divisions, and other segments which hold status positions in a hierarchical arrangement and usually crosscut localities to some extent. These too may represent segments which either have been differentiated during national development or have been incorporated from the outside (Steward 1956:47–48).

Five subcultures that reflected Puerto Rico's cultural diversity, four rural and one urban, were chosen for study. One was a sugar-growing community on the south coast characterized by corporate ownership, large-scale irrigation, and mechanization. The community was typical of the trend in Puerto Rico toward large absentee-ownership. Its population consisted largely of laborers and resident managers. Also studied were north coast communities where the government was the main owner of land and sugar mills but where there was no irrigation and little mechanization. Like the south coast sugar communities, these communities consisted largely of laborers. Third was a coffee-producing community in the western mountains. This district was characterized by traditional face-to-face relations between owners and workers, general lack of mechanization, considerable survival of old Hispanic patterns, and the concentration of land in the hands of Spanish-born owners. Fourth was a tobacco and mixed crop community in the central mountains. This region had privately owned farms, most of which were small. Finally, there was a study of the upper class elite of the city of San Juan. This class had very close connections with the United States, where its members spent considerable time. The elite was seen as a medium by which North American influence was transmitted to the island. Also, its prominent members were given special attention because of their economic, social, and political power in the society. The upper class of San Juan formed most of Puerto Rico's upper class (Steward 1950:126–139; Manners and Steward 1954). The four rural communities were seen as samples representing types of communities which were historically and ecologically significant in contemporary and historical Puerto Rico. These communities were seen as emerging from various political, economic, and ecological changes which Puerto Rico had undergone in the course of its history.

Each of the communities was analyzed in terms of both its internal structure and its relations to the larger society. The analysts used a common set of categories for their data, and their analyses also depended upon the use of common variables. Both the categories and the variables in turn were determined by the researchers' emphasis on economic and ecological variables as major determinants of culture (Strickon 1964:140).

The data from the particular communities, both from the time of the field study and from the historic past, were related to the policies of the great metropolitan powers, first Spain and then the United States, that controlled the island. Thus there developed a structural network which related ways of life in particular classes and communities to local conditions, to the island as a whole, and to the world outside the island. This was further reinforced by a consideration of some of the institutions and subcultures which were island-wide in distribution and which, therefore, cut across local systems (Strickon 1964:140–141). Only the study of the upper class of San Juan was not well integrated into the study, due to the dearth of information on elites at that time.

Steward (1956:9) suggests that there are two aspects of insular institutions, the formal and the local, that reflect the traditional division of labor among the social scientists. Anthropologists have studied the local, while sociologists, economists, political scientists, and others have studied the formal aspects. The following chart presents examples of how these aspects are distinct yet complementary (Steward 1956:9):

TABLE 5.1

Examples of insular institutions

Formal insular or extra-insular aspects	Local aspects
Government regulations and aid	Subsistence farming
Insular economy, world markets, sources of credit, etc.	Cash crop production and trade
Basic economy, land laws, inheritance system	Land tenure
Marriage and inheritance laws	Marriage and family
Insular social structure	Social classes
Economic system and insular specialization	Occupational groups
Labor unions	Labor union locals
National government	Local government
National parties and ideologies	Political affiliations and ideologies
National clubs and societies	Local associations
Organized churches	Church and supernaturalism
Educational system and mass media of communication	Schools of learning
Organized sports	Recreation
Government health measures	Hospitals, doctors, curers

Redfield (1962:388) has observed that if Steward had not chosen patterns of land use as the critical factor in selecting his communities, the representation of Puerto Rico would have been considerably different. Kushner (1969:110) carries the criticism even further by suggesting that "another anthropologist, even operating with Steward's units in mind, could very well have chosen other ways to think about Puerto Rico and could indeed have developed a very different portrait." Adams (1970:34) has further criticized Steward because the interrelationship of Puerto Rico and the United State was underplayed.

In spite of its weakness, Steward's study of Puerto Rico remains, as Strickon has observed (1964:141), "a model, though one which must be expanded upon and refined, for the sort of work that still remains to be done in most of Latin America."

Steward's approach to a complex situation, a nation, employed two important emphases which were lacking in Redfield's study. First, Steward used a cultural-historical approach. Unlike Redfield's reliance on trait distribution to reconstruct the past of Yucatán, Steward recognized that the historical analysis of a nation such as Puerto Rico cannot be handled in the same way that anthropologists had been reconstructing the past of the nonliterate primitive societies. In studying a nation, the anthropologist has to make use of a number of written sources: local records, archive data, newspapers, and so on, to piece together the historical development of the subcultures and their relationship to the total sociocultural system of which they are a part. Second, Steward viewed his subcultures as part of a large sociocultural system. Even Redfield's most primitive group, Tusik, cannot be understood unless one understands that its way of life is an adaptation to a larger sociocultural unit. By having cognizance of this fact, Steward has produced a greatly improved picture of a complex society in contrast to Redfield's study of Yucatán.

Wagley and Harris's Subculture Types   Another study undertaken shortly after Steward's Puerto Rico study, and also involving personnel from Columbia University, was the Columbia-Bahía Project, a study of the state of Bahía, Brazil. This was a cooperative effort between Columbia University and the Fundaçao para o Desenvolvimento da Ciencia na Bahía in 1950–1951 under the direction of Charles Wagley, Luis A. Costa Pinto, and Thales de Azevedo. Studies were undertaken of a community in the sugar-planting area near the coast (Hutchinson 1952, 1957), an old mining center in the central mountain zone (Harris 1952, 1956), and a community in the arid semidesert of the northeast (Zimmerman 1952). A later study was carried out in the cacao producing zone of southern Bahía (Leeds 1957).

On the basis of this research, Wagley and Harris (1965) developed a typology of subculture types in 1955. Subcultures are variations of a larger cultural tradition and represent the way of life of significant segments of the Latin American population. Distinguishing subcultures had a distinct advantage over Redfield's folk-urban continuum in that it was useful not only in describing differences *between* communities, but also internal cultural heterogeneity *within* communities. The folk-urban continuum was inadequate to describe nonurban communities which were heterogeneous. Wagley and Harris distinguished nine significant Latin American subculture types.

(1) *Tribal Indian Types.* This type is comprised of the few remaining aboriginal peoples. Only a small number of these groups remain today, and generally they are found in marginal areas such as the Chaco, the headwaters of the Amazon tributaries, or on isolated reservations and mission stations. As long as they remain carriers of their traditional culture they are not really a modern Latin American subculture, but rather carriers of distinct cultures within the geographic boundaries of Latin America. However, most of these groups have undergone some type of acculturation. Generally the tribal Indian types are remnants of groups that once inhabited the lowland areas during the pre-Contact period. Generally these groups lacked any large-scale political organization.

(2) *Modern Indian Types.* Unlike the lowlands, the highland regions of Latin America were inhabited by a dense aboriginal population organized into native states. These people were brought under the domination of the Spanish and formed the basic labor source for the conquerors. They borrowed freely from the European culture of the sixteenth and seventeenth centuries—a culture which in many respects contained as many "folk" fea-

tures as their own. By the beginning of the eighteenth century, through the fusion of aboriginal and colonial Spanish patterns, a new culture had emerged among these people. This culture persists today, unchanged in its main outlines, and constitutes an important variant of national patterns in many highland countries.

Modern Indians generally speak an aboriginal language; however, many are bilingual. Most are horticulturists planting native American crops, although European plants have also been adopted. The community is still the landholding unit and community cohesion generally persists at a high level despite the encroaching power of national states. Often native village officials are maintained alongside the national bureaucracy. While the Modern Indian is nominally Catholic, a large number of aboriginal beliefs have been fused with Catholic ideology. The Indians of each community generally think of themselves as ethnic groups separated from other Indian groups and from the nationals of the country in which they reside. Often they wear a distinctive costume which identifies them as Indians of a particular community. Many of these communities are endogamous. By Wagley and Harris's classification (1965:46), the Indians of Tusik would be included in the modern Indian type. In most communities inhabited by the modern Indian, there are also a few non-Indians (carriers of a peasant type subculture) who form an integral part of the community life. "Any full community study must treat not only the two subcultures of these communities but also the 'castelike' relationship between them" (Wagley and Harris 1965:46).

(3) *Peasant Types.* The people who live in the isolated agricultural villages of Latin America have a way of life which is analogous in many respects to that of peasants in other parts of the world. Latin American peasants are represented by American Indians, Negroes, or Europeans, or admixtures of these. They are called *mestizos* (in Mexico and other countries), *ladinos* (in Guatemala), *cholos* (in Peru), or *caboclos, tabareus, caipiras,* and *matutos* (in Brazil) (Wagley and Harris 1965:46). Like the modern Indian, the peasant is a horticulturist growing the same crops by the same techniques. The peasant subculture is also a syncretism of archaic European patterns and those of Amerind or African origin, however, unlike the modern Indians, peasants consider themselves to be nationals of the country in which they reside. In other words, instead of considering themselves Tzoltzil or Chamula, as the modern Indians would, the peasants consider themselves to be Mexicans, even though their integration with national institutions and economies is at the regional level. There is a fairly extensive participation in commercial transactions, usually at local or regional markets, where peasant farmers regularly sell their surplus crop for cash. Peasants generally speak the national language, though often a rural dialect of the language. The Catholicism practiced by the peasant tends to be more orthodox than that of the modern Indian. "Peasants share national fashions, values

and aspirations, although in all of these they are generally 'behind the times' since they tend to be isolated from the centers of diffusion" (Wagley and Harris 1965:47). There are persons living in most peasant communities who are neither peasants nor rural but townsmen with urban aspirations and urban patterns of behavior. An example of a community with a peasant subculture, as well as townsmen, is the village of Tepoztlán.

(4) *Engenho Plantation Types.* The *engenho* plantation was the family-owned type of sugar cane plantation which developed during the Colonial period in the lowlands of northern South America and in the Caribbean and was based on slave labor from Africa. The engenho plantation formed a closed social system in itself. The center of the plantation was the mansion in which the owner, his family, and his many servants lived. A chapel located nearby served as the church for the owner and his slaves. Behind the mansion were the slave quarters. The engenho plantation generally operated with no more than two hundred to three hundred persons. Leadership on the plantation was provided by the Portuguese and the Spanish and economics, religion, and almost all aspects of life were directed and controlled by the aristocratic owner or his administrators.

The abolition of slavery, the fluctuations of the international markets, and finally the industrialization of sugar refining brought about important changes in the colonial sugar plantations. However, many plantations are still found throughout Latin America which strongly resemble the old engenho plantation in their organization, despite the substitution of wage labor for slavery and other innovations. These present-day engenho plantations are similar to those which Wolf and Mintz (1957) and Julian Steward (1959:9–10) have called the hacienda in their typologies.

The modern engenho community consists of the carriers of two distinct subcultures, that of the workers and that of the owners. The engenho plantation owner is generally an urban Latin American cosmopolitan who is a part of the upper strata of the principal large cities. He is often a member of the old aristocracy. Since early colonial times his family has had both a house in the city and a place of residence in the country. His employees, formerly his family's slaves or peons (including domestic servants in the city, as well as the workers in the country), are treated by him with characteristic patriarchical, intimate, and benevolent concern. To this treatment the engenho plantation worker responds with loyalty and attitudes of dependence. It is this dependence and allegiance to the boss (*patrão*), together with the distinctive land tenure, occupational and communal arrangements peculiar to producing a monocrop, that distinguishes engenho plantation from peasant subcultures (Wagley and Harris 1965:48–50).

(5) *Usina Plantation Types.* The term *usina,* which characterizes the second plantation subculture of Wagley and Harris, comes from the Portuguese term used for the modern industrialized sugar mill. In this type of plantation system, the traditional pattern of intimacy and mutual depen-

dence between the workers and their employers found on the engenho plantation is replaced by a more intense economic relationship between the workers and the administrators and officials of the corporation. On the usina plantation, the number of workers increases and the social unit is more heterogeneous as new specialized occupations appear. The workers, without the old emotional ties to their fellow workers and to their employers, are more mobile than before, often leaving the plantations to seek higher wages elsewhere. The usina plantation, according to Wagley and Harris, is more clearly integrated with national institutions and culture patterns than is the engenho plantation. Labor unions are sometimes active among the workers, and social welfare legislation is enforced more often than on the engenho plantation. On the usina plantation, there may be modern facilities such as electric lights, schools, public health facilities, and excellent communications with the metropolitan centers. The workers have a way of life more similar to that of the growing urban-industrial proletariat of Latin America than to that of the workers on the older style engenho plantation (Wagley and Harris 1965:51–52).

The usina plantation type of Wagley and Harris is similar to Steward's field-and-factory combine type. Like Wagley and Harris, Steward emphasizes that national integration is typical of this type of plantation. He characterizes these combines as follows (Steward 1959:10–11):

(1) . . . they tend to be monocrop and provide no land for workers' subsistence plots; (2) they are highly mechanized and highly financed; (3) the laborers are entirely on a wage basis and depend wholly upon purchases for their food and other needs; (4) the worker's subculture is being affected not only by the economic arrangements but by education, mass communication, urban influences, and face-to-face contacts with other persons. The workers have a national rather than local orientation.

(6) *Town Types.* Towns where periodic fairs are held and which serve as the administrative and religious centers for rural districts have a long tradition in Latin America. Many are also regional market centers. In recent years these market centers have enlarged their range of trading with the improvement of transportation, thus becoming more closely integrated with national economic and political life. Life in these larger towns is becoming more like that of the urban centers by which they are influenced.

Yet there are still innumerable small towns that serve only an immediate rural area and preserve many traditional patterns. Within these towns there are two subcultures, the peasant and the town type. The town type is the local upper class. To the upper class inhabitants of the large cities, the local upper class are "hicks" or "country bumpkins." However, the life of the upper class townsman differs radically from that of the carriers of the peasant subcultures. The small-town upper class manifests in many respects an archaic version of the ideals and patterns of the big-city cosmopolitans and the plantation gentry of former times. They are often more familiar with the cities than with the rural areas of the community in which they live, and they try to emulate the dress, manners, and outlook of the cosmopolitan. Yet the town type is often thwarted in his ambitions by the incompleteness and inaccuracy of his notions of the contemporary standards of sophistication. For that reason the cultural patterns which he maintains are considered "old-fashioned" in the cities.

In general the upper class townsmen control most of the political and economic power in the local community. Upper class social life revolves around forms of entertainment from which the peasants are excluded. Catholicism is more orthodox than in either the peasant or modern Indian subculture.

The existence of Town subcultures in isolated communities furnishes the key to the problem of the relationship of Peasant subcultures to lines of national political and economic integration. Local standards are set and maintained by this sociocultural segment, and it is through the upper class of the town that changes emanating from national legislation and metropolitan influences must filter before reaching the peasant stratum (Wagley and Harris 1965:54).

(7) *Metropolitan Upper Class Types.* The people of the metropolitan upper class attempt to maintain the traditional patterns and ideals of an aristocratic landed gentry. This is the group which participates in and generally dominates local and national politics. Its members are absentee landlords, high-level government employees and officials, owners of industry and large commercial enterprises, and many well-to-do doctors, lawyers, and other professionals. The metropolitan upper class has a disdain for manual labor, an admiration for courtly manners, and a love of luxury. But, at the same time, it is this group that permits its daughters to have "dates" and allows them to enter the professions. They maintain contact with both Europe and the United States. Hence, the metropolitan upper class tends both to preserve old traditional forms and to be innovators, accepting new forms from abroad which then diffuse to the lower class of the city, to the peasants and the workers on plantations. To some extent the ideal patterns of the other Latin American subcultures are derived from metropolitan upper class patterns.

(8) *Metropolitan Middle Class Types.* This subculture is made up of first-generation professionals and of white-collar workers in business and government. The middle class maintains standards of material consumption such as housing, clothing, and prestige closely patterned after those of the metropolitan upper class. Its members seem to place a high value on freedom from manual labor. They employ domestic servants. Salaries are often insuffi-

cient in this subculture to maintain leisure-class standards. As a result, many middle-class wage earners hold down a multiplicity of jobs.

(9) *Urban Proletariat Types.* This group is the numerically dominant segment of the city. The last generation has seen considerable growth of urban centers due to migration from the rural areas. As a result, a large percentage of the urban proletariat are probably carriers of peasant, usina and engenho plantation, or town subcultures. Wagley and Harris considered this subculture the least known of all.

The Wagley and Harris typology was a considerable step forward from Redfield's folk-urban continuum; yet the subculture typology has its weaknesses as well. The various types are not always comparable units. Also, the subcultures seem to work best as a description of Brazil, even though they suggest the typology is valid for all of Latin America. As the usina-engenho subculture types are based primarily on the socioeconomic structure of the plantation, the typology does not take into account the relation of either the administrators or the workers to the cultural setting. For example, in Costa Rica, the foreign managers (primarily from the United States) of United Fruit Company employed West Indian Negroes to a much greater extent than it did Costa Rican nationals. Given the frequency with which foreign firms make use of migrant laborers from other cultural settings, the usina-engenho types are not an inclusive classification of plantation workers. In Costa Rica, as a result of the foreign managers, the mechanized plantation system functioned more like the engenho plantation in that the Costa Rican plantation system retarded the rate of acculturation and assimilation of the labor force in terms of integration to national institutions and cultural patterns. The foreign managers functioned as the buffer between plantation workers, national institutions, and cultural patterns of Costa Rica. As a result, the Negro laborers had little face-to-face contact with agents of Costa Rican national institutions or cultural patterns.

Adams's Cultural Components   Richard N. Adams attempted to develop a classification of Central America which better fit that area than did the Wagley and Harris typology. His classification was based on information collected in two surveys. In 1952 Adams and Harry Tschopik undertook an initial survey of eight communities in Costa Rica. Adams undertook more extensive general surveys of Panama and Nicaragua in 1953, Guatemala in 1954, and El Salvador and Honduras in 1955 for the World Health Organization. He had planned to carry out a comparable study in Costa Rica, but the Costa Rican Director General of Public Health refused permission for the survey in that country (Adams 1957:8). British Honduras and El Peten, in Guatemala, were largely omitted from the classification, as surveys had not been undertaken in those areas.

Adams (1956:904–906) criticizes the Wagley and Harris typology of

Latin American subcultures on four points. First, their classification does not include all of the population components to be found in Central America. Second, it suffers from the lack of comparability of categories. For instance, Wagley and Harris have placed themselves in the position of saying that laborers on large plantations and on small, family-owned plantations are as different from each other as each of them is from a Chocó Indian. Third, the classifications are based on different criteria for different subcultures. They emphasize structural differences in some, such as the town, peasant, usina plantation, and urban proletariat, as well as some broad culture type differences, e.g., the modern Indian and the tribal Indian. Fourth, the classification is based on information which was not collected for the specific purpose of formulating such a classification.

Adams suggests that the following factors should be considered in a classification: recognition of distinct historical traditions, recognition of assimilation, recognition of cultural differences, and recognition of social and economic relationships.

Adams's classification for Central America is based on a number of analytic units of varying degrees of abstraction. The empirical base is provided by the *population component*. This unit represents a specific aggregate of people who share a common culture, and manifest specific social and economic relationships with other population components.

The most important aspect of a population component is that it is a specific, empirically defined group of people; it is not an abstract category or type that includes a number of different people. A population component is not necessarily congruent with a community, e.g., San Luis Jilotepeque, Guatemala, having both ladinos and Indians as residents, would contain *two* population components.

A *regional variant* is a grouping of similar population components which are geographically contiguous.

A *cultural component* is comprised of all similar population components regardless of geographic location. The totality of ladinos, for example, would form a cultural component. A cultural component includes a number of specific population components but can be subdivided into regional variants if the subject so demands.

Crosscutting the component analytic units are the genetic relationships of these components as reflected in the concept of the cultural tradition and the regional tradition. A *cultural tradition* is composed of a class of cultural components which are distinguished by historically similar cultures. A *regional tradition* represents a number, but not all, of the components comprising a cultural tradition; thus the cultural components can be visualized in spatial terms as *horizontal* groupings while the cultural traditions represent the *vertical* dimension.

Table 5.2 lists the cultural components included in Adams's classification (Adams 1956:887):

TABLE 5.2

Cultural components	Cultural traditions
1. Cosmopolitan 2. Local Upper Class 3. Emergent Middle Class 4. Mobile Rural Labor 5. Stable Rural Labor 6. Independent Farmer 7. Urban Labor	A. Spanish-American
1. Traditional Indian 2. Modified Independent Indian 3. Modified Indian Labor 4. Ladinoized Independent Indian 5. Ladinoized Indian Labor 6. Torrupan 7. Yoro Jicaque 8. Paya 9. Miskito 10. Sumu 11. Rama 12. Guatuso	B. Mesoamerican
1. Matagalpa 2. Bribri 3. Boruca 4. Cabécar 5. Térraba 6. Guaymí 7. Cuna 8. Chocó	C. South America
1. Black Carib	D. Africo-American
1. Antillean Negroes	E. Africo-Euro-American
1. Anglo-American Islanders 2. Anglo-American Commerce 3. German-American 4. Mediterranean-American	F. Euro-American
1. Barrio Bacadillo	G. India-American
1. Chinese	H. Chinese-American

It is beyond the scope of this discussion to describe all of Adams's cultural components; however, a brief description of the cultural traditions will be presented.

Spanish-American Cultural Tradition   This tradition is found in the mestizo, creole, or modern Latin American societies. It contains three regional traditions within Central America: (1) the Ladino, which includes the Spanish-Americans of Guatemala, El Salvador, Honduras, Nicaragua, and the northwestern part of Costa Rica; (2) the Spanish-Americans of the central highlands of Costa Rica; and (3) the Spanish-Americans of the Panama interior. This cultural tradition would include most of Wagley and Harris's subcultures (metropolitan upper class, town, metropolitan middle class, usina plantation, engenho plantation, peasant, and urban proletariat).

Mesoamerican Cultural Tradition   This tradition refers to those groups descended from Mesoamerican aboriginal cultures or which have adopted their basic culture. These groups consider themselves Indian and are considered as such by neighboring Spanish-Americans. They maintain forms of social organization which are thought to be distinctively Indian. Most of these groups would be classified as modern Indian in the Wagley and Harris classification.

South American Cultural Tradition   The contemporary groups of this category, which include all the surviving Central American aboriginal groups outside of the Mesoamerican tradition, are rarely the direct social descendents of groups that existed at the time of the Conquest. Most of these groups would be included in either the tribal Indian or the modern Indian subculture types of Wagley and Harris.

Africo-American Cultural Tradition   This cultural tradition is made up of only a single cultural component, the Black Carib. Adams (1956:901) suggests that, "Within this component there are definite regional variants, with differences in multi-lingualism, occupation of men, and degree of adoption of the Spanish-American tradition traits."

Africo-Euro-American Cultural Tradition   This group includes the various West Indian Negroes who, over the last century or more, have drifted to Central America in search of labor. The population is usually English speaking with a culture involving a combination of some African survivals, strong European Caribbean backgrounds and, depending upon their length of residence in Central America, some adoption of Spanish-American traits.

Euro-American Cultural Tradition   This cultural tradition includes the non-Spanish Europeans who have moved into Central America and have maintained their own traditions as distinct from the Spanish-American tradition. There is some movement of these components to the cosmopolitan and emergent middle classes of the Spanish-American tradition. Where fairly large numbers of these people have come from one source, they have tended to perpetuate their own culture in the new environment.

India-American Cultural Tradition   There is only one population component which falls into this cultural tradition. This tradition is represented by the population of Hindu extraction which is found in one neighborhood in the town of Livingston, Guatemala.

Chinese-American Cultural Tradition   This population is scattered throughout the Spanish-American area and is composed of persons of Chinese ancestry who have retained a certain identification with their homeland. This population has generally become acculturated to the Spanish-American tradition but has retained certain distinctive culture traits, as well as an interest in the Chinese homeland. The Chinese are generally involved in commerical activities. This tradition is tending to become assimilated to the Spanish-American tradition.

Although Adams was able to include more of the population of Central America in his classification than Wagley and Harris, the Adams classification is weak for the areas in which no research was undertaken, namely, British Honduras and Costa Rica. Adams uses both ethnic group membership and social class stratification as criteria for his cultural components. Thus the cultural components of the Spanish-American tradition are various social classes, while the cultural components of the South American and Africo-American traditions are ethnic groups such as the Black Carib. Yet the Black Carib, at least in British Honduras, also have class stratification similar to, although not as complex as that of, the cultures in the Spanish American tradition.

Research in Costa Rica (Olien 1967, 1968, 1970) has suggested the need to modify the Adams classification for that country as well. For contemporary Costa Rica, Adams distinguishes six separate cultural traditions. The Spanish-American cultural tradition is divided into two regional traditions. The ladino tradition is found in the Northwest where the mestizo influence is strongest and the central highlands where the indigenous influence has been minimal. The Spanish-American cultural tradition is divided into seven different cultural components: cosmopolitan, local upper class, emergent middle class, mobile rural labor, stable rural labor, independent farmer, and urban labor.

A second cultural tradition, Mesoamerican, is represented by only one group, the Matambú, who form a ladinoized Indian labor cultural component. A South American cultural tradition is represented by two regional traditions: the Atlantic Lowlands (the Guatuso) and the Talamanca, made up of the Bribri, Boruca, Cabécar, and Térraba.

The other cultural traditions are less well known in terms of possible regional or cultural diversity within any of the groups. The Africo-Euro-American cultural tradition has only one cultural component, the Antillean Negroes. The Euro-American cultural tradition is made up of three cultural components: Anglo-American commercial, German-American, and Mediterranean-American. A sixth cultural tradition is the Chinese-American.

Although this classification adequately describes major traditions found in Costa Rica, there are a number of cultural components of these traditions which have not been included by Adams. Within the Spanish-American cultural tradition there must be added the Spanish-speaking whites of South American countries residing in Costa Rica, who numbered over twelve hundred in 1963, the majority from Colombia and Venezuela, as well as almost a thousand Spaniards. To the cultural components of this tradition must also be added the *parásitos* (squatters). These highly mobile, independent farmers number approximately thirty thousand.

Further distinctions should be made within the Africo-Euro-American cultural tradition, on the basis of West Indian island heritage. Although most blacks came from Jamaica, other islands are represented. Rivalry exists today in Puerto Limón between Negroes from Jamaica and those from Barbados. Other islands represented in Limón include Trinidad and Andros. Costa Rican Negroes from Haiti remain linguistically and culturally distinct from other Costa Rican Negroes. There are also Negroes in the lowlands who have migrated from Panama. The Costa Rican Negroes, like the whites, can also be classified on the basis of socioeconomic criteria. Although few, if any, Negroes would be considered upper class, some would be part of what Adams calls the emergent middle class. Others would be independent farmers, mobile rural labor, stable rural labor, and urban labor. The question must be raised, however, if a valid distinction can be made between rural and urban labor in the Costa Rican lowlands. Many Negroes easily move back and forth between the rural hinterland and Puerto Limón, the urban center, searching for any available work. Sometimes the difference between rural labor and urban labor is a seasonal one. Many Negroes work on rural plantations during the cacao harvest, near the city during the lobster season, and in the city when ships are in port. Other Negroes work full time in Puerto Limón but own subsistence or commercial farms in the hinterland which they visit on weekends.

Distinctions must also be made between various sectors of the Anglo-American commercial cultural component. Whereas many North Americans and English were situated in the lowlands during the United Fruit Company period, most North Americans and English are now located in San José. These segments make up the cosmopolitan cultural component of that tradition. The few who remain in the lowlands constitute a part of the local upper class cultural component.

Poles, Germans, French, and Italians each form foreign enclaves of about one hundred to about six hundred persons localized in San José. A few of each of these enclaves are found in other areas where they form part of the local upper class or the emergent middle class cultural component.

Most Chinese are concentrated in San José, the capital, or in the ports of Puntarenas and Puerto Limón. They form segments of the cosmopolitan and local upper class cultural component. Other Chinese are found in rural communities where they have great economic power but little social prestige.

Criteria for distinguishing cultural segments in contemporary Costa Rican society vary considerably from region to region. In the central highlands, racial and cultural diversity is minimal. Socioeconomic differences based primarily on occupation, education, and family background are of major importance. A diversity of occupations has developed with the onset of industrialization. Due to improved communications, rural urban differences are virtually nonexistent. Rural farmers frequently make the journey to San José and many *Josefinos* (people who live in San José) own farms in the country.

Wolf's Types of Latin American Peasantry   Eric Wolf's (1955) typology of Latin American peasants is another attempt to derive more empirically based types than the Wagley and Harris classification, which grouped together a number of different subcultures under the type peasant. Wolf bases his typology on similarities or dissimilarities of structure rather than on characteristics of culture content. Wolf defines a peasant as an agricultural producer who retains effective control of land and aims at subsistence, not reinvestment. Wolf gives the following criteria for a typology of peasantry (1955:455): (1) the subject matter must be defined as narrowly as possible; (2) structure rather than culture content should be stressed; (3) the initial criteria, while primarily economic or sociopolitical, should also include as many other features as possible; (4) types should be seen as component parts of larger wholes; and (5) some notion of historical trajectory should be included.

Wolf identifies seven different types of peasants but only two are discussed in detail: peasants of the corporate community inhabiting the upper highlands of Nuclear America and the peasants of the open community inhabiting humid lowlands and tropical lowlands.

Type One: the Corporate Community.   In the corporate peasant community intensive cultivation is practiced. Most of the production is for subsistence. Cash crops, when produced, are used to buy goods produced elsewhere. Integration of this type of peasantry into the colonial structure was achieved through the formation of communities which inhibited direct contact between the individual and the outside world but imposed between them an organized communal structure. The distinctive characteristic of the corporate peasant community is that it represents a bounded social system with clear-cut limits in relations to both outsiders and insiders. In other words, it has structural identity over time.

Seen from the outside, the community as a whole carries on a series of activities and upholds certain "collective representations." Seen from within, it defines the rights and duties of its members and prescribes large segments of their behavior. Although the peasant community is no longer held together by kinship, the members of the community are co-owners of a landholding corporation. This implies systematic participation in communal, political, and religious affairs. The corporate community has the following characteristics:

1. It is located on marginal land.
2. Exploitation of the land is through the means of traditional technology.
3. The community is poor.
4. The corporate structure is retained by community jurisdiction over the free disposal of land. (Where private property exists, there is a communal taboo on the sale of land to outsiders.)
5. There is a civil-religious system of power. Prestige is obtained by rising in this community structure from religious office to religious office along a prescribed ladder of achievement.
6. Any imposition of taxes, any increase in expenditures relative to the productive capacity of the community or the internal growth of the population on a limited amount of land must result in compensatory economic reactions in the field of production, such as wage labor, specialization, trade, and witchcraft.
7. Defensive ignorance, in which there is an active denial of outside alternatives that might threaten the corporate pattern, is present.
8. A cult of poverty exists in which the peasant will eat and consume less while working to maintain a steady state.
9. The nuclear family is the unit for the restriction of consumption and the increase of unpaid performance of work.
10. Institutionalized envy is manifested in gossip, attacks of evil eye, or fear and practice of witchcraft.

The employment of traditional technology keeps the land marginal and the community poor; it forces a search for supplementary sources of income and requires high expenditures of physical labor within the nuclear family. The technology is, in turn, maintained by the need to follow traditional roles in order to validate one's membership in the community, and this adherence is produced by the conscious denial of alternative forms of behavior, by institutionalized envy and by fear of being thrown out of equilibrium with one's neighbor.

Type Two: the Open Community. Wolf's second type of peasantry involves those who sell a cash crop which constitutes probably 50 to 75 percent of their total production. As mentioned above, these communities are distributed over humid and tropical areas. The peasants of this type of community receive capital from the outside but mainly on a traditional, small-scale, intermittent, and speculative basis. The open peasantry is only one of the subcultures of the community. There is continuous interaction with the outside world and the peasantry ties its fortune to outside demands. This type of community permits and expects individual accumulation and display of wealth and allows for periodic reshaping of social ties based on accumulation of wealth. Land is owned privately. As in the corporate community, the land of the open community is marginal and work is done by means of primitive technology. The actual amount of cash crops produced by each individual peasant is small. As a result, informal alliances between families and clients are formed. In this type of community there is great concern with status. The community is continually faced with alignments, circulation, and realignments, on both the socioeconomic and the political level. Since social, economic, and political arrangements are based primarily on personal ties, such fluctuations act to redefine personal relationships and such personal relationships are in turn watched closely for indices of readjustment. The disruption of social ties through the accumulation of goods which is inhibited in the corporate peasant community can go unchecked in the open community type.

Wolf suggests other types of peasant segments in Latin America but does not describe them in detail.

Type Three. In the same geographical area as the open community, there are peasants who commit 90 to 100 percent of their production to cash cropping. There is a greater stability of their market and more extensive outside capitalization. For example, United States capital flows into such peasant segments through organizations such as the United Fruit Company.

Type Four. This type includes peasants who habitually sell the larger part of their total production in restricted but stable local markets.

Type Five. Peasants located in regions which were formerly key areas of the developing system of capitalism, but which have since declined, make up this type. This region is located in the seasonally rainy tropical lowlands of northeastern Brazil and the West Indies. The economy of such areas has been contracting since the end of slavery with the result that this type of peasant seems to lean heavily toward the production of subsistence crops for home use or toward the production and distribution of very small amounts of cash produce.

Type Six. Foreign colonists introduced changes in technology into the forested environment of southern Brazil and southern Chile. Colonization was furthered by the respective central governments to create buffers against military pressures from outside and against local movements for autonomy. In both areas the settlers found themselves located on a cultural-ecological frontier. In both areas an initial period of deculturation and acculturation seems to have been followed by increasing integration into the national market through the sale of cash crops.

Type Seven. Peasants who live on the outskirts of the capitalist market, on South America's "pioneer fringe," form this type. This would include people who raise crops for the market in order to obtain strategic items of consumption such as clothing, salt, or metal which they cannot produce themselves. These peasants generally have a low level of technology and rather sporadic contacts with markets. Often these peasants are squatters on land not being used for commercial gain.

CURRENT APPROACHES TO COMPLEX SOCIETIES

Strickon's Folk Models   The various attempts to classify the Latin Americans that have been reviewed thus far have all been attempts to systematize into types what the researcher has observed. All have, to a certain extent, imposed a structure on the material. In general, none of the classifications were based on a consideration of how Latin Americans classify themselves. In cultural anthropology there has been an increasing concern with belief systems in which the anthropologist attempts to learn how the people themselves structure the world around them. The next classification to be discussed is important because it attempts to deal with categories actually used by the people being studied.

Arnold Strickon (1967), in attempting to classify the groups within a rural Argentine community, has added a folk dimension to the local level-national level distinction already suggested by Steward. At first Strickon found an apparent contradiction in the attitudes and expectations held by certain individuals toward other individuals of the same community. Some members of the community identified themselves either as *criollos* (literally, "born in the country") or as *descamisados* (literally, "shirtless ones"). These people expressed contradictory attitudes and expectations toward other people who were identified either as *Familia* (Family) or as *oligarquía* (oligarchy). On the one hand the criollo-descamisado held the Family-oligarchy to be exploiters of the poor who cared for nothing but their own selfish interests. On the other hand the criollo-descamisado also considered the Family-oligarchy to be patrons, protectors, and coparticipants in a highly valued way of life. In both examples it was the same individuals speaking about the same persons.

Upon closer examination it became clear that the two pairs of terms used to designate the various people were not in random variation with each other. Rather the terms Family and criollo were used together in the "positive" patronage context while the "negative," "class warfare" beliefs and expectations provided the context in which the descamisado-oligarchy terms were used. The discourse in which these pairings occurred differed. The class warfare, descamisado-oligarchy set was used in reference to national, or extralocal, conversational contexts. The patronage, criollo-Family set occurred in reference to local and personal interaction contexts. There were folk models of two social systems, one national and the other local. Both models were used to order the social phenomena that the people of the locality observed around them but neither one was used to arrange the total universe. An individual was assigned to at least one category in each of these models for different purposes. In one, the discourse referred to phenomena orderable within the context of a national level social system. These categories Strickon referred to as the "folk national system" (Strickon 1967:98). The system included the following categories: oligarquía (oligarchy), clase media (middle class), and descamisado (the poor). The other set of categories described by Strickon referred to phenomena orderable within the context of a local sociocultural system. This he referred to as "the folk local system." This system included the traditional categories: Familia, estanciero (literally, the owner of a large plantation organized cattle ranch), and criollo, as well as the nontraditional category, hijo de extranjero (literally, "son of a foreigner").

The folk local system can be summarized as follows:

1. All members of the Family were oligarchy.
2. All clase media were foreigners. Some were also estancieros.
3. All estancieros were also clase media and foreigners.
4. Some descamisados were foreigners, others were criollos.
5. Some foreigners were clase media, others were descamisados.
6. All criollos were descamisados.

While Strickon's model presents only a small number of the categories used in rural Argentina, it points to new and very fruitful direction for modern Latin American research.

Cochran and Reina's Study of Entrepreneurship   A second recent approach to the study of complex societies represents the combined efforts of an economic historian, Thomas C. Cochran, and a social anthropologist, Ruben E. Reina (1962). They analyzed the industrialization of Argentina by focusing on the career of one individual, Torcuato Di Tella, founder of the giant manufacturing firm S.I.A.M. (Sociedad Industrial Americana de Marquinarias). Di Tello was an Italian immigrant who introduced a new marketing approach to Argentine society based on aggressive selling techniques and generous credit terms.

The researchers discovered the importance of the kinship network in the operation of the company. As members of Di Tella's family came of age, they were drawn into company activity at the management level. As new openings of responsibility multiplied, individuals related through marriage also became company executives. Di Tella felt that in this way he could trust his executives and rely upon their loyalty and their willingness to remain with the company. Di Tella was further surrounded by a group of non-kin, his *hombres de confianza*, who were devoted to him. These ties existed in middle-to-upper management levels and in some cases, even in the lower-level management. Di Tella operated S.I.A.M. as a "family" based upon traditional patron-client types of relationships.

The study placed the career of the entrepreneur against the framework of a changing structure and economy in Argentine society. By studying an individual crucial to the society, Cochran and Reina have focused on some of the kinds of data necessary for understanding how decision making operates in complex societies.

Wolf's Studies of Relations in Complex Societies   Eric Wolf (1966) has been concerned with the hidden mechanisms of complex society. He states that "The anthropologist has a professional license to study . . . interstitial, supplementary, and parallel structures in complex society and to expose their relation to the major strategic, overarching institutions" (Wolf 1966:2). In particular Wolf has focused on three sets of parallel structures in complex societies: kinship, friendship, and patron-client relations.

Wolf has attempted to turn the anthropologist's attention from the study of communities as self-contained and integrated systems to the web of relations that extend through intermediate levels from the level of the community to that of the nation. In an early paper (Wolf 1965), he distinguished between relations of community-oriented and nation-oriented groups. The linkage between these groups is accomplished by individuals he termed "brokers"—those who mediate between community-oriented and nation-oriented groups. In serving some of the interests of groups on both the community and national levels, the brokers must cope with conflicts that often arise due to the opposition of interests in these different groups. The brokers maintain a role in society only as long as these tensions persist. At the same time, they cannot allow the conflict to get out of hand, lest more effective mediators take their place.

Wolf's work on complex societies attempts to expand upon the model utilized by Julian Steward for Puerto Rico. In the Puerto Rican study, the local and national level institutions were distinguished but the linkages between them were not well understood. Wolf's attention to the web of relations between these two levels helps to clarify these linkages.

Adams's Study of Power   Beginning in 1966, Richard N. Adams introduced another dimension, power, to the study of complex societies in Latin America. This initial statement was further elaborated in two theoretical works (Adams 1967a, 1967b) and developed in great detail in a case study of Guatemala (Adams 1970). In a social relationship, power is thought of as "the tactical control that one party holds over the environment of another party" (Adams 1967a:32). Power is considered independent when the superior party holds control without the need for help from another party; it is derivative when the superior party depends upon a third party for its power. In discussing the growth of Latin American governments, Adams suggests that this growth is not only due to an increase of available power *within* the countries but also to the continuing increase of derived power from various international and foreign sources (Adams 1967a:46). It is in the upper sectors of Latin American societies that one finds the greatest concentration of power. The internal structure of a Latin American society's upper sector is "a series of relationships established and altered by virtue of a constant concern for gaining and using power" (Adams 1967b:25).

While power is concentrated in the upper sector, it is actually an aspect of all social relationships. When various units of human society confront each other, they find themselves operating in superordinate-subordinate positions, or else they recognize each other as coordinates. If one exercises control over the other, they operate in a power domain. Where they are coordinates, the two units operate at the same level of articulation. Adams distinguishes between levels of articulation, presenting a somewhat more complex model of society than does Wolf. As Adams notes (1970:55):

> What occurs is a range of confrontations, oppositions, integrations; what we deal with conceptually is an arrangement of these for our convenience, one which we think has some theoretical utility. It is important to see these levels as the loci where articulations occur and to understand that such articulations may occur between a great variety of operating units. It is also important to clearly distinguish the level and the various units that operate within it from any particular kind of unit.

Thus, at what may be called generally a "local" level, there will be articulations among nuclear families, kinsmen, *compadres,* potential marital partners, potential in-laws, and so forth. There is no level that operates with only one kind of unit, and specific individuals may operate at a number of different levels.

While Julian Steward has tended to emphasize integration in his analyses, Adams emphasizes both integration and opposition.

There are still differences of opinion as to how Latin American society should be analyzed. While considerable effort was used to devise types of Latin American subgroups in the 1950s, new trends in the 1960s and 1970s have emphasized the study of belief systems and structural analyses.

RECOMMENDED READING

Díaz, Bernal, 1963, *The Conquest of New Spain.* Baltimore: Penguin Books, Inc.
A new translation of an eyewitness account of the Conquest of Mexico.
Durán, Fray Diego, 1971, *Book of the Gods and Rites and the Ancient Calendar.* Norman, Okla.: University of Oklahoma Press.
Ranks with the writings of Sahagún in its ethnographic importance. Durán lived in Mexico City shortly after the Conquest.
Gage, Thomas, 1929, *A New Survey of the West Indies. 1648: The English-American.* New York: Robert M. McBride Company, Inc.
Gage was the first Englishman in Latin America. He wrote a highly critical account of colonial life.
Gallenkamp, Charles, 1962, *Maya: the Riddle and Rediscovery of a Lost Civilization.* New York: Pyramid Publications, Inc.
An exciting account of the major discoveries of Mayan civilization.
Keen, Benjamin, 1971, *The Aztec Image in Western Thought.* New Brunswick, N.J.: Rutgers University Press.
This book appeared too late to be discussed in the text, but is highly recommended as an outstanding critical analysis of Aztec studies. It traces the various interpretations of the Aztecs by the Europeans through time.
Sahagún, Bernardino De, 1950–1963, *Florentine Codex: the General History of the Things of New Spain.* 13 vols. Salt Lake City, Utah: University of Utah Press.
A scholarly translation of the most extensive collection of information about the Aztecs recorded shortly after the Conquest. A basic reference.
Stephens, John L., 1841, *Incidents of Travel in Central America, Chiapas, and Yucatán.* 2 vols. New York: Harper and Brothers.
————, 1843, *Incidents of Travel in Yucatán.* 2 vols. New York: Harper and Brothers.
Both works still make interesting reading of the discovery of a lost civilization, the Maya.
Strickon, Arnold, 1964, Anthropology in Latin America. In Charles Wagley

(ed.), *Social Science Research on Latin America*. New York: Columbia University Press, pp. 125–167.
The only modern review of twentieth century anthropology in Latin America.
Thompson, Edward H., 1965, *People of the Serpent: Life and Adventure Among the Mayas*. New York: Capricorn Books.
Highly readable account of explorations among the Mayan ruins, including Thompson's famous dive into the Sacred Well of Chichén Itzá.
Thompson, J. Eric S., 1963, *Maya Archaeologist*. Norman, Okla.: University of Oklahoma Press.
Describes the trials and tribulations of the early days of Maya explorations and excavations.
Tozzer, Alfred M. (ed.), 1941, *Landa's Relación de las Cosas de Yucatán*. Cambridge, Massachusetts: Papers of the Peabody Museum of American Archaeology and Ethnology, vol. 28.
The basic source on the Maya by an eyewitness of the post-Contact Yucatecan Maya, combined with extensive footnoting by the editor.
Vega, Garcilaso de la [El Inca], 1965, *Royal Commentaries of the Incas and General History of Peru*. 2 vols. Austin, Tex.: University of Texas Press.
Although sometimes inaccurate, this work is still a basic source written by a mestizo of Spanish-Inca blood.
Von Hagen, Victor Wolfgang (ed.), 1959, *The Incas of Pedro de Cieza de León*. Norman, Okla.: University of Oklahoma Press.
An account of the Inca by one of the early chroniclers. Also a basic reference.
Wauchope, Robert, 1962, *Lost Tribes and Sunken Continents: Myth and Method in the Study of American Indians*. Chicago: University of Chicago Press.
Presents the major theories, scientific and otherwise, concerning the origin of the American Indian.
————, 1965, *They Found the Buried Cities: Exploration and Excavation in The American Tropics*. Chicago: University of Chicago Press.
An account of archaeological research with emphasis on the Maya area.

RECOMMENDED CASE STUDIES IN CULTURAL ANTHROPOLOGY

Basso, Ellen, 1973, *The Kalapalo Indians of Central Brazil*. New York: Holt, Rinehart and Winston, Inc.
A tribal Indian group living in an area ecologically similar to the Yąnomamö, but the Kalapalo are psychologically different.
Chagnon, Napoleon A., 1968, *Yąnomamö: the Fierce People*. New York: Holt, Rinehart and Winston, Inc.
Another tribal Indian subculture type, which is engaged in chronic warfare.
Chiñas, Beverly, 1973, *Isthmus Zapotecs: Sex Roles in Cultural Context*. New York: Holt, Rinehart and Winston, Inc.
Examines women's roles in a modern Indian subculture.

Faron, Louis C., 1968, *The Mapuche Indians of Chile.* New York: Holt, Rinehart and Winston, Inc.
A tribal Indian subculture type located on a reservation.
Kearney, Michael, 1972, *The Winds of Ixtepeji: World View and Society in a Zapotec Town.* New York: Holt, Rinehart and Winston, Inc.
The world view of a peasant subculture type living in a remote village.
Lewis, Oscar, 1960, *Tepoztlán: Village in Mexico.* New York: Holt, Rinehart and Winston, Inc.
A study of a peasant subculture in one of anthropology's most famous villages.
Turner, Paul R., 1972, *The Highland Chontal.* New York: Holt, Rinehart and Winston, Inc.
A modern Indian subculture type in Mexico.

CHAPTER 6

Major themes of Latin American life

Upon arrival in Latin America for the first time, many individuals experience "culture shock," a state of disorganization that one develops while first attempting to operate within the framework of another culture. The differences between North America and Latin America are not always immediately apparent. The climate of some areas of Latin America is comparable to various areas of the United States. The physical types one encounters, at least in the cities, generally fall well within the range of physical variation found in North America. Certainly the Amerind and Negro admixtures are more prevalent in Latin America, but in general the people are physically similar to the North Americans. Clothing of the urban inhabitant closely resembles that which is worn in the United States. On a superficial level, then, North America and Latin America are similar. Yet there are differences, some of which are obvious, such as language and foods, while others are more subtle and not as apparent to the North American. It is often these subtle differences which bring about the culture shock and cause the problems of disorientation.

Individuals are often not aware that the Latin operates with a set of behavioral cues different from those used in the United States, for example, the perception of what distance one maintains when speaking to another. While conversing, two Latins stand several inches closer together than would two North Americans of similar age, status, and sex. When a Latin and North American engage in conversation there is often a feeling of discomfort. The North American considers the Latin too close and thus feels crowded and reacts by moving a few inches away. The Latin, in turn, feels uncomfortable and moves closer to that distance which he deems comfortable for conversation. In so doing, he once again "crowds" the North American, causing him to feel uneasy. In one instance, a Latin American and North American diplomat were observed in conversation at a party at one end of a ballroom. By the end of the evening, with the Latin moving forward and the North American backing away, they had moved across the hall to the other end of the room.

Often behavior that is considered "natural" to the members of our own culture implies something different to the Latin Americans. To indicate height in the United States one uses a particular gesture which is almost an unconscious act. The hand is raised or lowered to the appropriate level, outstretched and palm down. This motion indicates the height of any and all matter. Because this gesture is so automatic, it never occurs to the North American that people in other cultures might use the same gesture but with not quite the same meaning. In Costa Rica three different gestures are used to indicate height. If he wishes to indicate the height of an animal (other than man), such as a prize bull, the Costa Rican will use a gesture identical to that of our culture. But to show the height of an inanimate object, for example, a car, a different gesture is used. The hand is again extended but with the palm face up. To indicate the height of a human being, the Costa Rican cocks an arm and cups the hand, palm down, and cups the other hand around the elbow of the cocked arm. The North American who is describing his son to a Costa Rican, and indicates that the child is three feet tall by using the proper gesture of North American culture, is conveying information which he had not intended. He is inadvertently telling the Costa Rican that his son is like a nonhuman animal!

One other example will suffice to illustrate the subtle types of differences one encounters while learning to understand Latin American culture. In Chile an American housewife wishing to purchase meat for her family will soon learn that she must visit a meat market on a Friday morning. This is the only day that fresh beef is available to the Chileans. Upon entering the store, she finds many women packed together at the counter. There are no lines in which she can wait her turn. To her the situation resembles a mob scene, yet it is not a mob. She is witnessing a group that is well organized and disciplined but one which is organized on different principles than she is accustomed to.

Each Chilean housewife approaches the salesperson directly and immediately, ignoring anyone else in the store (particularly other customers, who are her competitors), and quite intensely and vehemently forces the fact of her personal presence upon the quietly waiting salesman. She cites the existence of a remote kinship link between herself and him, or to the family of his employer, if possible; she narrates the facts of a long friendship or of a mutually rewarding relationship between herself, her husband, her family, and the clerk or his dueño; or she loudly recites the details of some special situation which requires that she receive immediate attention and service. Throughout, her manner is slightly imperious if not lordly, her tone forceful and insistent, and her attitude dominant and demanding. Meanwhile, she waves her shopping list in the clerk's face, elbows other customers out of her way, and forces herself to the center of the stage. Depending upon how well she does all this, and of course the facts of her case, she—sooner or only slightly later—makes her purchase and departs. Meanwhile, the gringa housewife, becoming more annoyed as the quarter-hours slip by, stands waiting on the outskirts of what she sees as a crowd of immature and tantrum-prone children. And the clerk of course does not even notice her presence. He is occupied with the task of sorting the persons who are very obviously customers into a line, not of those who arrived earlier or later, but one organized by differences in the manifest prestige and prominence of the competitors for his attention. The more successful customer is thus one who puts forward the better and more obvious claim for service (Clifton 1968:31).

While it is important to be aware of the numerous subtle differences between the Latin American and the North American, an introduction can examine only the major patterns in detail.

In the previous chapter the variety of Latin American types was discussed. Many elements have contributed to the Latin American cultural tradition. The primary contributions to this tradition derive from the Amerinds, the Spanish and Portuguese conquistadors, and the African slaves. During the Colonial period a unique blend of beliefs, customs, and institutions developed which reflected the accommodation of the Amerind, Iberian, and African cultures to the New World environment and to each other. If the Iberian traditions seem to dominate the modern Latin American heritage it is not surprising since the Iberians also dominated colonial Latin America. Yet even the customs and institutions of the rulers had to be bent and shaped to fit the New World situation, while other institutions and customs developed uniquely in the New World.

In this chapter, five patterns characteristic of much of Latin America will be described: the grid settlement pattern, Catholicism, concepts of health and illness, the double standard of sex morals, and the nature of interpersonal relations. It should be kept in mind that not every individual or subculture will share all of these patterns but that most Latin Americans share at least some of them, with the population of Mestizo-America probably sharing the greatest number.

THE GRID SETTLEMENT PATTERN

A certain sameness prevails between the communities of Latin America, in particular those of the highlands. When an author writes about "a typical Latin American community," he implies that the community shares the following characteristics with many other Latin American communities: (1) grid settlement pattern, (2) central plaza, (3) narrow streets, and (4) low houses built next to one another and to the sidewalk.

The Spaniards had been preoccupied with their war against the Moors in the centuries immediately preceding Columbus's voyage and, as a result, did not participate in the urbanization movement of western Europe where a growing awareness of the need for some form of town planning was developing. The idea that a town should be established according to a preconceived pattern was, therefore, foreign to the Spanish. Houses, streets, and alleys were built in a haphazard fashion in the fifteenth century Spanish community. The first New World Spanish settlements were established in a similar haphazard manner. In these early settlements on the Caribbean islands, little attention was given to the choice of sites, resources, or community plan. This chaotic approach worked only so long as the conquistadors were merely extracting tribute. But once the land itself became valuable, methods for measuring and apportioning were of the utmost importance (Stanislawski 1947:94–96).

Following the Conquest of Mexico, the instructions from the Spanish king for the establishment of settlements became increasingly explicit. The various laws of the Indies established consistent standards of design regulating the size and form of the main plaza, width of streets, orientation of gates and walls, location of public buildings, and subdivision of land into lots. As a result practically every city has exactly the same size of block, the same width of street and the same general urban pattern (Davis 1960:45).

The Spanish kings turned to the Romans and Greeks for concepts of city planning; the instructions of the Roman Vitruvius became their basic source. Copies of Vitruvius's *The Ten Books on Architecture* were printed in 1550, or earlier, and were used in the New World (Stanislawski 1947: 101). The Roman grid pattern with straight streets and rectangular blocks oriented around a central plaza became the pattern for colonial settlement in the Hispanic New World in contrast to the United States settlement pattern, where the orientation is around a main street. Not all the towns were built on a true grid; many were modified to adjust to various topographical features such as rivers and hills.

In Latin American towns today, the plaza remains the heart of the town. In the Colonial period the town's most important buildings surrounded the plaza—the administrative offices, the church, the houses of the wealthy, and often the market. Today commercial buildings have replaced some of the colonial structures, but the blocks surrounding the plaza are still considered highly desirable places in which to live. It is in the plaza where the *paseo* (or *revuelta*) still occurs once or twice every week. (The Sunday evening paseo is especially traditional.) Groups consisting of two or three girls walking arm in arm circle the plaza in one direction while small groups of young men walk the plaza in the opposite direction. Each time a procession of girls passes, the boys flirt with them. Initially the girls ignore them as they circle the plaza several times. Eventually, however, the girls may acknowledge the boys with smiles and allow themselves to be accompanied on their walk.

The streets of the Latin American community were often built during the Colonial period with carriages in mind and so today these same streets are very narrow for automotive traffic. Some cities contain streets wherein the pedestrian can touch buildings on either side simultaneously. The famous "Street of the Kiss" in Guanajuato, Mexico, derives its name from the fact that part of the street is so narrow, lovers in houses on opposite sides of the street are able to kiss from the overhanging balconies (Sjoberg 1960:92).

Houses are built flush with the sidewalk and are connected to each other. The houses of the wealthy frequently have elaborately decorated doors and grillwork adorning the windows facing the sidewalk. The houses of the poor usually have a simple wooden door and a simple wooden shutter in the window opening, or no window at all, which face the sidewalk. Homes of the wealthy are often two stories in height. The larger houses open onto a courtyard around which the rooms of the dwelling are oriented. Guests are usually entertained in a room at the front of the house. The dining room is used to accommodate guests for more informal occasions. The bedrooms are usually at the back of the house. A separate shed adjoining the back of the main structure is used for cooking. Generally, modern kitchen conveniences have been lacking until very recently. Food is prepared over a simple wood or charcoal burning stove. A refrigerator is not considered a necessity as food is purchased by the day or by the meal. The homes of the poor often consist of only one room with very few pieces of furniture on a dirt floor. Because they have few, if any, windows, the room is usually dark.

At noon time, businesses close for a long lunch hour that often lasts three or four hours. The Latin American enjoys a leisurely lunch, often the main meal, with a number of courses, followed by a nap (*siesta*). Businesses begin to reopen about four in the afternoon and remain open until eight or nine in the evening. A late supper follows the work day.

In recent years there has been a greater tendency for the larger stores in the cities of Latin America to adopt the North American "lunch hour."

Businesses closed during the traditional long afternoon meal time. Queré-taro, Mexico.

Stores remain open throughout the day while employees take staggered lunch breaks. A quick sandwich replaces the many-course dinner of the traditional lunch meal.

CATHOLICISM

The Catholic Church has played a large role in the development of the modern Latin American cultural tradition. Most Latin Americans are Catholic. Latin American Catholicism covers a wide range of practices and beliefs, the local varieties being more diverse than in the United States where Catholicism, whether in Milwaukee, Wisconsin or Portland, Oregon, is very much the same. In Latin America the local Catholicism is sometimes orthodox, but frequently it is a blend of Catholicism plus aboriginal practices and beliefs, or a syncretism with African practices and beliefs.

In many parts of Latin America the Catholic pantheon of saints was superimposed on a native pantheon of pre-Columbian gods. In both Meso-america and the Andean areas, pre-Columbian civilization had been accompanied by the development of organized state religions with an elaborate pantheon of gods and a priesthood. Religion was vital to the Amerind. As Tannenbaum (1962:53) has observed:

At the time of the discovery the American Indian was a profoundly religious and mystical human being. A great part of his daily existence

197

Easter Week processsion, Acuitzio del Canje, Michoacán, Mexico. (Courtesy of Raymond E. Wiest.)

was bound up in religious rites, in propitiating his many gods, in finding grace, justification, and peace. Every act had its religious significance, every wind, every change in the color of the moon, every appearance of the unexpected, had its religious portent. In such highly developed cultures as the Aztecs and the Inca, a large priesthood served to interpret the will of the gods.

The Spanish priests destroyed the native temples and built churches upon the ruins of the old temples. Yet the spot remained sacred to the native. In many instances only the names of the native gods were changed to those of Catholic saints. Some priests, for example, Sahagún and Landa, recorded native religious beliefs in order to facilitate the introduction of Catholicism through the native framework of belief. In this way the priests themselves were sometimes responsible for the syncretism. In other cases the local priest tolerated many pagan practices in local Catholicism. More frequently, though, the priest attempted to destroy completely any vestige of pagan religion. Sometimes he was successful, but often he merely drove the practices underground where they continued to flourish. Orthodox Catholicism has not been strong in many Latin American rural areas due to the fact that these areas have been unable to support a priest. Villages are serviced by a priest once every month, or even less frequently.

In the lowlands and the Caribbean, Catholicism blended with traditions carried from Africa by the Negro slaves, thus resulting in a variety of Afro-American cults. In some areas such as Haiti, the lower classes follow more than one set of religious practices and beliefs. Catholicism is the only religion of Haiti's elite and is the country's only approved religion. Yet the folk religion of Haiti, Vodun (sometimes referred to as Voodoo), is extremely widespread among the lower classes, most of whom are also Catholics (Leyburn 1966:113–114). The members of the lower classes are able to compartmentalize their religious beliefs into two sets which are not thought of as being in conflict.

The saints are the central powers of Latin American Catholicism. Each community and neighborhood has its own patron saint. There are miraculous saints, such as the Virgin of Guadalupe in Mexico and Nosso Senhor do Bonfim in Brazil, to whose shrines thousands of people come each year. Many families have a saint of special devotion whom they honor as a family custom. Also there are saints that are protectors of certain occupations or guardians of specialized groups, and others with special attributes and powers (Wagley 1968:64). For the Latin American the important occasion is not a child's birthday but the saint's day after whom the child is named—for example, Saint Thomas, Saint John, Saint Peter.

The day is like Christmas. It begins with going to mass accompanied by one's friends all in their best clothes. All through the day there are presents, music, and visits, and sometimes the dancing goes on late into the night. And as the families are large, there are numerous occasions for such festivities. Each member of the family—the grandparents, the parents, the children, and the grandchildren—has his own particular patron saint whose day is celebrated in similar fashion. Then there are the numerous first, second, third, and fourth cousins, the aunts and uncles, the school friends, the companions and associates in business or in the professions, and last but not least, the *compadres*—the godfathers and godchildren—who may literally run into the dozens (Tannenbaum 1962:64–65).

Religious brotherhoods (*cofradías* or *irmandades*) are another tie between the Latin American and Catholicism and are especially important in the smaller towns. The cofradías are often concerned with community tasks such as caring for the church and repairing public buildings, as well as organizing the annual festival of their patron saint. The religious brotherhoods are often the only voluntary associations the women consider joining. In a study of participation in voluntary associations in Guadalajara, Mexico, Floyd Dotson (1953) found that church-affiliated associations accounted for over 81 percent of the memberships of women. The participation in church-affiliated associations by men was approximately 15 percent. The church associations seem to provide the only socially sanctioned activity outside of the household for women, whereas men, having greater freedom outside the family, tend to join athletic and sport associations and labor unions more frequently.

Compadrazgo   An especially important institution of Catholicism in Latin America is compadrazgo (ritual coparenthood). According to Mintz and Wolf (1950:341), "This term designates the particular complex of relationships set up between individuals primarily, though not always, through participation in the ritual of Catholic baptism." In the United States the naming of godparents for baptism is a fairly widespread Christian custom. But the rights, duties, and obligations are somewhat different from those in Latin America. In the United States godparents tend to play a minor role in a child's life, agreeing to serve as guardians if the child's parents were to die and to raise the child in his faith. In most cases, though, the immediate family directs whatever, if any, religious training the child would receive, and the child would be raised by relatives rather than the godparents if something were to happen to the parents.

In Latin America the compadrazgo institution is particularly important and is a part of one's daily life. Three sets of relationships are involved. The first links parents and child and is set up within the confines of the immediate biological family. The second links the child and his ceremonial sponsor, a person outside the limits of his immediate biological family. This relation is familiar to most North Americans as the relations between godfather or godmother and godchild. The third set of relationships links the parent of the child and the child's ceremonial sponsor. In Spanish each calls the other compadre, literally coparent of the same child (Mintz and Wolf 1950:341). The diagram on page 201 shows this triad of relationships, as well as the reciprocal terminology used.

Compadrazgo is, or has been, confined to less industrialized parts of southern Europe and to those regions of the world to which the southern European version of Catholicism was introduced. The salient characteristic of New World compadrazgo is the prominence of the relationships established between sponsors and parents (the compadres). Compadre relationships hold this strategic position by their long-enduring mutual socioeconomic commitments, which are accompanied by the special terminology, imbued with respect and trust, and sustained by compelling sacred sanctions (Deshon 1963:57). Ties between compadres are not unknown in rural southern European forms of compadrazgo, but they either share their importance with sponsor-child relationships or assume a subsidiary position (Anderson 1956, 1957; Foster, 1953; Moss and Cappanari 1960; Pitt-Rivers 1958).

Some reviews of the ethnographic literature pertaining to compadrazgo have resulted in the formulation of several interesting hypotheses, most of which have never been tested in the field. Benjamin Paul, in a survey of

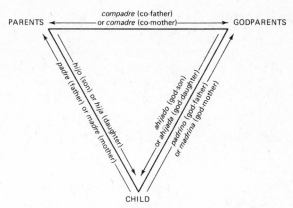

FIGURE 6.1 Compadrazgo relationships and reciprocal terminology. (Adapted from Mintz and Wolf 1950.)

ritual kinship forms in Middle America, described the principles of "intensification" and "extension" defined by the number of sponsors selected for baptism and other occasions and by the utilization of pre-existing relationships or of new ones for the various occasions for each child (Paul 1942: 56–57). Some families select relatives and thereby "intensify" already existing bonds. Others establish new relations with non-kin by requesting they serve as godparents, thereby "extending" their network of relationships outside the nuclear family. Mintz and Wolf (1950:359), in developing these points further in their analysis of past European forms and contemporary New World manifestations, proposed that the relationships between compadres assume various forms depending on the amount of sociocultural and economic mobility that is available to the individual in any given instance.

Compadre relationships tend to link members of the same group or class in single-class societies under relatively stable socioeconomic conditions. Mintz and Wolf term this a "horizontal" relationship. Relationships that link members of hierarchically-arranged groups of strata in well-established multiclass societies are term "vertical." They are multiplied through the selection of different sponsors for each child's baptism or for different rites (Paul's principle of extension) under conditions of accelerated culture change (Mintz and Wolf 1950:362–364).

Shirley Deshon, testing some of these hypotheses on a plantation in Yucatán, found that the variability characteristic of compadrazgo observed at the community level closely resembled Mintz and Wolf's description; however, the variables of land tenure, stratification, and so on, did not entirely explain the selection of baptismal godparents. Instead, she found that (Deshon 1963:582):

> The fit between the direction of sponsor mobility was better when the cyclical nature of the hacienda household was taken into account. As we proposed, selections were more vertical during the nuclear stage and

201

more horizontal during the extended stages. It is these latter stages, therefore, which have given compadrazgo in the hacienda community investigated its horizontal character, and maintained this character during the periods of accelerated culture change.

Requesting someone to serve as godparent to one's child requires careful consideration. It is a serious decision because it structures a relationship between the parent and the godparent. Many Latins believe there are few people they can trust or rely upon in time of need outside of the immediate family. Although occasionally a person may call upon a second cousin for a small favor or to help him celebrate a fiesta, only the close kin are obligated to assist with serious problems. By agreeing to serve as godparent, an individual accepts a responsibility not only to the child but also to the parents. The parents and godparents become almost blood brothers. Compadres and comadres must treat each other with respect, using the polite rather than familiar Spanish verb forms. They are considered to be so close they may not marry or have sexual relations with each other; such behavior would be considered incestuous. From the time a nonrelative agrees to serve as godparent, he acts as if he is a consanguineal (or blood) kin. However, there are exceptions to this ideal of closeness between compadres. For example, in a rural village in Paraguay, Elman and Helen Service (1954:170) found that many informants had difficulty recalling the surnames of many of their compadres.

In Latin American the ceremony of baptism is the most important occasion for selecting a godparent for one's child. The wealthier the family the more likely it is to ask a number of persons to serve as godparents. As the godparents are obligated to pay for the fiesta and often the child's baptismal outfit, the impoverished families feel reluctant to ask friends and neighbors to become godparents because of the economic burden. Instead a poverty-stricken individual might ask a brother to serve as sponsor; thus intensifying an already existing bond. Since the brother would already be obligated to contribute financially to the ceremony in his role as uncle of the child, the added costs are not as great as if a non-kin had accepted the sponsorship.

A family's network of compadrazgo ties can be expanded in one of three ways: (1) by proliferating the number of occasions on which compadres are chosen (e.g., Gillin [1947:105] reported fourteen occasions which call forth new compadrazgo ties in Moche, Peru); (2) by forming numerous compadrazgo ties on each occasion (e.g., Biesanz and Biesanz [1944] report that some of the upper class brides have numerous padrinos and madrinos chosen for their weddings, thus extending ties between the wealthy families); (3) by selecting different compadres for each occasion.

In Tzintzuntzan, Mexico, George Foster (1969) undertook the most extensive synchronic and diachronic analysis of compadrazgo. He found that roughly a third of the persons chosen by the villagers as godparents were relatives, frequently a sibling of one of the parents.

The decision of whether to choose relatives or friends as compadres seems to be related to the birth order of the children. Few individuals in Tzintzuntzan form compadrazgo ties prior to marriage. The real need for a social network of relatives, compadres, and friends develops with marriage and the beginning of a family. The compadrazgo system provides the most flexible and common device for building this social network. During the early years of marriage, a premium is placed on expanding a compadrazgo network through the use of friends, rather than relatives, that will provide the new couple with the aid and support it needs for daily living and to meet periodic personal crises. Though the newly married couple may have an insufficient number of reciprocal ties, the family eventually may come to have too many compadres if it continues to choose only friends as godparents. Every expectation of aid implies a reciprocal obligation thus creating a burden in terms of time, money, and emotional expenditures for relationships that bring reciprocal support not really needed. In other words, the ease in acquiring compadres in early married life can become a liability at a later time (Foster 1969:273). According to Foster (1969:273):

The very devices which facilitate the rapid development of a compadrazgo network constitute the weakest link in the system: it can overburden the parents of numerous progeny with excessive compadres. With an optimum compadrazgo network achieved, additional compadres call forth significant output, but little is obtained in return that is not already available from others. A compadrazgo system therefore requires manipulative devices which permit participants rapidly to expand ties when needed and also to hold them in check when they are not needed.

The network of compadres is kept in check by the following devices: (1) already existing social ties may be reinforced by asking relatives to baptize children or by asking the same compadres to baptize two or more children; (2) people select compadres with no real functional ties such as a godmother chosen to baptize a child. When a godmother alone baptizes a child, it is generally assumed that obligations will be minimal since much of the support that is valued requires male activities or the activities of a couple. After the family has a few children it generally extends the compadrazgo ties to the optimum number of friends. From then on until very late in the family cycle (when some compadres have to be replaced due to death) more and more relatives are asked to serve as kin thus reducing the possibilities of any further and unnecessary expansion of the family's social network (Foster 1969:274–275).

In some countries there are specialized ceremonies that are related to rites of passage for which godparents are chosen. In Colombia, godparents are named for the fiesta of Our Lady of Carmen; in Tzintzuntzan, Mexico, for Easter; a woman is asked to be a godmother in Mitla, Mexico, when a child becomes ill and in San Luis Jilotepeque, Guatemala, when a child suffers from magical fright. In some countries the Spanish custom of compadrazgo is linked with pre-Columbian traditions; for example, in Moche, Peru, and Saucio, Colombia, godparents are named for the child's first nail cutting, haircutting, and ear piercing.

Throughout Latin America the most influential persons tend to have the greatest numbers of compadres. A president of a country may have as many as several thousand godchildren. The patrón of the hacienda is the godfather of many of his peon's children, allowing the patrón to bind his workers to the hacienda and at the same time providing the workers with a person to turn to in time of need.

Fiestas   Another important component of Latin American Catholicism is the fiesta complex. The yearly calendar in most areas of Latin America is filled with fiestas. In addition to the celebrations which are a part of the orthodox calendar, there are special national fiestas, as well as those held only at the local community level. These are fiestas for the patron saints of barrios, as well as fiestas to celebrate the saint's day of each of one's relatives.

The fiestas are possibly the most colorful aspect of Latin American life. The fiestas break an otherwise monotonous work routine. As Octavio Paz (1961:49) so vividly observed of the Mexican fiesta:

> In all of these ceremonies—national or local, trade or family—the Mexican opens out. They all give him a chance to reveal himself and to converse with God, country, friends or relations. During these days the silent Mexican whistles, shouts, sings, shoots off fireworks, discharges his pistol into the air. He discharges his soul. And his shout, like the rockets we love so much, ascends to the heavens, explodes into green, red, blue, and white lights, and falls dizzily to earth with a trail of golden sparks. This is the night when friends who have not exchanged more than the prescribed courtesies for months get drunk together, trade confidences, weep over the same troubles, discover that they are brothers and sometimes, to prove it, kill each other. The night is full of songs and loud cries. The lover wakes up his sweetheart with an orchestra. There are jokes and conversations from balcony to balcony, sidewalk to sidewalk. Nobody talks quietly. Hats fly in the air. Laughter and curses ring like silver pesos. Guitars are brought out. Now and then, it is true, the happiness ends badly, in quarrels, insults, pistol shots, stabbings. But these too are part of the fiesta, for the Mexican does not seek amusement: he seeks to escape from himself, to leap over the wall of solitude that confines him during the rest of the year. All are possessed by violence and frenzy. Their souls explode like the colors and voices and emotions.

Special foods are consumed at fiestas. In many rural areas where cattle and pigs are raised only for market, the fiesta provides an opportunity for eating meat. Other fiesta foods include special sweets and sauces. For example, the descendants of Aztecs, the Nahua of central Mexico, restrict certain dishes to their most important fiestas. *Mole de guajolote* is an expensive and elaborate sauce which is generally prepared only once a year for the fiesta which honors the patron saint of the village. The sauce is made of three varieties of dark chiles, tortillas, peanuts, almonds, raisins, cinnamon-flavored chocolate and sesame and is served either with turkey or chicken. *Mole adobo* and *mole verde* are prepared for family fiestas, such as birthdays, baptisms, or confirmations. Mole adobo is made from red chiles which are boiled, skinned and ground and then fried with salt and sugar. The sauce is poured over sliced pork, chicken, beef, or tongue and topped with slices of raw onions. Mole verde is offered to dead relatives on the Days of the Dead at the beginning of November. This sauce is made from pumpkin seed paste, green chiles, green onions, green tomatoes, garlic, coriander (a vegetable of the carrot family), and broth made from turkey, chicken, or pork. It is served with tamales. For village fiestas, enchiladas (tortillas filled with mole de guajolote and cheese and chopped onion) are prepared (Madsen 1969:611).

The fiesta is a time for drinking. Latin Americans are social drinkers. Drinking cocktails at home without the company of friends is considered strange behavior in many parts of Latin America. Hans Buechler (1969) reports that in the peasant communities of Bolivia, alcohol is consumed only at fiestas. In this social context alcohol takes on special importance. One is not allowed to refuse alcohol when it is offered by the host; to do so would be insulting. At the same time, the host's prestige is often measured by the amount of alcohol he is able to serve to his guests. Among the Tarahumara of northern Mexico drinking is also a social affair. Their corn beer, *tesguino,* has a sacred character. The group that gathers for a beer drinking fiesta carries out all the functions of social life outside those of the household groups:

It is the religious group, the economic group, the entertainment group, the group at which disputes are settled, marriages arranged, and deals completed. It is here with his set of neighbors, and under the influence of alcohol, that the individual has a chance to play the role which has been dormant during his isolation. The man with leadership qualities or aspirations gets to his feet and gives a "sermon" which also functions to reinforce moral norms, as well as to dramatize status aspirations or position. Deals are made for animals or maize. A ceremony or race may be arranged. It is at the tesguinada (beer drinking fiesta) that the unmarried may find a mate, or the married vary his sexual experience. Kinship roles outside those of the nuclear family rarely find a chance or mood for expression except at one of these inebriated get-togethers. Here, also, the clown makes his reputation of being *muy diablo,* and much laughing follows stereotyped sexual jokes and horseplay. The ritual role of the native religious practitioner is also largely played out in this atmosphere. The tesguinada provides practically the only opportunity for the release of aggressive impulses, so frequently a fight occurs for one reason or another. This is in contrast to the fact that fighting virtually never occurs outside of the tesguinada (Kennedy 1963:629).

Sponsoring a fiesta is the primary means of achieving prestige in many Amerind and peasant communities. Male villagers often spend vast sums on fiestas in order to fulfill their religious obligations. These obligations form part of a system of ranked fiesta sponsorships found in parts of Amerind-America. Villagers move from one office to others of greater prestige by sponsoring more and more elaborate fiestas. This system is known as the civil-religious hierarchy or "cargo" system.

Protestantism   Protestants have lived in Latin America for centuries. Protestant missionaries did not become active in the area, however, until the twentieth century. Because Catholicism permeates so much of Latin American culture, it is difficult for the Latin American to convert to Protestantism. To do so would be to forsake something of his cultural heritage. The priests in many areas still actively fight against Protestant intrusion into their domain. In 1875 Gilbert Haven (1875:466), a Protestant traveling in Mexico, observed the following placard which expressed the hostility of the priests toward the early Protestant movement. Beneath a skull and crossbones was the message:

DEATH TO THE PROTESTANTS!!!
To the people of Toluca,—Either you are Catholic by name, or Catholics in fact. If you are Catholics in faith, give a terrible blow to these savages, intruders, and adventurers, who, to make themselves appear wise and important, and to assure themselves a future without labor, attempt that which they do not understand—that band of filthy scoundrels, deluded sons of all the devils. Let us rise *en masse* to finish at once this accursed race, whose proper place is in hell, which is not complete, without them. With one sure blow insure their death and the death of their families. Let a fiery death exterminate this sect of accursed wretches, who attempt to overthrow the Apostolic Roman Catholic religion, in which we will live and die.
Unfurl proudly the standard of the Faith, and shout, "Long live the religion! Viva la religion!! Death to the sons of Satan!!!!"

Although the dislike of Protestants is certainly not as pronounced as in 1875, one still sees signs in house windows which read "Somos Católicos" (We are Catholics), accompanied by a warning to Protestant missionaries. Latin America remains a Catholic area; however, the Protestants have been successful in converting a growing number of Latins. In many areas the Catholic Church has been demanding and exploitive. With a monopoly on religion in Latin America, the Catholic Church has not always been concerned with the needs of its people. In fact the Church has often been more concerned with the needs of the Church—larger offerings, new buildings, and so on, than with the needs of the congregation—mass, baptism, food, clothing, and so on. In many rural areas, the people are served only periodically by priests. Even though a community erects a church, it is not assured of a full-time priest. At the same time, few Latins are recruited into the clergy. Many of the priests are non-Spanish Europeans, some with considerable language problems. On the other hand, many of the Protestant churches project an image of being interested in the needs of people, helping them with agricultural techniques, handicrafts, and literacy.

In other cases, Protestantism has attracted converts because some people wish to break away from the traditional system of fiesta giving and the only way possible is through Protestantism. The peasant is encouraged to use any surplus he is able to accrue for the sponsorship of Catholic fiestas. The prestige given to the fiesta sponsor is reward enough as long as new wants for material goods do not arise. Among the Mayo and Yaqui of Sonora, Mexico, the fiesta performers cost a minimum of $72.00, and the expense of feeding the guests can cost as much as seven times the expense of the performers. The expense of a fiesta is comparable to a person in the United States earning a salary of $6,000 a year spending from $1,500 to $9,500 for a party. The inhabitants of this region find it increasingly difficult to bear the expense of sponsoring the fiesta on the one hand and to purchase consumer items on the other. As a result some of the people have joined Protestant churches in order to escape their obligations to the fiesta complex. Those who remain in the Catholic Church have attempted to reduce the tremendous costs of these fiestas. In some cases they will refuse to assume the sponsorship and at best will share the expense with co-sponsors. In addition, there has been a tendency for the individual sponsor to spend less for a fiesta (Erasmus 1961:183–305).

CONCEPTS OF HEALTH AND ILLNESS

The beliefs that Latin Americans hold concerning the causes and cures of illnesses are extremely diverse. Some of these beliefs are derived from pre-Contact Amerind customs, while others come from European and North American medical traditions and still others from African origins. The syncretism forms a "popular" medicine with a far greater number of alternatives for curing and explaining disease than is true of modern medicine. The contemporary popular medicine of Latin America includes folk medicine, modern medicine, patent remedies, homeopathic medicine (a system based on the idea that certain diseases can be cured by giving very small doses of drugs which in a healthy person would produce symptoms like those of the disease, i.e., like can cure like), naturopathy (a system in which the patient is cured through herbal remedies and other natural phenomena), and spiritualism.

Latin American popular medicine also includes a number of different types of healers including the folk curers (*curanderos*), the physicians (practicing modern medicine), the homeopaths, naturists, as well as licensed pharmacists. The pharmacists dispense not only patent remedies, but also antibiotics. Often they are preferred to the physicians because they will diagnose without charging the consultation fee of the physician.

Healers who have a nonempirical referent include saints to whom promises are made (for example, a woman might promise a saint that she will walk on her hands and knees to a shrine if the saint were to cure her son), spirits (often of famous doctors), and (for some of the Protestants) God. Instead of praying to a saint as the Catholic would do, the Protestant would be more likely to pray directly to God (Richardson and Bode 71:256–261). To many Latin Americans who might make use of any or all of these healers, the most important healer is still the curandero, or folk healer.

Illness in many parts of Latin America is divided into two categories, natural and unnatural. In Texas, among the Mexican-Americans, these illnesses are known as *mal natural* and *mal artificial* or *mal puesto* (Rubel 1966:156). On the Island of Chira, in Costa Rica, this same distinction of illnesses prevails but is referred to as sickness *hechos por la mano de Dios* (made by God's hand) and sickness *hecho por maleficios o brujería* (made by sorcery) (Orso 1970:24). Illnesses of the first category are caused by God, whereas the unnatural illnesses are produced by sorcerers. This distinction is also reported for Chichicastenango, Guatemala (Bunzel 1952: 143–144).

The folk medicine of Latin America is a blend of the formal medical beliefs held in Spain at the time of the Conquest, the Spanish folk medical beliefs of the rural Spanish peasants who settled in the New World, and a number of beliefs held by the Amerinds. Many of the Latin American folk concepts of illness originated from the Hippocratic doctrine of four "humors"—blood, phlegm, black bile, and yellow bile. Those humors formed the basis of Greek and Roman medical theory and were transmitted to Spain via the Arab world to become the basis of Spanish formal medicine. Each humor had its own "complexion": blood was thought to be hot and wet; phlegm was thought to be cold and wet; black bile, cold and dry; yellow bile, hot and dry. The three most important organs of the body were thought to have the following complexions: the heart was dry and cold, the brain wet and cold, and the liver hot and wet. The normal body was thought to have an excess of heat and moisture although the actual balance varied from one individual to another. Some individuals were thought to be hot, others humid, cold, or dry. This system of classification extended beyond the human body. Illness, medicines, foods, and most natural objects had particular complexions. Curing an illness consisted primarily of understanding the natural complexion of the illness or its cause and in restoring the fundamental harmony which had been disturbed. What survives of this medical system in the New World is the belief that there are hot and cold qualities inherent in nature. In some areas of Latin America a third quality, temperate, is also used (Foster 1953). The ideas of wet and dry and of the humors have been lost.

In the Nahautl village of San Francisco Tecospa (in the Valley of Mexico), the hot and cold classification has been expanded to include 2 degrees of cold and 2 degrees of hot as well as temperate (Madsen 1955). The classification includes the categories hot (*caliente*), very hot (*muy caliente*), fresh (*fresco*), very fresh (*muy fresco*), cold (*frío*), very cold (*muy frío*) and temperate (*templado*). The classification of hot, temperate, cold, or fresh usually has no reference to the actual temperature of the item classified. The quality of coldness comes from water (cold) and the quality of heat comes from the sun or the energy within an animal or plant. Although water is classified as cold even when boiling, its frozen forms are classified as hot.

The main function of the hot-cold complex is to determine the treatment of injuries and illnesses. In San Francisco Tecospa, a "hot" injury or sickness is treated with a "cold" remedy. For example, a sprain (which is a cold illness) is treated by tying a piece of raw weasel meat (which is hot) over it. A person stung by a black widow spider (which is cold) drinks black coffee (which is hot). Raw mushrooms (cold) are poisonous and can cause stomach pains which are cured by eating toasted garlic (hot). As new items come into San Francisco Tecospan culture, they are in turn incorporated into the system. For example, movies are classified as cold and Alka-Seltzer is fresh (Madsen 1960:161–179). The assignment of these new items into hot and cold categories is often arbitrary. By assigning items such as Alka-Seltzer to a category, they are able to make use of new, effective remedies without having to abandon their basic medical theory. Violation of this hot-cold principle is only one cause of disease.

In her analysis of the hot and cold complex of Chira Island, Costa Rica, Ethelyn Orso discovered that the basic hot-cold system was further complicated by rules of behavior determined by the different periods of the day. For example, a type of food which might be considered safe to eat during one part of the day, might be considered unsafe during another part. The following proverb clearly illustrates this point (Orso 1970:43):

La naranja en la mañana es medicina,
al mediodía le enferma,
en la tarde le mata.

An orange in the morning is medicine,
In the middle of day it makes you sick,
In the evening it kills you.

In Chira oranges are classified as a "cold" food. The morning hours (from sunrise to about ten o'clock) are considered the safest time for the body to have contact with cold temperatures and cold foods, such as oranges, due to the fact that the body's temperature is lower than usual as a result of sleeping and because the morning's temperatures are cool. In the middle of the day cold temperatures and cold items are avoided. The temperature of the air is very hot and the body's temperature is raised by the morning's work activities. Contact with cold items during this period of the day can result in sickness. In the evening, cold foods must be avoided. The temperature of the air is cool and the body is even hotter than in the middle of the day due to additional afternoon work activities. The combined forces of cold temperature and direct contact with cold foods are believed to produce a deadly shock on the very hot body (Orso 1970:43–44).

In Latin America the human body is conceived of differently than in North America. In Colombia, for example, every individual is thought to consist of four different parts: the "person" (*persona*), the "spirit" (*espíritu*), the "soul" (*alma*), and the "body" (*cuerpo*). The "person" is represented by the individual's congenital traits, as well as characteristics which have been culturally conditioned. It is his "personality" (*personalidad caracter*), his unique way of behaving. In some parts of Latin America it is thought that man is born evil and that it is this innate part of his person which contains evilness; whereas the acquired part ("education") tends to suppress this inclination. Doing good or evil depends exclusively upon the "person." The "spirit" is thought to control the person. It attempts to lead it and orient it and is much like "another person," but in essence a good one. It struggles against the "person's" innate tendency to evil. It directs the person toward what it ought to do. However, because it is believed that the person is essentially evil, the spirit often fails and then becomes evil itself (Reichel-Dolmatoff and Reichel-Dolmatoff 1961:275).

The soul (alma) is neither good nor evil. In fact, it holds no relationship whatsoever to the other components. Instead the soul represents a factor of vitality; it is that part of the being that has the capacity for giving or receiving love. While the person and the spirit are conceived of as individualized entities, the soul is thought to be very similar to all other souls. However, only souls that are "identical," or nearly so, feel love for each other. Only then can the soul make itself felt as an active power even though the person or the spirit resists this power. It is believed that the spirit and soul of the individual never change of themselves but only when the spirit becomes dominated by the person. However, the person is able to change greatly. The soul has its seat in the heart (and therefore in the blood), whereas the person and spirit inhabit the entire body (Reichel-Dolmatoff and Reichel-Dolmatoff 1961:275).

Throughout Latin America blood is thought to represent the essential life force. In many areas blood is believed to be nonregenerative. A person with all of the blood he was born with is considered a healthy person, but one who loses some of his blood due to an accident will be somewhat sickly the rest of his life. In other areas, blood in a healthy person is believed to be renewed by food and beverages but is slowed down or stopped entirely in a sick person.

In the mestizo village of Aritama, Colombia, it is believed that only blood in women circulates; the blood of men does not circulate and is described as "quiet." Susceptibility to disease depends primarily upon certain characteristics of the individual's blood. One's blood can be either "strong" or "weak." In general a man's blood is always stronger than a woman's blood because a man's blood is quiet. A woman's blood is weaker because it circulates. By circulating it acquires impurities that are eliminated every month by menstruation, which takes place to purify the blood. Some individuals, both male and female, are born with stronger or weaker blood than others of their sex. There are also certain occasions and situations during which a person's blood is "weak." During puberty boys and girls have weak blood. After sundown everyone's blood becomes "weak," reaching its previous level of strength only after dawn. Physical fatigue, sexual relations, menstruation, menopause, drunkenness, fear, rage, jealousy, exposure to the sun or the rain, or actually any type of physical or mental stress are occasions which temporarily "weaken" the blood (Reichel-Dolmatoff and Reichel-Dolmatoff 1961:276–279).

Social relationships are generally conceptualized by the Latin as bearing inherent dangers to the equilibrium of the individual. *Mal ojo* (evil eye) is a disease that weaker individuals receive from stronger ones. Women and children are thought to be inherently weaker than adult males and therefore more receptive to the disease.

This disease is not explained by the germ theory but rather by the exceptional "power" of some individuals. The power is believed to be located in the visual apparatus. Strong glances, covetous expressions, or excessive attention paid to one person by another, such as the tourist who stares or smiles at the Latin child playing in the street, exposes the individual to the dangers of an unnatural bond. The afflicted is thought to be drained of the will to act, which causes the entrance into his body of the "stronger power" of the other. The symptoms of the disease, at least for the Mexican-Americans, include sudden severe headaches, inconsolable weeping (by children), unusual fretfulness, and high temperature. The careful person recognizes a situation in which he or she has coveted someone by the appearance of a pain on one of the agent's temples and will break the spell by passing a hand over the forehead of the afflicted or by patting the temples (Rubel 1960:800).

The symptoms of mal ojo appear very abruptly. At the first signs of the illness the family of the afflicted party attempts to retrace the social contacts the individual had experienced in the previous few hours in the search for a significantly affective relationship. If such a relationship is recalled, the suspected agent is quickly asked to return and to attempt a rupture of the charm by which one of the individuals is held to the other (Rubel 1960: 800–801).

If the actual agent cannot be determined or found, the bond is broken and the intrusive power of the other is drained from the subject by means of sympathetic magic and religious prayers:

A hen's egg is taken and rubbed whole over the patient's body to absorb some of the heat and power which has disturbed the balance of the youngster. A water glass half-full of liquid is brought close to the sufferer and the egg tapped three times on the edge of the glass. On the third blow the shell is broken open, symbolizing the rupture of the bond between the patient and the stronger individual. The egg is emptied into the water glass where it is permitted to settle and assume a diagnostic form. If the form assumed by the egg in the glass suggests a "cooked" shape, i.e., sunny-side up, the condition is diagnosed as one of mal ojo. An elongated shape bespeaks a male cause, a round shape a woman agent (Rubel 1960:801).

If the egg presents a diagnosis of mal ojo, a treatment is given to drain the intrusive power of the stronger individual from the patient. The mixture of egg and water is placed under the head of the patient's bed until the following morning. Then the mixture is carefully disposed of by burying in the yard or flushing in a commode. Among the Mexican-Americans it is believed that mal ojo is not fatal unless it is improperly diagnosed or treated (Rubel 1960:801); whereas in Colombia it is always considered fatal in children (Reichel-Dolmatoff and Reichel-Dolmatoff 1961:284). In Paraguay the condition of evil eye extends beyond humans to become a type of bad luck in which the power will cause crops to fail, milk and eggs to curdle in cooking, and baking pottery to crack (Service and Service 1954:249).

Another common disease is *susto* (also called *pasmo, jani, espanto, pérdida de la sombra*). Susto results from incidents which have unstabilizing effects on individuals causing a part of the self, the espíritu (the spirit), to leave the body, or it arises if the spirit leaves the body during sleep while the individual is dreaming. Those who suffer from the disease include Amerind and non-Amerind, male and female, rich and poor, rural dwellers and urbanites. The basic susto syndrome appears as follows: (1) during sleep the patient evidences restlessness; (2) when awake the patient is characterized by listlessness, loss of appetite, disinterest in dress and personal hygiene, loss of strength, depression, and introversion (Rubel 1964: 270).

Susto can be caused by a number of factors. A shock sufficient to disengage one's espíritu may be caused by sudden, unexpected barking, falling from a horse, or tripping over an unnoticed object. A particularly unpleasant occurrence, such as the experience of sharing a hospital ward with a patient who has died during the night, is unbalancing and will in turn make the person liable to the loss of his espíritu. Equally frightening is a nighttime encounter with an apparition. Susto can also be caused by the impingement of society upon the individual. Social situations that produce a disquieting condition of anger or fear in the individual are avoided because they too might result in the wandering of one's espíritu (Rubel 1960:803).

In Paraguay it is believed that susto is in part caused by worms. Every child and adult is thought to have worms in his blood which may cause illness. If an individual has poor circulation, insufficient or "bad" blood, or "weak blood in the head," the worms are able to attack. Children, being generally weaker than adults, are considered most susceptible. Eating too many sweets, anemia, paleness, and nervousness are thought to be contributing factors. Any of the above causes, in combination with a frightening experience, may bring on an attack of susto. The remedies in Paraguay all involve killing and eliminating the worms by purgatives (Service and Service 1954:323).

Generally the curing involves a healing ritual similar to that described by Gillin (1948) among the Pokomam Maya of Guatemala. A group of persons who are important to the individual suffering from susto are organized to attend a nocturnal ceremony. Some of the group join the patient and healer in offering prayers to the Catholic saints of the village. Next hens' eggs are passed over the patient's body to absorb some of the illness. The eggs are later deposited at the place where the spirit loss had occurred, together with a collection of gifts, to propitiate the spirits who hold the patient's spirit and who are requested to release it. Following prayers and libations to the spirits, a procession is formed traveling from the place of the accident back to the patient's home. The healer makes noises to indicate to the espíritu the appropriate direction for returning to the patient's body. The patient is then undressed, "shocked" by cold liquor sprayed from the mouth of the curer, then massaged, and finally "sweated" on a bed placed over a brazier filled with burning coals.

Other causes of disease in the folk system of medicine are supernatural beings and witches. Among the Nahua speaking peoples, rain dwarfs (*yeyecatl* or *ahuatoton*) cause *aire*, a sickness brought about by the spirits blowing their breath on humans. The rain dwarfs are thought to be about a foot and a half in height and consist entirely of water. The symptoms of aire include paralysis, palsy, twisted mouth, skin pustules and aching joints. This type of aire must be cured by a specialist, a *curandero de aire*. The treatment includes a series of cleanings. The patient's body is brushed with a handful of herbs and an unbroken chicken egg. A second type of aire (*aire de noche* or *espanto*) is believed to be caused by ghosts. Its symptoms are loss of consciousness, loss of speech, chills, and trembling. It is also cured through cleansing and by rubbing a live black chicken over the patient's body. A third type of aire (*aire de basura*) is believed caused by loose women and prostitutes. It causes eye trouble in newborn babies and fetuses. A fourth type is believed caused by the imbalance of the hot and cold. Most commonly it is thought to be caused by the cold night air striking the warm body of a sleeping man (Madsen 1969:630–631).

Disease by bewitchment among the Nahua are of two types. One type, *tlacique,* is caused by vampires who suck the blood of their victims. The second type is brought about by the *nagual* (transformer). The nagual has the power to cause illness from a distance by magical means. The nagual can change from human into animal forms in order to spy on its victims. The techniques used by the nagual to bewitch its victim include sticking pins in a doll representing the victim and object intrusion, in which the nagual sends animals, worms, hair, or pebbles into the victim's stomach by magical means. The treatment of these diseases is often very difficult. The object has to be removed by a witch; the buried doll has to be found and then burned (Madsen 1969:630–631).

Other diseases are brought about by God and the saints. They are believed to send a variety of diseases to punish misdeeds such as breaking a religious vow. To cure this type of disease one must pray for forgiveness and make an offering. On Chira Island, Costa Rica, all nonsupernatural diseases are believed sent by God.

In the folk system of medicine the question, Why is *he* ill? supplants the question we ask in our society, *Why* is he ill? Our own system of medicine might explain the cause of a particular disease but it does not explain why the particular individual becomes ill. Practitioners of folk medicine not only attempt to cure individuals but seek to discover why these persons, rather than others, become ill. Often the "answer" can be found in the use of witchcraft by the enemies of these individuals. There is a saying, *"Nadie muere sin que le echen algo"* (No one dies without having been made to).

THE DOUBLE STANDARD OF SEX MORALS

The Latin Americans practice a double standard of sex morals which deems premarital and adulterous sexual intercourse socially acceptable when practiced by males but unpardonable and socially stigmatizing when practiced by females. The ideal pattern will be described though not all persons or social groups follow these patterns in their actual behavior.[1] An ideal pattern is one which is thought to be the proper action of a man and a woman.

The Latin male should be *macho* (manly)—domineering, aggressive, and uncompromising. Octavio Paz describes manliness in Mexico as never "cracking"—never backing down. Those who "open themselves up" are considered cowards. It is thought to be a sign of weakness or a betrayal. "The Mexican can bend, can bow humbly, can even stoop, but he cannot back down, that is, he cannot allow the outside world to penetrate his privacy. The man who backs down is not to be trusted, is a traitor or a person of doubtful loyalty; he babbles secrets and is incapable of confronting a dangerous situation" (Paz 1961:29–30). Following the same line of logic, women are considered inferior beings because in submitting to males they open themselves up.

One of Oscar Lewis's Mexico City informants, Manuel Sánchez, suggests the same concept of manliness when he says:

Mexicans, and I think everyone in the world, admire the person "with balls," as we say. The character who throws punches and kicks, without stopping to think, is the one who comes out on top. The one who has guts enough to stand up against an older, stronger guy, is more respected. If someone shouts, you've got to shout louder. If any so-and-so comes to me and says, "Fuck your mother," I answer, "Fuck your mother a thousand times." And if he gives one step forward and I take one step back, I lose prestige. But if I go forward too, and pile on and make a fool out of him, then others will treat me with respect. In a fight, I would never give up or say, "Enough," even though the other was killing me. I would try to go to my death, smiling. That is what we mean by being "macho," by being manly (Lewis 1964:38).

Usually parents desire a male child. The Reichel-Dolmatoffs (1961: 184) found in Aritama, Colombia that all of the women envied men and all of them, young and old, said they wished they had been born men and not women. Throughout his childhood the male is encouraged to "be a man." Boys are expected to get into mischief and to be daring. As a teenager the boy is given considerable freedom and expected to be sexually active. He becomes a potential threat to the household maids and the females of the neighborhood. It is also expected that he will demonstrate his masculinity by visiting prostitutes. While he may sometimes be scolded for his amorous

[1] Several forthcoming studies, *Female and Male in Latin America*, by Ann Pescatello, and the February 1973 issue of *The Journal of Marriage and the Family*, edited by Nora Scott Kinzer, will attempt to present the actual rather than the stereotyped, situation of the Latin female. Most discussions of the role of Latin American women thus far have come from male Latin Americanists. The forthcoming studies will present female Latin Americanists' interpretations.

adventures, his parents are usually secretly proud of their son's exploits. It is expected that a man will attempt to seduce a female whenever an opportunity arises. His sexual conquests do not end after marriage. Many men have mistresses and maintain at least two households (the *casa grande,* or "large house" of his nuclear family and the *casa chica,* or "little house" of his mistress).

The female is thought to be an opposite creature from the male. The woman is born into a life of suffering and of isolation from the world outside of the family. She sees herself as a martyr. The young girl has to be protected from males since ideally the female should be a virgin when she marries. The father, mother, and brother closely guard the female to prevent a situation which might result in the loss of the female's virginity. Dating is still not widespread in Latin America, and the female is generally chaperoned when escorted by a male. She is further encouraged to be accompanied by other girls whenever in public. It is thought that the female is incapable of resisting the advances of the male.

A girl is allowed little freedom in her parents' house. As a result she is usually anxious to marry and move out of the house. The male, on the other hand, is usually not interested in marriage at an early age. It means settling down with greater restrictions on his amorous affairs. Sometimes when a man is hesitant to set a wedding date the anxious young girl will meet secretly with her suitor, meetings which normally result in intercourse. When this happens the male usually refuses to marry the girl because she is no longer a virgin. He feels that if the girl will offer herself to him before they are married, then she may offer herself to others after they are married (Wagley 1968:72). These abandoned girls often become prostitutes or mistresses.

In some areas this Latin American pattern of a double standard is related to social class. In other words, only certain members of the society seem to emphasize this strong behavior dichotomy. In Brazil it does not seem prevalent in the lower class, yet remains strong in the upper and middle classes. Emilio Willems (1953:340–343) suggests that in these two classes the female role is centered around a cluster of values that he terms a "virginity complex," wherein the belief that females should abstain from premarital sexual experiences is rigidly maintained. On the other hand, the male role is centered around a set of values that Willems terms a "virility complex," in which the young man is expected to become actively interested in sex at the age of puberty. According to Willems (1953:341):

> Even before puberty the average boy becomes used to the sexual bravado of older companions. He learns that regular sexual intercourse is not only believed to be physically healthy, but above all an essential attribute of manhood. There is a generally accepted opinion that early and frequent sexual intercourse is stimulated by peculiar racial qualities and the

physiological effects of a tropical climate. This point of view, which is presumed to be scientific, entitles men to feel irresponsible in sex affairs. Marriage is not expected to channelize or to restrict his sexual activities. Normally a male feels free to have intercourse with as many different women as may be available.

The male is thought of as an active force while the female is seen as passive, receptive, as not intruding her will—in other words, self-sacrificing (*abnegada*). Marriage then becomes the joining together of two unlike units. It is not dramatized as something entered into by mutual consent but rather the event is celebrated as aggression on the one hand and submission on the other (Diaz 1966:55–56). In some communities this opposition of the traditional male and female roles is emphasized by the practice of bride stealing, in which a man "robs" a woman from her parents. On Chira Island, Costa Rica, this male-female opposition is equated with the hot-cold system of classification. Men are considered to be "hot" and to have "hot" sexual organs. Women are classified as "cold" and are thought to have "cold" sexual organs (Orso 1970:80).

When a female marries, her freedom actually does not increase significantly. She merely moves from one type of sheltered life to another. After marriage the double standard of expected behavior continues. The husband rules the family as a dictator. His word is not to be questioned. In a family dominated by a woman it is believed that the wife has bewitched her husband. Although the husband may not realize he is bewitched, his mother and sisters will recognize the "symptoms" and will attempt to break the "spell."

After marriage the male continues his activities outside the household, yet the woman is discouraged from any outside activities as she is still thought to be vulnerable to the advances of men. Therefore, if she remains within the confines of the house she will not have an opportunity to meet any men. This attitude is clearly expressed in two Spanish sayings: "A woman's place is in the home, with a broken leg" and "Between a female saint and a male saint, a wall of mortared stone" (Paz 1961:36).

Men desire a number of children—one right after another—so that their wives will find it difficult to maintain any outside activities. Even friendships with other women are discouraged because the friends might act as go-betweens for the wife and a lover. The ideal wife is one who bears children, submits to the demands of her husband, remains at home, and is not sexually demanding. A passionate wife is considered undesirable. She is a source of great concern to her husband. A man prefers a frigid wife because she is less likely to seek sexual satisfaction elsewhere. In Tepoztlán, Oscar Lewis (1949) found that some husbands deliberately refrain from arousing their wives sexually for fear that they may enjoy it too much and look outside the house for fulfillment. A man saves his love-making techniques for his mistress. The wife often feels self-righteous in her attitudes toward sexual relations with her husband. She sees herself submitting to her husband because it is an obligation. In fact coitus is sometimes verbalized on the part of the woman as an "abuse" (*abuso*), a humiliating and dis-agreeable act during which only pain is felt.

The male remains aloof from the rest of the family. He maintains a formal relationship with his children. As a result, mother and children often develop a close relationship. The children see their mother much as she sees herself—self-sacrificing in order that the other members of the family will have a better life.

Lewis (1949) reports that in Tepoztlán there is considerable discrep-ancy between the ideal patterns and actual behavior. Most marriages show some conflict between man and wife over the question of authority and the respective roles of the spouses. The most placid marriages generally are those in which the husband is not too overbearing and at the same time the wife does little to challenge the authority of the husband. The conflict between husband and wife is greatest in those families in which the husband is so insecure that he becomes violent and fear-inspiring, or in which the woman is openly aggressive and actively attempts to dominate the husband. There is an awareness among the villagers that there has been a growing assertiveness of wives and a continual struggle of husbands to keep them under control. The men say, "When the man relaxes, the woman takes over." The women believe, "When we give in, the men impose."

THE NATURE OF INTERPERSONAL RELATIONS

A basic social unit throughout parts of Latin America is the nuclear family. Each nuclear family household represents a social isolate. There is frequently a lack of larger, effective social units. As a result, in parts of Latin America there is a feeling that the only people one can really count on and trust are the members of one's own nuclear family. Within the walls of the household one feels safe and secure. The outside world is sometimes thought to be filled with danger from others. To describe a type of society in which the nuclear family constitutes the major social unit, Arthur Rubel, studying the Mexican-Americans, has used the term "atomistic social system." The atomistic social system has the following characteristics: (1) there is an absence of cooperation between nuclear families, (2) the qualities of con-tention, invidiousness, and wariness are uppermost in the perceptions which nuclear families hold of one another, and (3) social behavior and emotional qualities are consonant with normative expectations (Rubel 1966:207). There are no ideal expectations for harmonious extrafamilial interpersonal relations. Often with those individuals one can trust, which is an extremely limited number, there are shifting alliances. While the atomistic social system has been used to describe Mexican-Americans, the description is probably applicable to other subcultures of Latin America as well.

The Dyadic Contract   In the atomistic type of social system, the adult organizes his contacts outside the nuclear family by means of a special form of contractual relationships which George Foster (1961, 1963) has termed the "dyadic contract." The dyadic contract forms the basis of reciprocity in the atomistic social system. The contracts are informal, lacking a ritual or legal basis, and they occur only between two individuals—three or more persons are not brought together. The contracts are noncorporate in the sense that social units such as villages, neighborhoods, or extended families are never bound together through the contract.

In a society consisting of networks of social relations based on dyadic contracts, no two persons have exactly the same ties. As a result there are no groups of people to serve as the basis for either positive or negative action. Thus there is no unit to serve as a base for feuding nor is there a unit to serve as a base for cooperative work for mutual goals (Foster 1961:1191).

The dyadic contract, as expressed within the formal systems of the family, compadrazgo, and neighborhoodship-friendship, provides the institutional framework for organizing most interpersonal relations within the community. Each of these systems provides norms that define the ideal behavior appropriate to the settings in which people find themselves (Foster 1961: 1178).

The nuclear family itself can be seen as consisting of dyadic relations. Marriage tends to be a dyadic contract (albeit a formal contract) in some peasant communities. In Tzintzuntzan, the Mexican village studied by Foster, marriages are not thought of as the merger of two families but rather the establishment of a bond between two individuals; in fact elopement is a fairly common way of initiating marriage. The bride does not take her husband's last name but instead continues to be referred to by her maiden name. She may register property in her name and she may buy, sell, or take court action without the consent of her husband (Foster 1961:1179).

Each individual is born into an established network of relatives with whom there is a multiplicity of expected rights and obligations. Throughout his life he will continue to acquire relatives but with no choice in the selection. His only option is in picking a spouse, and in Catholic countries this is an indissoluble relationship. The individual's only real choice is the degree to which he will honor his obligations.

The compadrazgo institution is much like the family in that once the compadrazgo bonds are established they are considered indissoluble. By middle age a man has usually acquired many more compadrazgo ties than he can fully maintain. As a result he completely ignores some, maintains superficial ties with most and develops effective working relationships with only a few compadres (Foster 1961:1182–1183).

The fact that people live together in communities establishes at least minimal bonds of common interest between the inhabitants. A landslide that wipes out a road creates a problem for all of the inhabitants—as does a householder's vicious dog. Thus the neighborhood or community is the scene of certain necessary interaction. Sometimes the interaction is the basis for friendship, yet not all neighbors are friends nor are all friends neighbors. As two people realize their mutual interests and begin to like each other, they visit at each other's homes, offer each other food, and exchange favors (Foster 1961:1183).

Friendships often begin in childhood. An adolescent boy will refer to his best friend as *amigo carnal,* signifying that the friend is as close as a brother. An exchange of goods such as knives or tops usually marks the establishment of the friendship. The exchange of goods continues for as long as the tie is recognized. If the friendship lasts until one of the friends becomes married, the relationship may be turned into a compadrazgo tie. Girls are less likely to develop such close friendships, as they are allowed considerably less freedom outside the home.

There is always some reservation attached to friendship. It is best that one never reveals all of what he thinks and feels to a friend. Even between amigo carnales it is doubtful that confidences are such as to justify the term "buddies" to describe the pattern.

Friendship and "neighborhoodship" are considerably more flexible institutions than either kinship or compadrazgo. Through the use of friendship and neighborhoodship an individual is able to compensate for the problems of the other institutions. In a pinch, friendship and neighborhoodship can provide a mechanism for any situation normally provided for by kinship and compadrazgo ties. Friends and neighbors help in the kitchen; they go with a young man's father to make peace with a girl's family; they sit together at ceremonial tables; and together they engage in commercial transactions. In some cases they may even enjoy the same degree of confidences as a relative or compadre. Friendship is a highly adaptive institution, especially in situations of rapid change. While almost anything that can be accomplished within the framework of kinship and compadrazgo can be accomplished through friendship, long-range commitments are avoided. New friendships are easily formed while detrimental ones are dropped and forgotten; no messy ends are left as when an individual quarrels with a brother or stops speaking with a compadre (Foster 1961: 1183–1184).

In the village of Santa Cruz Chinaulta, Guatemala, two distinct patterns of friendship have been observed. One of the patterns, *cuello,* is practiced by the ladinos of the community; the other, *camaradería*, is practiced by the Amerinds. The cuello relationships represent convenient friendships from which some economic or legal benefit can be expected. These friendships fluctuate as new friends are added and old ties are forgotten (Reina 1959:44–45).

The Amerinds associate themselves under the *camarada* pattern which is entered into during youth. The camaradería ties represent bonds of intense friendship. This type of friendship is maintained not for economic, political, or practical purposes but for an emotional fulfillment. The Amerind demands reciprocal affection in his friendship and expects that the camarada will act only in a manner which will bring pleasure to his friend. Each individual is jealous and egotistical in this relationship. He wants undivided affection and he would prefer to lose everything rather than share a friendship with others. The Amerind does not have more than one camarada at a time (Reina 1959:45).

Through the extension of dyadic contracts the individual is able to choose a comparatively small number of people with whom he wishes to maintain reciprocity from his total network of kin, compadres, friends, and neighbors. This reciprocity is expressed in the continued exchange of goods and services. The reciprocity is complementary because each partner owes the other the same kinds and quantities of things. However, an exactly even balance between partners is avoided. "The dyadic contract is effective precisely because partners are never quite sure of their relative positions at a given moment. As long as they know that goods and services are flowing both ways in roughly equal amounts over time, they know their relationship is solidly based" (Foster 1961:1185).

Contractual ties are found in all societies. Their importance in atomistic social systems is that they exist in a type of society in which there is an absence or near absence of corporate ties. Meaningful contracts occur almost exclusively between pairs of individuals; they form a dyad and do not bind larger groups. By means of a great number of dyadic contracts with both colleagues and patrons, the individual maximizes his security in the uncertain world in which he lives (Foster 1963:1923). On the one hand the individual sees himself facing a hostile world in which the ideal male, the macho, can successfully defend himself, can live without obligations (*sin compromisos*), and does not need to rely on others. Still, as Foster (1963:1280) notes, paradoxically:

... the struggle to reach this goal can be made only by saddling one's self with a wide variety of obligations. Strength and independence—success in defending one's self—in fact always depend on the number and quality of the contractual ties one has incurred. Hence the whole course of life consists of manipulating and exploiting the institutions and behavior forms one knows to achieve desirable obligations, to tap social resources so that life's dangers will be minimized and its opportunities maximized.

In Brazil, Anthony Leeds (1965:387) observed a different type of extrafamilial grouping called the *panelinha* (literally, "little saucepan") which is "... a relatively closed, completely informal primary group, held together in common interest by personal ties and including a roster of all key socio-politico-economic positions." The typical panelinha is composed of individuals such as a customs official, an insurance man, lawyers, business-men, government officials, and a banker. Through the ties of the group, they are often able to circumvent the law. Likewise, this group is able to pool large quantities of money on short notice in order to win contracts and enter into various business speculations (Leeds 1965:393–395).

Palomillas   One form of organization found outside of the family among Latin Americans is the egocentric association formed by young men known as the *palomilla* or *amigazco* among the Mexican-Americans and *pandilla* in Colombia, Argentina, and Spain. "Palomillas are particularistic, personal, voluntary, and non-instrumental; they lack such corporate attri-butes as group name, identification with a particular territory, ingroup senti-ments, or even persistence over time" (Rubel 1965:93). The palomilla is a network of informal dyadic relations between agemates. These groups play an important role in the transition from boyhood to adulthood. Within many Latin families interaction is governed by a strict dichotomization of the sexes, emphasis on social distance between members, and the dictatorial con-trol by the father/husband. Respect deference is observed between those who are younger to their elders and between sexes. Frivolous actions such as laughter, drinking, smoking, and particularly any reference to sexual behavior are discouraged as disturbing the etiquette of family relations and are con-sidered an affront to the male head of the household. Young men are en-couraged to express the virile sides of their nature outside the house, but only to the extent that their conduct does not scandalize their parents and siblings, or later their wife and children. It is thus in the palomilla that a boy learns to become a man and to express himself as such. The participants of a palomilla spend their time telling stories, discussing one another's amorous adventures, drinking, arranging social events such as dances, and discussing problems in which they share concern. From the point of view of the family, these associations make possible the continuity of the tradition-ally autocratic relations which exist between fathers and their sons, since the fathers need not fully participate in their son's transition from childhood to manhood. At the same time, by allowing only males to engage in extra-familial non-kinship contacts, the mothers and sisters of the youths are insulated from worldly matters (Rubel 1965).

Male friendship group, Acuitzio del Canje, Michoacán, Mexico. (Courtesy of Raymond E. Wiest.)

A similar pattern of friendship known as the *cuate* (twins) was introduced into Tepoztlán, Mexico, during the Revolution. The cuate is a close alliance between two or more individuals of the same age group for a generalized companionship. The cuate is depended upon for loyalty and defense in time of trouble, for political support, and for companionship in drinking, in romantic undertakings, and in celebrating fiestas (Lewis 1951:292–293).

As an individual begins to reach forty years of age, he diminishes the frequency of his interaction with a palomilla and engages more actively in the management of his household affairs (Rubel 1966:214). It would seem that as a male reaches middle age in some Latin subcultures, he tends to withdraw from interpersonal relations and seeks safety in the haven of his home. This has been reported in several studies of Mexican-Americans (see Rubel 1966, Simmons 1961, and Romano 1960), and has also been found in Aritama, Colombia (Reichel-Dolmatoff and Reichel-Dolmatoff 1961:200–201). In Frontera, Texas, the Mexican-American middle-aged male is re-

223

Male friendship group, San José, Costa Rica.

warded by his neighbors for his withdrawal from interpersonal relations outside of the nuclear family. They bestow upon him the honorific title, "don," as an acknowledgement that he no longer constitutes a potential threat to his neighbors (Romano 1960).

Personalism In his interpersonal relations, the Latin American emphasizes personal ties (*personalismo*). Personalismo is a contractual tie between two people who feel they can help each other by ignoring, in large measure, the institutional context in which they meet (Foster 1961:1191). Personalism is possibly most extreme in the political realm where the *caudillos* (political bosses) and dictators run the polity as they wish, regardless of constitutions, and anyone wishing any governmental action goes directly to the political boss rather than working through the bureaucracy (for example see Tannenbaum 1948). According to John Santos (1967:7), a psychologist, the Latin American places great emphasis upon bypassing authority. The Brazilian writer Clodomir Vianna Moog (1964) has described a type of personalism characteristic of Brazil, the *jeito*. This is the "gimmick," the indirect and often complex means to an end. Another Brazilian, Jose Honorio Rodrigues (1967:57), a historian, observes that the Brazilian ". . . stresses direct personal relations, based on liking rather than on unconditioned, impersonal, practical relations. Personal liking is above the law." Rogelio Díaz-Guerrero (1959:186), a Mexican psychiatrist, suggests along somewhat the same lines that the Mexican evaluates an interpersonal relation on the basis of the immediate pleasure and satisfaction that it brings.

Ask a Mexican for street directions. He will often go into a complex series of explanations and gestures, frequently grinning; he will make you *feel* good. But, you may get nowhere with his directions! Simply because he cannot answer your question, the Mexican would never let the *real thing*, the pleasant interpersonal encounter, go to waste (Díaz-Guerrero 1959:186).

The emphasis on personalism seems to be related to another aspect of interpersonal relations in Latin America, the need to understand one another's souls.

In general a high value is placed on individuality. A person is valued because he is considered different from all other individuals. The soul (*alma* or *ánimo*) or inner uniqueness is the important feature that distinguishes one person from another. The individual defends this inner quality to the utmost of his ability in order that others will not think he has lost his manliness. The soul is constantly guarded against insults. The *mosca* (insult) is a type of verbal abuse that is continually anticipated. The Latin American often reacts with extreme emotion to such insult.

It is the stranger or non-kin of whom one is especially suspicious. Ceremonial politeness is used with all but one's close kin and close friends. By remaining extremely formal, a situation in which one's guard is lowered is avoided. The soul will not be subject to attack. The perception of the outside world as hostile also inspires the macho ideal male image. A true macho is someone who is aware of his inner worth and is willing to bet everything on his self-confidence (Gillin 1965:509). This outlook also encourages a pattern of noninvolvement outside the household. There is limited participation in formal associations, and involvement in community affairs is also minimal. Increasing the amount of interaction with others enhances the possibility of attack upon one's soul.

When interaction does take place, a personal or intimate relationship is desired. It is only with this type of relationship that a person is able to understand and appreciate another's inner quality. However, the types of persons with whom one might have such a relationship are severely restricted to blood kin, compadres, and true friends (individuals who understand each other's souls but do not want to invoke the compadrazgo relationship). Yet with true friends one must also use caution, because, as many Latin Americans believe, "Your friend today may be your enemy tomorrow," and if they reveal their true selves to a friend and the friendship ceases, intimate confidences might be used against them.

Social Control   In some communities individuals resort to the courts as a primary mechanism of social control, yet in many cases other techniques are used to keep another individual's behavior within certain limits. These involve the use of informal, personal controls. They are important in a social system such as the atomistic social system where there is a minimal number of structural bonds and where a considerable amount of behavior is unpredictable. If in an atomistic social system there is a general absence of extrafamilial alliances, it might then seem as though there are few if any means of bringing anyone who has deviated from the norms back into line; however, informal means, such as malicious gossip and witchcraft, are used to control interpersonal relations with a certain degree of success.

Ruben Reina (1966:268–279) describes five types of informal controls used by Amerinds of Chinautla, Guatemala, which have a wide distribution in Latin America, albeit in somewhat modified forms: malicious gossip (*habladurías*), quasi-witchery (*envidia*), the evil eye (*mal de ojos*), fright (*susto*), and witchery (*brujerías*).

Malicious gossip is a means of launching an anonymous, often vicious, attack on another. It is often successful because group cohesiveness is generally not sufficiently strong enough either to counteract what is being said or to support the person being gossiped about. The gossip attacks the individual's morals and often stigmatizes a person as a poor marriage partner. A bad reputation may limit how and whom one marries; it reduces the value of a marriage partner and in the most scandalous cases completely eliminates the best prospective mates. In fact, in Chinautla, malicious gossip has been utilized by mothers to destroy the reputation of a girl so that their sons might have a better chance of marrying her and the girl's parents be less demanding in the bargaining process (Reina 1966:268–270). Malicious gossip is part of a broader pattern of criticism. Foster (1967:91) remarked that of the behavior characteristics of the Tzintzuntzan villagers none is more striking than criticism. "No one is spared, within or without the village, and no one is given the advantage of a doubt. The worst is automatically assumed, unless and until overwhelming evidence to the contrary is forthcoming."

Envy is a means with which to strike back at someone. The envidia (a personal desire), causes evil to fall on another person. Acts of envidia occur in situations of personal friction, such as the rejection of a marriage proposal or when distrust exists among spouses, relatives, and friends. Techniques used include petitions to saints, the burning of candles, and doll burial in which an image of the individual is stuck with pins and buried. Acts of envidia are counteracted by rituals in the church (Reina 1966:270–271). Envidia is described by Rubel (1966) as a form of envy among Mexican-Americans, which, in its extreme forms, is assumed to result in witchcraft. Oscar Lewis (1951:281) reports that in Tepoztlán sorcery is used in courtship by unsuccessful suitors. The most feared type of sorcery is doll burial. Envy is also described by Foster (1967:153–166) in his study of Tzintzuntzan. In Aritama, Colombia, envy is seen as the prime cause of disease to the person envied (Reichel-Dolmatoff and Reichel-Dolmatoff 1961:278). The Peruvian social scientist Carlos Delgado O. (1969:135) has noted that the socially mobile Peruvian employs either flattery (*sobe*) or malicious gossip (*raje*) depending on the situation. Flattery is used for the powerful and influential—those who could help the individual rise to an improved position, while slander is used against all those he considers a real or potential competitor.

Mal de ojos and susto (described in the section on health and disease) at times also serve as checks on social interaction.

Finally witchery affects interpersonal relations. Serious evil can be wrought against enemies through the use of *brujos* (witches). The brujo is a paid specialist. When one wishes harm done to another, even death, he will pay a brujo to cause various things such as worms and inanimate objects to materialize inside the victim's body (Reina 1966:273).

All of these phenomena serve as means of controlling social behavior. Most of the phenomena are thought to be powerful enough to result in death unless the necessary counteractions are taken. While many of these controls operate most prevalently in the rural areas, they are also utilized by various subcultures of the cities.

This chapter has described some of the major themes of Latin American life. In examining these themes, it has been possible to glimpse at the belief systems by which the Latin Americans operate. It should be kept in mind, however, that it is difficult to generalize about nearly three hundred million people. Not all Latins think or behave in the manner described. Yet these characteristics are at the basis of the Latin American tradition.

RECOMMENDED READING

Foster, George M., 1953, Relationships between Spanish and Spanish-American Folk Medicine. *Journal of American Folklore* 66:201–217.
   An historical analysis of the basic elements of Latin American folk medicine and its Mediterranean antecedents.
Gillin, John, 1947, Modern Latin American Culture. *Social Forces* 25:243–248.
————, 1955, Ethnos Components in Modern Latin American Culture. *American Anthropologist* 57:488–500.
   Two of the most insightful articles on the Latin American tradition.
Mintz, Sidney W., and Eric R. Wolf, 1950, An Analysis of Ritual Co-Parenthood (Compadrazgo). *Southwestern Journal of Anthropology* 6:341–368.
   A structural and historical description of the function of compadrazgo in the Old and New Worlds.

Rubel, Arthur J., 1966, *Across the Tracks: Mexican-Americans in a Texas City.* Austin, Tex.: University of Texas Press.

The most extensive discussion of the relationship of the atomistic social system to Latin American society.

Wagley, Charles, 1968, *The Latin American Tradition: Essays on the Unity and the Diversity of Latin American Culture.* New York: Columbia University Press.

This book contains articles on a variety of topics related to Latin America. "An Introduction to the Culture" is especially informative.

Wolf, Eric R., and Edward C. Hansen, 1972, *The Human Condition in Latin America.* New York: Oxford University Press.

Provides important background material, especially on politics.

CHAPTER 7

The rural sector

〰〰〰〰〰〰〰〰〰〰〰〰〰〰〰〰〰〰〰〰〰〰〰

Despite the recent massive growth of cities in Latin America, more than 60 percent of the population is classified as "rural" by the census criteria used by various countries. Many of those classified as "urban" live in small communities of three thousand persons or fewer. Within the rural sector are many varieties of life styles ranging from those of unacculturated Amerinds to those of university-trained operators of large farms or plantations.

In some marginal areas of Latin America, small Amerind groups have managed to survive. While they have been able to perpetuate many of their traditional ways, they are subcultures of larger complex societies whose institutions have affected their lives. As long as the ecological niche they inhabit remains marginal to the developing national economies, institutional change is minimal. For example, in southern Venezuela and northern Brazil —areas marginal to both national economies—live a widely scattered tribal people known as the Yąnomamö. They have had sustained, permanent contact with outsiders since 1950. Most of these contacts have been with missionaries. Yet the Yąnomamö have been able to maintain their traditional ways such as continued, fierce intervillage warfare and the daily use of hallucinogenic drugs (Chagnon 1968). In other areas the Amerinds have been less successful in maintaining their heritage. For example the Mundurucú who live in the state of Pará, Brazil, were once considered the most warlike tribe of their region. Unlike the territory inhabited by the Yąnomamö, the region settled by the Mundurucú became a boom area for rubber production during the last half of the nineteenth century. As the area was opened for rubber tapping, the Mundurucú grew dependent on Brazilians for manufactured goods that became necessities in their society. Today they have lost a considerable part of their traditional culture. Agents of the modern world, including the Brazilian Indian Protection Service, the police of the town of Itaituba, a Franciscan mission, and the patrón they sell rubber to, have begun impinging on Mundurucú society. Individual members of the Mundurucú are in the process of becoming incorporated into Brazilian society as *caboclos* (lower-class backwoodsmen and peasants) as the tribe becomes increasingly fragmented (Murphy 1960).

Indians on Jicaque Reservation, Honduras. (Courtesy of Pedro A. Pequeño-Rossié.)

Many rural inhabitants live a peasant style of life. In terms of economic organization, two of the Wagley and Harris types—modern Indian and peasant—would both be included as peasants. Unlike "primitive" societies, which are conceptualized as closed systems, peasant subcultures are tied to larger political, economic, and social units. According to Eric Wolf (1966:3–4), peasants ". . . are rural cultivators whose surpluses are transferred to a dominant group of rulers that uses the surpluses both to underwrite its own standard of living and to distribute the remainder to groups in society that do not farm but must be fed for their specific goods and services in turn." The peasant is thus a rural cultivator who is subject to the

Market day in San Juan Chamula, Chiapas, Mexico. (Courtesy of Dean R. Snow.)

demands and sanctions of powerholders who exist outside of the peasant's own social stratum. While the peasant is able to provide for his own subsistence, he obligates a portion of his surplus to someone who exercises an effective superior power over him. Wolf calls this obligation a "fund of rent."

The basic economic unit of the peasant village is the nuclear family. It is involved in both production and consumption. Almost all of the services required by an individual are performed at the family level. This family unit is highly adaptive because it controls most of the peasant's needs. He is able to plan on the basis of family requirements and the obligations of the fund of rent owed to his superiors, as well as any ceremonial obligations.

Every community is faced with certain subsistence risks. Communities adapt to their environments in different ways depending on the level of technology and the nature of the environment. Some means of coping with the problems of the environment (fluctuations, vagaries, and so on) have to be discovered by the members of each given society. On the band level and in highly industrialized, urbanized societies we find two extremes— and in both a considerable need for dependence and cooperation. These are culturally derived mechanisms for coping with environmental problems. On the band level, people cooperate by sharing food so that no one will die of hunger. The successful hunter shares his kill with other members of the band to insure reciprocation. In highly complex societies cooperation is necessary due to the extreme specialization and compartmentalization of individuals. In peasant societies the situation is different. The family is a self-sufficient unit that builds its own house, grows its own food, and manufacturers its own clothing and utensils. On the family level, subsistence risk can be reduced in several ways. One way is through increasing production, the other through the reduction of consumption.

The Peasant and the View of Limited Good   Not only is the family a self-sufficient unit, but the peasant village, in turn, is self-sufficient. According to Foster (1965), the peasants view their total environment as one in which all the desired things in life such as land, wealth, friendship, love, good health, manliness, respect, power, security, and so on, exist in finite quantity and are always in short supply. At the same time there is no way in which the peasant is able to increase the available quantities. Therefore, if they view the system as a closed one, any family can improve its position (its share of desired things) only at the expense of other families in the village. As an analogy, the peasant village might be represented as a pie. A pie can be sliced into wedges, each representing a family's share of any desired thing. The pie has a fixed size, just as the amount of any desired "good" is finite. Therefore any change in a family's fortune is taken to mean that someone else's share has been reduced. In other words, if a family is getting a larger wedge others in the village are getting smaller wedges. Within the village there is considerable uncertainty over who is actually losing part of his share. Therefore, any significant improvement by a family in the village is seen not as a threat to some particular family but rather as a threat to the stability of the entire community.

Actually there is much in the peasant world that is limited. The peasant economy is generally not a productive one. Only a finite amount of wealth is produced within the village and no amount of extra work will *significantly* alter the figure. For example, the peasant's small plot may yield 100 bushels of corn a year if he spends 120 days out of the year working his plot. By working fervently 365 days a year the peasant may increase his yield very slightly—perhaps by an additional two bushels—due to the limited technology. Therefore the peasant sees little relationship between hard work and getting ahead. One works merely to eat, not to create wealth.

Each peasant family sees itself in a continual struggle with the rest of the villagers for what it considers to be its share of the limited good. The families of the village are in a position calling for extreme caution and reserve and are reluctant to reveal their true positions. A situation of suspicion and mutual distrust is thus created within the village; things are not always what they appear to be. If, for example, an individual acquired enough money to purchase an expensive item, he would bring it home under cover of darkness to keep his neighbors from learning of his new possession. From the outside, a man's family and his home retain the same shabby appearance. To the rest of the village the family seems as poor as it always had been. Yet one day the front door may accidentally be left open. If neighbors were to see the new item, they would wonder about other purchases the family might have made. They would question the family's sudden wealth—and wonder who, in the village, was deprived of his share because of this family.

An individual rising above the level of security for the village subjects himself to negative sanctions. The villagers attempt to bring the person back into line through gossip, slander, character assassination, witchcraft, and even physical assault. Public opinion is important to the peasant and a powerful social control. Occasionally an individual improves his position in the face of these negative sanctions. If this happens, an attempt is made to restore a balance by neutralizing the action. The person is encouraged to use up his gains through conspicuous giving. He is pressured into sponsoring costly fiestas that use up his money and may even put him in debt. His reward is prestige, which the village views as harmless. The fiesta is seen as a redistributive mechanism that permits a family to restore the status quo of the village.

The peasant village is not a completely closed system. However, the only chance the peasant generally sees of improving his lot is with luck and fate. In some villages stories are told and retold to explain how certain people have become wealthy in a system where acquired wealth is deemed an impossibility. Past tales dealt mostly with people who discovered buried treasure or sold their souls to the devil. Today these stories also include tales of winning lotteries and thievery. Whether past or present, the "luck or fate" facet is an integral part of the peasant storytelling.

In the Mexican village of Tzintzuntzan, there was a potter named Silverio Caro. With money he inherited from his father he built a pottery stand and sold his craftwork to tourists. As he prospered he became a middleman buying and selling pottery. In early 1961 he suddenly bought a large house, remodeled it and added a number of new rooms. The estimated expense was about $30,000. To the people of the village he was still a poor potter and they knew potters were not wealthy. A story began to circulate to explain his "sudden" wealth.

One night, while returning from Mexico City, Silverio was fortunate enough to sit next to a sleeping American woman tourist who just happened to be riding the second-class bus to Tzintzuntzan. As she slept Silverio reached into her purse and removed $40,000. Then he supposedly left the bus at the next stop and came home on another bus. The story is widely believed. While it is difficult for the Tzintzuntzeños to explain many of the details, it is even more difficult for the villagers to explain how else Silverio could be spending so much money.

Silverio continued to prosper, adding a second story to his house and purchasing a house for his daughter and son-in-law. The total cost of his expenses now were approximately $70,000. The original story obviously was not sufficient to explain his expenditures. In 1965 another story began to circulate with two versions. Silverio's niece, it was said, worked in a restaurant and acquired a substantial sum of money illegally. In one version she stole a wallet from a customer. In the second version, she found the owner's concealed profits when he died. In any case she gave the money (again a sizable sum) to Silverio for safekeeping and he spent part of it. Now with the two stories the villagers can explain how Silverio is able to live so much better than anyone else (Foster 1967:148–150).

The Rural Proletariat   Not all of rural Latin America is classified as peasantry. There are many who live by selling their labor on the market for wages. Often such people are found on plantations and have been termed "rural proletariat" by Sidney Mintz. The life of the rural wage laborer is more affected by outside forces than that of the peasant. The peasant is only partially controlled by others to whom he sells his crops or pays his rent. He has his family and land to fall back on. The plantation worker has only his ability to work. In areas with large-scale plantations, the plantation may be the only employer. If the laborer is to work at all—and to eat, since his food is purchased, not grown—he must work for the plantation, on their terms, or migrate. The large plantation is organized for the production of a single crop. Men are hired and fired according to the dictates of the growing season of the particular crop. In Cuba before the revolution, the large plantations were organized to produce sugar cane. A large number of workers were needed only during the peak season. During the off-season (the *tiempo muerto*), 20 percent of Cuba's entire labor force was unemployed. The off-season lasted from seven to nine months each year (Mintz 1964:xxxiv).

During the Colonial period the planters had been faced with labor shortages and competed for African slaves and indentured Europeans. The same situation existed following the emancipation of slavery wherever the Negroes refused to continue working on plantations. By the twentieth century a relatively small number of large corporation-type plantations controlled production of the major export crops. In many areas peasants lost their land and became a part of the plantation work force at the same time that the birth rate was increasing. Thus the situation became one in which a great number of individuals were competing for a limited number of jobs.

The highland hacienda retarded the growth of nationalism by promoting regionalism and the interests of the hacienda. Yet nationalism was possible because both the patrón and the peons were lifetime inhabitants of the state. In a few cases those of Amerind origin were considered foreigners in their own native land, but generally the hacienda-dominated countries have considered the creoles, mestizos, and Amerinds a part of the nation.

The areas of large plantations present a different picture. In the underdeveloped countries of Latin America, there is generally not enough capital available on the local level to establish and maintain the plantation. The demands of the plantation for capital are much greater than those of the hacienda as it is usually geared to production for large-scale markets. The capital, therefore, is supplied from outside the country by foreign sources. The labor force may be drawn from inhabitants of the country but frequently it is imported from other countries.

The plantations have their own effects on nationalism. First, the foreign investors have little concern with nationalism. However, they are concerned with influencing the political machinery of the country because of the investment they have at stake (Wolf and Mintz 1957:397). They are often able to dominate the areas of their holdings through the influence they exert; consequently, the state gives up effective control over a section of the country to the plantation corporations. If the workers are imported, they may not share the values of the country. If they consider their employment temporary, they may retard the growth of nationalism through apathy toward the host state. If the employment is seen as permanent and if the foreign workers form a sizable force, they may become a political force which agitates for change.

The plantation laborer is not the only type of rural worker who sells his skills on a labor market. Yet anthropological investigation has lagged behind in the study of the other types such as the mining communities, the worker in the oil field, the commercial fisherman, and cattle ranchers.[1] Nor are all workers easily lumped into the category of peasant or proletariat. On some of the smaller islands of the Caribbean, Richard Frucht (1967) has observed rural sharecroppers whose means of production are "peasant-like" but whose relations of production are "proletarian-like."

Nor should it be assumed that the means of livelihood of the rural sector is static. Instead there are many who change from peasant to proletarian and vice versa. Sometimes the change is a temporary one; however, it may be a seasonal or even a permanent change. Also there are other rural workers who fluctuate between rural and urban work.

Finally, there is a growing number within the rural sector who are

[1] An important exception is the recent study of ranchers in northern Brazil (Rivière 1972), as well as Strickon's (1965) article on the Euro-American ranching complex.

settling other people's land. These are the squatters. The squatter phenomenon has increased in recent years especially in areas with uncultivated land and absentee ownership. In some cases the squatter movement receives support from the government as an expedient type of land reform.

Squatter farm near Ciudad Quesada, Costa Rica.

In this chapter several different types of rural communities are described. Several of these communities retain a strong Amerind influence—in Chiapas, Mexico, and in the Andean highlands. Tepoztlán is a peasant community. The proletariats of the United Fruit Company banana plantations of lowland Costa Rica provide an example of the rural wage laborer. Finally, a less "typical" rural community, Minas Velhas, Brazil, is presented as a rural community with an urban orientation.

ZINACANTAN

The Setting The *municipio* (township) of Zinacantan is one of twenty-one Tzotzil Mayan-speaking Indian municipios of highland Chiapas, Mexico.[2] Zinacantan has a population of about eight thousand Indians living

[2] This section is based on Vogt (1969, 1970).

MAP 7.1 Communities of the rural sector.

in a settlement pattern of ceremonial center surrounded by fifteen outlying hamlets dispersed throughout the municipio. The municipio is bisected by the Pan American Highway. It is connected by road with the larger ladino town of San Cristobal Las Casas.

Zinacantan men on highway. Chiapas, Mexico. (Courtesy of Jaroslaw T. Petryshyn.)

Like other rural peoples of Mexico, the Zinacantecos are maize (native corn) cultivators. Maize is consumed at every meal. In fact, the overwhelming bulk of the native's daily calories comes from maize. The Zinacantecos grow their maize on three types of land: (1) small plots that are owned individually and are generally located near the person's home, (2) plots of *ejido* (government) land generally located in the lower elevations, and (3) larger plots of land rented from ladino landowners in the lowlands. Besides maize, other important food crops include squash and varieties of beans. The beans are planted in the same hole as the maize.

Squash, which is sometimes sown with the maize, is more frequently planted on the edge of the maize fields.

Few wild animals remain in the regions exploited by the Zinacantecos, although occasionally a rabbit or deer is killed. However, many other forms of wild life are important. Wild greens are collected and cooked. At least sixteen different varieties of mushroom are used for food. Snails and iguanas are also important food supplements. Honey is collected from wild beehives in the woods.

Most of the important types of domesticated animals in Zinacantan were introduced by the Spanish following Contact. Chickens are raised but seldom eaten, except during ritual meals. Eggs are not eaten but are sold to supplement the family's income. Horses and mules are used as pack animals. Sheep are raised for their wool.

Fictive Kinship In Zinacantan the compadrazgo system has been extended to include a large number of individuals in ritual ties. Godparents who have been named for baptism accompany the parents and the child to the church for the ceremony within a month after the baby's birth. Following the Catholic ceremony the godparents return home with the parents and are served a Mayan ritual meal which is also attended by the child's grandparents and other close relatives and sometimes even close neighbors. In Zinacantan, unlike most of Latin America, *all* of the individuals who participate in the ritual meal are considered ritual kinsmen of the godparents from that time on—thus creating a network of individuals to whom a person can turn for money, labor, credit, political support, and hospitality. Other compadres are added to this network through another ritual meal at confirmation.

Other occasions on which a number of Zinacantan compadres are added to the network of ritual kinsmen occur during courtship and marriage. Zinacantan courtship is both long and expensive, yet an individual is not considered an adult until he is married. The first courtship ceremony begins when a boy's relatives, represented by two "petitioners," visit a girl's relatives to make known the boy's interests and to ask for the approval of the girl's father. The boy's family brings chocolate, brown sugar, rolls, and a twenty-liter jug of rum. If the girl's parents approve of the match and accept the food and drink, a trial courtship period begins during which time the boy begins to pay a bride price. The payments are made in three forms: (1) by large nets of fruit and rum liquor that are presented to the girl's parents at major fiestas, (2) by smaller gifts of maize, beans, tortillas, and liquor presented every few weeks, and (3) by the boy's labor at the house and fields of his prospective father-in-law. Within two years (after the boy has made a sufficient investment in the girl), the "house entering" ceremony takes place. The girl's father is asked to name an "embracer" of the wedding. The petitioners ask the embracer to serve. If he accepts, the embracer and all the relatives living in his house at the time, become compadres to the petitioners and their wives.

The Cargo System   Adult life centers around the cargo system. This system is one of a religious hierarchy organized around the Catholic Church and saints. When a Zinacanteco speaks of *'abtel ta Hteklum*, he is referring to important "work" or "service" that is provided by men who hold positions in this hierarchy. *'Abtel* is conceived of as the bearing of a burden, much as a Zinacanteco carries a heavy load of maize on his back. In the context of carrying burdens in the cargo system, the concept is related to an ancient Mayan idea, the "Year Bearer," as the positions are held for only one year. Just as the ancient Maya gods carried the "year" with a tumpline and passed it along to their successors, a contemporary Zinacanteco carries the burden of office for a year and then passes it along to his successor. In Spanish these positions came to be called *cargos*. While the positions are conceived of as burdens, they also provide enormous prestige for the cargo-holders and hence are much sought after by Zinacanteco men. The Zinacanteco religious hierarchy consists of sixty-one positions grouped into four levels in a ceremonial ladder. Unlike similar systems found in Mesoamerica, the Zinacantan system is divorced from civil activities.

To pass through the positions of this ceremonial ladder the men must serve a year at each level. During the time they hold cargos, the Zinacantecos are expected to move from their hamlets into the ceremonial center and engage in a complex annual round of very expensive ceremonies. Some cargos cost the incumbents as much as $1,120 for food, liquor, and ritual paraphernalia such as candles, incense, and fireworks. This expense is roughly equivalent to ten years' income for a relatively prosperous Zinacanteco.

While filling their roles in the religious hierarchy, cargoholders wear special costumes and enjoy special prestige accorded no others in the community. When their service is completed they turn the post over to the next year's incumbents and move back to their hamlets to become full-time maize farmers once again. Many years elapse before they are able to pay off their debts from these cargos and accumulate enough wealth to ask for cargo positions on the next higher level. When they complete four levels of cargos, they become honored *pasados*.

The first level of the hierarchy contains several offices—*Mayores* and *Mayordomos*. The twelve Mayores are ranked from one to twelve and serve as policemen and errand boys for the civil officials. They also have important ceremonial functions. The twenty-eight Mayordomos care for specific saints in the Catholic churches of the ceremonial center or in one of the chapels of the outlying hamlets. Their cargos are named after the saints they serve.

The second level of this religious hierarchy is composed of fourteen offices known as *Alfereces,* also named for saints, that are organized into two ranked orders. Although the Alfereces may once have had caretaking duties for the saints, they now spend most of their year in office, feasting one another at ritual meals, and dancing for the saints.

The third level contains four offices of *Regidor* ranked from one to four. At the top of the hierarchy are the two *Alcaldes Viejos,* "Big" and "Little" Alcalde. The Alcaldes and the Regidores form a group at the top of the hierarchy known collectively as the *Moletik,* the "Elders." It is the duty of the Elders to manage the cargo system. In addition the Regidores have the duty of collecting money to pay the Catholic priests for performing masses.

Elderly men who have not managed to serve at each level are sometimes appointed to the position of *Alcalde Shuves* when it is evident that they are not going to be able to serve in a top *Acalde Viejo* post.

A man's first years of marriage are spent paying back the debts incurred by his marriage. He then begins planning for a house of his own. Between the ages of twenty-five and thirty he begins to consider serving in the cargo system.

When a Zinacanteco calculates that he will be ready for his first cargo some years in the future, he takes a bottle of liquor and presents it to the Moletik on the eighth of August. On this date each year the Moletik sit outside the church of San Lorenzo and receive requests for cargos. The "waiting lists" are kept by Scribes in hardcover notebooks that have a page or two devoted to each year in the future for which there is a cargo requested. The first man to appear with his bottle and request a particular cargo for a given year has his name recorded for that date. For example, in 1966 a man might request the cargo of Senior Mayordomo Rey for 1980, only to be told that 1980 is already spoken for but that he may have the position in 1986. Alternatively if he wishes to accept a less prestigious cargo such as the Junior Mayordomo of San Sebastian, he may be able to have the year 1970.

Once his name is recorded in the sacred book, the applicant must reappear each eighth of August, present another bottle of liquor and reaffirm his intention to serve. If he does not appear his name will be crossed out and the post will open to others.

As soon as a Zinacanteco has his name on the waiting lists, he acquires new prestige in the eyes of the community. He may not serve for fifteen or twenty years, but it is widely known that he has made the crucial move of requesting the cargo. This defines him as a man of respect who is helping to carry on an important Zinacanteco tradition.

The costs of sponsoring cargos vary from approximately $4 for the lowly Mayor who serves as errand boy and policeman to more than $1,120 for the Senior Mayordomo Rey. These costs and the traditional rank determine the prestige a man derives from serving in a cargo. Since both the cost and the traditional rank of a cargo are public knowledge, the cargo becomes a means of communicating the abilities and image of a man to his fellow Zinacantecos.

To pass through the cargo system at the highest level of prestige depends not upon inherited land or money per se, but upon the successful manipulation and management of one's economic and social life. The resources to pay for the expenses of the cargo require that a man must be able to obtain help from his kinsmen and that he serve as godparent for a number of baptisms and as a ritual official of many weddings so that he will have many ritual kinsmen to help support him. The process tends to be circular: a respected man who has served in one or two cargos is likely to be asked to serve as a godparent or as a ritual specialist in a wedding and thereby acquire more compadres. With the aid of these compadres he is able to call upon the support of more people to help him with his next cargo. In turn he then becomes more sought after to serve in more baptisms and weddings and acquires still more compadres.

A career in the cargo system also requires that a Zinacanteco be expert not only in maize-farming by his own efforts but that he become an entrepreneur acquiring and managing other land. He will need to call upon his kinsmen, including his compadres, not only for assistance in his maize-farming but also as helpers when he serves in cargo positions. Even if he finds success as an entrepreneur in farming, he will still have to borrow large sums of money in order to meet the expenses of cargos. Again his kinsmen are the primary persons to whom he will turn for cash loans.

Souls The Zinacantecos believe that two types of "souls"[3] are possessed by each human being: a *ch'ulel* and a *chanul*. The ch'ulel is an inner, personal "soul" located in the heart of each person; it is also found in the blood which is connected with the heart. The ch'ulel is believed to be placed in the body of an unborn embryo by the ancestral deities.

The Zinacanteco "inner soul" is thought to possess special attributes. It is composed of thirteen parts, and a person who loses one or more parts must undergo a special curing ceremony in order to recover them. The "inner soul," while temporarily divisible into parts if "soul-loss" occurs, is believed to be eternal and indestructible. At the point of death the "inner soul" leaves the body. It is associated with the individual's grave for the period of time that the deceased person lived on earth and then it joins the "pool" of "inner souls" that are kept by the ancestors to be utilized later

---

[3] The term "soul" is used in quotes to indicate that the European concepts of "souls" and "spirits" are inadequate for a precise definition of these ideas.

by another person. While the person is alive the "inner soul" is able to leave the body during sleep and visit with "inner souls" of other Zinacantecos or the deities. It can also "drop out" of the body temporarily in periods of intense excitement such as sexual intercourse. The "inner soul" tends especially to leave the body of a small child because it is not yet accustomed to its new receptacle. As a mother with a small child in unfamiliar settings leaves, she sweeps the ground on which the child has been sitting (with her shawl) thereby making certain to gather up all the parts of the "inner soul" of her infant. Parents are expected to treat a small child with utmost care and affection lest its "inner soul" become frightened and leave. One of the major purposes of the baptismal ceremony is to "fix" the "inner soul" more firmly in the child's body.

Baptism cannot prevent "soul-loss" from occurring through fright later in life. There are many immediate causes of "soul-loss"—falling down suddenly, seeing a "demon" on a dark night, and so on. The Zinacantecos still relate vividly how a large number of people experienced "soul-loss" when the first airplane swept low over Zinacantan twenty years ago; the curers were busy for weeks afterwards performing ceremonies to gather up the pieces of "inner souls."

At a more profound level of causation, "soul-loss" is believed to be caused by the ancestral gods who punish bad behavior by causing a person to fall down, by sending a lightning bolt to knock out one or more parts of the "inner soul," or by an evil person who performs witchcraft ritual in a cave to "sell" one or more parts of his victim's "inner soul" to the Earth Owner.[4] The Earth Owner then proceeds to use the victim as a servant.

Without all thirteen parts of the "inner soul" a person cannot remain healthy, instead he feels or possesses *chamel* ("sickness"). A shaman (curer) must be summoned to diagnose the sickness and to perform a ceremony to recover the missing parts and to place them back into the body of the patient.

The phenomenon of the "inner soul" is by no means restricted to the domain of human beings. Virtually everything that is important and valuable to Zinacantecos also possesses an "inner soul": domesticated animals and plants; salt, which possesses a very strong "inner soul"; houses and the household fires; the wooden crosses erected on sacred mountains, inside caves, and beside waterholes; the saints whose "homes" are inside the Catholic churches; musical instruments used in ceremonies; and all the various deities in the Zinacanteco pantheon. In Zinacantan the most impor-

---

[4] The Earth Owner is the most important deity, next to the ancestral gods. He is pictured as a large, fat ladino living under the ground with piles of money and many animals. He is thought to own or control everything of importance to the Zinacantecos—waterholes, rain, land, and so on. Offerings must be made when the land or any of its products are used.

tant interaction is not between persons, nor between persons and objects, but rather between "inner souls" and material objects.

The second type of "soul" is the chanul which is an "animal spirit companion" or "spiritual alter ego." A volcano, located east of Zinacantan, named "Senior Large Mountain," rises to a height of over nine thousand feet and contains a series of supernatural corrals with eight thousand "animal spirit companions," one for each person in Zinacantan. One of these corrals contains jaguars, a second one coyotes, a third one ocelots, and a fourth one smaller animals like opossums. These "animal spirit companions" are watered, fed, and cared for by the ancestral gods under the direction of the supernatural "Big Acalde" who is the celestial counterpart of the highest ranking member of the religious hierarchy in Zinacantan and whose house is located inside the mountain and whose household cross is the shrine that Zinacantecos visit for ceremonies on top of the volcano.

The Zinacantecos believe that they and their "animal spirit companions" share the same "inner soul." This means that when the ancestors install an "inner soul" in the embryo of a Zinacanteco they simultaneously install the same "inner soul" in the embryo of some animal. The moment that a Zinacanteco baby is born, a jaguar, coyote, ocelot, or other animal is born. Throughout life whatever happens to the Zinacanteco happens to his "animal spirit companion" and vice versa. If, for example, an "animal spirit companion" is released from the corral and left to wander alone in the forest he may be injured or shot and then his Zinacanteco counterpart feels the same injury. It follows that if the "animal spirit companion" is released from the corral, and is thereby not being cared for properly by the ancestors, a Zinacanteco is in mortal danger. A shaman must be summoned to perform the proper ceremony, asking the pardon of the ancestral deities and persuading them to round up the lost "animal spirit companion" of the patient and place it safely back in its supernatural corral.

There is a clear relationship between the beliefs in these two "soul" concepts and social control in the Zinacanteco code of life. Anything that invokes the wrath of the ancestors against a particular Zinacanteco can lead quickly and directly to punishment by causing the person to suffer "soul-loss" or in more serious cases, by having his "animal spirit companion" turned outside its corral to wander alone and uncared for in the woods. The types of deviant behavior that can lead to these "soul" troubles include the breaking of the important moral rules or the flouting of the central values of Zinacantan—an individual who fights with his kinsmen, a man who does not accept community service in the cargo system, a man who fails to care for his maize fields properly or a woman who mishandles the maize after it is brought to her house, a person who fails to wash regularly and change into clean clothes, or a man who fails to make contributions when the officials arrive to collect "taxes" for fiestas—are prime candidates.

HIGHLAND PERU

The highlands of Peru are dominated by small mestizo towns, large haciendas, and Indian villages (*comunidades indígenas*). A rigid hierarchy exists ostensibly based on biological differences but in reality based primarily on cultural differences. A person who wears sandals, lives in a mud-walled, thatch-roofed house, maintains "pagan" beliefs, and speaks Quechua or Aymara is classed as "Indian." One who wears shoes, has a tile-roofed house, practices "orthodox" Catholicism, and speaks Spanish is generally classified as "mestizo," or, if he has light skin or is a near-white descendant of well-to-do criollos, he is classified as "white." Even those classified as "Indian" have changed considerably from aboriginal times. As Steward and Faron observed (1959:161–162), "None of the highland people, however, are truly Indian in the aboriginal sense. They not only acquired many sixteenth-century Spanish features, such as oxen, plows, religious brotherhoods, a long series of church festivals, and new crops and animals, but, more importantly, their whole pattern of life has been modified by their relationship to the larger world of commerce." Some of the Indians have been assimilated as skilled or unskilled workers in the mestizo towns; more are hacienda workers and peasant farmers.

While some of the highland Indians have been able to subsist on the crops from the village lands, many have become dependent on the haciendas for extra work and extra land and are tied to the hacienda through indebtedness, which compels the Indian to renew his contract with the hacendado annually. Employment on the coast (in the city and on the plantations) is beginning to provide an alternative to work on the hacienda and also is affecting the relationship of the village to the outside world. There are still many Amerind villages that can be classed as corporate, or closed, communities in Wolf's classification (see Chapter 5). In this section three highland communities (Vicos, Hualcán, and Recuayhuanca) will be described, each with a different response or adaptation to the problems of limited land and overpopulation.

Vicos Possibly the poorest and lowest ranked Indians of the highland social hierarchy are the hacienda Indians. They generally have had the least contact with the outside world. Vicos is a hacienda in the Callejón de Huaylas Valley, approximately two hundred fifty miles northeast of Lima. This hacienda was established some four hundred years ago during the Colonial period and changed little until 1952.[5]

[5] Beginning in 1952 the hacienda was rented by social scientists as a part of the Cornell-Peru Project that attempted a program of directed culture change. This account describes pre-Project life.

Vicos belongs to the state and is leased out to the highest bidder every ten years as are some two or three hundred other properties. Attached to the land but owning none of it are some eighteen hundred fifty Quechua-speaking Indians, most of whom live on small scattered subsistence farmsteads on the lower slopes of the hacienda. Approximately 90 percent of the arable land is farmed by these Indians; 10 percent is farmed for commercial purposes. One adult member of each household pays a labor tax of three days' work on the commercial land each week in return for a small plot of land which is furnished by the landlord and upon which the family subsists. The family is obligated to perform other tasks for the hacienda. Various members of the family serve as cooks, grooms, watchmen, shepherds, and servants. If the Indian fails to fulfill his obligation to the hacienda, the hacendado can dispose of the worker's tools, his animals, or his plot of land, thus creating a situation in which most, if not all, families are in a constant struggle to maintain their security and integrity (Holmberg 1960:79–80).

Fiestas remain an important aspect of Vicos life. They include national religious holiday celebrations, patriotic celebrations, local saint-cult festivals, life crises ceremonies (such as baptism, first haircuttings, birthdays, weddings, and so on), rituals centering on political office, cooperative work group celebrations, plant curing and harvest ceremonies. In terms of the time spent in an activity, fiestas rank with agriculture and the making of clothes as one of the most time consuming of all activities. Moreover a great deal of the time involved in agriculture and clothesmaking is directly related to the fiestas. The fiestas are usually accompanied by ceremonial eating and ceremonial drinking of alcoholic beverages, music, dancing, processions and pageants, and some prescribed sexual and social license (Mangin 1961: 84–85).

The fiestas are sponsored by the officeholders of the civil-religious hierarchy. These fiesta offices and the political offices are the positions most highly desired by Vicosino adult males and the positions that Vicosino women want their husbands and male consanguineal relatives to fill. The offices are subordinate to two other local centers of authority: the mestizo government located at Marcara and the patrón of the hacienda. The fiesta has remained stable during the past ten years in spite of marked changes in the hacienda system.

Hualcán   Hualcán is another Quechua-speaking Indian village in the Callejón de Huaylas.[6] Both the Vicosinos and the people of Hualcán are thought of as conservative Indians by the mestizos. The village has a population of about eight hundred persons. The life of the village is based upon subsistence agriculture, but agricultural capital is insufficient to support the

[6] This section is based on Stein's (1957, 1961) studies of Hualcán.

entire population. Some have attempted to solve this problem in much the same way as the Indians of Vicos. The Indians bind themselves in a peón-patrón relationship to a hacienda which obligates them to work three or four days a week on the hacienda in return for fields to plant, pasture for livestock, and free firewood.

For those who wish to participate in fiesta sponsoring, the work on the hacienda does not provide sufficient capital accumulation to purchase the necessary supplies. Those oriented toward the fiesta system have found two means of accumulating capital—work in the mestizo town of Carhauz and migration to the coast.

When their time permits, some Hualcainos will work in town for a day or two. Such work not only provides the extra money to purchase necessities and luxuries but also allows a person to build up a reserve of cash for the sponsorship of fiestas. Assuming the responsibility for a fiesta remains an important channel for achieving prestige in the community.

Another important supplement to the income of the native results from working on the cane fields of the large agricultural-industrial plantation enterprises on the coast. Workers receive wages that are more than double those paid in and around Hualcán.

In general, many Hualcainos feel uncomfortable working on the coast with its warm climate and Spanish culture and often stay only a week or two before returning to the highlands. However, some of the young men remain as long as a year or two.

On the coast, the Indian is exposed to a larger and more sophisticated world than that of the village from which he migrates. At the same time, he is often moving from the social isolation of the highland community to the social isolation of the plantation. While on the coast the Indians tend to insulate themselves from Spanish culture. Laborers' residential areas are laid out in blocks of apartments. In these blocks Indians who are related or who are friends tend to locate near each other—in other words, Hualcainos live near other Hualcainos. In this way a type of voluntary segregation based on kinship and place of origin in the highlands is established. The Quechua language is heard on the streets more frequently than Spanish, and the Indian costume prevails over coastal clothing.

In Hualcán, innovations from the outside world are not readily accepted—the exception being coastal food products, which are considered treats. An Indian who returns from coastal work wearing coastal-style clothes soon removes them and returns to Indian costume because coastal clothing is considered inappropriate in Hualcán. The innovator is ridiculed and sometimes accused of witchcraft.

Coastal labor, then, is not a means of social mobility in Hualcán. Like the Vicosino the Hualcaino accepts his position at the bottom of a rigid highland hierarchy. The money from the coast is used to perpetuate the already existing values, especially those associated with the fiesta and the civil-religious hierarchy.

Recuayhuanca   Recuayhuanca is another Indian community of the Callejón de Hualyas.[7] Unlike Vicos and Hualcán, Recuayhuanca is rapidly changing. The village is smaller, with a population of about four hundred persons. In outward appearance it resembles the other Indian communities of the area, a scattered settlement based on subsistence agriculture and herding. Politically it is organized as a comunidad indígena, a legal status that places it under the jurisdiction of the Ministry of Labor and Indian Affairs in Lima. Land tenure follows a pattern of small plots owned by individuals.

In a number of important characteristics Recuayhuanca resembles a mestizo village rather than an Indian one. In Vicos and Hualcán only a few men, and no women, speak Spanish. In Recuayhuanca, while few women speak Spanish, 78 percent of the males over twenty are able to converse in Spanish. (The figure is actually 90 percent in the twenty to twenty-nine age group.) The Recuayhuanquinos also differ sharply from the other communities in their level of formal education. In Vicos and Hualcán a child may spend one or at most two years attending school irregularly when not herding animals for the family. Among Recuayhuanquinos more than a third of all men as well as a smaller number of the women have spent at least three years in school with fairly regular attendance. Some have attended school for as long as twelve years. In addition to the usual Indian celebrations, some Recuayhuanquinos give birthday parties, a mestizo custom. Music and drink also follow the mestizo style: the guitar is used rather than the flute and drum, and cognac is served instead of *huashco* (raw native alcohol).

To the mestizos of Marcara, the Recuayhuanquinos are "Indians" and are conveniently lumped with all other Indians of the highlands as a separate race. To maintain his supremacy, the mestizo looks down on the Indian, who must show him respect. He is kept in his place and is spoken to in Quechua (the Indian native language) whether or not the Indian knows any Spanish. In religious activities the mestizos maintain segregation.

In comparison to Vicos and Hualcán, the resources of Recuayhuanca are poorer even though the land is privately owned. At the same time, the men of Recuayhuanca are freer to leave the area because they have no labor obligations to haciendas keeping them in the village. The end result is that the people of Recuayhuanca cannot support themselves with an agricultural economy. Instead they have become specialists, traders, and, more recently, coastal laborers. Eighty percent of the men and 25 percent of the women have been to the coast—the majority in search of work. Whereas the Hualcainos use coastal money for fiesta participation, the Recuayhuanquinos use the money for basic necessities—food and clothing.

[7] This section is based on Snyder (1957).

While the Hualcainos who return from the coast remain fairly insulated from the outside world, the Recuayhuanquinos encounter a wider range of experiences. Many come back from the coast with a fairly accurate picture of other nations and definite knowledge of the customs of other people. More importantly, they are beginning to identify themselves as "Peruvians" rather than "Recuayhuanquinos" or "Quechua." They have gained considerable sophistication with respect to national institutions. They have learned the functions of organizations such as labor unions and political parties.

Those who go only to the coastal plantations are sheltered from the coastal style of life for the same reason as the Hualcainos. Half of the Recuayhuanquino men and 25 percent of the women who have been to the coast have also been to Lima. In the city they have come as individuals and are not insulated by friends and neighbors. Those who have lived in the cities are the most acculturated.

The Recuayhuanquinos are considered only a little more civilized than the Vicosinos by the mestizos of Marcara. To the mestizos, the Recuayhuanquinos were born Indian and will remain Indian. To the Vicosinos, the Recuayhuanquinos represent a group somewhat more advanced than themselves. They tend to look for wives from Recuayhuanca. But the Recuayhuanquainos do not classify themselves by the traditional highland caste hierarchy. Instead they use a national referent. They are *paisanos* (fellow countrymen) or *obreros* (workers). They cannot move upward in the traditional caste system which does not allow mobility and so they leave the system. Of those who have left Recuayhuanca, 90 percent have moved to the coast, yet they have not migrated in groups. It is not the community of Recuayhuanca that is changing. Rather, social change occurs as the rejection of a society labeled "Indian" by individuals leaving to join "Peruvian" society. The shift from "Indian" to "Peruvian" occurs in two ways: (1) the more acculturated the individual the less likely he is to participate in community activities, either sponsoring fiestas or holding civil office, and (2) the Recuayhuanquino has little interest in the movements that promise to raise the position of his group as a whole within the caste society. Movements such as the Peasant League of Ancash, which attracted members in Vicos, found no support in Recuayhuanca.

Instead Recuayhuanquinos are leaving their community, physically or psychologically, to become Protestants, participants in national labor unions, and members of national political parties. They are beginning to live in a national rather than a local society.

TEPOZTLÁN

The Mexican village of Tepoztlán is located about sixty miles south of Mexico City.[8] It is a peasant village whose history begins prior to the

[8] This section is based on Lewis (1951, 1960).

Spanish Conquest. Under the Aztec, Tepoztlán was a center of paper production. Paper was supplied to the Aztec lords as part of the village's tribute payments. Thus the village's participation in a complex society extends back over five hundred years. The village has been of special anthropological importance because it was the setting for the methodological and conceptual debates between Robert Redfield and Oscar Lewis concerning the nature of peasant communities.

Tepoztlán was first studied in 1926–1927 by Robert Redfield. He attempted to apply the concepts of social anthropology and ethnography to a peasant community. Oscar Lewis began a restudy of the village in 1943 and later returned in 1956–1957 to observe the changes which had taken place since his earlier study. Working with a larger staff and a broader theoretical framework, Lewis has produced a more complete picture of the village, including a life history of one of its inhabitants, "Pedro Martinez" (Lewis 1964).

The Setting   The present-day population of Tepoztlán numbers approximately forty-eight hundred. Although there has been a general trend toward learning Spanish, many of the inhabitants are bilingual and speak Spanish but retain Nahuatl, the ancient language of the Aztecs. Like many Latin American communities, the town of Tepoztlán is built around a plaza with park, bandstand, shade trees, and benches. Surrounding the plaza are the various government buildings. Yet the plaza area is not a hub of activity as one might find in other communities. Instead the official buildings are in disrepair and the few shops in the center of town are seldom frequented. The streets leading from the center of town are rustic and quiet and mark the community as a rural village. At night there are no street lights and few people venture out after dark.

The houses of Tepoztlán can be classified as one of three basic styles: the *jacal,* the adobe house, and the larger dwellings that are found in the center of the community. Only 5 percent of the families of Tepoztlán live in the jacal, which is constructed of cornstalks or bamboo with a thatched roof and dirt floor. This type of house is found in the outlying areas. Almost 90 percent live in adobe houses with tile roofs, most with dirt floors. The jacal generally consists of only one room. The adobe may have more than one room and many of the families living in adobe houses have separate bamboo lean-tos with tile roofs that serve as kitchens and are located at the rear of the houses. The third type of house is owned by wealthier families and is built of brick or stone, covered with plaster and whitewashed. These houses are generally much larger than the first two types and are surrounded by high outer walls that are built flush to the street. Set into the walls are windows and small balconies of iron grillwork.

Few houses in Tepoztlán have running water or toilets and none have any means of heating other than the kitchen fire. Only one house has electricity; the rest use candles or kerosene lamps. More marked than the differences in house types is the variety of house furnishings. Often a house will contain a combination of modern and primitive household items. While many women continue to cook on a pre-Contact style hearth, they may listen to soap operas over a Japanese transistor radio. For sleeping, the family uses *petates* (straw mats) that are laid on the floor; *tepexcos* (raised beds made of bamboo sticks tied together and placed on a wooden frame or on two sawhorses); or metal bedsteads with metal springs over which a petate is placed. Most of the families use either the petates on the ground or a tepexco.

Diet   The basic diet of the Tepoztecans is based upon corn, beans, and chile as is the case with other rural Mexicans. The diet is supplemented by other foods that are grown locally, collected from wild plants or purchased in the village. These diet supplements include such foods as banana, orange, lemon, lime, grapefruit, hog plum, papaya, mango, prickly pear, avocado, squash, tomato, sapodilla, acacia seeds, sugar cane, cherimoya, peanuts, coffee, honey, spices, herbs, beef, pork, chicken, turkey, milk, eggs, cheese and clotted cream, wild greens, bread, salt, sugar, rice, noodles, chocolate, powdered milk, and several varieties of fish such as codfish, canned sardines, tomato herring, and so on. The amount of the supplements increases as the family's income increases. The poorest families restrict their food consumption almost exclusively to corn, which is in some cases as much as 70 percent of the diet. Food is especially scarce in the months immediately preceding harvest. For many families even the basic diet is reduced to an absolute minimum. When families need cash for fiesta expenses they will also minimize food consumption in order to be able to sell some of their corn, beans, eggs, and chickens. Meat is scarce in Tepoztlán. In winter some cattle are slaughtered when pasture is scarce. Eggs are saved for the men of the family. Chickens and turkeys are saved for special occasions such as fiestas, weddings, baptisms, and birthdays. Normally the members of the family eat three meals a day but they seldom eat together. The father and older sons eat an early breakfast before leaving for their fields. They eat their lunch in the field at noon and dinner anywhere from 5:00 to 8:00 P.M., once they return home. The women and children eat a later breakfast after the men have been fed, usually at 7:00 or 8:00 A.M. Dinner is eaten about 1:00 P.M. and supper at dusk. If the family were to eat together the men would be served first. In those families with a limited amount of furniture, men sit on low chairs or stools while women and children sit on the floor. Tables, knives, and forks are used only with guests during fiestas. While spoons are used more frequently, most food is eaten with a tortilla (which is used as a spoon).

Dress   Both old and new styles are reflected in the clothing worn by the Tepoztecans. Items of Spanish origin, as well as certain elements from pre-Contact times, represent the older style. The woman's dress consists of a long, dark colored skirt, a white underskirt, a collarless undershirt, a highnecked blouse, a half-apron, a sash, and a *rebozo* (shawl). The women will often wear earrings, sometimes of gold, and a short string of beads made from red seeds. Generally their feet are bare. Men who dress in the older style wear white cloth pants, long white cotton underdrawers, white undershirt, a white collarless overshirt, a white cotton jacket, leather sandals, and a straw sombrero. A *serape* (woolen blanket) is carried for warmth and for protection against the rain. The machete is also carried as part of the costume. The newer style of dress has been adopted by members of all socioeconomic statuses, but most commonly by the wealthiest members of the community. Women wear one-piece dresses, full-length skirts and long aprons. Sweaters and jackets replace the rebozo. A more recent style for men consists of factory-made pants, a shirt with collar and buttons, a jacket with a collar, and shoes. A narrowbrimmed felt hat is replacing the sombrero. The serape is being replaced by sweaters and jackets.

Economy   The economy is basically a household economy of small producers, peasants, artisans, and merchants whose primary concern is subsistence. The resources for agriculture in Tepoztlán are quite poor. Only 15 percent of the total land can be cultivated by plow and an additional 10 percent by slash-and-burn agriculture based on the hoe. The average landholding is one and one-half acres of cultivable land and about eight acres of forest and grazing land. The land is not equally divided so many have considerably less land than the average. There is no irrigation and only one harvest a year. These factors produce a situation in which the Tepoztecans are unable to support themselves by farming alone. They are forced to seek other sources of income and engage in a wide variety of jobs during different seasons of the year.

The Tepoztecan economy is a complex one. There are well-developed concepts of private property, a high degree of individualism, a free market, a definition of wealth based on land and cattle, a fairly wide range in wealth differences, the use of money, a highly developed system of marketing and trade, interest in capital accumulation, wage labor, pawning of property, renting of land, the use of plow and oxen, and specialization in part-time occupations.

There is a clearly defined division of labor by sex. The men of the village are expected to support their families by working in the fields caring for the cattle, horses, oxen and mules, by making charcoal and cutting wood, and by engaging in all important business transactions. Most specialized occupations are filled by men. At home the men are expected to provide wood and water, make or repair furniture and work tools, repair the house, and help pick fruit. Politics and local government, as well as the organization and management of religious and secular fiestas, are also handled by men. On the other hand, a woman's work is centered about the house and family. Duties performed by the women include cooking, cleaning, washing and ironing, daily shopping at the market, shelling corn, and caring for the children. Daughters help their mothers from an early age in order to learn the skills which will help to make them desirable wives. To supplement the family income women also raise chickens, turkeys, and pigs. The women of Tepoztlán do not work in the fields and hold the women of surrounding villages who do so in low regard.

The land of the village is divided into 3 types of holdings: communal land, ejidos, and private land. Almost 80 percent of the land is considered communal property. Communal land became an important issue during the Revolution. Local bosses (*caciques*) had taken control of the communal land and prohibited the other villagers from using it. Less than 5 percent of the land are ejido holdings. Whereas the communal lands are controlled by the regular municipal authorities, the ejido lands are under the control of locally elected ejido officials. The ejido lands are used primarily for plow agriculture. These holdings are divided into small plots and assigned to individuals according to the rules for eligibility established by the National Ejido Program. The title to ejido land rests with the nation, while the title to the communal land is a municipal responsibility. The ejido system was an outgrowth of the Revolution. It was an attempt to redistribute land. In 1929 the village received twenty-one hundred hectares of ejido land which had come from a large hacienda. An ejido plot cannot be purchased or sold. Private holdings, which account for roughly 15 percent of the land, are also used primarily for plow agriculture. These holdings are in fee simple, and ownership must be proved by legal title.

Approximately 31 percent of the families now hold ejido lands. All of these holdings are less than three hectares in size. Only 36 percent of the families own private land. This is the ideal land tenure type, yet 64 percent of the villagers do not own land. Ninety percent of the holdings of owned land are less than nine hectares and most of these are actually under four hectares. At the same time, those who own cornfields have holdings that are fragmented into a number of tiny plots.

There are no tractors in Tepoztlán. Instead two traditional systems of agriculture are used: the plow and oxen or the hoe. The organization of each type of technology is quite different. The hoe is used on steep and rocky land. Hoe agriculture is practiced on communal land and requires a great deal of time and labor but little capital. With this technology, land is farmed exclusively by family labor. With hoe agriculture the yields are much higher than with plow agriculture; however, the amount of corn planted to begin with is extremely small. Rotation of land is also necessary every few years.

Plow cultivation is used primarily on less sloping, relatively treeless land. This land is privately owned and requires little time and labor but considerable capital. Much of the work is performed by hired help. The fields cultivated by plow can be planted year after year. Hoe culture is primarily geared to production for subsistence while plow culture is better geared to production for market. However, one cannot make a general statement and say that only the poor farm the communal land, and the rich farm the private land. Farmers who own small plots of land may also work some communal land to supplement their income. In fact some of the wealthiest farmers rent out their privately owned land and work communal land.

Other differences between hoe and plow farming include the cycle of work, the tools, the type of corn, the work techniques, and even the terminology. Tools and techniques used with hoe agriculture are derived from Nahuatl names, while in plow agriculture the Spanish names prevail. The lands that are cultivated by plow tend to be much closer to the village than those cultivated by hoe. Therefore the farmers who operate the communal land must allow two to three extra hours just to reach their fields every day and the same amount of extra time returning at the end of the work day.

Fiestas   The year-long cycle of work is broken by the occurrence of many festivals. Benefiting from two traditions, each characterized by many calendric festivals (the elaborate ceremonial calendar of the Aztecs and the many saints' days of Catholicism), the Tepoztecans enjoy a great number of festivals that are in part sacred but in greater part secular. Redfield (1930) recorded eighty-two days of festivals throughout the year—in other words, almost one out of every four days is a festival day. The number is actually closer to one-third of all days because Tepoztecans are invited to participate in festivals outside the community within the valley of Tepoztlán. Of course not all fiestas involve full-scale celebrations. Four-fifths of the holidays occur between December and June. Toward the middle of June the rainy season begins and a new period of work starts on the farms. Fields are planted at the beginning of the rainy season. By December the crops are harvested and once more the fiestas begin in earnest.

Although a large fiesta may last only one day there are often many days of preparation. Money has to be collected, the fireworks tower has to be built, dancers have to be trained, wax candles and wax flower decorations are crafted, and festive dishes are prepared. In the case of festivals honoring saints, the day is a pleasurable one in which the villagers wear their finest clothes and eat fiesta dishes (one of the few chances for a change in the bean and corn diet), watch or participate in religious dancing, drink, and sing. These aspects are even more emphasized in the secular fiestas such as carnival and *Altepe-ilhuitl* ("the day of the *pueblo*"). The important taboo days are those imported by the Spanish priests—the last three days of Lent. Even during this period however the taboos are broken ceremonially at a lesser carnival by getting drunk and eating meat *tamales*.

Altepe-ilhuitl is a most important fiesta and one of the few in which the Church is not directly involved. The celebration is much like Carnival, with eating, drinking, and buying and selling in the plaza. Ancient ritual recalls the past glories of the village. A man assuming the role of the semi-mythical leader of the Tepoztecans defies the forces of the enemy pueblos and successfully defends the ancient citadel against attack. It is the most important patriotic holiday and is considered the Independence Day of Tepoztlán.

The holidays of Tepoztlán are unique, each with its own special ritual. For the fiesta of Los Reyes the fireworks tower must be made in a certain shape; for the fiesta of Ixcatepec it is traditional for particular dances to be performed. The food for festive occasions is differentiated from everyday cooking and assumes a sacred character. On Palm Sunday one eats meat tamales; on the Day of the Dead several special dishes are prepared; on days honoring saints, and on no others, one eats mole verde, the special fiesta sauce.

The Family The biological family is the basic productive unit of the village. Families are strong and cohesive, held together by traditional bonds of loyalty, common economic strivings, mutual dependence, the prospect of inheritance, and the absence of any other social group to which an individual might turn in time of need. Cooperation within the immediate family is essential, for without a family the individual stands unprotected and isolated, prey to every type of aggression, exploitation, and humiliation known in Tepoztlán. Thus it is within the bounds of the nuclear family that the Tepoztecans seek personal security. Over 70 percent of the village housesites are occupied by nuclear families living alone.

According to ideal cultural patterns the husband should be authoritarian and patriarchal; he should be master of his household. He is responsible for the support of the family and for the behavior of its members and makes all major decisions for the household. It is his prerogative to be given obedience, respect, and service by his wife and children. On the other hand, the wife is expected to be submissive, faithful, and devoted to her husband and to ask for his advice and permission before venturing on any but the most minor enterprises. She should be industrious and manage to save money regardless of her husband's income. She is expected not to be critical, jealous, or to display any curiosity regarding her husband's activities outside the home. In actual practice, few husbands are the dominant figures they seek to be and few wives are completely submissive.

Many marriages reveal conflict over the question of authority and the roles of the spouses. Conflicts of this kind are fostered by a basic discrepancy between ideal roles and actual roles in the organization of the family. Although the wife is supposed to be subordinate to her husband, it is she who has the central role within the house. She is responsible for planning, organizing, and managing the household and for training and caring for the children. The husband generally turns over all of his earnings to her. The husband's actual participation in family and household affairs is minimal. His work is outside the home. The men are gone a good part of the day, sometimes for several days at a time depending on their work and the particular season of the year. Those who work for the haciendas are often away four to six months during the dry season and visit their homes once a week.

Even more important than a husband's absence is his behavior when he is at home. He avoids intimacy with the members of the family in order to gain their respect. In many homes the husband's sense of security derives from the extent to which he can control his wife and children or make them fear him. Wife beating is still widespread and is resorted to for offenses that range from not having a meal ready on time to suspicion of adultery.

In sexual relations as in social relations the husband is expected to take the initiative and his wife to submit to his demands. The Tepoztecan does not expect his wife to be sexually demanding or even passionate, nor does he consider these to be desirable traits in a wife. Women who "need" men are referred to as *loco* (crazy) and are thought to be under the influence of black magic. Some husbands deliberately refrain from arousing their wives sexually because it is thought that a passive or frigid wife will be more faithful. For the most part sexual play is a technique husbands reserve for the seduction of other women, not for their wives. Promiscuity is a male prerogative and men have affairs to prove their manliness. Usually they have extramarital relations with widows or unmarried women, less frequently with married women.

Beyond the nuclear family an individual can sometimes turn to other blood or affinal relatives for help. Possibly more important than the kin is the system of compadrazgo. Godparents address their godchildren in the familiar *tu* and are addressed by the respectful *Usted*. The more important relationships are those between the compadres. Compadres address each other with the respectful Usted. Their relationship is a reciprocal respect relationship in which there is an avoidance of intimacy or undue familiarity such as any subject of a very personal nature. Compadres are not allowed to drink together. They often exchange favors, and borrowing between compadres is more frequent than between kin. When one compadre dies the other is expected to contribute toward funeral expenses. Compadres invite each other to fiestas and treat one another with deference. The villagers prefer compadres who are neither relatives nor neighbors.

The three most important occasions for which godparents are named are baptism, confirmation, and marriage. The husband's parents usually select godparents of baptism for at least their first child. These godparents are obliged to assist at the baptism, to buy the infant's clothing for the ceremony, and to pay the priest's fee. They also accompany the mother and child to the first mass, forty days after the birth. If the child dies the godparents are expected to help with the funeral. It is also their duty to see that the parents send their child to school when the time comes. Godparents may play a role in punishing the child. The godparents of confirmation are selected by the godparents of baptism. The godparents of marriage assist at the wedding and later act as mediators if the couple has quarrels or separates.

In Tepoztlán the compadrazgo system has been extended far beyond the original Catholic form to include godparents of *miscotón* (a Nahuatl term that refers to a small sweater the godparent puts on the child to protect him from illness); godparents of *medida* or *listón* (a small piece of ribbon, blessed by the priest, which is placed on a sick child as a charm); godparents of *evangelio* (a woman of "bad" reputation is asked to become godmother of an ill child and to pray in the church for his recovery); godparents of scapulary (two small pieces of cloth joined by strings worn on the chest and back as a token of religious devotion); godparents of the Child Jesus, and so on. The compadrazgo system has been extended to secular activities as well. At soccer and basketball games each team has its own "godmother" who dresses in white, carries flowers, acts as the sponsor, and hands out prizes to the winners. At social dances there are "godmothers" who act as chaperons.

Social, economic, and political factors sometimes enter into the operation of the compadre system. The poorer families look for godparents of higher socioeconomic standing for their children. The Tepoztecans think it is desirable to have a compadre in Mexico City. The more godchildren a man has the more compadres and the wider the circle of persons who can be counted on for favors. Anyone who aspires to a position of leadership in Tepoztlán must have many godchildren.

World View   The traditional world view of the Tepoztecans has been conditioned by the limitations of their physical environment, technology, and economy, by their turbulent history, by their three hundred years of colonial status, by their poverty and high death rate, and finally by the haphazard nature of social changes caused by urban influences. To the villagers, the world and nature present a constant threat of calamity and danger. The world is filled with hostile forces and punishing figures that must be propitiated if their goodwill and protection are to be secured: (1) El Tepozteco withholds rain if he is neglected, (2) *los aires* (bad air sicknesses), (3) the spirits who live in the water send illness to those who offend them, and (4) *naguales* (humans in pact with the devil) can turn themselves into pigs or dogs to do harm at night. Even the Catholic figures are seen as threatening. God is a punishing figure rather than one of love and most misfortunes are ascribed to Him. He brings good fortune only rarely. The saints are seen as intermediaries between God and man, and the Tepoztecans devote themselves to cultivating their favor. The saints with the greatest punishing powers are the most diligently worshipped.

Most Tepoztecans do not distinguish clearly between the punishments of God and the work of *el pingo* (the devil), nor do the Tepoztecans have a clear conception of the Catholic heaven and hell. Hell is thought to be a purgatory only for the greatest sinners. Ordinary people do not fear hell and usually have no concern with sin, confession, or life after death.

According to Oscar Lewis, the Tepoztecans are not an easy people to know, for they are neither outgoing nor expressive. Most interpersonal relationships are characterized by reserve and carefully guarded behavior. The peasant who speaks little, minds his own business, and maintains some distance between himself and others is considered prudent and wise. The people are somber and quiet. Boisterousness and noise coming from a house soon earns the family an unpleasant reputation. Women and girls are expected to walk with eyes modestly downcast; those who smile freely may be thought of as flirtatious. Those who smile at other people's babies are suspected of "evil eye." Men, in particular, tend to be undemonstrative and limited in their ability to express warmth and affection and the more tender emotions. As one Tepoztecan observed of his fellow villagers, *"Somos muy secos"* ("We are very dry") (Lewis 1960:88).

The villagers rely on formality and intermediaries to facilitate interpersonal relations. Any direct expression of aggression is discouraged and competition between individuals is rare. Underlying the smooth surface, however, is a feeling of oppression, particularly for those individuals who are trying to improve themselves or who deviate from strict conformity. A good deal of suppressed hostility finds indirect release in malicious gossip, stealing, secret destruction of other's property, envy, deprecation, and sorcery. The *indirecta* or indirect criticism is a common, accepted form of aggression. Assault in the form of surprise attack and murder occurs from time to time. Men in positions of wealth, power, or authority often carry a gun for protection and prefer not to venture out at night. The most feared, although perhaps the least common, form of indirect aggression is sorcery.

LIMÓN

During the Colonial period, white settlement in Costa Rica was concentrated in the temperate highlands. The Spanish made little effort to establish effective control over the eastern lowlands. For the most part the lowlands remained a refuge area for Indians who resisted conquest—many of whom had been displaced from the highlands by white settlement. Only a few of the Spanish ever ventured into the lowlands, usually for the purpose of establishing small cacao plantations as absentee landlords (Olien 1970:22).

Coffee was developed in the highlands following Independence. It became the country's major export crop and was transported to the west coast to Costa Rica's only port, Puntarenas, and shipped around the tip of South America to Europe. This process of coffee exportation was both time consuming and expensive. In 1871 the government initiated construction of a port on the east coast and a railroad connecting the port with the highlands.

Banana cultivation was begun in the lowlands to provide business for the railway as it was being constructed. Minor C. Keith, the railroad's builder, began exporting bananas in 1880. By 1889 Keith owned twenty-seven banana plantations in the lowland region. All of the bananas grown in the lowlands were exported through Keith (Stewart 1964:158–159). With these holdings Keith merged with the Boston Fruit Company and formed the United Fruit Company in 1899.

The majority of the laborers used on the construction of the railway were Jamaican Negro peasants. Once the railway was completed, these blacks sought new forms of employment. Many joined the United Fruit Company as plantation proletarians. The United Fruit Company dominated the eastern lowlands of Costa Rica, an area known as Limón, from 1871 to 1941. The West Indians who came to Limón worked for the Company on its banana plantations, its railway, or in its port town, Puerto Limón. As employees of the United Fruit Company the plantation system permeated all aspects of their lives.

The Limón region attracted a considerable number of West Indians so that by 1927 the majority of people living in the lowlands were black. Almost the entire West Indian Negro population of Costa Rica, approximately nineteen thousand persons, was situated in Limón by this time. The West Indian Negro immigrant filled positions both in the middle and at the bottom of the economic hierarchy. The white managers of the Company, from the United States, held positions at the top. White peons from the highlands generally held positions at the bottom of the hierarchy. A limited number of highland whites assumed managerial positions.

Nature of the Plantation System   The economic structure of the lowland plantation contrasted greatly with that of the highlands. Whereas the coffee farms of the highlands were often owned by local Costa Rican families, the banana plantations of the Limón lowlands were absentee-owned, with managers who were technicians from foreign countries. The managers had no ties with the local society except as employers. Padilla's (1960:26) description of the Caribbean corporation-owned plantation is applicable to the Limón situation:

The corporation has been institutionalized in different industrial countries to meet the capital scope of large industrial and commercial developments and is an internationally-based and internationally-operating enterprise. In the Caribbean area it appears in the form of a variety of business enterprises requiring large capital outlays, such as the large-scale agricultural production and processing of sugar cane, the marketing and shipping of crops and manufacturing goods, the banks, and the large-scaled exploitation of mineral resources, such as oil. Capital resources for this corporate enterprise may be partially supplied by local capital; however, the larger enterprises are based on foreign-drawn capital and are usually controlled by absentee stockholders and companies. Corporations are legal persons, that is, no particular individual or individuals own them. It is a collective body empowered by the laws to enter into business transactions as if it were a person or a single entity.

The plantation system in Costa Rica was a closed system. All of the black's needs were fulfilled by "Mamita Yunai."[9] The structure of the system was clearly established. The relationships between the laborer and the Company and between the Company and the government were clearly outlined in formal contracts. The new worker entered into not only a new economic position upon his arrival in Costa Rica but also a new social system.

The West Indian Negroes lived in Company houses, received Company health service, and purchased supplies at Company stores. Their rent was nominal or free, and every occupant of a Company house or cabin had a rent-free garden patch on which he could raise vegetables (F. Adams 1914: 176).

Generally the housing consisted of one-room or two-room two-family houses with corrugated iron roofs. These dwellings were elevated on stilts. Families frequently occupied single rooms which were about twelve feet square. Although these quarters were congested, some of the families took in boarders. The houses usually had small unscreened front and back porches. The stove (or oven) for cooking was usually under the back porch.

The Company also provided medical facilities for its employees. However, whereas the managers were treated in the Company hospital, a large portion of cases of illness among the West Indian laborers were treated at home.

The banana plantation workers purchased most of their articles and food from the Company's commissary stores. (The commissary department

[9] According to the famous Costa Rican novelist Carlos Luis Fallas (1941:246), this was a popular term for United Fruit among the workers. *Mamita* is an affectionate diminutive form of *mama* (mother) and *Yunai* is the Spanish pronunciation of "United."

House along railway in eastern lowlands of Costa Rica like those used by workers of United Fruit.

of the Company had twenty-four stores by 1929.) These stores did an annual business of approximately one and one-half million dollars (Crowther 1929:251). In general the prices were less than that of non-Company stores; however, toward the end of the United Fruit Company period in Limón, prices rose considerably because of import duties on many items such as canned goods and tools. The West Indian workers celebrated the major North American holidays such as Thanksgiving and the Fourth of July, as well as many of the Costa Rican holidays.

The Company railway provided the main, and in most cases the only, means of transportation for the workers of the lowlands. As Nunley (1960: 45) has pointed out:

It is difficult for residents of a country so well supplied with surface transportation as the United States, to visualize an area in which practically all transportation depends upon the railroad, a road on which only company-owned vehicles could run. In the Caribbean lowlands of Costa Rica school children go back and forth to school on the train. The sick man is carried to the hospital on the train. And, even in the city of Puerto Limón, the dead man is carried to the cemetary [sic] on a special funeral train!

Because the *linieros* (the Costa Rican term for the banana plantation workers) were a part of the plantation social system they became integrated with the Company's institutions and culture patterns. These institutions and culture patterns often contrasted with those of Costa Rica.

The Costa Rican whites of the highlands had never been able to exploit or settle the lowlands successfully. As a result, the United Fruit Company was not seen as economic competition because it restricted its operations to previously uncultivated areas of Costa Rica and was importing its own labor supply. Frederick Palmer (1910:220) described the situation in Costa Rica in 1910 as follows: "Most of the planters in Costa Rica are Americans. The Costa Ricans themselves are too happy growing coffee in the cool highlands to undergo the punishing climate of the lowlands, where endurance and killing time are really the chief requisites." Environmental determinism provided a rationale for the highlanders. The tropics were said to be a place in which white men could not survive. George Putnam (1913:88) probably summarized the feelings of the average highland Costa Rican when he wrote, "To leave the invigorating uplands of San José and plunge down into the banana belt along the Atlantic is like abandoning the Alps for a Turkish bath. That sounds overdrawn, doesn't it? It isn't."

Organization of the Plantation Economy Prior to the Depression about two hundred sixty different categories of workers were employed on the United Fruit Company's tropical properties. Within the supervisory force were included division managers; superintendents of transportation, agriculture, commissary, and other departments; farm overseers and time-keepers; accountants; and chief inspectors. Among the white-collar employees were clerical assistants and storekeepers. Skilled labor included farm foremen, axmen, railroad mechanics, surveyors, construction engineers, and operators of steam shovels and dredges. Among the semiskilled were ditch diggers and road makers, cutters who harvested the fruit and cleaned and pruned the cultivations, and members of loading gangs who packed the bananas in railroad cars. Unskilled laborers were employed, some permanently and others temporarily, on the wharves, in the railroad yards, and on the farms (Kepner 1936:125).

Workers of different categories were paid in various ways. White-collar workers (North Americans) received monthly salaries. Negroes and other employees were paid differently. Members of railroad gangs received weekly wages; casual, unskilled laborers received daily or hourly wages. Longshoremen who carried bananas from the freight cars to the loading machines on the ships were paid by the bunch. Work on ditch-digging or road-building projects was measured by the distance covered. When the Company required the clearing of virgin land it gave contracts not to individual workers but to foremen who made their own terms with their men. The bulk of farm maintenance and harvesting was performed by workers holding individual contracts to do certain specified tasks (Kepner 1936:125–216).

In 1929 the United Fruit Company payroll that was distributed in all the tropical divisions totaled $28,420,060 to a labor force of about sixty-five thousand men. This gave an average annual return per man of $437.23. Since departmental superintendents, farm superintendents, overseers, and other higher ranking employees had salaries that were considerably above average, most manual laborers received less than the equivalent of $1.25 per day, six days a week, throughout the year. Some received more than this amount and many received much less. In the latter group were large numbers of part-time laborers who were employed only during rush periods. If part-time laborers were able to find other types of employment when not working for the Company, their plight was not serious; however, near the United Fruit Company's banana centers there was no other large-scale employer. Some of these part-time laborers were squatters who sold an average of three to ten bunches of bananas to the Company weekly. Their total earnings both as part-time laborers and as small planters were meager (Kepner 1936:128–129). In 1918 the Company employed sixty-five hundred men with a payroll of nearly three million dollars in Costa Rica (Crowther 1929:250).

The port of Limón developed as an extension of the United Fruit Company's banana plantations. Many Negroes worked in the port rather than on the plantations. Puerto Limón was the North American administrative center for the entire region.

Putnam (1913:107) records that the West Indian Negroes received fifteen cents an hour on the docks for night work and ten cents an hour for day work. The Spanish-speaking whites, on the other hand, received twelve and one-half cents an hour for night work and eight and one-half cents an hour for day work.

Fringe benefits such as old-age pensions did not exist in the banana zones. The United Fruit Company induced some of the retired Jamaican laborers to return to their island by providing free transportation on a Company-owned ship (Kepner 1936:145).

Although not everyone worked on the United Fruit Company plantations, everyone in the Limón region was directly affected by the Company. The private planters were forced to sell their bananas to the Company for export and were forced to use the Company railway to transport their fruit to the port. The Company was able to establish effective control over the people of Limón through direct force, such as using police to drive squatters off Company-owned land, and through indirect force, such as increasing the amount of rejected fruit from any planter not cooperating.

The United Fruit Company as an international organization was able to exert pressure on the political leaders by threatening to move out of Costa Rica whenever the government attempted to raise the export tax on bananas. Keith would suggest that it might be better if the United Fruit Company developed its interests in Guatemala or Honduras rather than in Costa Rica, and the Costa Rican government would be forced to abandon its idea of raising the tax. Keith would then use a similar threat in other countries dominated by United Fruit to control prices there. Putnam (1913:102) quoted a United Fruit Company employee remarking on Keith's ability to manipulate the Costa Rican powerholders as having said, "God and Minor C. Keith alone know what goes on behind the scenes."

In Costa Rica, not only were the capital investment and the managers foreign, but the labor supply was foreign as well. Most of the Negro laborers who came to Costa Rica remained foreigners throughout the United Fruit Company period. They did not consider themselves "Costa Ricans"—one of the reasons the West Indians did not become integrated with Costa Rican institutions or culture. The blacks came to Costa Rica primarily because of the employment opportunities and not because they intended to settle permanently. They expected to return to Jamaica as soon as they had collected sufficient savings. Blacks working for the United Fruit Company were free to visit or to return to Jamaica whenever they pleased. Frederick Adams (1914:193) wrote that thousands of Negroes made the trip to Jamaica annually. The United Fruit Company maintained its own shipping line between Puerto Limón and Jamaica and most West Indians sailed on Company ships.

Patterns of Emulation   A study of Limón undertaken in the early 1900s revealed that 128 banana planters were Costa Rican whereas 589 were foreigners. Most of the foreigners had not become naturalized citizens of Costa Rica. Among them were citizens of the United States, the British Empire, Spain, and other European countries. Many of the small planters were Jamaican Negroes and were thus British subjects. The study found that a large proportion of the foreign planters were sending their savings to their countries (Kepner and Soothill 1935:256). The majority of the people living in Limón Province in 1927 were foreigners. There were 2.2 foreigners for every Costa Rican. In all other provinces of the country, the majority were citizens of Costa Rica (Ministerio de Economía y Hacienda 1960:63).

Other demographic data also suggest that the laborers who were living in Limón did not expect to remain in Costa Rica permanently. Most were unmarried males. The sex ratio and household size of the Limón population was quite distinct from that of any other Costa Rican province, with 9.4 percent more males than females (Ministerio de Economía y Hacienda 1960:62–63). Data from the urban centers of each of the provinces show that Puerto Limón was the only urban center in Costa Rica with more males than females. Only 24 percent of the population in Limón over the age of fifteen were married (Ministerio de Economía y Hacienda 1960:43).

The average household size for Limón Province was only 2.7 persons. The average household size of all other provinces of Costa Rica was nearly double that figure. Almost 41 percent of all households in Limón consisted of a single person. Twenty-one percent of all households in Limón consisted of only two persons. These data indicate that the majority of the Negroes were temporary residents of Costa Rica. Without citizenship the Negro had no voice in Costa Rican government; however, Costa Rican politics were not important to the West Indian as the United Fruit Company foreign managers were able to control Limón as they wished, with little outside interference from the government. The United Fruit Company constituted *de facto* authority in Limón.

As long as the blacks remained in the lowlands, the highland whites did not object to their living in Costa Rica, though they did object to the blacks migrating into the highlands. In the tropical lowlands, the West Indians provided a labor force that filled the vacuum created by Costa Ricans who were unwilling to work in the Limón region. If the blacks were to move to the highlands it was thought that they would directly compete with the lower class whites for available jobs. It was also felt that blacks were particularly susceptible to some of the diseases of the lowlands such as malaria and yellow fever and would bring these diseases with them if they migrated to the highlands. As a result of these fears, considerable pressure was exerted to prohibit blacks from settling further west than the town of Turrialba on the periphery of the highlands.

Because the Costa Rican government was unable to exert *de facto* control over the lowlands, the West Indian Negro was able to retain his West Indian form of education, his English language, and his Protestantism.

The government built public schools in the Limón region once the area was settled; however, the Spanish instruction of these public schools was difficult for the English-speaking West Indian children of the United Fruit Company employees. With the Company's aid, private English-speaking schools came into existence as a substitute for the public schools. The Secretary of Education in Costa Rica, Ricardo Fournier, commenting on the private schools in 1930, said (Kepner 1936:166–167):

Because of the language difficulty, the children of English speaking Jamaican Negroes frequently go to private schools, in which they often have to pay tuition.

The private schools are really an acute problem for the public education system—it being hard to exercise supervision over them because of the language, and because they do not follow government regulations. Some of the schools are in very small villages; thus the only way to force them to conform to governmental requirements would be to increase the number of inspectors. They tend to denationalize their areas. In them the government is unable to teach national ideas and the sentiments of Costa Rica.

After almost fifty years of living in Costa Rica, the West Indian Negro was still described as lacking national ideas and sentiments.

In 1927 there were at least thirty-three private schools in Limón with a total enrollment of fifteen hundred students, most of whom were black. Many of these schools were associated with the Protestant churches of the region (Ministerio de Economía y Hacienda 1960:79).

Throughout the United Fruit Company's domination of the lowlands, the blacks were able to retain their West Indian language, a dialect of English common throughout the Caribbean known as "pidgin English" or "banana English." The Jamaican newspaper, *The Daily Gleaner,* written in English, was imported from Jamaica and read by workers in Limón.

To a certain extent the United Fruit Company encouraged the retention of English by offering higher wages to English-speaking workers. The foreign, English-speaking managers found it easier to communicate with the Negroes than with other workers who could speak only Spanish. The ability to speak English also probably played a role in the recruitment policies of the Company. With English as the language used by the foreign Company managers, it was the prestige language of the province. There was no motivation for the West Indian to learn Spanish. As a Company employee he did not have to deal directly with the Spanish-speaking government officials. The foreign managers of the United Fruit Company acted as intermediaries between the government officials and the Negro laborers.

There was no advantage for the West Indians, as temporary immigrants, in joining the Catholic Church. Although the Catholic Church was the State church, it seldom directly affected the lives of the Negro workers. Most of the plantation laborers retained their membership in Protestant churches. The Protestant churches had followed the West Indian laborers from the Caribbean to Costa Rica. The largest Anglican church in Central America was established in Puerto Limón. Methodist and Baptist churches were also established in Limón, as well as a number of smaller sects. The Protestant churches maintained the English schools.

In the final analysis there is little evidence to suggest that the West Indian Negro was integrated with the Costa Rican national institutions or culture patterns during the United Fruit Company's domination of the lowlands. Instead the West Indian's life was intimately associated with the United Fruit Company, managed by North Americans. The West Indians and the North American managers shared much in common. They were both foreign to Costa Rica, they spoke the same language, many persons from both groups were Protestant, and they were employed by the same company.

Plantation Subcultures: the Costa Rican Case The laborers who form the usina plantation subculture (see Chapter 5) on plantations in other countries are often integrated with national, rather than local, institutions and culture patterns because they are typically free laborers in a free labor market. As free laborers of the usina plantation subculture they normally have considerable geographic mobility when compared to the laborers of the engenho plantation subculture. Also in many countries, national labor unions are active among usina plantation subculture workers. Neither of these factors was important on the Costa Rican banana plantations.

The blacks were prevented from moving out of the lowlands and into the highlands by the Costa Rican whites. At the same time, the United Fruit Company was really the only employer in the lowlands. For these reasons the West Indian Negroes in Costa Rica did not constitute a mobile work force. The only real choice the black could make was to remain in Limón with the United Fruit Company or to return to the West Indies. In this respect the Costa Rican plantation resembled the engenho type plantation found in Brazil or the Mexican hacienda where geographical mobility was restricted. A few blacks managed to sustain themselves outside Company employment; however, they almost always remained in Limón. Some of the Negroes became squatters on Company land and were able to make a living through subsistence agriculture; yet even these squatters were often part-time employees of the Company during the peak seasons and often supplemented their incomes by selling several bunches of bananas to the Company each week. In short, they continued to live under the shadow of the United Fruit Company. Few of the West Indians ever migrated into the highlands (only 795 by 1939). Some of the blacks were employed as bellboys in San José hotels that catered to North American visitors. Waibel (1939:549) wrote that the majority of the highland Negroes lived in San José. They were concentrated near the railway terminal and formed a district in that section of the city.

Unlike the situation on some modern field-and-factory combine plantations in other areas of Latin America, the labor unions were never important on the United Fruit Company banana plantations of the Atlantic lowlands. Following the First World War there were strikes in many parts of the world including strikes on various United Fruit Company holdings. In Costa Rica the strikes were unorganized and spontaneous. They resulted from indignation against working conditions on the plantations rather than from the efforts of outside agitators. During the 1920s, union organization did not exist in the banana region among the plantation, railway, or dock workers of the United Fruit Company. The Company was able to break strikes by playing one ethnic group against another, persuading certain sections of strikers to return to work (Kepner 1936:180).

The first major attempt to organize the workers failed. A union organization known as the *Federación General de Trabajadores* was able to unite workers of various crafts for a while. It too eventually failed as a result of unsuccessful political activity. In the early 1930s the banana workers were organized by the *Sindicato de Trabajadores del Atlántico*, which was sponsored by the Communist Party of Costa Rica (Kepner 1936:183). This organization backed a major strike in 1934; the strike was unsuccessful. The strikers were able to reach an agreement with various small planters but the United Fruit Company neither participated in the conciliatory conference nor signed the agreement. Consequently some of the workers struck a second time against the Company but without effect (Kepner 1936:188, 201).

Wolf and Mintz (1957:403–404) have described the problems of unionization on modern plantations:

Unionization . . . often founders on the very problem that brings it into being: too many men competing for too few opportunities to work. It thus rarely remains purely on the economic plane but tends to develop political ends. If the labor union can gain enough strength to influence politics on the national level, it can work for an increase of institutionalized services provided by the government or forced on the plantations through government intervention. This political role of unions of plantation workers is especially important in societies which are politically and economically dependent on dominant powers. The union may have opportunities to ally itself with groups operating on the national level to restrict the power of the dominant power. Agitation against foreign-owned and foreign-operated plantations may form part of a political effort, and political success of anti-colonial political groups may result in an extension of services of the plantation population.

As previously mentioned, the Negro workers of Limón had little or no voice in politics because they were not Costa Ricans. Certain highland groups that operated on a national level did attempt to restrict the power of the United Fruit Company. The fact that the United Fruit Company controlled export taxes and made long-term contracts with the government that were advantageous to the Company but not to the country was viewed by these highland groups as a violation of their country's sovereignty. They made the renegotiation of the United Fruit Company's banana contracts a major political issue. As these power groups had little effect on the situation, the contracts remained as they had been until after the Revolution of 1948. On the whole, labor unions were of little importance in the lowlands.

Although the national labor unions were never strong, the banana plantation workers did receive some benefits from national legislation. In particular the Negro plantation workers eventually came under the Costa Rican workmen's compensation law. This law was passed in 1925 and obligated employers to report all accidents and made them solely responsible for payment of all liabilities. The law provided for fines or criminal prosecution in cases where employers tried to pass their new expense on to their workers by deductions from wages or in other indirect ways. It also included provisions for compensation for occupational diseases. However, the legislation still had not been successfully enforced in the lowlands by 1934. As a result a strike occurred in 1934 involving workers' demands for the guarantee of proper compensation for accidents.

The Limón area was unlike most plantation areas in Latin America in that its workers were restricted in their freedom of movement, and they were not supported by strong national union organizations. These factors, along with the presence of foreign intermediaries, kept the West Indian blacks from becoming integrated with Costa Rican institutions and culture.

In summary, the fact that the plantation system was based almost entirely on foreign labor and management produced ramifying effects on Costa Rican society. The North American managers took over important positions in both highland and lowland areas, which resulted in a redistribution of wealth, authority, and prestige within Costa Rican society as a whole. For the West Indian Negro, however, the situation was quite different. Because he was restricted to the lowland area his position in Costa Rican society was limited to the context of a regional lowland wealth, authority, and prestige hierarchy. As long as the plantation system continued to operate, and as long as the highland population refused to accept the West Indian as a legal equal, the position of the black in Costa Rica remained static. It was not until the collapse of the banana plantations, caused by banana diseases and the social reforms of 1948, that significant structural changes took place in Costa Rican society. These structural changes resulted in an acceleration of West Indian acculturation and assimilation.

Collapse of the Plantation System   The Panama disease (*Fusarium cubense*) was the first and most serious of two diseases that struck the banana plantations (as early as 1890 in some areas). The Panama disease attacked the banana plants through the root system causing the leaves to wilt and the plants to rot off at the ground. By 1926 the United Fruit Company had abandoned 29,500 acres of banana land in eastern Costa Rica because of the disease (Jones and Morrison 1952:6–7).

In 1938, Sigatoka (*Cercospora musae*), a leaf spot disease, made its initial appearance in Costa Rica. This particular disease attacked the leaves of the plant and prevented the plant from producing large bunches of high quality bananas (Jones and Morrison 1952:6–7).

By 1940, as a result of Sigatoka, it became less and less profitable for the United Fruit Company to purchase bananas from the Atlantic lowland area for export. Although the United Fruit Company had abandoned plantation production of fruit in eastern Costa Rica before Sigatoka appeared, this disease hastened the withdrawal of the Company from all major activities in the area. So far as the purchase and export of bananas was concerned, the United Fruit Company pulled out entirely from the Limón region of Costa Rica in 1942, moving their operations to the Pacific coast of Costa Rica.

As early as 1935 the United Fruit Company had decided that the plantation was no longer the most successful means of exploiting the region. Production was being maintained only through the continued development of new land. These new plantations were short-lived because of the banana diseases. From that time on, and until the Company moved, United Fruit encouraged independent growers to plant bananas for sale. The Company, in turn, contracted to purchase the stems and also leased Company land to the growers.

As the United Fruit Company began to move its operations from Limón, some attempt was made to help the West Indian immigrants who had been employed in the lowlands. The Company offered to relocate the blacks on the Pacific coast as banana divisions were opened there. The Costa Rican government refused to allow the West Indians to be relocated on the grounds that it would "upset the racial pattern of the country and possibly cause civil commotion" (May and Plaza 1958:208). Costa Rica no longer suffered from a labor shortage as it had when the United Fruit Company first began its operations. By refusing to allow the Negroes to be relocated, the government was able to provide jobs for highland whites with United Fruit in the Pacific lowlands. As a result, the Company's Pacific coast division employs whites or mestizos almost exclusively. Approximately 70 percent are Costa Rican and the remainder are Nicaraguan (May and Plaza 1958:207).

With the exodus of United Fruit and its white, North American administrators came the beginning of the West Indian's culture change. As a result of the collapse of the plantation system, the blacks who remained were more dependent upon the land than ever before. As they became land holders and then citizens their pattern of acculturation and assimilation changed. They no longer had foreign administrators forming a buffer between the plantation and the nation, nor did they have a social system which provided for all of their needs outside of the Costa Rican institutions. Once the United Fruit Company moved, the West Indians came into direct contact with the Costa Rican national institutions and culture patterns and from that time on they became progressively more integrated with these patterns. In the process, they were transformed from a plantation subculture type to a rural proletariat type.

As the white managers and planters left the lowlands of Limón, the West Indian Negroes took over sections of Company land. Shouse's (1938) descriptions of various farms in the Limón hinterland in 1938 show that the Negroes assumed positions of ownership and supervision on these land holdings, as well as that of manual laborer. In some cases a black landowner employed white laborers.

The modern plantation is usually highly specialized and generally only one crop is grown. In Limón the plantation system was based on the production of bananas. Unlike the engenho plantation or the hacienda, where there is a tendency to diversify the crops produced, the modern field-and-factory combine plantation bases its fate on the outcome of its major crop. When the major cash crop fails, the plantation fails (Wolf and Mintz 1957: 398–399). The period immediately following the collapse of the plantation system was one in which the inhabitants of the region experimented with other types of cash crops that, it was hoped, might provide alternatives to banana production.

Experiments with cacao were begun as early as 1914 by the United Fruit Company. Cacao production requires full-time labor only during the first five or six years until the trees begin to bear fruit, and then laborers are required only at harvest time. Most of the cacao grown in the late 1930s was on small-scale farms rented to tenants by the United Fruit Company. These tenant farmers and small-scale planters turned over their produce to several exporting firms that were located in the cacao growing centers (Keithan 1940:79–85). Cacao production was only partially successful due to fluctuating prices on the world market and the growing competition from Africa.

In 1936 the Goodyear Rubber Company started a one thousand acre rubber plantation at El Cairo on the Old Line of the railroad; however, because labor costs in Costa Rica were higher than in the East Indies, and because of South American leaf blight, rubber production never developed into an important industry in the Limón lowlands (Jones and Morrison 1952:9).

During the Second World War the United States government signed a contract with the *Compañía Bananera de Costa Rica*, a subsidiary of the United Fruit Company, to develop a Manila hemp (*abacá*) producing center at Bataan on the railroad route from Puerto Limón to San José. This production was abandoned in 1959 (Instituto de Tierras y Colonización 1963:8).

Attempts were made during the Second World War to develop the production of cinchona, the bitter bark of the tree of the same name, from which quinine, quinidine, and other medical alkaloids are obtained; however, disease greatly hindered this production (León 1948:454–455). Other crops were also experimented with including pineapples, balsa wood, coconuts, and maize (Shouse 1938:74–85). None became significant commercial crops in the region.

Another North American-owned company attempted to grow bananas in the region. The Standard Fruit Company took over some of the older areas previously owned by United Fruit. They began banana plantations with new methods of production. The Sigatoka disease was eventually controlled by spraying with chemicals. The Company introduced a new variety of banana, the Giant Cavendish, which was more disease resistant than the Gros Michel banana which had been grown by United Fruit. The Company's holdings, however, are considerably smaller than those of United Fruit (Nunley 1960:45).

The collapse of the plantation system and the abandonment of the Limón area by foreign plantation managers of the United Fruit Company marked the initial step in the integration of the West Indian Negroes with Costa Rican institutions and culture patterns. It marked the end of the United Fruit Company's *de facto* control of the lowlands and the beginning of the domination of the region by the Costa Rican government. Shortly after the fall of the plantation in the lowlands the Costa Ricans made sweeping changes in their constitution giving the blacks equal legal status in Costa Rican society.

MINAS VELHAS

The Eastern Highlands   The eastern highlands of Brazil are formed by most of the state of Minas Gerais, the western part of Espírito Santo, and the southern part of Bahia.[10]

During the eighteenth century this region produced 44 percent of the world's supply of gold. Gold was discovered in 1698 and diamonds by 1729. The gold attracted many new settlers, in particular a new wave of Portuguese immigrants numbering as many as one-half million. The mines were generally small operations worked by individuals or small groups with little capital. The gold rush coincided with the decline of sugar plantations in the northeast. Many plantation owners sold their Negro slaves to the miners.

Within a few decades following the discovery of gold a number of urban settlements had been established in the eastern highlands. The most famous was Vila Rica (now Oura Prêto) which at one time had a population of approximately one hundred thousand persons. These urban areas

[10] This section is based on Harris (1956).

were often situated in places ill-adapted to agriculture, and food was expensive and difficult to obtain. Mules were the most important means of transportation for food, merchandise, and gold. Tens of thousands of these pack animals were used. The gold rush lasted approximately one hundred years.

The urban centers began to adapt to the disappearance of gold by evolving new economic resources: handicrafts, cattle raising, coffee growing, mixed farming, and fireworks manufacturing. Some individuals managed to continue mining on a small scale. Many people left the area entirely.

The eastern highlands today are still rich in mineral resources, especially iron ore; however, the principal economic activities are stock raising and agriculture. Population has once again increased although the size of former urban centers has not. Many now live in small towns with a population of under five thousand. Most of the agricultural production of the region is carried out on the *fazenda mineira,* the typical plantation of the area, or on small farms. Unlike the sugar plantations of the northeast, the fazenda mineira is not based on monocrop production; instead, it is remarkably diversified. The tenants on the fazenda mineira are not concentrated in a plantation village but are scattered widely throughout the countryside.

The people of the eastern highlands are characterized by other Brazilians as conservative and traditional. The region maintains the traditional ideal patterns of Brazilian national culture such as religious brotherhoods (*irmandades*). There is a middle class that perpetuates older patterns of behavior such as *compadresco* (coparenthood). Extensive kinship webs still dominate local politics (Wagley 1963:53–59).

Minas Velhas   The town of "Minas Velhas" (a fictitious name) in the state of Bahia was one of the prosperous urban centers of the eighteenth century that fell into decay. It was studied in 1950–1951 by Marvin Harris. In the eighteenth century Minas Velhas was the administrative center of a large *municipio.* During the nineteenth and twentieth centuries, thirty-four new counties were created from the original county. Today the municipio of Minas Velhas, of which the town of Minas Velhas continues to be the county seat, is one of the poorest and one of the smallest in size of area and population in the entire state of Bahía.

While the town of Minas Velhas has a population of only fifteen hundred, it maintains an awareness of and interest in the outside world. The citizens of the town consider themselves urban and superior in all ways to the surrounding rural populations. It is the inhabitants of the tiny rural villages who produce the food that maintains Minas Velhas.

Economy   Since the decline of mining, the inhabitants of the town have turned to manufacturing, commerce, and civil service for their livelihoods. In the surrounding villages everyone is a farmer of one type or another with the exception of one or two storekeepers or a priest. In the town there is considerable occupational diversity. There are thirty-nine metal-workers, twenty-eight leatherworkers, sixteen commercial travelers, sixteen storekeepers, thirty-two civil servants, six lacemakers, nine dressmakers, plus several brickmakers, tinsmiths, goldsmiths, carpenters, tailors, hotel oper-ators, and also a pharmacist, priest, dentist, fireworks maker, flower maker, and luggage makers. There are also seven landlords who own farm lands but do not actually farm themselves. In addition sixty household heads make their living through menial tasks, often a combination of a variety of tasks including work as cooks, woodcutters, beggars, prostitutes, miners, general laborers, and on road gangs. In only 14 percent of the households does the head of the family earn his living through farming.

Manufacturing, such as metal and leatherworking, is operated on a small scale as home shop industries. Knives, shoes, whips, and cheap lamps (made from small glass bottles, with wicks, set into metal frames made from kerosene cans), and other goods are sold in the hinterland by peddlers trav-eling by foot and mule. The dominant pattern of craft manufacturing is one of a large number of independent, duplicative, and competitive installations. The same can be said of commerce. There are eighteen stores that depend upon the sale of foodstuffs for their mainstay. All of the stores carry the same type of food.

Owning a store does not bring wealth. The shopkeepers buy their food products at the same open fairs on Saturdays where townspeople purchase food for themselves and for the same prices. Stores are able to survive because one third of the families of the town are not able to purchase enough food at the fair to carry them through the week. These families are continuously in debt. Their income is irregular and they must buy their food from day to day. The storekeeper will also grant a certain amount of credit. Although storekeepers do not accrue large fortunes they have what is con-sidered one of the most desirable occupations in the community, as there is a strong disdain for manual labor. The shopkeepers spend most of their time sitting on chairs in front of their stores chatting with townspeople through-out the day. To the people of the community the life of the shopkeeper is both stimulating and romantic.

Race and Class   Although small in population, Minas Velhas is a highly rank-conscious community. The townspeople divide the population into two classes: (1) "the whites" or "the rich" (*brancos-ricos*) and (2) "the Negroes" or "the poor" (*pretos-pobres*). However, the stratification is actually considerably more complex. Those who are truly "white" *and* "rich" are in the top stratum, those who are "Negro" *and* "poor" are in the bottom stratum. In between those two extremes are a number of possibili-ties based on economic, occupational, educational, and racial criteria.

The middle strata are formed by mulattoes, poorer whites, and wealthier Negroes. The Negroes do not attempt to "pass" by posing as white, but rather by posing as anything but a Negro—i.e., they refer to themselves as dark *morenos, chulos, caboclos,* and so on, or even invent new categories. One Negro storekeeper, for example, prefers the euphemistic term *roxinho* (a little purple) and refers to his son as, "that slightly purple fellow over there." It is possible for an individual Negro to obtain an education, as well as financial success, but the Negro group is generally considered inferior to the white. High rank can be achieved in spite of, but never because of, the fact that one is black.

The Clube Social is an indicator of the differences in rank and how these differences operate. The Clube dances provide an opportunity for the highest ranking to appear—they are often referred to as "the whites." Those who are excluded from the Clube and have to watch the festivals from windows are "the Negroes." The Clube membership includes people with the following characteristics: (1) white and wealthy, (2) white and of average wealth, (3) white and poor, (4) mulatto and wealthy, (5) mulatto and of average wealth, (6) Negro and wealthy. Those excluded from the Clube and lumped in the category "Negro" are people with the following characteristics: (1) white and poverty-stricken, (2) mulatto and poverty-stricken, (3) mulatto and poor, (4) Negro and poverty-stricken, (5) Negro and poor, (6) Negro and of average wealth. Approximately 90 percent of Minas Velhas's Negroes, 50 percent of its mulattoes, and 10 percent of its whites are not allowed to dance at the Clube.

This social cleavage of *brancos-ricos* versus *pretos-pobres* is carried over into Carnival, the high point of the social calendar. The Clube Social organizes its own festival. As a result the poorer people organized their own club, *Sociedade dos Pobres* (Society of the Poor) in order to celebrate their own carnivals. Rivalry has developed between the two groups and the Society of the Poor is especially concerned with besting the Clube Social by exhibiting the most lavish celebrations.

Politics   The townspeople are fully aware that they are members of a larger nation: most know the Brazilian national anthem or can at least recognize it when they hear it; Independence Day is celebrated in the schools; and news about the outside world is received via newspaper, radio, and word of mouth. The most important institutionalized links with the rest of the nation, however, are through formal government and political parties. Local government is a powerful urbanizing force, while politics produce intense schisms which, like differences in race and class, bring about a low level of community cohesion.

The money that is allotted by the government for the entire county tends to be used for public works within Minas Velhas. The villages of the countryside see very little of the money. Money is spent on the construction of bridges, roads, markets, and schools. The townspeople consider public works construction a sign of progress. At the same time little, if any, money is spent on matters of public health, for example, to hire doctors or to purify the water. The local government, while having a great degree of autonomy, is nevertheless responsible to the larger centers of power. At the same time local government is now, and always has been, deeply emersed in state-wide and nation-wide political events.

The political history of Minas Velhas is intimately linked with the political history of Bahia State and Brazil. The rise and fall of leaders in the government of the county reflect the fortunes of the state and national politics. The town is divided into several political factions. There are three parties represented in town—P.S.D. (Social Democracy Party), P.T.B. (Brazilian Workers' Party), and U.D.N. (National Democratic Union). The P.S.D. and the U.D.N. are the strongest in the county. Each has its local *chefe* (political boss). Patronage is the binding force within the party structure. The local chefes promise votes for the state bosses; the state bosses promise assistance in all matters requiring mediation between the county and the state.

Most of the posts in the local government are handed out by the victorious local party to the most active partisans. This disposition of spoils is capable of generating intense, and at times violent, party allegiances. With the power to pass out jobs at his command, the local chefe has the means to surround himself with a core of dedicated partisans.

In the local campaigns there is no question of opposing party platforms or dedication to specific reforms. Personalities are the only visible issues. The contest between the chefe and his challenger inevitably assumes the aspect of a struggle for power between two personal enemies. According to Harris (1956:196–197):

> It is often hard to tell whether people are enemies because they belong to different political parties or whether they belong to different parties because they are enemies. Townspeople with specific grievances against each other seem to identify with the opposite camps. In this way social snubs and hundreds of interpersonal and interfamily frictions eventually come to be seen as part of the political struggle.

> In both camps there are partisans who look upon the opposition as people without honor. This conflict between personal enemies compounded with the struggle for spoils is sufficiently widespread to involve the whole town. The party line bisects the heart of Minas Velhas like an open wound.

In Minas Velhas, there are two barbers, and many people choose between barbers on the basis of their political preference. Similarly, the store an individual shops at is very likely to be determined by the owner's political preference.

The political schism has some effect on almost every aspect of town life. Even churchgoing has its political facet. The current priest is extremely active in political matters. He was formerly the mayor of a neighboring county. In Minas Velhas he is president of the P.S.D. and a member of the town council. Many members of the U.D.N. do not frequent the church on this account.

Political campaigns afford the townspeople a great deal of welcomed action. The principal stores serve as informal party headquarters where the men gather in the evening to listen to news bulletins and campaign speeches on the radio. As election day nears, tension mounts between the two parties. Walls and sidewalks are painted during the night with campaign slogans and names, only to have them crossed out and replaced with contrary slogans and names the next night. Posters are put up, torn down, put up again. Firecrackers and rockets are set off almost without letup. Sometimes small bombs are thrown onto the roofs of houses owned by particularly active partisans. After the election returns are announced there are victory parades, dances, and speeches. On the day that the new mayor is inaugurated he is expected to provide food and drink to those who appear at his home.

The end of balloting, however, does not bring an end to political strife in Minas Velhas. Tension may even increase if the victorious local party does not also win the state-wide election. The local chefe who has lost the election begins asking favors from state officials of his party who have control of the state and its funds. He may even attempt to have the elected mayor ousted from his post on one pretext or another.

CONCLUSIONS

The chapter has presented glimpses of the diversity of the Latin American rural sector. The shortage of land has become a vital issue in this rural sector. The inhabitants of villages lacking sufficient land have traditionally met land crises either by working the land of others (in some form of patron-tenant relationship) or through migration.

Until recently, land reform programs have been initiated not by the landless farmers, but by powerholders within the government. In many cases these programs have been unsuccessful as only small portions of land have been turned over to the peasants. Within recent years, however, new pressures are being exerted as the small farmers of many regions have begun to form organizations to bring about more rapid reforms. The study of these changes is beginning to add a new dimension to the anthropology of the rural sector as reform programs, peasant organizations and the linkages between peasant organizations and government agencies are becoming phenomena to which anthropologists and other social scientists are now devoting their attention.[11]

RECOMMENDED READING

Foster, George M., 1967, *Tzintzuntzan: Mexican Peasants in a Changing World.* Boston: Little, Brown & Company.
The application of many of Foster's theories to the ethnographic data collected over a number of years in a Mexican village.
Landsberger, Henry A. (ed.), 1969, *Latin American Peasant Movements.* Ithaca, N.Y.: Cornell University Press.
A collection of papers dealing with peasant involvement in contemporary complex societies.
Mintz, Sidney W., and Eric R. Wolf, 1957, Haciendas and Plantations in Middle America and the Antilles. *Social and Economic Studies* 6:380–412.
A comparison of the economic and social relations of two major colonial and postcolonial institutions.
Stavenhagen, Rodolfo (ed.), 1970, *Agrarian Problems and Peasant Movements in Latin America.* Garden City, N.Y.: Anchor Books.
Like the Landsberger collection, these articles deal with peasants in the modern world. It brings together in a single volume a number of approaches to the vital issues involving peasants today.

RECOMMENDED CASE STUDIES
IN CULTURAL ANTHROPOLOGY

Rivière, Peter, 1972, *The Forgotten Frontier: Ranchers of Northern Brazil.* New York: Holt, Rinehart and Winston, Inc.
A rural population that is neither a plantation subculture nor a rural proletariat.

RECOMMENDED CASE STUDIES
IN EDUCATION AND CULTURE

Modiano, Nancy, 1973, *Indian Education in the Chiapas Highlands.* New York: Holt, Rinehart and Winston, Inc.
Deals with the process of socialization in a modern Indian area of Mexico.

---

[11] See for example Buechler 1968, Carroll 1964, Chevalier 1967, Chonchol 1965, de la Peña 1964, Dew 1969, Fals Borda 1965, Heath, Erasmus and Buechler 1969, Hobsbawm 1967, Kantor 1953, Landsberger 1969, Mendieta y Nuñez 1960, and Stavenhagen 1970.

CHAPTER 8

The urban sector

Since the Second World War parts of Latin America have undergone rapid urbanization. The growth of interest in the urban sector by anthropologists has been slow; however, considerable momentum developed in the 1960s. The first major anthropological study of a Latin American city was the study of Mérida, Yucatán by Redfield and Hansen in the late 1930s (see Chapter 5). In the early 1950s Ralph Beals (1951) provided a social charter for the anthropological study of the urban sector and Oscar Lewis (1952) revised some of Redfield's notions of urbanization based on his study of Tepoztecans who moved to Mexico City. In 1959 Lewis provided the first detailed description of slum life in Mexico City. Julian Steward's study of Puerto Rico included a study of San Juan's elite class by Raymond Scheele (1956). During the 1950s Andrew Whiteford (1960, 1964) applied Lloyd Warner's concepts of social class to his comparative description of Popayán, Colombia (a provincial capital of thirty-three thousand) and Querétaro, Mexico (a provincial capital of fifty thousand), publishing the first detailed description of stratification in Latin American cities by an anthropologist.[1]

While the study of the Amerind and the peasant community has generally been the exclusive domain of the anthropologist, the same is not true of the city. Other sciences, sociology in particular, have had a more extensive interest in Latin American cities and social stratification. Some of the important early research includes John Biesanz's studies of Heredia, Costa Rica

[1] For a review of urban studies in recent years see Kemper (1971) and Morse (1965, 1971).

(1944) and Panama City (1949, 1950; Biesanz and Biesanz 1955; Biesanz and Smith 1951), Theodore Caplow's study of Guatemala City (1949), Floyd Dotson's study of voluntary associations in Mexico City (1953), the Dotsons' study of Guadalajara, Mexico (1954), the Hawthorns' study of Sucre, Bolivia (1948a, 1948b), Norman Hayner's study of Oaxaca, Mexico (1944) and Mexico City (1945, 1946, 1948), and Olen Leonard's study of La Paz, Bolivia (1948). Of special importance was the publication of a five volume study of the Latin American middle class in a number of countries (Crevenna 1950–1951).

For the most part the anthropologists have limited their urban interests to the study of those urban peoples who are most like the rural sector—the lower class. With the exception of Whiteford's studies, there has been little attempt to view the total context of the city. Instead the anthropologist has focused on the Amerind and the peasant as he moved from the country to the city. A great deal of interest has been generated in the study of the adjustment of migrants to the city. In some ways it is unfortunate that anthropologists have limited themselves to the study of the lower sector. Often these individuals are socially isolated from the city in which they live. Studies of middle- or upper-class groups might provide a better understanding of the urban phenomenon. In any case, the case studies that are described in this chapter show a definite bias toward lower-class phenomena. This is due to the abundance of data on the lower-class slums and the sparsity of information relating to other sections of the Latin American city.

Why the Lower Class?   The newly arrived in the city and those who remain in the lower class share much in common with their rural counterparts. In an important article, George Foster (1953) demonstrates persuasively the similarities between the urban proletariat and the rural peasant not only in material culture but also in world view.

In many cases the anthropologist has undertaken research in the city due to the fact that so many of his informants have migrated there rather than because of an initial interest in the city itself. The anthropologist is faced with a wide range of variables making the traditional type of study attempted in the rural village impossible in the city. Finding it necessary to limit his universe, the anthropologist has generally restricted his study to a slum neighborhood, a shantytown, a housing project, or an even smaller unit such as a *vecindade* (apartment building) or, in the case of Oscar Lewis, individual families.

The emphasis on the urban poor seems a natural outcome of anthropological research in the rural areas. The anthropologist operates most effectively through personal contacts. As the people he knew in the country migrate to the city, it is logical that they and their friends and relatives will be his contacts and the people he will choose to study. They are often the only people he knows intimately in the city or they are city relatives of people he knew intimately in the rural area. His rural informants can speak for the anthropologist's inner soul (*dignidad*). It is sometimes advantageous for the informants to have an anthropologist living with the lower sector as friend and neighbor. He is a person with connections; someone of influence in a network of individuals who have no connections in the larger city as a whole and the rest of the nation. This aspect of urban research is especially well described by Lisa Redfield Peattie (1968) in her study of the La Laja barrio of Ciudad Guayana in Venezuela. During a controversy surrounding the placement of a sewer by outside agencies, she was asked to serve as one of three individuals representing the barrio to deal with the national agencies and their local representatives. She remarks, ". . . I was of unique usefulness to La Laja in being a person with some roots in the barrio who was, at the same time, clearly a member of the *gente buena* (established middle class), a 'Doctora,' a person of upper-class level." (Peattie 1968:87). Although anthropologists have not often reported the effects of their presence in the urban setting, it seems likely that in many cases the anthropologist is viewed as a patrón, a person of considerable wealth, power, and prestige—at least in contrast to the inhabitants of the slums.

There is a second factor that has focused the attention of the anthropologist on the lower class, that is, the difficulty of studying the middle and the upper classes. The more prestigious families of the Latin American city live in a closed network of kin and compadres. Friendships do not normally extend beyond business meetings. The non-kin are not invited into the home. Anyone coming to the door is looked upon with great suspicion and quite possibly not invited in. An anthropologist could live in an upper-class neighborhood and *never* become acquainted with many of his neighbors.

Development in Urban Latin America   Urban development in Latin America predates much of the urban development in Europe. The greatest cities of pre-Contact Latin America were Teotihuacán and Tenochtitlán in Mexico, Tikal in Guatemala, and Chan-Chan in Peru. At the same time, Spain was one of the leading urbanized areas of Europe between the ninth and the eighteenth centuries. Thus there were both native and Spanish groups merging in the New World who preferred the urban setting. The Spaniards who settled in the cities were the encomenderos who had been awarded the labor of various Indians who became the agricultural force that supported the urban Spanish.

During the first half of the sixteenth century many of the great cities of Latin America were developed under a systematic policy of urbanization directed by ordinances from the Crown.[2] Some were established on the sites

[2] See Hardoy and Schaedel (1969), W. Harris (1971), and Morse (1962) for recent discussions of urban development in Latin America.

of older Indian communities; others were new sites chosen specifically for their locations. When a new town was established the founding fathers were given the title of *vecinos* (neighbors). The vecinos were granted the encomiendas. Later, immigrants from Spain who settled in these communities were referred to as *habitantes* or *moradores* to distinguish them from the vecinos. The habitantes did not share the rights and privileges of the original settlers (Moore 1954:140–144). In 1740 it was estimated that in the average New World city there were eight habitantes for each vecino (Enríquez 1938: 31–36). The encomendero class eventually became the hacendado class, and throughout most of post-Contact Latin American history this group has remained the dominant social, economic, and political group.

The great cities of the Colonial and early Republican periods were preindustrial cities (see Sjoberg 1960). In other words these cities developed prior to the introduction of industry into Latin America. In more recent years a new style of urbanization has been taking place. It manifests the following characteristics: urban growth, industrialization, the rise of nationalism as the dominating and unifying political ideology, and in some cases the emergence of a middle class into power (Reissman 1964:168).

The preindustrial cities existed primarily as places of residence for aristocrats, the nobility, artisans, intellectuals, clerics, and merchants; there was no sustained economic pressure for expansion. With industrialization came rapid urban growth. The development of factories requires a relatively large and permanent labor force. The large concentrations of people require increased services to maintain them such as housing, sanitation, food, clothing, and amusements, all of which in turn create more jobs (Reissman 1964: 169–175).

Industrialization comprises a major economic shift from agriculture to manufacturing with important changes in capital formation, labor force composition, credit structure, and so on. Sometimes there is also a restructuring of power relationships. The emergent middle sector supplies the agents of change who challenge the existing power structure and in a few cases have brought about a social restratification. In other cases the elites merely transfer the center of their power from agriculture to industry (Reissman 1964:175–179).

Traditionally only a minority desires social change in the Latin American society. The majority of the population, the peasants and Amerinds at the bottom of the social hierarchy and the elite at the top, cling to things as they are. The middle sector is, however, highly committed to change in the established order so that it might reach new positions of power and effectiveness. In order to mobilize a society behind that movement there must be an ideology: a body of plausible beliefs that justifies the change for the good of society as a whole. The idea of nationalism is the most important such ideology. Differences between tribes, groups, individuals, and localities become submerged in favor of the nation as an entity which in turn becomes the focal point for one's primary loyalty (Reissman 1964:188–194).

THE SOCIAL STRATIFICATION OF CITIES

The nature of social stratification in Latin America is far from clearly delineated. Considerable controversy has raged over the importance of the concept "social class" as a descriptive device for Latin American societies and, in particular, the problem of conceptualizing the middle class.

Controversy of the Middle Class The early work of the sociologists led to the direct application of North American or European concepts of social stratification to Latin American nations without consideration of the differences in historical development between these culture areas. In most, if not all, countries of Latin America a middle class can be described if one considers only economic and occupational differences in the populations. Most of the middle classes described in *Materials para el estudio de la clase media* (Crevenna 1950–1951) were of this type. An important exception was raised by Lowry Nelson's (1950) description of Cuba, in which he denies the existence of a middle class at least in terms of how the Cubans perceived of themselves in 1950. It is the self-perception or identity that must be taken into account when discussing the middle class in Latin America. It is only in southern South America, where there was a large immigration of Europeans during the nineteenth century, that a middle class of the classic variety developed comparable to the middle class of Euro-American industrialism. For the balance of Latin America a basic cultural dichotomy persists between the "haves" and the "have-nots," each sector with its distinctive value system and different bases for social mobility (R. Adams 1967a:47–48).

In the lower sector the goal is wealth and the recognized means of obtaining it is work—physical labor. The upper sector has a variety of prestige symbols as its goal and the means of achieving them lie in the manipulation of power. Most of the groups identified as "middle classes" by the sociologists do not recognize themselves as such but rather operate in terms of the dual sectors that have existed in Latin America since early post-Contact. During all periods there were groups of individuals who did not identify with the lower sector, yet were not accepted as members of the upper sector. In the Colonial period the mestizos and mulattoes formed such groups.

Today, with industrialization in many parts of Latin America, a number of groups labeled "middle sectors" or "middle classes" have come into being due, in part, to the growing multiplicity of occupations. In some cases these individuals are former members of the lower sector who have become wealthy through work—often as a result of industrialization; however, they have not been accepted in the upper sector. In other cases there are individuals who were formerly members of the upper sector who have lost their wealth and are unable to maintain the traditional upper sector style of life. With the exception of the southern South American countries (and probably Costa Rica), those identified as middle class on the basis of economics and occupation generally do not have a specific class ideology of their own. Instead, as Ralph Beals (1953:330) has observed, "the orientation of the middle-status groups is toward traditional aristocratic upper-class values, although typical bourgeois attitudes and values are found."

While the middle class does not ordinarily have class self-identification, it does have a number of problems unique to the middle sectors. The middle class attempts to lead an upper sector way of life with what is often a lower sector income. While the lower sector uses its income for maintenance, the middle class must both subsist and conspicuously consume in order to maintain its chosen way of life. While the members of the lower sector survive through physical labor, the middle-class individual disdains such labor. His status is insecure. By avoiding working with his hands he hopes others will identify him with the upper rather than the lower sector. Besides maintaining a white-collar position, the middle-class individual must spend a large part of his income on status-maintaining items. The middle-class family employs maids, is well clothed, and lives in a respectable neighborhood. The middle class, because it consists of many with fixed salaries, fares poorly in an era of rapid inflation. To make ends meet individuals usually hold more than one job at a time, and most members of the family work as well. Money is not spent on items that do not affect status. For example, the family may spend very little money on food, living on a diet of beans and tortillas.

In contrast to the literacy of the middle class, the members of the lower sectors are illiterate. Because of electoral laws in many Latin American nations requiring literacy, the middle class joins with the upper sector as the voting members of the society. Literacy is important in promoting an awareness in the middle class not only of events but also of new consumer products. While the middle class is increasing in number and importance since the advent of industrialization, the lower and upper sectors still represent a basic dichotomy in Latin American society reaching back into the Colonial period.

The Culture of Poverty   As mentioned earlier, the lower sector has received the greatest amount of attention from the anthropologist. The poor are attracted to the city by hopes of acquiring great wealth. Many have come from rural areas where they barely survived through subsistence agriculture. Many fare no better in the cities and live in a state of "subsistence urbanization," to use Gerald Breese's term (1966:5), in which the individual has only the bare necessities and sometimes not even those for survival in the urban environment.

The populations of the large cities of Latin America have more than doubled in the past few decades and the growth of adequate housing and sanitation facilities has lagged far behind the massive exit from the rural areas. New slum areas have literally sprung up overnight. Many of the poor live in shantytowns in houses made from scraps of wood and cardboard. The poor are illiterate and generally unskilled. As a result, many of the destitute compete for a limited number of jobs. More than half of the employment force of the lower sector may be unemployed at any given time. Those employed are often paid to perform a particular task rather than being paid by the hour or by the week. Others consider themselves self-employed; however, in reality this may be a form of disguised unemployment. The man who sits on a doorstep eight hours a day selling three or four pairs of shoe-strings a week can hardly be considered gainfully employed. Yet with the almost insurmountable problems of surviving in the city, the members of the lower sector do not live in utter disorganization. They have evolved a way of life quite different from that of the upper sector that allows them to adapt to and survive in their particular environment. Oscar Lewis refers to this way of life as the "culture of poverty." The culture of poverty "represents an effort to cope with feelings of hopelessness and despair that rise from the realization by the members of the marginal communities in these societies of the improbability of their achieving success in terms of the prevailing values and goals" (Lewis 1966:5). According to Lewis, once the culture of poverty comes into existence it tends to perpetuate itself as do other cultures.[3] By the time slum children are six or seven they have generally absorbed the basic attitudes and values of their subculture. Lewis (1965:xlv–xlviii) has described four basic characteristics of the culture of poverty that he found in Mexico City, San Juan, and among the Puerto Ricans of New York City. First there is a lack of effective participation and integration of this lower sector in the major institutions of the larger society. (This was also characteristic of the inhabitants of the La Laja barrio of Ciudad Guayana described by Lisa Redfield Peattie.)

People with a culture of poverty produce very little wealth and receive very little in return. They have a low level of literacy and education, usually do not belong to labor unions, are not members of political parties, generally do not participate in the national welfare agencies, and

[3] There has been negative reaction to Lewis's concept (cf. Valentine 1968) by those who feel that Lewis is suggesting that people born into poverty can never really change. In this sense the concept has racist overtones. It is not meant to be used in such a deterministic manner in this text but rather as an adaptation to deprivation that will cease when the conditions being adapted to cease.

make very little use of banks, hospitals, department stores, museums or art galleries (Lewis 1965:xlvi).

Persons existing within the culture of poverty may be aware of some of the values of the upper sector but they do not live by them.

Second, there is a minimum of organization beyond the level of the nuclear and extended family. It is the absence of organization that keeps this sector marginal.

Third, on the family level there is the absence of childhood as a particularly prolonged and protected stage in the life cycle found in the upper sector; there is early initiation into sex, free unions or consensual marriages, a relatively high incidence of the abandonment of wives and children, a trend toward matrifocal families and consequently a much greater knowledge of maternal relatives, a strong predisposition to authoritarianism, lack of privacy, sibling rivalry, and competition for limited goods and maternal affection.

The fourth characteristic is one of helplessness; feelings of fatalism, dependence, and inferiority may be reflected in the large proportion of income spent on religious objects by the very poor. Oscar Lewis (1969) found that in the *vecindades* of Mexico City the poorest families had more invested in religious objects than in anything else. In one family the religious possessions represented nearly twice the total value of the furniture.

In its marginal position the culture of poverty has developed various means of adapting to its position within society. The individual in the midst of subsistence urbanization has the best chance of surviving if he is able to develop a network of individuals who will share with him. In the culture of poverty, as well as in the primitive band, sharing is a necessity. The rural peasant family may be able to operate quite independently of kith and kin; however, the peasant who migrates to the city finds himself forced to depend on others. While there is a certain amount of risk and possible failure in growing subsistence crops, the peasant usually has a patrón he can turn to if his crop fails. In most cases the peasant is at least assured of having food to eat. In the city the situation changes, and the migrant finds himself completely dependent on wage labor in a highly irregular labor market. Urban land is too valuable to be used for growing crops. Raw materials are not available to the family for making their own clothes, utensils, or houses, and the peasant family must rely upon money for the necessities. These factors create a situation in which those who are working support those who are not working. In the La Laja barrio of Ciudad Guayana, each individual who was working supported an average of five persons, not necessarily kin, who were not working (Peattie 1968:35). Those who have some type of housing share it with those who do not. Sharing is a form of insurance based on anticipated reciprocity. The individual shares with others because if tomorrow he is out of work and evicted from his rented home, he will have to rely on others to feed and house him. In the city the people of the lower sector have developed a large network of close and distant relatives and compadres who can be counted upon in time of need and to whom one must, in turn, give help.

The members of the lower sector of the city also adapt to their marginal economic position through considerable flexibility of occupation. Any and all means of producing an income are exploited: begging, collecting scraps of paper or metal, collecting old bottles, using the front of the house as a small store, and so on. Everyone works when he can. Boys shine shoes and guard automobiles. A young girl helps her mother by packaging peanuts or taking in washing. A woman who scrubs floors for a living may also become an "instant prostitute" if the opportunity arises.

In rural areas the poor channel their small surpluses into ritual extravagance. Money is spent on the sponsorship of fiestas by which a person gains prestige within the community. In the city the traditional forms of recreation are replaced by commercial forms of recreation such as movies, radios, and so on. The very poor drink alcoholic beverages as a major form of recreation. Commercial alcoholic beverages replace the native-made brew.

Just as there is flexibility in occupation, there is flexibility in family organization, and this allows the poor to adapt more successfully to their marginal position within the society. Common-law marriages are more frequent than formal marriages. Men and women live together until one or the other moves out. Normally the children remain with the female. But it is not uncommon for children to be farmed out to other relatives. This feature plus the sharing of household space with other relatives and compadres results in household arrangements quite different from the nuclear family of the upper sector. There is a considerable movement of individuals from one household to another. The situation is further complicated by imbalances in the sex ratio in various cities. In the city the woman, as well as the man, is a wage laborer. As a result a woman who is able to work is capable of supporting herself and any children she may have. She may receive monetary help at various times from different men but quite often will not form a stable relationship with any of them. These family arrangements are often called "disorganized" or "broken." Yet if they are to be viewed from a positive point of view they are merely adaptive forms in a situation of great economic uncertainty.

The Culture of Affluence   Land has formed the basis of wealth in the upper sector of Latin American society since the Colonial period. With land reform programs dispossessing some of the land belonging to the wealthy, they diversified by involvement in industrialization. As mentioned previously in this chapter, the literature on the upper sector is limited. Wagley and Harris's description of the metropolitan upper class type (see

Chapter 5) and Raymond Scheele's study of the upper class of San Juan, Puerto Rico (which will be described later in this chapter), were early attempts to analyze the upper sector. Whiteford's 1960 study described the upper class of Querétaro and Popayán. More recent studies include a biography of Julio di Tellio, the Argentinian industrialist (Cochran and Reina 1962), a study of Brazilian careers by Anthony Leeds (1965), and several studies of Latin American elites by anthropologists, sociologists, and political scientists (Bonilla 1970, Goldrich 1966, Lipman 1969, Lipset and Solari 1967, Stephens 1971, and Whiteford 1969).

The upper sector differs from the lower sector not only in wealth but also in power. Richard Adams (1967a:57) emphasizes that "It would not be too exaggerated to say that the entire internal structure of the upper sector may be seen as a series of relationships established and altered by virtue of a constant concern for gaining, retaining, and using power." The upper sector individual has a network of relatives and compadres he can depend upon—not for subsistence as is the case in the lower sector but for tactical advantage in order to maintain or expand his power base.

The upper sector dominates local and national politics as well as the economy. Women of this group are least likely to be employed. The family organization is one of stable nuclear families that have legal sanctions. The double sex standard is also followed, with many males maintaining more than one household. This group is the best educated; their children attend private schools locally or in foreign countries. The upper sector is also the most cosmopolitan.

Rural-Urban Migration   For migrants the process of urbanization actually begins in the rural areas. People become exposed to city ways long before they move to the city. In some rural areas an urban world view has developed, as for example in Minas Velhas, Brazil, which was described in the previous chapter. A similar phenomenon has been reported in Flores, Guatemala (Reina 1964) and in Costa Rica (Goldkind 1961; Olien 1967). In other rural areas the migrant entering the city experiences a shock resulting in various forms of disorganization such as alcoholism and mental illness.

The rural Indian or peasant who moves directly to the city is not the only migrant. Other types of migrants include those Indians and peasants who first move from villages to towns and smaller cities and then to the larger cities. Sometimes this movement takes a family several generations. In other words, the parents and children will move to the town and the children will later move to the city. Other than Rollwagen's (1968) study of the migration patterns of middle-class entrepreneurs in Mexico, little is known of the migration of the local middle and upper classes from rural towns and small cities to large cities.

Where does the migrant settle once he reaches the city? Generally the initial settlement is in one of three areas of the city: (1) the old center of the city usually composed of large colonial buildings that have been converted into apartment-type dwellings such as the vecindades in Mexico City (the settings for Oscar Lewis's studies); (2) the newly developed suburban areas where single-family dwellings (Dotson and Dotson 1956:46–47) predominate; and (3) the squatter or invasion settlements[4] usually located on the extreme urban fringe and generally lacking regular urban services. The housing is usually single-family dwellings placed on land to which the settler has no legal title but which is nevertheless purchased and sold. Most anthropological attention has been focused on the city center or squatter settlements. Little is known about the suburban developments of the middle and upper classes that are growing almost as rapidly as the slums within Latin American urban centers (Kemper 1970:4–5).

To understand the nature of urban migration in Latin America requires the collection of many life histories of migrants and probably the life history of families over several generations. Since the migration process involves the towns as well as the cities, migration patterns must be studied on a wider scale than has heretofore been the case. There is evidence that some migrants make temporary forays to the city before moving permanently (see the discussion of highland Peru in Chapter 7).

There is also evidence that the rural peasants who move to intermediate centers fill positions at the bottom of the socioeconomic structure, though many eventually improve their positions. As they move up the hierarchy they crowd others up and out who in turn move to the larger cities, while new migrants move into the intermediate centers to fill the positions at the bottom of the socioeconomic scale (Kemper 1970:6).

Several different types of urban subcultures are described in this chapter: life in the lower sector of Lima, Peru; Ciudad Guayana, Venezuela; and New York City; the middle class of Querétaro, Mexico; and the upper sector of San Juan, Puerto Rico.

THE BARRIADAS OF LIMA

While the slums of some Latin American cities are populated by people filled with despair, this is not true of all slums. Recent studies (summarized in Mangin 1967a) suggest that some of the slums, especially those that are squatter settlements, are quite different from previous characterizations. The standard myths about these settlements are as follows (Mangin 1967a:66):

---

[4] These settlements are referred to by a number of terms, such as *barriadas* in Peru, *favelas* in Brazil, *callampas* in Chile, *villas miserias* in Argentina, *cantegriles* in Uruguay, *barrios proletarios* in Mexico, *ranchos* in Venezuela, *barrios brujas* in Panama, and so on, throughout Latin America (Matos Mar 1966:13).

MAP 8.1 Communities of the urban sector.

1. They are formed by rural people coming directly from their farms.
2. They are chaotic and unorganized.
3. They are slums with high rates of crime, delinquency, prostitution, family breakdown, illegitimacy, and so on.
4. The slum dwellers represent a tremendous economic drain on the nation since unemployment is high and they are the lowest class economically.
5. They do not actively participate in the life of the city.
6. The slums are rural peasant or Indian communities reconstituted in the cities.
7. They are "breeding grounds" for radical political activity, particularly communism, because of resentment, ignorance, and a longing to be led.

From the studies of the barriadas (squatter settlements) of Lima, Peru by Doughty (1970), Mangin (1967b, 1970a, 1970b, 1970c), Matos Mar (1961, 1966, 1968), and John Turner (1965, 1970), the above mentioned impressions of the squatter settlements do not seem correct.

The barriadas of Lima, Peru, have grown from forty-five thousand in 1940 to four hundred fifty thousand of Lima's population of two million. Unlike the inner city slums that seem to attract the migrant initially, the squatter settlements are made up of individuals who were born in the provinces but had previously spent an average of nine years in Lima before moving into the barriadas (Mangin 1967a:68).

Rather than being chaotic, the barriadas show a relatively high degree of organization. When a group decides to start a new barriada considerable planning and cooperation are involved. The leaders must recruit enough families to move to the selected plot of land at one time to make the move a success. Lawyers are engaged to search land titles to find a site owned by some public agency, preferably the national government. The organizers visit the site at night and mark off lots. Building supplies for temporary housing must be purchased. A friendly newspaper and prominent political and religious figures who might be friendly to the invasion are informed. On the appointed day, often the eve of a major national or religious holiday, the people recruited for the invasion, numbering in the hundreds or even thousands, rush to the site in taxis, trucks, buses, and even on delivery cycles. Once at the site the families immediately put up shelters (made of matting) on their assigned lots. More than one hundred such invasions have taken place in Lima during the past twenty years. Once settled the barriadas maintain committees that screen incoming applicants and perform other duties. All of these activities require considerable organization (Mangin 1967b).

Although barriadas are sometimes described as centers of organized crime, the empirical evidence does not bear this out. Instead, they contain families who work hard and aspire to get ahead legitimately. The crimes that do occur are petty thievery, children damaging others' property, wife and child beating, and drunkenness. There are also some interfamily disputes over land titles, small debts, dogs, and so on. But in general this is social disorganization on a low level. Family and kinship relationships are strong and provide a degree of insurance in times of crisis (Mangin 1967a).

Rather than representing an economic drain on the nation, the squatter settlement actually makes important contributions to the national economy. First, the investment in housing and land improvement runs into millions of dollars. Although the initial housing is temporary and hastily built, the residents begin using their capital for constructing permanent houses, as well as for improvement of streets, lighting, and sanitary facilities. A second contribution is in the job market. Squatter settlements are seldom one-class communities. The inhabitants cover a wide range of occupations from garbage collectors through government employees, policemen, bank employees, store owners, teachers, lawyers, and doctors. Matos Mar (1961:180) also found that 71 percent of the active population of Lima's barriadas had stable employment and another 27 percent had casual employment. Most of these individuals are employed outside the barriadas in the city. The needs of the barriadas provide additional opportunities for employment for construction workers. Third, there is a tremendous proliferation of small enterprises. Once a barriada becomes established and accepted by the government, banks, movie theaters, and chain stores begin to appear. Fourth, the community makes possible investment in housing and neighborhood improvements and in the numerous small enterprises. The community also involves the inhabitants of the barriada in the life of the nation with a small but increasingly effective power base (Mangin 1967a:74–77).

The particular conditions created by the squatter settlements forcibly involve the inhabitants with the city. They keep up with news, become sophisticated in manipulating the national and international bureaucracies, play one political party against another, and become real estate and legal specialists. Jobs, marketing, schools, and kinship and voluntary associational ties keep most people in close touch with the city. Many of the squatters are literate and are quite concerned that their children receive a proper education (Mangin 1967a:78–79).

Although the squatter settlements have most frequently been described as rural communities in the city, this is not the case. The settlements are urban phenomena resulting from sophisticated urban decisions made by long-time urban residents, and the internal political organization is new and does not follow any rural pattern (Mangin 1967a:80–82).

The barriada does not appear to be a breeding ground for radical political behavior. The dominant ideology of most of the active barriada people appears to be very similar to the beliefs of the small businessman in nineteenth century United States and can be summed up in the familiar and accepted maxims: work hard, save your money, trust only family members, outwit the state, vote conservatively if possible—but always in your own economic self-interest, educate your children for their future and as old-age insurance for yourself. Aspirations are toward improvement of the local situation with the hope that children will enter the professional class. Aspiration levels for many of the adult migrants are relatively low and many of them feel that when they have a steady income, a house of their own, and their children in school, they have achieved more than they had believed possible (Mangin 1967a:82–85).

Why do people move to the barriada? Space at relatively low cost appears to be the main reason. The person moving to the barriada comes most frequently from inner-city slums where housing is extremely congested. Space is at a premium, therefore rents are extremely high. Few can afford to own their own home. At the same time the living conditions are miserable. These factors become especially crucial for young couples as they begin having a family. The squatter settlement offers the chance for free land with sufficient space to build a larger dwelling. The initial step following settlement is to build walls around one's property. Once the space is enclosed, then a roof can be added, rooms divided, permanent brick walls constructed, and a second floor added. While the barriadas are often great distances from places of employment, the money saved by not paying rent is usually more than enough to pay transportation costs to and from work as well as for building equipment.

Pampa de Cuevas: a Case Study   Pampa de Cuevas is a Lima barriada that was established in 1960.[5] It has a population of twelve thousand persons, most of whom had spent approximately ten years living in the city slums. The great majority of Cuevas settlers were motivated to become squatters by the desire to escape the high rents, the miserably poor conditions, the tyranny and the insecurity of slum life. For the average family of five or six, with an average monthly income of $90 (U.S. dollars), there are only two *legal* alternatives—to wait until the family's income has risen sufficiently (or until the family has accumulated sufficient savings) to buy and build in the lowest-priced subdivisions, or to wait for the chance to get a subsidized government project house. Many families reject the latter alternative even when they are among the small minority to whom the opportunity is presented. The great majority prefer the illegal alternative of squatting if the prospects of obtaining *de facto* possession are good, even if very considerable sacrifices must be made to obtain a plot and to build.

In December of 1959 the original Cuevas settlers, approximately five hundred adults from different parts of Lima, formed the "Associación de Padres de Familia Pro Vivienda," a community association for housing.

After considerable planning the Cuevas invasion took place the night of November 17, 1960. The police forced them off the land and the invaders (several hundred men, women, and children) camped along a nearby railway embankment while their leaders negotiated with the authorities. The government at that time was particularly anxious to avoid further invasion because it was about to promulgate a law designed to prevent further invasions and squatting by providing low-cost building land. The owner of the adjacent land, a wealthy man with political influence, was strongly opposed to the invasion that he saw as a threat to his property. As a "temporary measure" the invaders were permitted to set up an encampment on part of the land on Christmas Eve, five weeks later.

Either unknown to the authorities or disregarded by them, the associa-

5 This section is based on Turner (1970).

tion contracted five topographers to set out the blocks and individual plots. The plots were to have been ten by twenty meters (about two thousand square feet), but the majority were in fact only eight by sixteen and one-half meters. The association paid approximately $1,000 for the work that took two months to complete. Apparently permission granted the invaders to camp on the land was temporary but would allow time for the allocation of an alternative site. Over Christmas it was hardly considered humane, or even politic, to let so many apparently desperately poor families continue to live in the open. The families themselves had timed the operation well and had correctly calculated that once on the land they would have *de facto* possession. The invaders, therefore, risked their funds for the layout plan and as soon as it was completed each family transferred its temporary shack (made from woven cane mats wired to a light bamboo frame) to the plot allocated to it by the organizers.

During the first five weeks the squatters had literally lived in the open. Although it was during the summer, when there is no rain in the Lima area, camping with no equipment was a considerable hardship. Given the hope of a building plot of acceptable size on level land, reasonably near the city and adjacent to a public transport route, great numbers of people were encouraged to sit it out indefinitely rather than return defeated and demoralized to the city slums and the high rents from which they had escaped. As soon as the encampment on the site was established the association organized a school that provided primary education for adults as well as children. Many set up shops for vermicelli, candles, inca-cola, and other essentials. At first everything including water had to be carried up a footpath; however, once the families had moved to their plots, an access road was made through the cultivated land that separated the site from the main road in spite of the landowner's protests. Many felt themselves to be far better situated than they had been in the slums. Even with such primitive beginnings, a major part of their housing needs were satisfied. Each family had a fair size plot of land rent free and little or no fear of eviction. In terms of space, sunlight, and unpolluted air, their shacks were a vast improvement over the dark, unventilated, and crowded rooms on narrow, smelly, and noisy slum courts. There are hardships and expenses in Cuevas, such as having to buy water from doubtful sources at exorbitant rates (usually about fifteen U.S. cents per gallon drum). The lack of electric lighting reduces the opportunity for social life and study and increases a sense of physical insecurity. On the other hand, the absence of extremely inadequate, poorly maintained communal toilets with which the slum courts are equipped is of little or no disadvantage when there is a great deal of space for individual pit latrines. Transportation costs for the family as a whole are generally greater than before, though the extra cost rarely surpasses the savings made from not paying rent, as long as additional expenses are not required for travel to school and shopping facilities. Therefore, even for the minority of families whose cash expenditures are slightly greater than before (because of having to purchase water or to spend a greater amount of money on fares), the net gain in improved conditions is generally appreciable. With regard to personal security, it is invariably considerable.

CIUDAD GUAYANA: A PLANNED CITY

The discussion of life in the lower sector thus far has described life in settlements that grew fairly recently in a city established hundreds of years ago. Often these settlements developed in response to the government's attempts to provide planned low-cost housing. What happens to the lower sector when an entire city is planned?

Ciudad Guayana is a new city being built in the lower Orinoco Valley of Venezuela to stimulate the development of eastern Venezuela. Unlike other Latin American cities, Ciudad Guayana is a recently planned city; the project was formulated in Caracas, the nation's capital. Ciudad Guayana is being designed as if the planners were converting wilderness into a city; however, there are several small towns at the site that were in existence long before the original idea was on a drawing board. The architects have not considered the small towns in their plans for Ciudad Guayana. A steel mill and a copper mill were also present in the area before planning of the city. The population of four thousand in 1950 grew to surpass seventy thousand by 1964. Ciudad Guayana's projected population is approximated at over six hundred thousand by 1980.

Migrants create a particular problem for the government's planning agency, the Corporación Venezolana de Guayana (C.V.G.). Shantytowns are springing up at a much faster rate than the agency is able to compensate for in their planning. With nothing to lose by moving, the *campesinos* (rural inhabitants) come to the city. Thousands are pouring into Ciudad Guayana without education, skills, or the experience of urban industrial living. They come with the prevailing opinion that they have nothing to lose, and in large measure they are correct. Less apparent to them is the fact that they have very little to offer but their hands, arms, and backs. In a complex industrial setting there is little demand for unskilled labor. In Ciudad Guayana there is also the problem of single migrant women with families who have even less possibility of finding employment in heavy industry. There is little opportunity for a woman to earn money other than as a shopkeeper, domestic servant, or prostitute. The result of this lack of employment opportunity for the rural migrant is frustration, fear, and apathy. When adjustment is made and employment found, there are other problems to overcome. The city promises much but it exacts a toll by limiting freedom to live as one pleases. To the migrant the unoccupied land seems to be for the taking; yet this is not the case. The Corporación Venezolana de Guayana (C.V.G.) has its long-range plans for the city. Migrants are posted off land that is reserved for highways, parks, and industrial centers, and if they squat on the reserved areas the bulldozer will eventually move them (McGinn and Davis 1969:11).

Venezuela has one of the highest population growths in the world. The majority of the Guayana migrants, however, have not been crowded off farms by increased population pressures. In most cases they left low-yield *conucos* (small farms) many years ago to work in oil exploration and construction in the coastal areas, and as employment opportunities slackened, they moved to Ciudad Guayana. Word of mouth reports of brisk economic activity in Guayana have had a pronounced effect on migrants. Throughout eastern Venezuela rumors suggest that jobs are plentiful in Guayana. Yet migrants do not realize that the educational and technical skill demands of Ciudad Guayana's industrial job market are higher than the traditional qualifications of eastern Venezuelan camps. Workers often remain unemployed for lengthy periods after their arrival because of their lack of specialized training (McGinn and Davis 1969:46–47).

Why do the migrants remain? Ciudad Guayana has promise in the eyes of inhabitants. Often the very inconveniences that they suffer demonstrate the promise as old roads are torn up to make way for sewer and utility lines or for larger new roads. There is dust and mud because the bulldozers are always at work excavating sites for new housing. Urbanization is taking shape. The population of the planned housing is growing faster than that of the shack barrios in the ratio of three to two. The housing of many is improving, and people are moving out of the barrios and into planned housing in increasing numbers. Development housing was more plentiful for the higher and middle income groups when building first began, though it is now beginning to open to the lower income groups. Government sponsored housing is not available for the very low income households or for the unemployed, only for the wage earners with just below average incomes (McGinn and Davis 1969:63).

The settlers of the shantytowns present a legal complication to the C.V.G. which hopes to clear the shanty areas for their planned city. The legal rights of squatters are protected by the Venezuelan doctrine of *bienhechurías* (improvements). Under Article 557 of the Venezuelan Civil Code any person who improves, in good faith, the land of another is entitled to compensation upon removal from the land. Historically Venezuela has been a land-rich country, especially the eastern region. Under such circumstances the law has tended to favor the man who uses the land constructively. While the law on bienhechurías does provide for the element of good faith, it is in essence favorable to an improver on the grounds that the person whose land is improved would otherwise be receiving unjust enrichment. Thus when squatters are relocated they must be compensated by the government. If the cleared land is not reused immediately, it is occupied by a new group of squatters who must also be removed and compensated. For this reason the C.V.G. has tried to control all building, although unsuccessfully. At the same time, the squatters, recognizing the lack of clarity in official policy, continue their building knowing that they possess no real title and may be displaced at any moment but hopeful that condemnation will bring monetary compensation, thus converting their accumulated labor into hard cash (Doebele 1969:282–289).

William Doebele (1969:289) recounts how in one of the barrios he observed:

... a large rough barn-like structure in a squatting area, inside which, with infinite pains, a relatively successful immigrant family was constructing (in semi-darkness) a rather fine house. The plan was to escape the notice of the authorities during the sensitive period of construction, and then, when the proper moment came, to pull down the barn and reveal a *fait accompli* of such proportions that official counteraction would be embarrassingly difficult.

The View from La Laja   The anthropologist Lisa Redfield Peattie spent two and one-half years living in a slum neighborhood of Ciudad Guayana known as La Laja. This barrio came into existence in the 1940s through the settlement of wage laborers from the Iron Mines Company of Venezuela, an American-owned subsidiary of Bethlehem Steel. The barrio is situated just outside the Company fence. Only a small number of residents work for the Iron Mines Company today and many of the barrio's earlier founders have moved elsewhere. In 1962 it consisted of four hundred ninety inhabitants living in eighty household groups.

Houses in La Laja are constructed of one of the two main building materials, cement blocks or *bahareque* (earth mixed with manure and straw). Of these two materials, bahareque represents the traditional and rural, cement blocks the more modern and urban. The cement block houses are universally esteemed as the superior of the two. Houses built originally with bahareque may be rebuilt in cement block by building the new walls around or inside the old and then removing the bahareque. The first cement block house was built in La Laja ten years ago. Today over one-third of the dwellings are cement block (Peattie 1968:15).

Houses have strong "presentation" aspects oriented toward the street or public side, the exception being the homes of the very poor. The back yard, which is fenced with wire or opaque fencing, is the area for outhouses, washing, and similar outdoor activities rather than for social interaction with neighbors. Visiting with neighbors usually takes place on the paved strip in front of each house. The front door opens onto a *sala* (living room) which may be furnished, if economically possible, with a suite of plastic-covered upholstered chairs and a small "coffee table" on which the occupant will usually place plastic flowers in a plaster vase and perhaps a plaster statuette; on the walls hang enlarged photographs of family members, perhaps a picture of the "miraculous doctor," possibly framed photographs of smiling American girls leaning on new motor cars. In the kitchen and more "service" oriented areas to the rear of the house, the floor is most likely to be earth and here even a family that is able to afford plastic-upholstered furniture for the sala is likely to use the straight unpainted skin-seated chairs and plain tables. Almost all families in La Laja have at least one veneered bed and wardrobe that serve somewhat the same prestige and image-defining functions as the living room "set." However, there are often neither beds nor sleeping space for the entire family, the overflow usually being accommodated in hammocks that tend to be hung toward the rear of the dwelling, in the kitchen or yard (Peattie 1968:17).

Of the employed persons living in La Laja, the largest group (twenty-one) work at the steel mill. Eleven others are employed by the Orinoco Mining Company, a U.S. Steel subsidiary. Seven work for the Iron Mines Company, which had been the first impetus for the settlement. Eleven are in commerce, either as owners of small grocery and refreshment businesses or as ambulant salesmen. Twelve women are either domestic servants or take in washing and ironing. Nineteen persons have various occupations from school teacher to cab driver (Peattie 1968:35).

A great deal of the commercial activity takes place in La Laja itself. The barrio has six businesses, one for every twelve households. One is a small stand where produce and groceries are for sale and is owned by a family living in a small earth-daub house in the most physically and socially marginal part of the barrio; the proprietor is one of the four car owners in La Laja, having purchased a secondhand vehicle to use for hauling goods. Four businesses have more substantial *abastos* (stands) at which such staples as bread, plantains, sugar, margarine, powdered milk, soft drinks, and beer are sold in small quantities. These stands serve as social centers where men might play dominoes or pool, or drink beer. The proprietor of one of the abastos has almost relinquished his grocery business, being perpetually out of stock, and is now operating a small pool hall in its place. The sixth business is a licensed "bar," with dancing to jukebox music in the evenings, especially on weekends. Owners of these businesses are residents of the barrio. A seventh business, a small one-freezer meat market, was formerly located in the barrio but it was too marginal to survive even in the very small-scale commercial world of La Laja; the quantity of meat eaten in La Laja is not great and people preferred to carry their supply from the market or the company commissaries where the quality was better and the prices were lower (Peattie 1968:35–36).

Company wages not only support commercial life but are generally the sources of capital that make it possible for the worker to establish himself in business. Those whose earnings are more than enough to cover family expenses attempt to invest in equipment that will bring more money into the family. On a small scale this may mean buying a refrigerator that would take care of the family's food storage needs, as well as provide added income from the sale of ice and Pepsi-Cola. To start a small grocery takes very little more than the initial investment. Another common way of translating money capital into a source of income is to build or buy a house for rental. Approximately twelve persons living in the barrio own houses that they rent to others. Some people own houses in other barrios and receive rent in amounts of up to four hundred bolivares a month. The companies are important in capital formation at the individual level not only as a source of capital but as agglomerators of capital; it is the lump sum payment made annually under Venezuelan labor law, or, on a larger scale, the substantial payment to employees upon termination of employment that is characteristically translated into refrigerators and rental houses (Peattie 1968:37).

La Laja definitely thrown its lot in with the city and the cash economy. The poor of La Laja may raise chickens but they cannot really earn a living doing so. They are, in fact, earning their way using others. They become dependent upon the persons in the barrio who have found themselves niches in the modern sector of the economy. Their cognitive orientation is toward the modern world of mass-produced consumption goods and toward the world of personal relations giving them access to it. Because they do not have the skills, they cannot be full participants in the modern world, but they are hangers-on.

People who live at the margins of the urban economy seem to develop variants of the life style identified as the "culture of poverty" in widely different parts of the world. In the life situation of the La Laja barrio, long-term planning of resources becomes not only difficult but nonadaptive. People living in the cash economy and having no skills or social position with which to derive security find their only possible security to be social relations with others. In the short run it may be more useful for the unemployed laborer to spend the afternoon drinking beer and keeping up his contacts than it would be for him to spend the time looking for a job he is quite unlikely to find.

THE HISPANOS: PUERTO RICANS IN NEW YORK

While the Mexican-Americans of the United States are usually stereotyped as a rural agricultural population, the Puerto Ricans of the United States are stereotyped as an urban slum population. To a very great extent the stereotype is correct. Prior to the Second World War there had been a small but steady migration from Puerto Rico to the mainland, especially to New York City. Most came by steamship from San Juan—New York being the cheapest and most direct route. The least expensive passage was $40 and the voyage took from three and one-half to five days (Chenault 1938:56). By 1930 there were fifty-three thousand Puerto Ricans living in the United States, of which forty-five thousand lived in New York City. Between 1940 and 1950, with a labor shortage in the United States caused by the war, immigration increased 206 percent in New York and 443 percent in other states. By 1955 there were some five hundred fifty thousand Puerto Ricans in New York City and one hundred seventy-five thousand outside of New York. This rapid increase in migration was made possible by inexpensive air travel. It now takes only a few hours to travel from San Juan to New York City.

Why have so many Puerto Ricans migrated? First, there has been a tremendous population increase in Puerto Rico creating a limited job market, particularly for unskilled labor. The migration frequently takes place in two steps. First the small farmer leaves the countryside and migrates to San Juan, Puerto Rico's largest city. In Lewis's (1968:121) sample of fifty Puerto Rican families in New York City, two out of three family heads had been born in rural areas and later moved to San Juan. Most lived in a San Juan slum. Eighty-two percent of the families had migrated from a San Juan slum, 6 percent from an urban nonslum region, and only 12 percent came directly to New York from a rural area of Puerto Rico. While the slum dweller of San Juan experiences a push to migrate from Puerto Rico, he also experiences a pull from New York. Most of the individuals in the sample had relatives living in New York City. The Puerto Ricans of New York generally paint a rosy picture of life in the city. It is true that the wages are much higher in New York than San Juan; however, so is the cost of living.

In Puerto Rico, families own their own homes, even if they are one-room shacks. In New York City one has to rent an apartment. Since the 1950s apartments have been scarce and at a premium. The rent is high and it is not unusual to be told that an additional $1,500 in cash is expected for the privilege of moving in and for the use of the furniture contained in the apartment. A renter of an unfurnished apartment may have to spend an amount of up to $800 for the key before he is able to move in (Padilla 1958:7).

The Puerto Rican has an added expense for clothing in New York City that he would not have had in San Juan. Puerto Ricans arrive without the proper clothing for the city's winter months. Clothes are an important status symbol in the mainland setting. In Lewis's New York City subsample (1968:173) of nine families, it was found that they had spent anywhere from 1 percent to over 50 percent (a 34 percent average) of their total income on clothing.

When the Puerto Rican arrives in New York City he settles in a section of the city with a large concentration of Puerto Ricans. Spanish Harlem is the largest of the Puerto Rican. settlements. The migrant learns to refer to himself as a "Hispano" or a "Latino" rather than a Puerto Rican. In the past, Hispanos or Latinos were a small minority of intellectuals and middle-class professionals from Puerto Rico, Spain, and Latin America living in New York City. By 1950 the Spanish-speaking socially mobile persons of lower-class origins, who now considered themselves to be of a higher social position than the recent lower-class migrants from Puerto Rico, were calling themselves Hispanos. More recently the term has been extended to include all Spanish-speaking persons who reside in New York City regardless of their social and economic class (Padilla 1958:33).

The Hispanos classify themselves into three major groups with reference to life experience and time spent in New York City. Those who have lived there for many years (*los que llevan muchos años aquí*) are the first group. Those who grew up in this country, including the second generation, *nacidos y criados* (born and brought up), and those born in Puerto Rico who came to New York City in early childhood comprise the second group. Migrants who have arrived from Puerto Rico in recent years constitute the third group and are referred to as "Marine Tigers"[6] by members of the first two groups (Padilla 1958:35).

Many Hispano households and family forms often do not conform to the patterns of the larger society. In Puerto Rico a consensual marriage that meets the standards of a good marriage gains as much social approval as a legal one and those involved in such a relationship are not considered to be "living in sin." The same is true within the Hispano society in New York City. Yet in relation to local and national governments, there are direct sanctions from the larger society against the consensual form of marriage. Lack of proof of legal marriage may disqualify a low-income person from obtaining an apartment in city-owned low-rental buildings. Professionals may take it upon themselves to deny service to a child unless his parents marry legally (Padilla 1958:102).

Family ties are extremely important in the Hispano community. Most Hispanos have some relatives already living in New York City when they arrive from Puerto Rico. Relatives are especially necessary in the early adjustment to the city. Frequently the immigrant will move in with relatives

---

[6] *Marine Tiger*, a derogatory term, was the name of one of the Liberty ships that made a number of trips between San Juan and New York City after the war, bringing many thousands of Puerto Ricans to the States. It lent its name to the newly arrived and the name has continued to be used.

until he finds work and an apartment of his own. Lewis (1968:132) found that 70 percent of the family heads in his sample stayed with relatives; another 16 percent lived with friends. The arrival of immigrants places new strains on the often crowded living conditions of the Hispanos. Immigrants expect their relatives to take them into their homes when they arrive. The arrival of either parents or children is generally harmonious; the arrival of siblings creates the greatest tension. Sibling relatives tend to move out more quickly than either parents or children. The ties between relatives are, however, less intense than in San Juan, where almost no request from a relative would be refused.

The ties of compadrazgo (coparenthood) are also found in New York, though they are less binding than in San Juan. Unless the Hispano is a relative, the immigrant often does not know much of the person's background. In San Juan the potential compadre is well-known, but this is not possible in New York City. The Hispanos believe it is important for a child to have godparents for baptism. Thus the focus is shifted from the ties between parent and godparent, as is the case in most of Latin America, to the relationship between the child and godparent. Yet even here the relationship is not a strong one. Often the child doesn't know who his godparents are, especially if the fictive kin should move from the neighborhood.

In the poorer families there are serious adjustments to the new educational system. Many of the Hispano children drop out of New York schools at an early age. A major problem for many immigrants is learning English, and generally only the children tend to be fluent in the language. One who has migrated during his adult lifetime often has poor control of English and, as a result, is severely limited in searching for a job. His lack of technical training has already limited the type of work he can do. His inability to speak English, or at least sufficient English, means he can be hired by only the few Hispano operated companies in the city or at a job where there is someone who can act as a translator. Women are often slower than men in learning English and are limited only to jobs requiring sewing skills or as domestics for other Hispanos. Sometimes Spanish is purposely used by Hispanos with considerable Negro admixture to keep from being mistaken for the American Negroes of the same slums.

The Hispanos distinguish between "ancient" (*a la antigua*) and "modern" families. The family that is rigidly ruled by the father or the mother is called "ancient" and is different from the "families of today." The ideal of greater leeway and tolerance for the children is more distinct among young adults whether they are recent Puerto Rican arrivals or raised in New York City. As a rule the younger parents are better educated than their parents, have broader outlooks, and uphold the idea that there should be fewer restrictions placed on children by the parents. Among adults whose fathers were of the "ancient" type and whose mothers suffered either by infidelity, mistreatment, physical punishment, or desertion of the family, there is outspoken criticism of the "ancient" type of family. Yet even in the "modern" families, decisions about family affairs reside in a central authority, usually the father. The difference is that the authority is more flexible, less restrictive, and less formidable (Padilla 1958:150). For many immigrants, the increased freedom of the children and the wives is seen as a negative, and in some cases the worst, feature of living in New York City.

In San Juan, the housewife makes frequent daily trips to a nearby store to purchase a few items at a time and in very small quantities. Often shopping is done before each meal. This pattern is impossible to follow in New York City. The grocery stores are often several blocks away and it is tiring to climb the flights of stairs in the tenements. With the exception of a few small local grocery stores, food cannot be purchased on credit (Lewis 1968:142–143).

The Hispanos not only interact within the neighborhood but also have contacts with the larger society. Hispanos are invariably in a position subordinate to that of the official or the professional. The relationship between them is based on the service the professional or official renders. Barely do they consider each other friends. The official is in a position that gives him authority over the Hispano, and he enjoys a high social status and greater prestige than does the Hispano in the society. It is usually as a job seeker, an applicant to a social agency or in some other status of the underprivileged of the society that Hispanos appear to the professional or white-collar worker (Padilla 1958:249–250).

THE MIDDLE CLASS OF QUERÉTARO, MEXICO

The Bajío[7] of central Mexico is one of the country's richest farming areas. During the Colonial period it was a frontier mining area. León, Guanajuato, Silao, Irapuato, Salamanca, San Miguel Allende, Celaya, and Querétaro formed a nucleus of cities that attained great wealth in commerce, mining, agriculture, and industry and developed a cultural and administrative complex independent of the central government in Mexico City. Querétaro became an important textile manufacturing center. It was founded in 1531 and serves as the capital of the State of Querétaro.[8]

With limited control over Querétaro from Mexico City a local aristoc-

[7] The region known as the Bajío extends from León in Guanajuato to the city of Querétaro in the State of Querétaro. See Wolf (1957) for a discussion of the historical setting of Querétaro.
[8] Unless otherwise noted, this section is based on Whiteford's (1960 and 1964) study of Querétaro. At the time of the study, Querétaro had a population of fifty thousand inhabitants.

racy and a large proletariat developed. A middle class of merchants, entrepreneurs, artisans, and others also developed. However, the middle class of Querétaro today is not the direct descendant of this colonial middle class. Instead the middle class has fluctuated, sometimes becoming almost obliterated and then growing again with new personnel and in somewhat different directions. As times changed, as revolutions toppled one group and raised another, different kinds of people filled the ranks of the middle class; clever peons moving up, aristocrats whose fortunes had dwindled. This does not mean that the middle class in Querétaro consists simply of a loose amalgam of ambitious lower class people and declining members of the upper class. It is not merely an undefined area between the extremes of society. It actually possesses in itself a reality that gives its members a sense of identification and position. Its members interact with each other, conscious of the social position they share. They are proud of the characteristics that distinguish them from the other classes (Whiteford 1964:98–99).

The middle class of Querétaro can be classified into three subdivisions: the *clase media acomodada* (comfortable middle class), hereafter referred to as the upper middle class; *clase media sin dinero* (middle class without money), hereafter referred to as the middle middle class; and the *clase media sin cultura* (middle class without culture), hereafter referred to as the lower middle class. In outlook the upper middle and middle middle are very similar, differing mainly in the amount of money available to carry out their desired life styles.

The upper middle class includes lawyers, doctors, engineers, merchants who own prosperous businesses, bank managers, and some moderately wealthy farmers. Characteristically these families own their homes, possess a car, and dress well. Education is regarded as important by these families and most of the men have attended a university and are sending their sons to private secondary schools. The homes of the upper middle class families are well furnished, food is plentiful and varied, and most own such luxuries as refrigerators, radios, phonographs, and television sets. Sons enter their fathers' businesses or study for the professions, and daughters help their mothers in the home or attend commercial institutes to learn to become secretaries in their relatives' offices or in one of the new industrial concerns. Every family has at least one maid.

The middle middle class includes those families who in spite of meager income ($32 to $80 per month in contrast to $240 to $400 per month for the upper middle) strive to maintain a respectable middle class style of life patterned after the upper middle class: dressing carefully, maintaining good manners, valuing the cultural aspects of life, and exerting themselves to procure an education for their children. This is the "white-collar class" of Querétaro and includes public schoolteachers, many merchants with small businesses, and a growing number of clerks and accountants who work in the banks, the offices of local industries and the various agencies of the municipal, state, and federal governments. The members of this group emulate the upper middle class as much as their inadequate incomes will permit. They fear that they will lose their identification with the upper sector as a result of insufficient funds to maintain what they consider the proper style of life and that they will decline into the lower sector. The designation "*sin dinero*" (without money) expresses the most significant and most compelling single factor in the middle middle class.

The subdivision of the middle class called *clase media sin cultura*, the lower middle class, includes those families with incomes roughly the same as the middle middle class but who do not suffer as much from their deficiencies because they use their money for different ends. They are high ranking members of the working sector. Thus the greatest gap is between the lower middle and middle middle class. The middle middle identifies with the upper sector; the lower middle with the lower sector. The members of the lower middle class tend not to be intimately exposed to the upper middle class style of living and hence are not motivated to emulate the life style. While they do respond to the obvious value of material possessions, their level of education is generally considerably lower than that of the men of the middle middle class. A few of them are lower level government clerks, though the majority are skilled workers or artisans: watchmakers, postal employees, midwives, typesetters, electricians, printers, cabinetmakers, mechanics, and skilled workers on the railroad or in one of the industries such as the Singer Sewing Machine Company. Some of the owners or operators of small stores are included in this category (R. Adams 1967a:48–50; Whiteford 1964:105).

Almost all subdivisions of the middle class support civic and church organizations in one way or another. The men of the upper middle class frequently express a sense of civic and moral responsibility and take an active interest in the Lions Club, the Rotary, and, to a lesser extent, in the Knights of Columbus. Some of the younger men belong to a hunting and shooting club, a few belong to the chess club, and the membership of the small tennis club that sends representatives to play against the clubs of other cities is almost completely upper middle class. Both the young men and their elders play cards, dominoes, or billiards at the Casino Club which is maintained by the Lions. There are a few cafes or taverns where men of various occupations meet in the afternoon to discuss business and other items of mutual interest. The men of this class, though more particularly the women, participate in the lay associations of the Church, the program of Catholic Action, in charitable enterprises and in the fairs and bazaars that are given to raise funds for the Church or for the parochial schools. These activities are valued by the women, not only because it gives them an accepted reason for activities outside the household but also because it

Upper middle class family on Sunday picnic, Querétaro, Mexico.

brings them into contact with the families of the upper class and gives them an opportunity to participate in "good works."

In the upper middle class families, as in the families of the upper upper class, girls are strictly chaperoned. Because most of the eligible young men of this class and the lower upper class (the nouveau riche) are away at school, young girls have difficulty finding escorts who meet with their parents' approval. Many of the girls enroll in various courses at the university or the commercial institute in order to relieve their boredom and perhaps eventually to find respectable stenographic positions that will give them some freedom. In Querétaro the presence of university students does very little to mitigate the situation as most are regarded as lower middle class. Cut off from the most attractive young women of the city and apparently not absorbed by the weight of their studies, the students move about in gangs looking for excitement and in the process frequently conduct themselves in ways that make parents even more determined to shield their daughters from the students' unwelcomed attentions.

The upper middle class of Querétaro is progressive in ideal and conservative in fact, deeply concerned with the attitudes of others toward it yet determined to maintain certain modes of life and manners of thinking that it is convinced represent "the good life" for itself and for the community. It regards intellect and education as the means to eventual salvation, and it honors liberty while restraining it in the interests of the preservation of the family with its almost Victorian code of morals and womanly honor.

Of those Querétanos who belong to the broad middle class, the members of the middle middle class category are probably most acutely aware of their position in the total society. These are the people who are referred to, and who refer to themselves, as the *clase media sin dinero*. They are white-collar workers; people who generally do not work with their hands, who usually have at least a secondary school education, whose pride demands that they dress neatly although they can rarely afford to dress well, who stretch their meager incomes by almost every device to maintain respectability, and who share the value system and behavior pattern of the upper middle class to the extremes of their ability. This subdivision does not constitute a completely homogeneous bloc. The Revolution was responsible for one major ingredient of the middle middle class, the former hacendados and families of wealth and education who now find themselves reduced to low-income clerical positions. The second major ingredient consists of talented and/or ambitious members of the lower class and lower middle class who have worked their way up the social ladder and find a sense of achievement in the new forms and values that introduce them into the culture of the upper segments of Querétaro society. This group encounters a strange new world that demands different behavioral patterns from those to which they are accustomed. Some social climbers find it completely alien and in rejecting it are diverted into the lower middle class, though some see it as a challenge of self-improvement and carefully absorb it to bury themselves as inconspicuously as possible in the beliefs and manners of their newly achieved social status. They are circumspect, they are genteel, they are moderate and basically conservative, they support the Church and its associations, join the Knights of Columbus, and aspire to membership in the Rotary. Increasingly they take pride in their middle class status, espouse education, culture, and good works and develop a disdain for the uncouth lower class and the uncultured lower upper class.

Everything in the life of a member of the middle middle class is bound by the restrictions of his meager financial income. As a respectable member of the middle class he has to maintain his personal appearance and to dress his family well. Even with the most careful selection and the cooperation of the women of the family in making their clothing, a substantial part of the family's monthly salary is absorbed in keeping the family clothed. With rent payments and the expenses of sending children to school, little money is left for food or recreation. Meat appears on the table infrequently. Tortillas and beans form the staple elements in the diet. Very few families can afford automobiles. Evening strolls around the plaza, public band concerts, and the activities of church organizations serve as major pastimes. An occasional movie or a soft drink at one of the restaurants on the plaza is considered a special treat. Occasionally the men play chess and dominoes at home or at the chess club.

The cultural discontinuity that exists between the middle middle class and the lower middle class is probably a reflection of the traditional Spanish disdain for hand labor. Most of the men in the lower middle class are workers; some are clerks or white-collar office workers of the lowest ranks in the post office or similar institutions. The most typical examples are the owners of small shoe stores, clothing stores, and other modest enterprises in which a few clerks or workers are employed at very low wages. Some entrepreneurs work in their small printing shops setting type and operating the presses; others hire men to help them to do mechanical work in their garages, to assist them in their plumbing or masonry work, or to work with them in their carpentry shops. These men of the lower middle class all work at their trades, but they are also businessmen in that they hire labor, contract for work, and purchase supplies. All of them have an investment in equipment, and their major assets are their own experience and training.

The heritage of the lower middle class is the culture of poverty, the tradition of peonage and ignorance. The members of this class have moved into a new world, one that had been completely closed to their fathers, bringing with them almost nothing but ambition and energy. Their lack of education closes many doors, yet their ignorance of Spanish traditional culture is a major advantage because they are unaware of the many taboos, and by naive insolence and perseverance are able to achieve success. Continued progress and improvement for them lies not so much in the propriety and intellectualism of the upper sections of the middle class but in the more materialistically oriented, property- and power-respecting circles of the lower upper class (the nouveau riche). The very successful families in the lower subdivision of the middle class simply grow richer and richer, and usually more and more gaudy, until they suddenly find themselves in the lower upper class by virtue of their potential financial power, their ambition, and the sheer weight of their possessions. Often they acquire better houses, more clothes, and bigger cars than any of the middle middle class and many of the upper middle class. They are still uneducated and crude, yet they are envied, emulated, and respected by almost all members of the lower class who accord them considerable prestige.

There appear to be two distinct modes of social mobility in Querétaro. Traditionally the first is the climb from the lower class up through the subdivisions of the middle class to ultimate acceptance in the upper class, through the acquisition of education and culture concurrently with at least a limited accumulation of wealth. This traverse is sometimes accomplished in a single lifetime, though more frequently it requires several generations. The second mode of mobility, the material, occurs when a man or a family moves from the lower class to the lower upper class through the exercise of good fortune, great skill, superior intelligence, bold opportunism, or some potent combination of them all. The precedent for such a mode was established by the military figures and politicians who, since the epoch of revolution, suddenly moved into positions of power, acquired great wealth and became the leading figures of society—all without benefit of education and proper etiquette.

No group is more concerned with social mobility than the members of the middle middle class. Almost all of them nurture hopes of someday moving upward. They aspire to membership in the upper class, or at least in the upper middle class. At the same time, they struggle to suppress their fears of declining into the lower middle class or even the lower class. Generally their fears are more realistic than their aspirations, as their financial positions are often quite precarious. A misfortune such as illness in the family or loss of employment because of changing conditions might easily result in social disaster if they are forced to turn to some type of hand labor in order to sustain themselves. Such a decision is strenuously resisted, for these people possess few skills that will allow them to become artisans and failure to find work as an *empleado* (white-collar worker) often means physical labor and reduction to the lower class. Social decline is rarely so drastic, though it sometimes occurs when daughters rebel against their families and marry mechanics or young construction workers, or when sons resent their families' pretensions and accept jobs beneath their status—but from which they earn a decent living. Many middle middle class families are relatively static in terms of mobility. For example, some families produce teachers and others produce clerks and accountants generation after generation. They are oriented toward the upper sector of the social scale but rarely able to effect any substantial improvement in their position. To move upward from this position is very difficult. Their acceptance of upper middle class mores that emphasize discretion, gentility, intellectualism, and morality makes it almost impossible for them to participate in any of the few activities that might produce wealth. However, any of these people who can acquire wealth are assured of acceptance in the upper middle class and some even in the upper upper class.

Many members of the upper middle class do not permit themselves to become socially ambitious because of their pride in the superiority of their class, yet none of this group is resistant to acquiring greater wealth. An upper middle class merchant or doctor who does become wealthy is faced with the dilemma of maintaining his middle class standards of moderation and cultivated lack of ostentation or using his wealth for clothes and cars and houses—in which case he claims a new status in the lower upper class.

THE AFFLUENT OF PUERTO RICO

Following the Spanish-American War, the Island of Puerto Rico became a possession of the United States. Until this time Puerto Rico held the same traditions as other Latin American countries. Following the turn of the century, North American business with its North American culture and technology began making inroads into Puerto Rico. The American way of life now has prestige on the island. The ordinarily conservative upper sector has been affected to a considerable degree by North American influences. Most of the transformation has taken place since 1940. In 1952, with the approval of the Congress of the United States and with the support of more than 80 percent of the voters of Puerto Rico, the island became the Commonwealth of Puerto Rico, voluntarily associated with the United States.

Puerto Rico is a small island, approximately thirty-five miles wide by one hundred and five miles long, and it is dominated by the city of San Juan. The city has almost four hundred fifty thousand of the island's total population of two million eight hundred fifty-four thousand. Almost all of the upper sector is concentrated in San Juan. Traditionally wealth was based on ownership of land. Sugar cane, tobacco, and coffee were the major commercial crops. With the Americans came industrialization, and a new managerial class was formed that merged with the old landed aristocracy, some of whom have extended their interests into industry to form a new upper sector. As is true of most upper class groups in Latin America, less is known about the upper class of San Juan than is known about the slums or the rural communities. So far there have been only two brief analyses of the Puerto Rican upper sector, a study of one hundred businessmen by Thomas C. Cochran (1959), an economic historian, and a study of two hundred households of prominent families by the anthropologist Raymond L. Scheele (1956) as part of Julian Steward's Puerto Rico Project.[9]

The affluent of San Juan are represented by a core consisting of approximately two hundred extended families and eight hundred nuclear or conjugal families. The prestige and status of these families rest upon wealth from an acceptable source, racial and ethnic characteristics, family background, correct behavior and attitudes, and education.

These families reported a minimum income of $6,000 annually; some reported $200,000 and over. To maintain some semblance of living standards acceptable for prominent people, a minimum of $6,000 is required. The major sources of income are from commerce, the professions, and finance. Additional sources include sugar production, government service, and to a much lesser extent coffee production and cattle. There are many

[9] Unless otherwise noted, this section is based on Scheele (1956).

who have gained their wealth rapidly and lack the social prestige necessary to be a part of the prominent families. Sometimes the nouveaux riches are rejected by the prominent families in spite of their wealth, either because they acquired their wealth too recently or because it came from dubious sources such as bootlegging.

On the island most of the population shows all manner of mixture of white, Negro, and some Indian. "Whiteness" has become associated with the upper sector. A person who has marked Negro physical characteristics and is therefore described as a Negro may have high income, great political power, and an advanced education, yet on racial grounds he may be excluded from the inner circles of intimate family life, Greek letter sorority or fraternity membership, and the more select social clubs. He may attend political affairs, be a guest at the Governor's palace and receive invitations to political cocktail parties because people wish to cultivate his friendship; however, he probably would not be invited to more private functions.

A college education has become a basic requirement for men in this subculture because the business and professional skills needed cannot be acquired without training. Many of the young people attend college or graduate school in the United States, although many others attend the University of Puerto Rico, at least for a few years. While Scheele emphasizes the widespread use of English in his sample, Cochran questions the ability of many of his informants to speak English. In any case, the use of English and the motivation to master it is greater among the elite than in any other group in San Juan.

There are a few individuals who have the characteristics required for acceptance in upper class circles yet are not interested in involvement with this group. Others are excluded or expelled because they disregard its conventions. Thus one who marries a person classed as a Negro or an undesirable for other reasons may lose his position.[10]

Conformity with all of the criteria for group participation does not suffice for admission into the upper class. Even good taste in clothing, art, music, and other esthetic features is not enough. Apparently the crucial factor or criterion is a sensibility to the very finely graded prestige system within the group itself, the ability to rank everyone within the upper class. This ability can be acquired only through intimate knowledge of the in-group, through participating in its social functions and above all being counseled by women in-the-know. Another aspect of the required sensibility to social nuances within the class is the ability to recognize and maintain social distance between classes. Since social functions vary in their inclusion of

---

[10] One of the exclusive upper class clubs in San Juan decrees that when a member marries a nonmember, he must apply to have his wife accepted as a member. If the application for the spouse member is refused the member may resign, thus admitting loss of status.

limited cliques and larger groups within the upper sector, it is necessary to treat the participants in appropriate degrees when associating with in-group participants. Since the larger social context within which the upper sector lives is rapidly changing, the importance of these new sensibilities has increased.

The business life of the Puerto Rican executive differs from that of the North American. The Puerto Rican executive maintains a patriarchal position over his employees. All matters not covered by routine procedures are brought to him. His subordinates are not free to make independent decisions. There is a tremendous dependency on the owner-executive. As employees seek the aid of the head of the firm in any and all problems, including some personal ones that do not involve the business, established routines tend to collapse, causing friction between employees and between departments. Because of the personalism involved in business relations, the Puerto Rican executive is acquainted with all or most of his employees on a face-to-face basis. Occasionally the executive's relatives represent a large percentage of his employees. In smaller organizations employees who are not related to the head often ask him to serve as a best man of their marriage or as a godfather of their child. The employment of relatives and of ritual kin is used by the executive principally to foster the feeling that his concern is a family one. The introduction of ritual kinship relations into a business organization gives the employee added emotional security. Ritual kinship in this context appears to insure a good personal relationship with the executive and thus enhances the employee's security and position.

The importance of speaking fluent English and of understanding American behavior cannot be exaggerated. It is a prime factor in commercial success. The American businessman on the island is simply a variation of a tourist. He selects a Puerto Rican representative with whom he thinks "he can do business," which means a person like himself. Many American businessmen express disapproval of certain Puerto Rican business establishments that do not meet their standards. Puerto Rican executives are aware of the Americans' preferences and many make great efforts to conform to the demands to Americanize their life style. They can do this more easily than any other group on the island because of their wealth and social contacts.

The way of life of the businessman is largely conditioned by his occupation. The executive is rewarded for his work by achieving goals that are highly valued in modern society: money, material wealth, social prestige, social esteem, fulfillment of self-conception—all expressions and attributes of power in society. This fulfillment of self-conception might be regarded as somewhat segmented since economic success is not the only factor in assuring success in other realms of life. Throughout his life, beginning with expectations acquired during his childhood and passing through later phases of indoctrination within the subculture, an individual learns to view himself as a successful adult businessman. He believes he can obtain his goals through superior intelligence, training, and hard work. Usually he either attains or approximates these goals. His status affords him every advantage for realizing his self-expectancies. This fulfillment of self-concept is extremely important to Puerto Ricans because it is intimately bound up with the cultural value of dignidad (dignity), one of the most important values on the island. To have dignidad, one must conceive of himself and believe others conceive of him as successfully fulfilling the expectancies of his various statuses.

At the age of fifteen, boys and girls are introduced into adult society and from that time on attend numerous formal balls, wedding receptions, cocktail parties, and other social events. Girls are initiated into their new roles through membership in sororities and through lavish coming-out parties. The social events serve the threefold purpose of social display, recreation, and an opportunity for courtship. Marriage in her early twenties will partially remove the young woman from the social arena. Until then, social events dominate her life. Before and after every festivity, she and her friends spend their time discussing clothes, boys, food, decorations, and the social statuses involved at the balls. Of greatest interest to girls just entering social life is the selection of the queen of the annual carnival, the queens of other events, and their ladies in waiting. To be chosen queen is a girl's supreme ambition. Choice of the carnival queen, the most prized of all, is by no means a popularity contest. Since the carnival has become commercialized, a self-appointed committee of interested businessmen together with society editors, managers of hotels where the balls will be held, and one or two socially prominent persons simply announce the queen for the year. The *ad hoc* committee's selection is based upon the family's financial ability to support the girl in her queenly role as well as upon her appearance and poise.

Initiation into one of the five major sororities, together with being presented at a society ball, is the final step in the coming of age. The sororities, however, are more than recreational groups. Formed in the late twenties but in no way connected with educational institutions, they have formalized social cliques. With approximately one hundred members each, the sororities have become status groups primarily of young, unmarried women. When a member marries, she may become inactive or "passive" in sorority chapters for married women. These "alumnae" chapters play an active role in the major social events of the island.

The young men of the upper class are exposed to a very different recreational pattern than that which affects most of the young women. They usually attend college in the United States. Their participation in Puerto Rican life is largely limited to summer vacations. Attending college in the

United States gives the young man certain interests and attitudes that differ somewhat from those of traditional Puerto Rico. He displays a greater inter-est in sports (and may even participate in them) than he did previously in Puerto Rico and is now often led towards making the game something of an end in itself. But he is also taught team play, cooperation and winning for the sake of winning. These are basic American patterns found in the com-mercial world in which the young man will soon function. This pattern combines individual competition and cooperation within an established set of rules. It requires initiative and leadership which the young man acquires gradually and hesitantly. His new attitudes have not yet greatly modified his participation in and acceptance of the more traditional recreational patterns based on values learned outside the school.

While marriage is the crucial point in the individual's life cycle, it is also an important religious ceremony. The wedding and the wedding recep-tion are primarily significant as "social" occasions. The premarriage parties and the final wedding reception are among the most important social events in a person's life. The announcement of the wedding initiates a series of cocktail parties, teas, showers, bachelor dinners, and evenings of drinking. Minor presents may be presented to the bride-to-be at these affairs, though the principal gifts are sent to the bride's home just before the wedding and are displayed for a number of days. While the wedding is largely a religious function, the wedding reception, usually held at one of the better hotels or clubs, is a purely social event. The guest lists, based upon prestige, reveal the Puerto Rican social hierarchy. The lavish and costly weddings and receptions are discussed constantly. A modest wedding accommodating two hundred guests will necessitate an expenditure of approximately $3,000 or more. Large weddings of five hundred or six hundred guests may entail an expense of over $10,000.

While the social activity reaches its peak in youth, it does not cease with marriage. Young married couples continue to attend balls, though not as frequently as before. The character of social life changes somewhat, how-ever, as persons of this age group begin to give cocktail parties in their own homes or in hotels or clubs. The significance of this change lies in the fact that those who give parties carry full adult responsibility as hosts. They function as individuals, not as members of families in which the parents are dominant nor as members of sororities that have collective responsibility. Although adults still continue to enjoy such earlier interests as moving pic-tures, sports, radio, and visiting friends, they turn increasingly to smaller in-group activities such as playing cards, gambling, social drinking, and home life. The present-day husband and wife share recreational patterns to a greater extent than in former generations.

The members of the upper class are great joiners. Besides providing prestige, clubs furnish recreation and further economic, religious, and community objectives. Men belong principally to the Rotary Club, Lions Club, Elks Club, and the Chamber of Commerce. Women join such secular organizations as the Red Cross and certain civic clubs. Among religious clubs are the Catholic Daughters of America, Catholic Sons, and Knights of Columbus. There are also a number of exclusive social clubs.

When children become old enough to attend balls and other social affairs, parents begin to enjoy their children's lives vicariously. Once again they are drawn into great balls and festivals as chaperons. They attend engagement parties, wedding receptions, baptisms, and other functions. Even when their children are married, the parents continue to participate in the social life of the community in various ways.

In urban areas of Latin America there are many different life styles. Vast differences in background and wealth prevail. This chapter has presented a few of the many subcultures. Many others remain to be explored.

RECOMMENDED READING

Jesus, Carolina Maria de, 1963, *Child of the Dark*. New York: Signet Books.
A rare account of the favelas of São Paulo by one of its inhabitants. This diary presents a vivid description of slum life.
Kemper, Robert V., 1970, The Anthropological Study of Migration to Latin American Cities. *Kroeber Anthropological Society Papers* 42:1–25.
A critique of various anthropological research on migration and the theories that have emerged from this research.
Mangin, William (ed.), 1970, *Peasants in Cities: Readings in the Anthropology of Urbanization*. Boston: Houghton Mifflin Company.
A series of articles, many on Latin America, dealing with the adjustment of rural peoples to urban centers.
Whiteford, Andrew H., 1964, *Two Cities of Latin America: a Comparative Description of Social Classes*. Garden City, N.Y.: Anchor Books.
The most detailed comparison of social class in Latin American cities. Compares Querétaro, Mexico with Popayán, Colombia.

RECOMMENDED CASE STUDIES
IN CULTURAL ANTHROPOLOGY

Pi-Sunyer, Oriol, 1973, *Zamora: Change and Continuity in a Mexican Town*. New York: Holt, Rinehart and Winston, Inc.
Deals with the place of the town in the larger complex society.

CHAPTER 9

Conclusions

🁢🁢🁢🁢🁢🁢🁢🁢🁢🁢🁢🁢🁢🁢🁢🁢🁢🁢🁢🁢🁢🁢🁢

Anthropology stands at a new threshold in understanding the Latin Americans. The material presented has considered what *is* known today about the Latin Americans. In these conclusions the future of anthropological research in Latin America will be considered.

Anthropological research has thus far centered primarily on the Amerinds. Most of the research has been ethnographical, in which the primary concern of the investigator has been the description of cultural traits. Research has focused on the pre-Contact traits and traditions. Colonial or more recent influences have frequently been ignored as irrelevant to the study of Amerinds. The study of trait distributions, developed in the United States, was applied by North American anthropologists to the non-Western peoples of Latin America in an attempt to reconstruct pre-Contact traits. Yet it was not until the development of scientific archaeology, within the past few decades, that an understanding of pre-Columbian cultures was attained. In addition to archaeology, three new fields of cultural anthropology are expanding our knowledge of the Latin American tradition: ethnohistory, the study of complex societies, and the study of belief systems.

ETHNOHISTORY

The subdiscipline of cultural anthropology known as "ethnohistory" has come into its own within the last ten years. Latin American historians

316

have concentrated on Spanish cultural development, drawing their generalizations concerning Amerinds from anthropology. It is the ethnohistorian who can bridge the gap between the traditional interests of history and the traditional interests of anthropology. Latin America is rich in historical documents, many of which have never been examined by anthropologists. Unlike the situation faced by anthropologists studying the Amerinds of the United States, in which written documents do not begin until the seventeenth, eighteenth, or even the nineteenth century, the written tradition in Latin America extends back to the end of the fifteenth century. In Mesoamerica it extends into pre-Contact times.

In the past, anthropologists have frequently confused two concepts of time. In our own society, and in Western civilization in general, history is thought of in terms of an absolute chronology of unique events. It is considered important to determine whether one event occurred before or after another and to find the actual number of intervening years between events. Primitive societies have other ways of interpreting the past. Time is telescoped or collapsed and events are interchanged so that history "makes sense" in the present-day context. Because the events do not fit the "true" chronological ordering, as it is viewed in our own society, other peoples' histories are labeled as myths and legends. When the anthropologist first began studying the perception of the past in other societies ("folk history," so to speak), he confused this type of history with his own culture's perception of the past and found the folk history to be inaccurate. Confusing the two types of history led to a general abandoning of historical research by the anthropologist. In other words, the anthropologist was asking questions concerning folk history when he was really interested in learning about history as it is perceived in our society. This confusion led to a disinterest in the study of mythology and legends and the development of a new orientation that emphasized the study of Latin American Amerinds either synchronically through the structural-functional approach or through archaeology. This attitude tended to underplay the changes that took place in these societies as a result of contact with the Spanish. It has already been shown that many societies had undergone considerable change during the first one hundred years of contact. By not asking historically oriented questions, a large mass of data was ignored. Although most of the Amerinds may not have had written history, this should not imply that other sources of information can be ignored. Historical data are to be found in the European archives, as well as in the archives of the various Latin American countries. This material is necessary for the study of past and present subcultures. The ethnohistorian will be able to supplement the work of the archaeologist, the ethnographer, and the historian by looking at archival data through a conceptual framework different from that employed by the historian studying the same material.

Archaeology has provided a wealth of material on the pre-Contact period, yet "historical archaeology" (the archaeology of the Colonial and Republican periods) is almost nonexistent in Latin America. Just as the historian has left the pre-Contact period to the archaeologist, the archaeologist has left the Colonial and Republican periods to the historian. Cooperation between the two types of scientists could result in fruitful investigation. Historical documents contain only certain types of data, and archaeological excavation of historical sites could clarify a number of gaps in the historical records. Too, there seems to be much greater prestige attached to the excavation of a pre-Contact pyramid than to the excavation of a colonial fort. Archaeologists generally do not think of the latter type of research as "real" archaeology. Yet the excavation of just one colonial fort might add considerable information needed to answer a number of historical questions. If the anthropological contributions to the understanding of the Colonial and Republican periods have been poor, the anthropological contributions to the understanding of the cultural processes of the last half of the nineteenth and first half of the twentieth century have been almost nonexistent. This era of Americanization, Panamericanization, and nationalization seems to be a *terra incognita* for anthropology, yet these processes are crucial to anyone viewing the Latin Americans today.

In summary, one necessary trend in the study of Latin Americans is the expansion of the historical orientation of anthropology from the pre-Contact period to include colonial, republican, and modern events of anthropological interest.

COMPLEX SOCIETIES

A second trend taking place in the study of Latin Americans is a change in the units of analysis. Previously, with the emphasis on studying non-Western man, the anthropologist focused on the small homogeneous society as a closed unit of observation with little consideration of any external influences. The use of this unit of analysis was perpetuated in the study of Latin Americans because: (1) the stereotype held in North American anthropology of the folk society as isolated and static, (2) there existed a lack of interest in and familiarity with the historical resources that documented the considerable external influences, and (3) there was a lack of interest in and understanding of modern processes such as the development of nationalism.

The perception of Latin American states as complex societies has led to the development of more appropriate units of analysis for studying the Latin American. Even Amerind groups can be understood more fully if viewed in the context of a larger complex society. The ethnographer can no longer describe a single tribe or highland village and ignore the outside effects of traders, missionaries, teachers, government officials, modern material culture, highways, and so on. That the complex society is a unit that many of today's anthropologists still feel perplexed about is expressed in their concern with the fact that their discipline has no unique contributions to offer to the study of modern nations. However, it would seem that anthropologists *can* make a vital contribution. Institutions have many manifestations. The ideal form is generally that which occurs on the national level and at this level the sociologist, political scientist, the economist and the historian make their contributions. Anthropologists, on the other hand, are best equipped to analyze the various manifestations of these institutions at the local level, as well as to analyze the intermediate agents who operate between the two levels (the "cultural brokers"). With this shift in emphasis the anthropologist is beginning to study many types of Latin Americans who have never been studied before: the urban squatter, the revolutionary, the business executive, minority groups, and so on.

BELIEF SYSTEMS

For years anthropologists have concentrated on the "study of culture" with little agreement as to what should be studied. Many of the early studies focused on the "material culture" or artifacts of the Amerinds. The ethnographers focused on inanimate objects and technological processes, particularly during the era of trait distribution studies. Native languages were often only casually learned, as a considerable amount of information was collected through observation. As social structure was studied, this too was based primarily on observation of interaction patterns. The study of the belief systems of Latin Americans has lagged behind.

While anthropologists studied various outward manifestations of culture, few centered their research on the belief system itself. The concern has been primarily with the "-etic" system, to use an analogy from linguistics. In other words, there has been a concern with describing a way of life with the categories of our own society—whether or not these categories have any significance for the people themselves. Only very recently have ethnographers begun to analyze systematically the belief systems of the people they study. This approach, to continue the analogy from linguistics, can be described as the "-emic" approach in which a way of life is described according to the categories that have significance for the people themselves. The study of belief systems is extremely difficult. One must have a command of the language of the people he is studying because almost all information concerning a society's system of beliefs has to be collected through depth interviewing. Little can be learned through observation alone. At the same time, one gains insights into belief systems only through extensive fieldwork with the same group of people. Yet it is only through greater concentration on the belief systems of the Latin Americans that a fuller understanding of their cultural tradition will be derived.

Ethnohistory, the study of complex societies, and the analysis of belief systems point the way to a new dimension in the anthropological study of the Latin American way of life.

References*

Acosta, José de, 1590, *Historia Natural y Moral de Las Indias*. Sevilla. Reprinted in 1962, Mexico City: Fondo de Cultura Económica.

Adams, Frederick Upham, 1914, *Conquest of the Tropics: The Story of the Creative Enterprise Conducted by the United Fruit Company.* Garden City, N.Y.: Doubleday & Company, Inc.

Adams, Richard N., 1956, Cultural Components of Central America. *American Anthropologist* 58:881–907.

———, 1957, *Cultural Surveys of Panama-Nicaragua-Guatemala-El Salvador-Honduras.* Washington, D.C.: Pan American Sanitary Bureau, Scientific Publications, no. 33.

———, 1964, *Introducción a la Antropología Aplicada.* Guatemala City: Seminario de Integración Social Guatemalteca, Publicación no. 13.

———, 1967a, *The Second Sowing: Power and Secondary Development in Latin America.* San Francisco: Chandler Publishing Company.

———, 1967b, Political Power and Social Structures. In Claudio Véliz (ed.), *The Politics of Conformity in Latin America.* London: Oxford University Press, pp. 15–42.

———, 1970, *Crucifixion by Power: Essays on Guatemalan National Social Structure, 1944–1966.* Austin, Tex.: University of Texas Press.

Aguilar, Francisco de, 1963, The Chronicle of Fray Francisco de Aguilar. In Patricia de Fuentes (ed. and trans.), *The Conquistadors.* New York: The Orion Press, Inc., pp. 136–164 [c. 1580].

Alvardo Tezozomoc, Fernando, 1949, *Crónica Mexicayotl.* Mexico City: Universidad Nacional Autónoma de Mexico, Instituto de Historia [1609].

* Numbers between brackets indicate original date of publication or original date of a document.

Anderson, Gallatin, 1956, A Survey of Italian Godparenthood. *Kroeber Anthropological Society Papers* 15.

————, 1957, Il Comparaggio: The Italian Godparenthood Complex. *Southwestern Journal of Anthropology* 13:32–53.

Anonymous, 1944, *Códice Ramírez: Relación del Origen de los Indios que Habitan esta Nueva España, Según sus Historias.* Mexico City: Editorial Leyenda.

Anonymous Conqueror, 1917, *Narrative of Some Things of New Spain and of the Great City of Temestitan, Mexico.* New York: Cortes Society [1556].

Aponte Figueroa, Juan de, 1867, *Memorial que Trata de la Reformación del Reino del Perú.* Madrid: Colección de Documentos Inéditos del Archivo de Indias, vol. 51, pp. 521–562.

Arriaga, Pablo José de, 1920, *La Extirpación de la Idolatría en el Perú.* . . . Lima: Colección de Libros y Documentos Referentes a la Historia del Perú, 2nd Series, vol. 1 [1621].

Atkinson, William C., 1960, *A History of Spain and Portugal.* Baltimore: Penguin Books, Inc.

Augelli, John P., 1962, The Rimland-Mainland Concept of Culture Areas in Middle America. *Annals of the Association of American Geographers* 52(2): 119–129.

Ávila, Francisco de (compiler), 1967, *Hombres y Dioses de Huarochirí.* Lima: Museo Nacional de Historia, Instituto de Estudios Peruanos [1608].

Bagú, Sergio, 1952, *Estructura Social de la Colonia: Ensayo de Historia Comparada de América Latina.* Buenos Aires: El Ateneo.

Baily, Samuel L. (ed.), 1971, *Nationalism in Latin America.* New York: Alfred A. Knopf.

Baker, Paul T., 1969, Human Adaptation to High Altitude. *Science* 163(3872): 1149–1156.

Barrett, Samuel A., 1925, The Cayapa Indians of Ecuador. *Indian Notes and Monographs* 40. New York: Museum of the American Indian (2 vols.).

Basauri, Carlos, 1940, *La Población Indígena de México: Etnografía.* Mexico City: Secretaria de Educación Pública (3 vols.).

Bastide, Roger, 1971, *African Civilisations in the New World.* New York: Harper & Row, Publishers [1967].

Beals, Ralph L., 1946, *Cherán: A Sierra Tarascan Village.* Washington, D.C.: Smithsonian Institution, Institute of Social Anthropology, Publication no. 2.

————, 1951, Urbanism, Urbanization and Acculturation. *American Anthropologist* 53(1):1–10.

————, 1953, Social Stratification in Latin America. *American Journal of Sociology* 58:327–339.

————, 1961, Community Typologies in Latin America. *Anthropological Linguistics* 3(1):8–16.

————, 1967, Acculturation. In Manning Nash (ed.), *Handbook of Middle American Indians.* Austin, Tex.: University of Texas Press, vol. 6, pp. 449–468.

Becker, Howard P., 1930, *Ionia and Athens: Studies in Secularization.* Unpublished Ph.D. dissertation, University of Chicago.

Bernal, Ignacio, 1964, Introduction. In Fray Diego Durán, *The Aztecs: The History of the Indies of New Spain.* New York: Orion Press, pp. xxi–xxxii.

Bernal, Ignacio, 1969, *The Olmec World*. Berkeley, Calif.: University of California Press.

Betanzos, Juan de, 1880, *Suma y Narración de los Incas*. Madrid: Biblioteca Hispano-Ultramarina, vol. 5 [c. 1551].

Biesanz, John B., 1949, Cultural and Economic Factors in Panamanian Race Relations. *American Sociological Review* 14:772–779.

————, 1950, Race Relations in the Canal Zone. *Phylon* 11:23–30.

Biesanz, John B., and Mavis Biesanz, 1944, *Costa Rican Life*. New York: Columbia University Press.

————, 1955, *The People of Panama*. New York: Columbia University Press.

Biesanz, John B., and Luke M. Smith, 1951, Race Relations in Panama and the Canal Zone. *American Journal of Sociology* 57:7–14.

Blaffer, Sarah C., 1972, *The Black-Man of Zinacantan: A Central American Legend*. Austin, Tex.: University of Texas Press.

Blanchard, R., 1910, Encore sureles tableaux de métissage du Musée de Mexico. *Journal de la Société des Américanistes* 7:37–60.

Bonilla, Frank, 1970, *The Failure of Elites*. Cambridge, Mass.: M.I.T. Press (*The Politics of Change in Venezuela*, vol. 2).

Borah, Woodrow, 1962, América como Modelo? El Impacto Demográfico de la Expansión Europea sobre el Mundo no Europeo. *Cuadernos Americanos,* Años 21, vol. 125, no. 6, pp. 176–185.

Breese, Gerald, 1966, *Urbanization in Newly Developing Countries*. Englewood Cliffs, N.J.: Prentice-Hall, Inc.

Brundage, Burr C., 1963, *Empire of the Inca*. Norman, Okla.: University of Oklahoma Press.

Buechler, Hans C., 1968, The Reorganization of Counties in the Bolivian Highlands: An Analysis of Rural-Urban Networks and Hierarchies. In Elizabeth M. Eddy (ed.), *Urban Anthropology: Research Perspectives and Strategies*. Athens, Ga.: Southern Anthropological Society, Proceedings no. 2, pp. 48–57.

————, 1969, The Social Position of an Ethnographer in the Field. In Frances Henry and Satish Saberwal (eds.), *Stress and Response in Fieldwork*. New York: Holt, Rinehart and Winston, Inc., pp. 7–19.

Bunzel, Ruth, 1952, *Chichicastenango: A Guatemalan Village*. Seattle: University of Washington Press.

Burma, John H. (ed.), 1970, *Mexican-Americans in the United States: A Reader*. Cambridge, Mass.: Schenkman Publishing Company, Inc.

Bushnell, G. H. S., 1963, *Peru*. rev. ed. New York: Frederick A. Praeger, Inc.

Caldwell, Joseph R., 1964, Interaction Spheres in Prehistory. In Joseph R. Caldwell and Robert L. Hall (eds.), *Hopewellian Studies*. Springfield, Ill.: Illinois State Museum Scientific Papers, vol. 12, pp. 135–143.

Cancian, Frank, 1965, *Economics and Prestige in a Maya Community: The Religious Cargo System in Zinacantan*. Stanford, Calif.: Stanford University Press.

————, 1972, *Change and Uncertainty in a Peasant Economy: The Maya Corn Farmers of Zinacantan*. Stanford, Calif.: Stanford University Press.

Caplow, Theodore, 1949, The Social Ecology of Guatemala City. *Social Forces* 28:113–133.

Carr, Robert F., and James E. Hazard, 1961, *Map of the Ruins of Tikal, El Petén, Guatemala*. Philadelphia: University of Pennsylvania, The University Museum, Museum Monographs, Tikal Report, no. 11.

Carroll, Thomas F., 1964, Land Reform as an Explosive Force in Latin America. In J. J. Te Paske and S. N. Fisher (eds.), *Explosive Forces in Latin America*. Columbus, Ohio: Ohio State University Press, pp. 81–125.

Caso, Alfonso, 1954, Instituciones Indígenas Precortesiana. In Alfonso Caso, et al., *Metodos y Resultados de la Política Indigenista en México*. Mexico City: Memorias del Instituto Nacional Indigenista, no. 6, pp. 13–27.

_____, 1963, Land Tenure Among the Ancient Mexicans. *American Anthropologist* 65:863–878.

Catherwood, Frederick, 1844, *Views of Ancient Monuments in Central America, Chiapas and Yucatan*. New York: Berlett and Weldford.

Cavazzi, G. A. da Montecuccolo, 1687, *Istorica Descrizione de'Tre Regni Congo, Matamba et Angola*. Bologna: Per G. Monti.

Chagnon, Napoleon A., 1968, *Yąnomamö: the Fierce People*. New York: Holt, Rinehart and Winston, Inc.

Chenault, Lawrence R., 1938, *The Puerto Rican Migrant in New York City*. New York: Columbia University Press.

Chevalier, François, 1967, The *Ejido* and Political Stability in Mexico. In Claudio Véliz (ed.), *The Politics of Conformity in Latin America*. London: Oxford University Press, pp. 158–191.

Chonchol, Jacques, 1965, Land Tenure and Development in Latin America. In Claudio Véliz (ed.), *Obstacles to Change in Latin America*. London: Oxford University Press, pp. 75–90.

Cieza de León, Pedro de, 1943–1945, *La Crónica del Perú*. Buenos Aires: Espasa-Calpe Argentina (part 1); Ediciones Argentinas Solar (part 2) [1553–1554].

Clifton, James A. (ed.), 1968, *Introduction to Cultural Anthropology*. Boston: Houghton Mifflin Company.

Cobean, Robert H., et al., 1971, Obsidian Trade at San Lorenzo Tenochtitlán, Mexico. *Science* 174(4010):666–671.

Cochran, Thomas C., 1959, *The Puerto Rican Businessman: A Study in Culture Change*. Philadelphia: University of Pennsylvania Press.

Cochran, Thomas C., and Ruben E. Reina, 1962, *Entrepreneurship in Argentine Culture: Torcuato Di Tella and S.I.A.M.* Philadelphia: University of Pennsylvania Press.

Coe, Michael D., 1962, *Mexico*. New York: Frederick A. Praeger, Inc.

_____, 1966, *The Maya*. New York: Frederick A. Praeger, Inc.

Coe, William R., 1965, Tikal, Guatemala, and Emergent Maya Civilization. *Science* 147(3664):1401–1419.

Cohen, Lucy M., 1971, The Chinese of the Panama Railroad: Preliminary Notes on the Migrants of 1854 Who Failed. *Ethnohistory* 18(1):309–320.

Cole, Fay-Cooper, and Fred Eggan, 1959, Robert Redfield, 1897–1958. *American Anthropologist* 61(4):652–662.

Collier, June, 1968, *Courtship and Marriage in Zinacantan*. New Orleans: Tulane University, Middle American Research Center.

Collins, Robert O. (ed.), 1968, *Problems in African History*. Englewood Cliffs, N.J.: Prentice-Hall, Inc.

Comas, Juan, 1964, *La Antropología Social Aplicada en México*. Mexico City: Instituto Indigenista Interamericano, Serie: Antropología Social no. 1.

Crevenna, Theo. R. (ed.), 1950–1951, *Materiales para el Estudio de la Clase Media en la América Latina*. Washington, D.C.: Unión Panamericana, Departamento de Asuntos Culturales (6 vols.).

Crowther, Samuel, 1929, *The Romance and Rise of the American Tropics*. Garden City, N.Y.: Doubleday & Company, Inc.

Curtin, Philip, and Jan Vansina, 1964, Sources of the Nineteenth Century Atlantic Slave Trade. *The Journal of African History* 5:185–208.

Davidson, Basil, 1961, *The African Slave Trade: Precolonial History 1450–1850*. Boston: Atlantic Monthly Press.

Davis, Kingsley, 1960, Colonial Expansion and Urban Diffusion in the Americas. *International Journal of Comparative Sociology* 1(1):43–66.

Delgado O., Carlos, 1969, An Analysis of "Arribismo" in Peru. *Human Organization* 28(2):133–139.

Deshon, Shirley, 1963, Compadrazgo on a Henequen Hacienda in Yucatan: A Structural Re-Evaluation. *American Anthropologist* 65(3):574–583.

Despres, Leo A., 1967, *Cultural Pluralism and Nationalist Politics in British Guiana*. Chicago: Rand McNally & Company.

Dew, Edward, 1969, *Politics in the Altiplano: The Dynamics of Change in Rural Peru*. Austin, Tex.: University of Texas Press, Latin American Monographs No. 15.

Diaz, May N., 1966, *Tonalá: Conservatism, Responsibility, and Authority in a Mexican Town*. Berkeley, Calif.: University of California Press.

Díaz del Castillo, Bernal, 1956, *The Discovery and Conquest of Mexico, 1517–1521*. New York: Farrar, Straus & Giroux, Inc. [written c. 1560; first published 1632].

Díaz-Guerrero, Rogelio, 1959, Mexican Assumptions about Interpersonal Relations. *ETC.: A Review of General Semantics* 16(2):185–188.

Dibble, Charles E., 1966, The Aztec Writing System. In Jesse D. Jennings and E. Adamson Hoebel (eds.), *Readings in Anthropology*. 2nd ed. New York: McGraw-Hill, Inc., pp. 270–277.

Dobyns, Henry F., 1963, An Outline of Andean Epidemic History to 1720. *Bulletin of the History of Medicine* 37(6):493–515.

———, 1966, Estimating Aboriginal American Population: An Appraisal of Techniques with a New Hemispheric Estimate. *Current Anthropology* 7(4):395–416, 440–449.

Doebele, William A., Jr., 1969, Legal Issues of Regional Development. In Lloyd Rodwin and Associates, *Planning Urban Growth and Regional Development*. Cambridge, Mass.: M.I.T. Press, pp. 286–298.

Dotson, Floyd, 1953, A Note on Participation in Voluntary Associations in a Mexican City. *American Sociological Review* 18:380–386.

Dotson, Floyd, and Lillian Ota Dotson, 1954, Ecological Trends in the City of Guadalajara, Mexico. *Social Forces* 32:367–374.

Dotson, Floyd, and Lillian Ota Dotson, 1956, Urban Centralization and Decentralization in Mexico. *Rural Sociology* 21–22:41–49.

Doughty, Paul L., 1970, Behind the Back of the City: "Provincial" Life in Lima, Peru. In William Mangin (ed.), *Peasants in Cities.* Boston: Houghton Mifflin Company, pp. 30–46.

Durán, Fray Diego, 1964, *The Aztecs: The History of the Indies of New Spain.* New York: The Orion Press, Inc. [written c. 1581; first published 1867–1880].

————, 1971, *Book of the Gods and Rites and the Ancient Calendar.* Norman, Okla.: University of Oklahoma Press [written c. 1576–1579; first published 1867–1880].

Durkheim, Émile, 1932, *De la division du travail social.* Paris: F. Alcan.

Enríquez B., Eliecer, 1938, *Quito a Través de los Siglos.* Quito: Imprenta Municipal.

Erasmus, Charles, 1961, *Man Takes Control: Cultural Development and American Aid.* Minneapolis: University of Minnesota Press.

Evans, Clifford, Betty J. Meggers, and Emilio Estrata, 1959, *Cultura Valdivia.* Guayaquil, Colombia: Museo Víctor Emilio Estrada, Publication no. 6.

Exquemelin, Alexander O., 1969, *The Buccaneers of America.* Baltimore: Penguin Books, Inc. [1678].

Fallas, Carlos Luis, 1941, *Mamita Yunai.* San José, Costa Rica: Editorial Soley y Valverde.

Fals Borda, Orlando, 1965, Violence and the Break-up of Tradition in Colombia. In Claudio Véliz (ed.), *Obstacles to Change in Latin America.* London: Oxford University Press, pp. 188–205.

Faron, Louis C., 1968, *The Mapuche Indians of Chile.* New York: Holt, Rinehart and Winston, Inc.

Fernández, León, 1889, *Historia de Costa Rica Durante la Dominación Española, 1502–1821.* Madrid: Tipografía de Manuel Ginés Hernández.

Fernández de Oviedo y Valdés, Gonzalo, 1944, *Historia General y Natural de las Indias, Islas y Tierra-Firme del Mar Océano.* Asunción, Paraguay: Editorial Guarania (14 vols.) [1535].

Forbes, Jack D., 1970, Mexican-Americans. In John H. Burma (ed.), *Mexican-Americans in the United States: A Reader.* Cambridge, Mass.: Schenkman Publishing Co., Inc., pp. 7–16.

Foster, George M., 1948, *Empire's Children: The People of Tzintzuntzan.* Washington, D.C.: Smithsonian Institution, Institute of Social Anthropology, Publication no. 6.

————, 1953a, What is Folk Culture? *American Anthropologist* 55(2):159–173.

————, 1953b, Cofradía and Compadrazgo in Spain and Spanish America. *Southwestern Journal of Anthropology* 9:1–26.

————, 1953c, Relationships between Spanish and Spanish-American Folk Medicine. *Journal of American Folklore* 66:201–217.

————, 1960, *Culture and Conquest: America's Spanish Heritage.* Chicago: Quadrangle Books, Inc.

————, 1961, The Dyadic Contract: A Model for the Social Structure of a Mexican Peasant Village. *American Anthropologist* 63(6):1173–1192.

Foster, George M., 1963, The Dyadic Contract in Tzintzuntzan, II: Patron-Client Relationship. *American Anthropologist* 65(6):1280–1294.

————, 1965, Peasant Society and the Image of Limited Good. *American Anthropologist* 67(2):293–315.

————, 1967, *Tzintzuntzan: Mexican Peasants in a Changing World*. Boston: Little, Brown & Company.

————, 1969a, *Applied Anthropology*. Boston: Little, Brown & Company.

————, 1969b, Godparents and Social Networks in Tzintzuntzan. *Southwestern Journal of Anthropology* 25:261–278.

Fretz, Joseph W., 1962, *Immigrant Group Settlements in Paraguay: A Study in the Sociology of Colonization*. North Newton, Kan.: Bethel College.

Freyre, Gilberto, 1964, *The Masters and the Slaves: A Study in the Development of Brazilian Civilization*. New York: Alfred A. Knopf [1946].

Fried, Morton H., 1956, Some Observations of the Chinese in British Guiana. *Social and Economic Studies* 5(1):54–73.

————, 1958, The Chinese in the British Caribbean. In Morton H. Fried (ed.), *Colloquium on Overseas Chinese*. New York: International Secretariat, Institute of Pacific Relations, pp. 49–58.

Frucht, Richard, 1967, A Caribbean Social Type: Neither "Peasant" Nor "Proletarian." *Social and Economic Studies* 16(3):295–300.

Gage, Thomas, 1929, *A New Survey of the West Indies, 1648: The English-American*. New York: Robert M. McBride Company, Inc. [1648].

Gamino, Manuel, 1922, *La Población del Valle de Teotihuacán*. Mexico City: Dirección de Talleres Gráficos (2 vols.).

Gibson, Charles, 1966, *Spain in America*. New York: Harper & Row, Publishers.

Gibson, Charles (ed.), 1971, *The Black Legend: Anti-Spanish Attitudes in the Old World and the New*. New York: Alfred A. Knopf.

Gillin, John, 1936, *The Barama River Carib of British Guiana*. Cambridge, Mass.: Papers of the Peabody Museum of Archaeology and Ethnology, vol. 14, no. 2.

————, 1945, Parallel Cultures and the Inhibitions to Acculturation in a Guatemalan Community. *Social Forces* 25:243–248.

————, 1947, *Moche: a Peruvian Coastal Community*. Washington, D.C.: Smithsonian Institution, Institute of Social Anthropology, Publication no. 3.

————, 1948, Magical Fright. *Psychiatry* 11:387–400.

————, 1949, Mestizo America. In Ralph Linton (ed.), *Most of the World*. New York: Columbia University Press, pp. 156–211.

————, 1965, Ethos Components in Modern Latin American Culture. In Dwight B. Heath and Richard N. Adams (eds.), *Contemporary Cultures and Societies of Latin America*. New York: Random House, Inc., pp. 503–517 [1955].

Goldkind, Victor, 1961, Sociocultural Contrasts in Rural and Urban Settlement Types in Costa Rica. *Rural Sociology* 26:365–380.

————, 1965, Social Stratification in the Peasant Community: Redfield's Chan Kom Reinterpreted. *American Anthropologist* 67(4):863–884.

————, 1966, Class Conflict and Cacique in Chan Kom. *Southwestern Journal of Anthropology* 22:325–345.

————, 1970, Anthropologists, Informants and the Achievement of Power in Chan Kom. *Sociologus* 20(1):17–41.

Goldrich, Daniel, 1966, *Sons of the Establishment: Elite Youth in Panama and Costa Rica.* Chicago: Rand McNally & Company.

Gómez de Orozco, Federico, 1961, Introduction. In Anonymous Conqueror, *Relación de Algunas Cosas de le Nueva España y de la Gran Ciudad de Temestitan Mexico, Hecha por un Gentilhombre del Señor Fernando Cortés.* Mexico City: Fernández Editores.

Greenleaf, Richard E., 1961, *Zumárraga and the Mexican Inquisition, 1536–1543.* Washington, D.C.: Academy of American Franciscan History, Monograph Series, no. 4.

Hansen, Asael T., 1934, The Ecology of a Latin American City. In E. B. Reuter (ed.), *Race and Culture Contacts.* New York: McGraw-Hill, Inc., pp. 124–142.

Hardoy, Jorge E., and Richard P. Schaedel, 1969, *The Urbanization Process in America from its Origin to the Present Day.* Buenos Aires.

Haring, C. H., 1963, *The Spanish Empire in America.* New York: Harcourt Brace Jovanovich, Inc. [1947].

Harris, Marvin, 1952, Race Relations in Minas Velhas: A Community in the Mountain Region of Central Brazil. In Charles Wagley (ed.), *Race and Class in Rural Brazil.* Paris: U.N.E.S.C.O., pp. 47–81.

————, 1956, *Town and Country in Brazil.* New York: Columbia University Press.

————, 1964, *Patterns of Race in the Americas.* New York: Walker and Company.

Harris, Walter D., Jr., 1971, *The Growth of Latin American Cities.* Athens, Ohio: Ohio University Press.

Haven, Gilbert, 1875, *Our Next-Door Neighbor: A Winter in Mexico.* New York: Harper and Brothers, Publishers.

Hawthorn, Harry B., and Audrey Hawthorn, 1948a, The Shape of a City: Some Observations on Sucre, Bolivia. *Social Research* 33:87–91.

————, 1948b, Stratification in a Latin American City. *Social Forces* 27:19–29.

Hayner, Norman S., 1944, Oaxaca, City of Old Mexico. *Sociology and Social Research* 29:87–95.

————, 1945, Mexico City, Its Growth and Configuration. *American Journal of Sociology* 50:295–304.

————, 1946, Criminogenic Zones in Mexico City. *American Sociological Review* 11:428–438.

————, 1948, Differential Social Change in a Mexican Town. *Social Forces* 26:381–390.

Heath, Dwight B., Charles J. Erasmus, and Hans C. Buechler, 1969, *Land Reform and Social Revolution in Bolivia.* New York: Frederick A. Praeger, Inc.

Helms, Mary W., 1971a, The Miskito Indians: Indios, Zamboes or Frontier Population? Paper presented at the Annual Meeting of the American Society for Ethnohistory, Athens, Ga.

————, 1971b, *Asang: Adaptations to Culture Contact in a Miskito Community.* Gainesville, Fla.: University of Florida Press.

Herring, Hubert, 1968, *A History of Latin America from the Beginnings to the Present.* 3rd ed. New York: Alfred A. Knopf [1955].

Herskovits, Melville J., 1937, *Life in a Haitian Valley*. New York: Alfred A. Knopf.

————, 1958, *The Myth of the Negro Past*. Boston: The Beacon Press, Inc. [1941].

————, 1971, *Life in a Haitian Valley*. New York: Anchor Books [1937].

Herskovits, Melville J., and Frances S. Herskovits, 1934, *Rebel Destiny: Among the Bush Negroes of Dutch Guiana*. New York: Whittlesey House.

————, 1947, *Trinidad Village*. New York: Alfred A. Knopf.

Hill, Clifford S., 1963, *West Indian Migrants and the London Churches*. London: Oxford University Press.

Hill, Lawrence F., 1932, *Diplomatic Relations Between the United States and Brazil*. Durham, N.C.: Duke University Press.

Hobsbawm, Eric J., 1967, Peasants and Rural Migrants in Politics. In Claudio Véliz (ed.), *The Politics of Conformity in Latin America*. London: Oxford University Press, pp. 43–65.

Holmberg, Allan R., 1950, *Nomads of the Long Bow: The Sirionó of Eastern Bolivia*. Washington, D.C.: Smithsonian Institution, Institute of Social Anthropology, Publication no. 10.

————, 1960, Changing Community Attitudes and Values in Peru: A Case Study in Guided Change. In Richard N. Adams, *et al., Social Change in Latin America Today*. New York: Vintage Books, pp. 63–107.

————, 1966, *Vicos: Método y Práctica de Antropología Aplicada*. Lima: Editorial Estudios Andinos, S.A.

Huddleston, Lee Eldridge, 1967, *Origins of the American Indians: European Concepts, 1492–1729*. Austin, Tex.: University of Texas Press, Latin American Monograph Series, no. 11.

Humboldt, Alexander von, 1814, *Researches Concerning the Institutions and Monuments of the Ancient Inhabitants of America, with Descriptions and Views of Some of the Most Striking Scenes in the Cordilleras*. London: Longmans (2 vols.).

Humphreys, Robert A., 1946, *The Evolution of Modern Latin America*. Oxford: Clarendon Press.

Hutchinson, Harry W., 1952, Race Relations in a Rural Community of the Bahian Recôncavo. In Charles Wagley (ed.), *Race and Class in Rural Brazil*. Paris: U.N.E.S.C.O., pp. 16–46.

————, 1957, *Village and Plantation Life in Northeastern Brazil*. Seattle: University of Washington Press.

Instituto de Investigaciones Sociales, 1957, *Etnografía de México: Síntesis Monográficas*. Mexico City: Universidad Nacional Autónoma de México.

Instituto de Tierras y Colonización, 1963, *Proyecto de Colonización de Bataan*. San José, Costa Rica: Instituto de Tierras y Colonización.

Izumi, Seiichi, and Toshihoko Sono, 1963, *Andes 2, Excavations at Kotosh, Peru 1960*. Tokyo: Kadokawa Publishing Company.

James, Preston E., 1959, *Latin America*. 3rd ed. New York: The Odyssey Press, Inc. [1942].

Johnston, Sir Harry, 1969, *The Negro in the New World*. New York: Johnston Reprint Corporation [1910].

Jones, Clarence F., and Paul C. Morrison, 1952, Evolution of the Banana Industry of Costa Rica. *Economic Geography* 28(1):1–19.

Kadt, Emanuel de, 1967, Religion, the Church, and Social Change in Brazil. In Claudio Véliz (ed.), *The Politics of Conformity in Latin America*. London: Oxford University Press, pp. 192–220.

Kantor, Harry, 1953, *The Ideology and Program of the Peruvian Aprista Movement*. Berkeley, Calif.: University of California Press, University of California Publications in Political Science vol. 4, no. 1.

Keithan, Elizabeth F., 1940, Cacao in Costa Rica. *Economic Geography* 16:79–86.

Kemper, Robert V., 1970, The Anthropological Study of Migration to Latin American Cities. *Kroeber Anthropological Society Papers* 42:1–25.

———, 1971, Bibliografía Comentada sobre la Antropología Urbana en América Latina. *Boletín Bibliográfico de Antropología Americana* 33–34:86–140.

Kennedy, John G., 1963, Tesguino Complex: The Role of Beer in Tarahumara Culture. *American Anthropologist* 65(3):620–640.

Kent, R. K., 1965, Palmares: An African State in Brazil. *Journal of African History* 6(2):161–175.

Kepner, Charles David, Jr., 1936, *Social Aspects of the Banana Industry*. New York: Columbia University Press.

Kepner, Charles David, Jr., and Jay Henry Soothill, 1935, *The Banana Empire: A Case Study of Economic Imperialism*. New York: Vanguard Press, Inc.

King, Arden R., 1965, Hamburg Financial Houses and German Coffee Growers in Guatemala, 1870–1940. *Year Book of the American Philosophical Society* 1965:402–405.

———, 1967, The Persistence of Cultural Identity: The Ineffectiveness of Repeated Foreign Cultural Dominance. Paper presented at the Annual Meeting of the American Society for Ethnohistory, Lexington, Ky.

King, Edward, (Lord Kingsborough), 1830–1848, *Antiquities of Mexico*. London: A. Aglio (9 vols.).

Kirchhoff, Paul, 1952, Mesoamerica: Its Geographic Limits, Ethnic Composition and Cultural Characteristics. In Sol Tax, *et al.*, *Heritage of Conquest: The Ethnology of Middle America*. New York: The Free Press, pp. 17–30 [1943].

Klass, Morton, 1961, *East Indians in Trinidad*. New York: Columbia University Press.

Krieger, Alex D., 1964, Early Man in the New World. In Jesse D. Jennings and Edward Norbeck (eds.), *Prehistoric Man in the New World*. Chicago: University of Chicago Press, pp. 23–81.

Kubler, George, 1946, The Quechua in the Colonial World. In Julian H. Steward (ed.), *Handbook of South American Indians*. Washington, D.C.: Smithsonian Institution, Bureau of American Ethnology, Bulletin no. 143, vol. 2, pp. 331–410.

Kuczynski, Robert R., 1936, *Population Movements*. Oxford: Clarendon Press.

Kushner, Gilbert, 1969, The Anthropology of Complex Societies. In Bernard J. Siegel (ed.), *Biennial Review of Anthropology*. Stanford, Calif.: Stanford University Press, pp. 80–131.

Kwong, Alice Jo, 1958, The Chinese in Peru. In Morton Fried (ed.), *Colloquium on Overseas Chinese*. New York: International Secretariat, Institute of Pacific Relations, pp. 41–48.

Landsberger, Henry A. (ed.), 1969, *Latin American Peasant Movements*. Ithaca, N.Y.: Cornell University Press.

Lanning, Edward P., 1967, *Peru before the Incas*. © 1967, Prentice-Hall, Inc., Englewood Cliffs, N.J.: Prentice-Hall, Inc.

Leeds, Anthony, 1957, *Economic Cycles in Brazil: The Persistence of a Total Culture Pattern*. Unpublished Ph.D. dissertation, Columbia University.

――――, 1965, Brazilian Careers and Social Structure: A Case History and Model. In Dwight B. Heath and Richard N. Adams (eds.), *Contemporary Cultures and Societies of Latin America*. New York: Random House, Inc., pp. 379–404 [1964].

León, Jorge, 1948, Land Utilization in Costa Rica. *The Geographical Review* 38(3):444–456.

León, Nicolas, 1924, *Las Castas de Mestizaje del México Colonial o Nueva España*. Mexico: Talleras Gráficos del Museo Nacional, Publicaciones del Departamento Antropología Anatómica, no. 1.

Leonard, Olen E., 1948, La Paz, Bolivia: Its Population and Growth. *American Sociological Review* 13:448–454.

Lewis, Matthew G., 1929, *Journal of a West Indian Proprietor,* London: John Murray [1834].

Lewis, Oscar, 1949, Husbands and Wives in a Mexican Village: A Study of Role Conflict. *American Anthropologist* 51:602–610.

――――, 1951, *Life in a Mexican Village: Tepoztlán Restudied*. Urbana, Ill.: University of Illinois Press.

――――, 1952, Urbanization without Breakdown: A Case Study. *The Scientific Monthly* 75:31–41.

――――, 1953, Tepoztlán Restudied: A Critique of the Folk-Urban Conceptualization of Social Change. *Rural Sociology* 18:121–134.

――――, 1959, *Five Families: Mexican Case Studies in the Culture of Poverty*. New York: Basic Books, Inc.

――――, 1960, *Tepoztlán: Village in Mexico*. New York: Holt, Rinehart and Winston, Inc.

――――, 1961, *The Children of Sánchez: Autobiography of a Mexican Family*. New York: Random House, Inc.

――――, 1964, *Pedro Martínez: A Mexican Peasant and His Family*. New York: Random House, Inc.

――――, 1965, *La Vida: A Puerto Rican Family in the Culture of Poverty—San Juan and New York*. New York: Random House, Inc.

――――, 1966, The Culture of Poverty. *Scientific American* 215(4):19–25.

――――, 1968, *A Study of Slum Culture. Backgrounds for La Vida*. New York: Random House, Inc.

――――, 1969, The Possesssions of the Poor. *Scientific American* 221(4):114–124.

Leyburn, James G., 1966, *The Haitian People*. rev. ed. New Haven, Conn.: Yale University Press [1941].

Liebman, Seymour B., 1970, *The Jews in New Spain: Faith, Flame and the Inquisition.* Coral Gables, Fla.: University of Miami Press.

Lipman, Aaron, 1969, *The Colombian Entrepreneur in Bogotá.* Coral Gables, Fla.: University of Miami Press, Hispanic-American Studies no. 22.

Lipset, Seymour Martin, and Aldo Solari (eds.), 1967, *Elites in Latin America.* London: Oxford University Press.

Livermore, Harold, 1960, *A History of Spain.* New York: Grove Press, Inc. [1958].

Lorente, Sebastián, 1867–1872, *Relaciones de los Vireyes y Audiencias que han Gobernado el Perú.* Lima and Madrid (3 vols.).

MacNutt, Francis Augustus (ed.), 1908, *Letters of Cortes: The Five Letters of Relation from Fernando Cortes to the Emperor, Charles V.* New York: G. P. Putnam's Sons (2 vols.).

Madsen, William, 1955, Hot and Cold in the Universe of San Francisco Tecospa, Valley of Mexico. *Journal of American Folklore* 68:123–139.

_____, 1957, *Christo-Paganism: A Study of Mexican Religious Syncretism.* New Orleans: Tulane University, Middle American Research Institute, Publication no. 19, pp. 105–180.

_____, 1960, *The Virgin's Children: Life in an Aztec Village Today.* Austin, Tex.: University of Texas Press.

_____, 1969, The Nahua. In Evon Z. Vogt (ed.), *Handbook of Middle American Indians.* Austin, Tex.: University of Texas Press, vol. 8, part 2, pp. 602–637.

Maine, Sir Henry J. S., 1861, *Ancient Law: Its Connection with the Early History of Society and Its Relation to Modern Ideas.* London: John Murray.

_____, 1887, *Village Communities in the East and West.* London: John Murray.

Mangin, William, 1961, Fiestas Among Andean Indians. In Viola E. Garfield (ed.), *Proceedings of the 1961 Annual Spring Meeting of the American Ethnological Society,* Seattle: University of Washington Press, pp. 84–92.

_____, 1967a, Latin American Squatter Settlements: A Problem and a Solution. *Latin American Research Review* 2(3):65–98.

_____, 1967b, Squatter Settlements. *Scientific American* 217(4):21–29.

_____, 1970a, Tales from the Barriadas. In William Mangin (ed.), *Peasants in Cities.* Boston: Houghton Mifflin Company, pp. 55–61 [1968].

_____, 1970b, Urbanization in Case History in Peru. In William Mangin (ed.), *Peasants in Cities.* Boston: Houghton Mifflin Company, pp. 47–54 [1963].

_____, 1970c, Similarities and Differences Between Two Types of Peruvian Communities. In William Mangin (ed.), *Peasants in Cities.* Boston: Houghton Mifflin Company, pp. 20–29 [1965].

Manners, Robert A., and Julian H. Steward, 1954, The Cultural Study of Contemporary Societies: Puerto Rico. *The American Journal of Sociology* 54:123–130.

Martyr d'Anghera, Peter, 1912, *De Orbe Novo; the Eight Decades of Peter Martyr d'Anghera.* New York: G. P. Putnam's Sons (2 vols.) [1516].

Masing, Ulv, 1965, *Foreign Agricultural Colonies in Costa Rica: An Analysis of Foreign Colonization in a Tropical Environment*. Ann Arbor, Mich.: University Microfilms.

Mason, J. Alden, 1957, *The Ancient Civilizations of Peru*. Baltimore: Penguin Books, Inc.

Matos Mar, José, 1961, Migration and Urbanization—The "Barriadas" of Lima: An Example of Integration into Urban Life. In P. M. Hauser (ed.), *Urbanization in Latin America*. New York: U.N.E.S.C.O., pp. 170–190.

————, 1966, *Estudio de las Barriadas Limeñas*. Lima: Instituto de Estudios Peruanos.

————, 1968, *Urbanización y Barriadas en América del Sur*. Lima: Instituto de Estudios Peruanos.

May, Stacy, and Galo Plaza, 1958, *The United Fruit Company in Latin America*. Washington, D.C.: National Planning Association.

McGinn, Noel F., and Russell G. Davis, 1969, *Build a Mill, Build a City, Build a School: Industrialization, Urbanization and Education in Ciudad Guayana, Venezuela*. Cambridge, Mass.: M.I.T. Press.

Mendieta y Núñez, Lucio, 1960, Efectos Sociales de la Reforma Agraria en Tres Comunidades Ejidales. *Revista Mexicana de Sociología* 23(2):350–384.

Millon, Rene, 1967, Teotihuacán. *Scientific American* 216(6):38–48.

————, 1970, Teotihuacán: Completion of Map of Giant Ancient City in the Valley of Mexico. *Science* 170(3962):1077–1082.

Ministerio de Economía y Hacienda, 1960, *Censo de Población de Costa Rica, 11 de Mayo de 1927*. San José, Costa Rica: Dirección General de Estadística y Censos.

Mintz, Sidney W., 1953, The Folk-Urban Continuum and the Rural Proletarian Community. *American Journal of Sociology* 59:136–143.

————, 1961, Review of Elkin's *Slavery. American Anthropologist* 63(3):579–587.

————, 1964, Forward. In Ramiro Guerra y Sánchez, *Sugar and Society in the Caribbean: An Economic History of Cuban Agriculture*. New Haven, Conn.: Yale University Press, pp. xi–xliv.

Mintz, Sidney W., and Eric R. Wolf, 1950, An Analysis of Ritual Co-Parenthood (Compadrazgo). *Southwestern Journal of Anthropology* 6:341–368.

Mitchell, J. Clyde, 1966, Theoretical Orientation in African Urban Studies. In Michael Banton (ed.), *The Social Anthropology of Complex Societies*. London: Tavistock Publications, pp. 37–68.

Montesclaros, Juan de Mendoza, y Luna, Marquis de, 1859, *Memorial . . . Memorias de los Vireyes*. Lima: F. Bailly, vol. 1, pp. 1–69.

Monzon, Arturo, 1949, *El Calpulli en la Organización Social de los Tenochca*. Mexico City: Publicaciones del Instituto de Historia, no. 14.

Moog, Clodomir Viana, 1964, *Bandeirantes and Pioneers*. New York: George Braziller, Inc. [1954].

Moore, John P., 1954, *The Cabildo in Peru under the Hapsburgs: A Study in the Origins and Powers of the Town Council in the Viceroyalty of Peru, 1530–1700*. Durham, N.C.: Duke University Press.

Morgan, Lewis H., 1877, *Ancient Society, or Researches in the Lines of Human Progress from Savagery, through Barbarism to Civilization.* New York: Henry Holt and Company.

Morley, Sylvanus G., 1956, *The Ancient Maya.* 3rd ed., rev. George W. Brainerd. Stanford, Calif.: Stanford University Press [1946].

Mörner, Magnus, 1967, *Race Mixture in the History of Latin America.* Boston: Little, Brown & Company.

Morse, Richard M., 1962, Some Characteristics of Latin American Urban History. *American Historical Review* 67(2):317–338.

————, 1965, Recent Research on Latin American Urbanization: A Selective Survey with Commentary. *Latin American Research Review* 1(1):35–74.

————, 1971, Trends and Issues in Latin American Urban Research, 1965–1970. *Latin American Research Review* 6(1):3–52; (2):19–75.

Moss, Leonard, and Stephen Cappanari, 1960, Patterns of Kinship, Comparaggio and Community in a South Italian Village. *Anthropological Quarterly* 33:24–32.

Munro, Dana G., 1950, *The Latin American Republics.* 2nd ed. New York: Appleton-Century-Crofts [1942].

Murdock, George P., 1959, *Africa: Its Peoples and their Culture History.* New York: McGraw-Hill, Inc.

Murphy, Robert F., 1960, *Headhunter's Heritage: Social and Economic Change Among the Mundurucú Indians.* Berkeley, Calif.: University of California Press.

Murra, John V., 1970, Current Research and Prospects in Andean Ethnohistory. *Latin American Research Review* 5(1):3–36.

Nelson, Lowry, 1950, The Social Class Structure in Cuba. In Theo. Crevenna (ed.), *Materiales para el Estudio de la Clase Media en la América Latina.* Washington, D.C.: Unión Panamericana, vol. 2, pp. 45–73.

Nimuendajú, Curt, 1939, *The Apinayé.* Washington, D.C.: Catholic University of America, Anthropological Series, no. 8.

————, 1942, *The Serente.* Los Angeles: Southwest Museum, Publication of the Frederick Webb Hodge Anniversary Publication Fund, vol. 4.

————, 1946, *The Eastern Timbira.* Berkeley, Calif.: University of California Press.

Nun, José, 1967, The Middle-Class Military Coup. In Claudio Véliz (ed.), *The Politics of Conformity in Latin America.* London: Oxford University Press, pp. 66–118.

Nunley, Robert F., 1960, *The Distribution of Population in Costa Rica.* Washington, D.C.: National Academy of Sciences—National Research Council, Publication no. 743.

Olien, Michael D., 1967, *The Negro in Costa Rica: The Ethnohistory of an Ethnic Minority in a Complex Society.* Unpublished Ph.D. dissertation, University of Oregon.

————, 1968, Levels of Urban Relationships in a Complex Society: A Costa Rican Case. In Elizabeth M. Eddy (ed.), *Urban Anthropology: Research Perspectives and Strategies.* Athens, Ga.: Proceedings of the Southern Anthropological Society, no. 2, pp. 83–92.

————, 1970, *The Negro in Costa Rica: The Role of an Ethnic Minority in a Developing Society.* Winston-Salem, N.C.: Wake Forest University, Overseas Research Center, Developing Nations Monograph Series, no. 3.

Orso, Ethelyn, 1970, *Hot and Cold in the Folk Medicine of the Island of Chira, Costa Rica.* Baton Rouge, La.: Louisiana State University, Latin American Studies Institute, Monograph and Dissertation Series, no. 1.

Padden, R. C., 1967, *The Hummingbird and the Hawk: Conquest and Sovereignty in the Valley of Mexico, 1503–1541.* New York: Harper & Row, Publishers.

Padilla, Elena, 1958, *Up from Puerto Rico.* New York: Columbia University Press.

————, 1960, Contemporary Social-Rural Types in the Caribbean Region. In Vera Rubin (ed.), *Caribbean Studies: A Symposium.* 2nd ed. Seattle: University of Washington Press, pp. 22–29 [1957].

Palmer, Frederick, 1910, *Central America and its Problems.* New York: Moffat, Yard and Company.

Paul, Benjamin D., 1942, *Ritual Kinship, with Special Reference to Godparenthood in Middle America.* Unpublished Ph.D. dissertation, University of Chicago.

Paz, Octavio, 1961, *The Labyrinth of Solitude: Life and Thought in Mexico.* 2nd ed. New York: Grove Press, Inc. [1950].

Pearcy, G. Etzel, 1965, *The West Indian Scene.* Princeton, N.J.: D. Van Nostrand Company, Inc.

Peattie, Lisa Redfield, 1968, *The View from the Barrio.* Ann Arbor, Mich.: University of Michigan Press.

Peña, Moisés T. de la, 1964, *El Pueblo y Su Tierra; Mito y Realidad de la Reforma Agraria en México.* Mexico City: Cuadernos Americanos.

Pendergast, David M. (ed.), 1967, *Palenque: the Walker-Caddy Expedition to the Ancient Maya City, 1839–1840.* Norman, Okla.: University of Oklahoma Press.

Pendle, George, 1963, *A History of Latin America.* Baltimore: Penguin Books, Inc.

Pitt-Rivers, Julian, 1958, Ritual Kinship in Spain. *Transactions of the New York Academy of Sciences,* Series 2, vol. 20, pp. 424–431.

Pizarro, Pedro, 1921, *Relation of the Discovery and Conquest of the Kingdoms of Peru.* 2 vols. New York: The Cortes Society [written 1571; published 1844].

Polo de Ondegardo, Juan, 1873, *Narrative of the Rites and Laws of the Incas.* London: Printed for the Hakluyt Society [1559–1571].

————, 1916, Relación de los Fundamentos Acerca del Notable Daño que Resulto de No Guardar á los Indios Sus Fueros. . . . *Colección de Libros y Documentos Referentes á la Historia del Perú.* Lima: Sanmarti, Series 1, vol. 3, pp. 45–188, [1571].

Poma de Ayala, Felipe Guaman, 1936, *Nueva Crónica y Buen Gobierno (Codex Péruvien Illustre).* Paris: Institut d'Ethnologie, Université de Paris à la Sorbonne, Travaux et Mémoires, vol. 23 [1580–1620].

Poppino, Rollie E., 1968, *Brazil: the Land and People.* New York: Oxford University Press.

Porter, Muriel Noé, 1953, *Tlatilco and the Pre-Classic Cultures of the New World.* New York: Viking Fund Publication, no. 19.

Price, Thomas J., 1970, Ethnohistory and Self-Image in Three New World Negro Societies. In Norman E. Whitten, Jr. and John F. Szwed (eds.), *Afro-American Anthropology.* New York: The Free Press, pp. 63–73.

Putnam, George Palmer, 1913, *The Southland of North America: Rambles and Observations in Central America During the Year 1912.* New York: G. P. Putnam's Sons.

Recinos, Adrian (ed.), 1950, *Popol Vuh: The Sacred Book of the Ancient Quiché Maya.* Norman, Okla.: University of Oklahoma Press.

Recinos, Adrian, and Delia Goetz (eds.), 1953, *The Annals of the Cakchiquels.* Norman, Okla.: University of Oklahoma Press.

Redekop, Calvin, and Charles P. Loomis, 1968, Ethnic Social System Survival: A Case Study. Paper presented at the Annual Meeting of the American Anthropological Association, Seattle.

Redfield, Margaret P., 1935, *The Folk Literature of a Yucatecan Town.* Washington, D.C.: Carnegie Institution of Washington, Contributions to American Archaeology, no. 13.

Redfield, Robert, 1930, *Tepoztlán, a Mexican Village: A Study of Folk Life.* Chicago: University of Chicago Press.

————, 1941, *The Folk Culture of Yucatán.* Chicago: University of Chicago Press.

————, 1947, The Folk Society. *American Journal of Sociology* 52:293–308.

————, 1950, *A Village that Chose Progress: Chan Kom Revisited.* Chicago: University of Chicago Press.

————, 1962, Civilizations as Societal Structures? The Development of Community Studies. In Margaret P. Redfield (ed.), *Human Nature and the Study of Society: The Papers of Robert Redfield.* Chicago: University of Chicago Press, vol. 1.

Redfield, Robert, and Margaret P. Redfield, 1940, *Disease and Its Treatment in Dzitas, Yucatán.* Washington, D.C.: Carnegie Institution of Washington, Publication no. 523, Contributions to American Anthropology and History, no. 32.

Redfield, Robert, and Milton B. Singer, 1954, The Cultural Role of Cities. *Economic Development and Cultural Change* 3:53–73.

Redfield, Robert, and Alfonso Villa Rojas, 1934, *Chan Kom: A Maya Village.* Washington, D.C.: Carnegie Institution of Washington, Publication no. 448.

Reichel-Dolmatoff, Gerardo, and Alicia Reichel-Dolmatoff, 1961, *The People of Aritama.* London: Routledge & Kegan Paul.

Reid, Ira de, 1937–1938, Negro Immigration to the United States. *Social Forces* 16:411–417.

Reina, Ruben E., 1959, Two Patterns of Friendship in a Guatemalan Community. *American Anthropologist* 61(1):44–50.

————, 1964, The Urban World View of the Tropical Forest Community in the Absence of a City, Peten, Guatemala. *Human Organization* 23(4):265–277.

————, 1966, *The Law of the Saints: A Pokomam Pueblo and Its Community Culture.* Indianapolis: The Bobbs-Merrill Company, Inc.

Reissman, Leonard, 1964, *The Urban Process: Cities in Industrial Societies.* New York: The Free Press.

Ricard, Robert, 1933, *La conquête spirituelle du Méxique. Essai sur l'apostolat et les méthodes missionaires des ordres mendiantes en Nouvelle Espagne, de 1523 à 1572.* Paris: Institut d'Ethnologie, Université de Paris à la Sorbonne, Travaux et Mémoires, vol. 20.

Richardson, Miles, and Barbara Bode, 1971, *Popular Medicine in Puntarenas, Costa Rica: Urban and Societal Features*. New Orleans: Tulane University, Middle American Research Institute, Publication no. 24, pp. 249–275.

Río, Antonio del, 1822, *Description of the Ruins of an Ancient City Discovered near Palenque in the Kingdom of Guatemala*. London: H. Berthoud and Suttahy, Evance and Fox.

Rivière, Peter, 1972, *The Forgotten Frontier: Ranchers of Northern Brazil*. New York: Holt, Rinehart and Winston, Inc.

Robertson, William Spence, 1961, *Rise of the Spanish-American Republics as Told in the Lives of Their Liberators*. New York: Collier Books [1918].

Robinson, Harry, 1967, *Latin America: a Geographical Survey*. rev. ed. New York: Frederick A. Praeger, Inc.

Rodrigues, José Honório, 1967, *The Brazilians, Their Character and Aspirations*. Austin, Tex.: University of Texas Press.

Rollwagen, Jack R., 1968, *The Paleteros of Mexticacan, Jalisco: A Study of Entrepreneurship in Mexico*. Unpublished Ph.D. dissertation, University of Oregon.

Romano, Octavio Ignacio, 1960, Donship in a Mexican-American Community in Texas. *American Anthropologist* 62(6):966–976.

Rosenblat, Ángel, 1945, *La Población Indígena de América desde 1492 hasta la Actualidad,* (rev. ed.). Buenos Aires: Institución Cultural Española [1935].

————, 1954, *La Población Indígena y el Mestizaje en América*. Buenos Aires: Editorial Nova (2 vols.).

Rowe, John H., 1946, Inca Culture at the Time of the Spanish Conquest. In Julian Steward (ed.), *Handbook of South American Indians*. Washington, D.C.: Smithsonian Institution, Bureau of American Ethnology, Bulletin no. 143, vol. 2, pp. 183–330.

————, 1965, The Renaissance Foundations of Anthropology. *American Anthropologist* 67(1):1–20.

Roys, Ralph L., 1933, *The Book of Chilam Balam of Chumayel*. Washington, D.C.: Carnegie Institution of Washington, Publication no. 438.

Rubel, Arthur J., 1960, Concepts of Disease in Mexican-American Culture. *American Anthropologist* 62(5):795–814.

————, 1964, The Epidemiology of a Folk Illness: *Susto* in Hispanic America. *Ethnology* 3(3):268–283.

————, 1965, The Mexican-American Palomilla. *Anthropological Linguistics* 7(4):92–97.

————, 1966, *Across the Tracks: Mexican-Americans in a Texas City*. Austin, Tex.: University of Texas Press.

Sahagún, Bernardino de, 1950–1963, *Florentine Codex: The General History of the Things of New Spain*. Salt Lake City: University of Utah Press (13 Books) [16th century].

Sahlins, Marshall D., 1968, *Tribesmen*. Englewood Cliffs, N.J.: Prentice-Hall, Inc.

Sanders, William T., and Joseph Marino, 1970, *New World Prehistory: Archaeology of the American Indian*. Englewood Cliffs, N.J.: Prentice-Hall, Inc.

Sanders, William T., and Barbara J. Price, 1968, *Mesoamerica: The Evolution of a Civilization.* New York: Random House, Inc.

Santo Tomas, Domingo de, 1951a, *Gramática o Arte de la Lengua General de los Indios de los Reynos del Perú.* Lima [1560].

————, 1951b, *Lexico o Vocabulario de la Lengua General del Perú.* Lima [1560].

Santos, John, 1967, Personal Values. In Samuel Shapiro (ed.), *Integration of Man and Society in Latin America.* Notre Dame, Ind.: University of Notre Dame Press, pp. 3–11.

Sapper, Karl, 1924, Die Zahl und die Volksdichte der Indianischen Bevölkerung in Amerika von der Conquista und in der Gegenwart. *Proceedings of the 21st International Congress of Americanists.* The Hague, pp. 95–104.

Sauer, Carl O., 1959, Age and Area of American Cultivated Plants. *Actas del XXXIII Congreso Internacional de Americanistas,* Tomo 1, pp. 215–229. San José, Costa Rica: Lehmann.

Scheele, Raymond L., 1956, The Prominent Families of Puerto Rico. In Julian H. Steward (ed.), *The People of Puerto Rico: A Study in Social Anthropology.* Urbana, Ill.: University of Illinois Press, pp. 418–462.

Schmidt, Wilhelm, 1939, *The Culture Historical Method of Ethnology: The Scientific Approach to the Racial Question.* New York: Fortuny's.

Schurz, William Lytle, 1964, *Latin America: a Descriptive Survey.* rev. ed. New York: E. P. Dutton & Co. [1941].

Schwerin, Karl H., 1970, *Winds across the Atlantic.* Carbondale, Ill.: Southern Illinois University, University Museum, Mesoamerican Studies, Research Records no. 6.

Scobie, James R., 1964, *Argentina: a City and a Nation.* New York: Oxford University Press.

Service, Elman R., 1954, *Spanish-Guaraní Relations in Early Colonial Paraguay.* Ann Arbor: University of Michigan, Museum of Anthropology, Anthropology Papers, no. 9.

————, 1955, Indian-European Relations in Colonial Latin America. *American Anthropologist* 57:411–425.

Service, Elman R., and Helen S. Service, 1954, *Tobatí: Paraguayan Town.* Chicago: University of Chicago Press.

Shouse, Melvin E., 1938, *The Lowland Hinterland of Limón, Costa Rica.* Unpublished M.S. thesis, University of Chicago.

Silvert, K. H., 1965, *Chile: Yesterday and Today.* New York: Holt, Rinehart and Winston, Inc.

Simmons, Ozzie G., 1961, The Mutual Images and Expectations of Anglo-Americans and Mexican-Americans. *Daedalus* 90(2):286–299.

————, 1965, The *Criollo* Outlook in the Mestizo Culture of Coastal Peru. In Dwight B. Heath and Richard N. Adams (eds.), *Contemporary Cultures and Societies of Latin America.* New York: Random House, Inc., pp. 518–530 [1955].

Simpson, Lesley Byrd, 1950, *The Encomienda in New Spain.* Berkeley, Calif.: University of California Press.

————, 1963, Foreword. In François Chevalier, *Land and Society in Colonial Mexico.* Berkeley, Calif.: University of California Press, pp. v–ix.

Sjoberg, Gideon, 1960, *The Preindustrial City: Past and Present.* New York: The Free Press.

Smith, Alfred Edgar, 1933, West Indians on the Campus. *Opportunity, Journal of Negro Life* 11(8):238–241.

Smith, C. T., 1970, Depopulation of the Central Andes in the Sixteenth Century. *Current Anthropology* 11(4–5):453–464.

Smith, G. Elliot, 1916, The Origin of the Pre-Columbian Civilization of America. *Science* 44(1128):190–195.

————, 1933, *The Diffusion of Culture.* London: C. A. Watts & Co., Ltd.

Smith, M. G., 1965, *Stratification in Grenada.* Berkeley, Calif.: University of California Press.

Smith, T. Lynn, 1954, *Brazil: People and Institutions.* 2nd ed. Baton Rouge, La.: Louisiana State University Press.

Snyder, Joan, 1957, The Changing Context of an Andean Community. In Verne F. Ray (ed.), *Proceedings of the 1957 Annual Spring Meeting of the American Ethnological Society.* Seattle: University of Washington Press, pp. 20–29.

Soustelle, Jacques, 1970, *Daily Life of the Aztecs on the Eve of the Spanish Conquest.* Stanford, Calif.: Stanford University Press [1955].

Spinden, H. J., 1928, The Population of Ancient America. *Geographical Review* 18:641–660.

Squier, E. George, 1877, *Peru: Incidents of Travel and Explorations in the Land of the Incas.* London: Macmillan and Company.

Stanislawski, Dan, 1947, Early Spanish Town Planning in the New World. *Geographical Review* 37:95–105.

Starr, Frederick, 1899, *Indians of Southern Mexico: an Ethnographic Album.* Chicago: By the Author.

————, 1900–1902, *Notes upon the Ethnography of Southern Mexico.* Davenport, Iowa: Proceedings of the Davenport Academy of Natural Science, vols. 8 and 9.

Stavenhagen, Rodolfo (ed.), 1970, *Agrarian Problems and Peasant Movements in Latin America.* New York: Doubleday & Company, Inc.

Steck, Francis Borgia, 1944, *El Primer Colegio de América, Santa Cruz de Tlaltetlolco.* Mexico City: Centro de Estudios Franciscanos.

————, 1951, *Motolinia's History of the Indians of New Spain.* Washington, D.C.: Academy of American Franciscan History, Documentary Series, vol. 1.

Stein, William W., 1957, Outside Contact and Cultural Stability in a Peruvian Highland Village. In Verne F. Ray (ed.), *Proceedings of the 1957 Annual Spring Meeting of the American Ethnological Society.* Seattle: University of Washington Press, pp. 15–19.

————, 1961, *Hualcan: Life in the Highlands of Peru.* Ithaca, N.Y.: Cornell University Press.

Stephens, John L., 1841, *Incidents of Travel in Central America, Chiapas, and Yucatán.* New York: Harper and Brothers (2 vols.).

————, 1843, *Incidents of Travel in Yucatán.* New York: Harper and Brothers (2 vols.).

Stephens, Richard H., 1971, *Wealth and Power in Peru.* Metuchen, N.J.: Scarecrow Press, Inc.

Steward, Julian H., 1950, *Area Research: Theory and Practice.* New York: Social Science Research Council, Bulletin no. 63.

————, 1955, *Theory of Culture Change: the Methodology of Multilinear Evolution.* Urbana, Ill.: University of Illinois Press.

————, 1959, Perspective on Plantations. In *Plantation Systems of the New World.* Washington, D.C.: Pan American Union, Social Science Monographs, no. 7, pp. 5–12.

Steward, Julian H. (ed.), 1946–1959, *Handbook of South American Indians.* Washington, D.C.: Smithsonian Institution, Bureau of American Ethnology, Bulletin no. 143 (7 vols.).

————, 1956, *The People of Puerto Rico: A Study in Social Anthropology.* Urbana, Ill.: University of Illinois Press.

Steward, Julian H., and Louis C. Faron, 1959, *Native Peoples of South America.* New York: McGraw-Hill, Inc.

Stewart, Norman R., 1967, *Japanese Colonization in Eastern Paraguay.* Washington, D.C.: National Academy of Sciences—National Research Council, Publication no. 1490.

Stewart, Watt, 1951, *Chinese Bondage in Peru: A History of the Chinese Coolie in Peru, 1849–1874.* Durham, N.C.: Duke University Press.

————, 1964, *Keith and Costa Rica: a Biographical Study of Minor Cooper Keith.* Albuquerque, N.M.: University of New Mexico Press.

Strickon, Arnold, 1964, Anthropology in Latin America. In Charles Wagley (ed.), *Social Science Research on Latin America.* New York: Columbia University Press, pp. 125–167.

————, 1965a, Hacienda and Plantation in Yucatán: An Historical-Ecological Consideration of the Folk-Urban Continuum in Yucatán. *América Indígena* 25(1):35–63.

————, 1965b, The Euro-American Ranching Complex. In Anthony Leeds and A. P. Vayda (eds.), *Man, Culture, and Animals.* Washington, D.C.: American Association for the Advancement of Science, Publication no. 78, pp. 229–258.

————, 1967, Folk Models of Stratification, Political Ideology, and Socio-Cultural Systems. In Paul Halmes (ed.), *Latin-American Sociological Studies.* Staffordshire, England: University of Keele, The Sociological Review Monograph, no. 11, pp. 93–117.

Sunkel, Osvaldo, 1965, Change and Frustration in Chile. In Claudio Véliz (ed.), *Obstacles to Change in Latin America.* London: Oxford University Press, pp. 116–144.

Tannenbaum, Frank, 1946, *Slave and Citizen: The Negro in the Americas.* New York: Alfred A. Knopf.

————, 1948, Personal Government in Mexico. *Foreign Affairs* 27(1):44–57.

————, 1962, *Ten Keys to Latin America.* rev. ed. New York: Vintage Books [1959].

————, 1963, *Slave and Citizen: The Negro in the Americas.* New York: Vintage Books [1946].

Tapia, Andres de, 1950, Relación de Algunas Cosas de las que Acaecieron al Muy Ilustre Don Hernando Cortés. In *Crónicas de la Conquista.* Mexico City: Universidad Nacional Autónoma, Biblioteca del Estudiante Universitario.

Tax, Sol, 1937, The Municipios of the Midwestern Highlands of Guatemala. *American Anthropologist* 39(3):423–444.

———, 1939, Culture and Civilization in Guatemalan Societies. *Scientific Monthly* 48:463–467.

———, 1941, World View and Social Relations in Guatemala. *American Anthropologist* 43(1):27–42.

Thayer Ojeda, Luis, 1919, *Elementos Étnicos que Han Intervenido en la Población de Chile.* Santiago.

Thompson, Edward H., 1965, *People of the Serpent: Life and Adventure among the Mayas.* New York: Capricorn Books [1932].

Tönnies, Ferdinand, 1935, *Gemeinschaft und Gesellschaft: Grundbegriffe der reinen Soziologie.* Leipzig: H. Buske.

Tovar, Juan de, 1860, *Historia de los Yndios Mexicanos.* Mexico City.

Tozzer, Alfred M., 1907, *A Comparative Study of Mayas and Lacandones.* New York: The Macmillan Company (for the Archaeological Institute of America).

Tozzer, Alfred M. (ed.), 1941, *Landa's Relación de las Cosas de Yucatán.* Cambridge, Mass.: Papers of the Peabody Museum of American Archaeology and Ethnology, vol. 18 [written c. 1566; first published 1864].

Tschopik, Harry, Jr., 1948, On the Concept of Creole Culture in Peru. *Transactions of the New York Academy of Sciences,* Ser. 2, 10:252–261.

Turner, John C., 1965, Lima's Barriadas and Corralones: Suburbs versus Slums. *Ekistics* 19(112).

———, 1970, Barriers and Channels for Housing Development in Modernizing Countries. In William Mangin (ed.), *Peasants in Cities.* Boston: Houghton Mifflin Company, pp. 1–19 [1967].

Valentine, Charles, 1968, *Culture and Poverty: Critique and Counter-proposals.* Chicago, Ill.: University of Chicago Press.

Vega, Garcilaso de la [El Inca], 1961, *The Incas: the Royal Commentaries of the Inca.* New York: The Orion Press, Inc. [1609].

———, 1966, *Royal Commentaries of the Incas and General History of Peru.* Austin, Tex.: University of Texas Press (2 vols.) [1613].

Véliz, Claudio, 1965, Introduction. In Claudio Véliz (ed.), *Obstacles to Change in Latin America.* London: Oxford University Press, pp. 1–8.

———, 1967, Introduction. In Claudio Véliz (ed.), *The Politics of Conformity in Latin America.* London: Oxford University Press, pp. 1–14.

Villa Roja, Alfonso, 1945, *The Maya of East Central Quintana Roo.* Washington, D.C.: Carnegie Institution of Washington, Publication no. 559.

Vogt, Evon Z., 1969a, Introduction. In Evon Z. Vogt (ed.), *Handbook of Middle American Indians.* Austin, Tex.: University of Texas Press, vol. 7, part 1, pp. 3–17.

———, 1969b, *Zinacantan: A Maya Community in the Highlands of Chiapas.* Cambridge, Mass.: The Belknap Press of Harvard University Press.

———, 1970, *The Zinacantecos of Mexico: A Modern Maya Way of Life.* New York: Holt, Rinehart and Winston, Inc.

Waal Malefijt, Annemarie de, 1963, *The Javanese of Surinam: Segment of a Plural Society.* Assen, Netherlands: Van Gorcum and Company.

Waddell, D. A. G., 1961, *British Honduras: A Historical and Contemporary Survey.* London: Oxford University Press.

Wagley, Charles, 1960, Plantation-America: A Culture Sphere. In Vera Rubin (ed.), *Caribbean Studies: A Symposium* (2nd ed.) Seattle: University of Washington Press, pp. 3–13.

————, 1963, *An Introduction to Brazil*. New York: Columbia University Press.

————, 1968, *The Latin American Tradition: Essays on the Unity and the Diversity of Latin American Culture*. New York: Columbia University Press.

Wagley, Charles, and Marvin Harris, 1965, A Typology of Latin American Subcultures. In Dwight B. Heath and Richard N. Adams (eds.), *Contemporary Cultures and Societies of Latin America*. New York: Random House, Inc., pp. 42–69 [1955].

Waibel, Leo, 1939, White Settlement in Costa Rica. *Geographical Review* 29(4): 529–560.

Waldeck, Jean Frédéric, 1838, *Voyage Pittoresque et Archéologique dans la Province d'Yucatan*. Paris: B. Defour et Cie.

Waldeck, Jean Frédéric, and C. E. Brasseur de Bourbourg, 1866a, *Recherches sur les ruines de Palenqué*. Paris: A. Bertrand.

————, 1866b, *Monuments Anciens du Mexique: Palenqué et Autres Ruines de l'ancienne Civilisation du Mexique*. Paris: A. Bertrand.

Warren, Fintan B., 1963, *Vasco de Quiroga and His Pueblo-Hospitals of Santa Fe*. Washington, D.C.: Academy of American Franciscan History, Monograph Series, no. 7.

Wauchope, Robert (ed.), 1965–, *Handbook of Middle American Indians*. Austin, Tex.: University of Texas Press (11 vols.).

West, Robert C., and John P. Augelli, 1966, *Middle America: Its Lands and Peoples*. Englewood Cliffs, N.J.: Prentice-Hall, Inc.

Whitaker, Arthur P., and David C. Jordan, 1966, *Nationalism in Contemporary Latin America*. New York: The Free Press.

Whiteford, Andrew H., 1960, *Two Cities of Latin America: A Comparative Description of Social Classes*. Beloit, Wis.: Logan Museum Bulletin no. 9.

————, 1964, *Two Cities of Latin America: A Comparative Description of Social Classes*. New York: Anchor Books [1960].

————, 1970, Aristocracy, Oligarchy and Culture Change in Colombia. In A. J. Field (ed.), *City and Country in the Third World: Issues in the Modernization of Latin America,* Cambridge, Mass.: Schenkman Publishing Company, Inc., pp. 63–91.

Whitten, Norman E., Jr., 1965, *Class, Kinship and Power in an Ecuadorian Town: The Negroes of San Lorenzo*. Stanford, Calif.: Stanford University Press.

Whitten, Norman E., Jr., and John F. Szwed (eds.), 1970, *Afro-American Anthropology: Contemporary Perspectives*. New York: The Free Press.

Wicke, Charles R., 1971, *Olmec: An Early Art Style of Precolumbian Mexico*. Tucson, Ariz.: University of Arizona Press.

Wilgus, A. Curtis, and Raul D'Eça, 1963, *Latin American History*. 5th ed. New York: Barnes & Noble, Inc. [1939].

Willems, Emilio, 1953, The Structure of the Brazilian Family. *Social Forces* 31(4):339–345.

Willey, Gordon R., 1953, *Prehistoric Settlement Patterns in the Virú Valley, Peru*. Washington, D.C.: Smithsonian Institution, Bureau of American Ethnology, Bulletin no. 155.

Willey, Gordon R., 1962, The Early Great Styles and the Rise of the Pre-Colum-
bian Civilizations. *American Anthropologist* 64(1):1–14.
_____, 1966–1971, *An Introduction to American Archaeology*. Englewood
Cliffs, N.J.: Prentice-Hall, Inc. (2 vols.).
Winsberg, Morton D., 1964, *Colonia Baron Hirsch: A Jewish Agricultural Colony
in Argentina*. Gainesville, Fla.: University of Florida Press, Monographs in
Social Sciences, no. 19.
Wirth, Louis, 1938, Urbanism as a Way of Life. *American Journal of Sociology*
44:1–24.
Wolf, Eric R., 1955, Types of Latin American Peasantry. *American Anthropologist* 57(3):452–471.
_____, 1957, *The Mexican Bajío in the Eighteenth Century: An Analysis of
Cultural Integration*. New Orleans: Tulane University, Middle American Research Institute, Publication no. 17, pp. 177–200.
_____, 1959, *Sons of the Shaking Earth*. Chicago: University of Chicago Press.
_____, 1965, Aspects of Group Relations in a Complex Society: Mexico. In
Dwight B. Heath and Richard N. Adams (eds.), *Contemporary Cultures and
Societies of Latin America*. New York: Random\House, Inc., pp. 85–101
[1956].
_____, 1966a, Kinship, Friendship, and Patron-Client Relations in Complex
Societies. In Michael Banton (ed.), *The Social Anthropology of Complex
Societies*. London: Tavistock Publications, pp. 1–22.
_____, 1966b, *Peasants*. Englewood Cliffs, N.J.: Prentice-Hall, Inc.
Wolf, Eric R., and Sidney W. Mintz, 1957, Haciendas and Plantations in Middle
America and the Antilles. *Social and Economic Studies* 6:380–412.
Zárate, Augustin de, 1933, *A History of the Discovery and Conquest of Peru*.
London: Penguin Press [1555].
Zavala, Silvio A., 1937, *La "Utopia" de Tomás Moro en la Nueva España y otros
Estudios*. Mexico City: Antigua Librería Robredo, de J. Porría e Hijos.
_____, 1962, *The Colonial Period in the History of the New World*. Mexico
City: Instituto Panamericano de Geografía e Historia, Comisión de Historia,
Publication no. 239.
Zelinsky, Wilbur, 1949, The Historical Geography of the Negro Population of
Latin America. *Journal of Negro History* 34:153–221.
Zimmerman, Ben, 1952, Race Relations in the Arid Sertão. In Charles Wagley
(ed.), *Race and Class in Rural Brazil*. Paris: U.N.E.S.C.O., pp. 82–115.

APPENDIX A

Collections of articles on Latin America

Adams, Richard N., *et al.*, 1960, *Social Change in Latin America Today*. New York: Vintage Books.

Burma, John H. (ed.), 1970, *Mexican-Americans in the United States: A Reader*. Cambridge, Mass.: Schenkman Publishing Company, Inc.

Foster, George M. (ed.), 1965, *Contemporary Latin American Culture: An Anthropological Sourcebook*. New York: Selected Academic Readings.

Frucht, Richard (ed.), 1971, *Black Society in the New World*. New York: Random House, Inc.

Goldschmidt, Walter, and Harry Hoijer (eds.), *The Social Anthropology of Latin America: Essays in Honor of Ralph Leon Beals*. Los Angeles: U.C.L.A., Latin America Center, Latin American Stupdies no. 14.

Heath, Dwight B., and Richard N. Adams (eds.), 1965, *Contemporary Cultures and Societies of Latin America: A Reader in the Social Anthropology of Middle and South America and the Caribbean*. New York: Random House, Inc.

Horowitz, Irving Louis (ed.), 1970, *Masses in Latin America*. New York: Oxford University Press.

Horowitz, Michael M. (ed.), 1971, *Peoples and Cultures of the Caribbean: An Anthropological Reader*. Garden City, N.Y.: The Natural History Press.

Johnson, John J. (ed.), 1964, *Continuity and Change in Latin America*. Stanford, Calif.: Stanford University Press.

Landsberger, Henry A. (ed.), 1969, *Latin American Peasant Movements*. Ithaca, N.Y.: Cornell University Press.

Leonard, Olen E., and Charles P. Loomis (eds.), 1953, *Readings in Latin American Social Organization and Institutions*. East Lansing, Mich.: Area Research Center, Department of Sociology and Anthropology, Michigan State College Press.

Lipset, Seymour Martin, and Aldo Solari (eds.), 1967, *Elites in Latin America.* London: Oxford University Press.

Mangin, William (ed.), 1970, *Peasants in Cities.* Boston: Houghton Mifflin Company.

Pan American Union, 1959, *Plantation Systems of the New World.* Washington, D.C.: Social Science Monographs, no. 7.

Rubin, Vera (ed.), 1960, *Caribbean Studies: A Symposium* 2nd ed., Seattle: University of Washington Press [1957].

Rubin, Vera (consulting editor), 1960, *Social and Cultural Pluralism in the Caribbean.* New York: Annals of the New York Academy of Sciences; vol. 83, art. 5, pp. 761–916.

Stavenhagen, Rodolfo (ed.), 1970, *Agrarian Problems and Peasant Movements in Latin America.* New York: Anchor Books.

Te Paske, John J., and Sydney N. Fisher (eds.), 1964, *Explosive Forces in Latin America.* Columbus: Ohio State University Press.

Véliz, Claudio (ed.), 1965, *Obstacles to Change in Latin America.* London: Oxford University Press.

————, 1967, *The Politics of Conformity in Latin America.* London: Oxford University Press.

Wauchope, Robert (ed.), 1970, *The Indian Background of Latin American History: the Maya, Aztec, Inca, and Their Predecessors.* New York: Alfred A. Knopf.

Whitten, Norman E., Jr., and John F. Szwed (eds.), 1970, *Afro-American Anthropology: Contemporary Perspectives.* New York: The Free Press.

APPENDIX B

Reference material on Latin America

Abonnenc, Emile, J. Huralt, and R. Saban, 1957, *Bibliographie de la Guyane Française*. Paris: Editions Larose.

Adams, Eleanor B., 1953, *A Bio-Bibliography of Franciscan Authors in Colonial Central America*. Washington, D.C.: The Academy of American Franciscan History.

Alcina Franch, José, 1955, Fuentes indígenas de México: ensayo de sistematización bibliográfica. *Revista de Indias* 15(61–62):421–521.

_____, 1960, *Bibliografía básica de arqueología americana*. Servilla: Universidad de Sevilla, Publicaciones del Seminario de Antropología Americana, vol. 1.

Alcina Franch, José, and Josefina Palop Martínez, 1958, *América en la época de Carlos V: aportación a la bibliografía de este periodo 1900*. Madrid: Associación Hispanoamericana de Historia.

American Geographical Society of New York, 1930–1933, *A Catalogue of Maps of Hispanic America*. New York (4 vols).

Antonio, Nicolás, 1672, *Bibliotheca hispana*. Rome: Ex Officina N. A. Tinassii (2 vols.).

Araujo, Orestes, 1912, *Diccionario geográfico del Uruguay*, 2nd ed. Montevideo: Tipo-litogr. Moderna.

Archivo de Indias, 1951, *Planos de ciudades iberoamericanos y filipinas existenes en el Archivo de Indias*. Madrid (2 vols.).

Arnade, Charles W., 1958, A Selected Bibliography of Bolivian Social Sciences. *Inter-American Review of Bibliography* 8(3):256–265.

Baginsky, Paul H., 1938–1942, *German Works Relating to America, 1493–1800*. New York: Bulletin of the New York Public Library, vols. 42–44.

Baldus, Herbert, 1954, *Bibliografía comentada da etnologia brasileira. 1943–1950*. Rio de Janeiro: Editora Souza.

————, 1954, *Bibliografía crítica da etnología brasileira*. São Paulo: Comissão do IV centenáio da cidade de São Paulo.

————, 1968, *Bibliografía critica da etnología brasileira, vol. 2*. Hanover: Niedersachsische Landes-Museum, Volkerkundliche Abhanglungen Band 4.

Bandelier, Adolph F. A., 1800, Note on the Bibliography of Yucatán and Central America. *American Antiquities Society Proceedings* (n.s.), 1:82–118.

Bartley, Russell H., and Stuart L. Wagner, 1966, *A Working Guide to the History of European and American Depositories*. Stanford, Calif.: Hoover Institution Press.

Basilio, Concepción, 1959, Bibliografía sobre cultura náhuatl, 1950–1958. *Estudios de Cultura Náhuatl* 1:125–166.

————, 1960, Bibliografía sobre cultura Náhuatl: 1959. *Estudios de Cultura Náhuatl* 2:209–217.

Bayitch, Stojan Albert, 1961, *Latin America: A Bibliographical Guide to Economy, History, Law, Politics and Society*. Coral Gables, Fla.: University of Miami Press, Interamerican Legal Studies, no. 6.

————, 1967, *Latin America and the Caribbean: A Bibliographical Guide to Works in English*. Coral Gables, Fla.: University of Miami Press, Interamerican Legal Studies, no. 10.

Bazzanela, Waldemiro, 1956, *Estratificãcão e mobilidade social no Brasil: fontes bibliográficas*. Rio de Janeiro: Centro Brasileiro de Pesquisas Educacionais.

————, 1960, *Problemas de urbanização na América Latina: fontes bibliográficas*. Rio de Janeiro: Centro Latino-Americano de Pesquisas em Ciências Socials, no. 2.

Behrendt, Richard Fritz Walter, 1949, *Modern Latin America in Social Science: A Selected, Annotated Bibliography of Books, Pamphlets, and Periodicals in English in the Fields of Economics, Politics, and Sociology of Latin America*. Albuquerque, N.M.: University of New Mexico Press.

Benito, Miguel, 1971, *Latinamerika i Svensk Bibliografi/America Latina en la bibliografía sueca 1959–1969*. Stockholm: Kungliga Biblioteket and Latinamerika-Institutet i Stockholm.

Beristain de Souza, José Mariano, 1883–1897, *Biblioteca Hispano America Septentrional*. Amecameca, Chile: Tip. del Colegio Católico (4 vols., 2nd ed.) [1816–1821].

Bernal, Ignacio, 1962, *Bibliografía de arqueología y etnografía Mesoamerica y el norte de México, 1514–1960*. Mexico City: Instituto Nacional de Antropología e Historia, Memorias no. 7.

Bernal Villa, Segundo, 1969, *Guía bibliográfica de Colombia de interés para el antropólogo*. Bogotá: Ediciones Universidad de los Andes.

Beyer, Hermann, 1923, *Sucinta bibliografía sistemática de etnografía y arqueología mejicanas*. Mexico City: Secretaria de Educación Pública.

Birkos, Alexander S., and Lewis A. Tambs, 1971, *Academic Writer's Guide to Periodicals, vol. 1, (Latin American Studies)*. Kent, Ohio: Kent State University Press.

Blay, Maria Luisa de, 1964, *Contribución a la bibliografía de viajes y exploraciones de Venezuela*. Caracas: Universidad Central de Venezuela, Colección Geografía, no. 1.

Boggs, Ralph S., 1940, *Bibliography of Latin American Folklore*. New York: The H. W. Wilson Company, Inter-American Bibliographical and Library Association, Series 1, vol. 5.

Borba de Moraes, Rubens, 1958, *Bibliographia Brasiliana: Bibliographical Essay on Rare Books on Brazil Published from 1504 to 1900 and Works of Brazilian Authors Published Abroad before the Independence of Brazil in 1882*. Amsterdam: Colibrís Editora (2 vols.).

Brasseur de Bourbourg, Charles E., 1871, *Bibliothèque Mexico-Guatémalienne*. Paris: Maisonneuve.

Burrus, E. J., 1955, An Introduction to Bibliographical Tools in Spanish Archives and Manuscript Collections Relating to Hispanic America. *Hispanic American Historical Review* 35:443–483.

Butler, Ruth L., 1937, *A Check List of Manuscripts in the Edward E. Ayer Collection*. Chicago: Newberry Library.

Cáceres Freyre, Julián Bernardo, 1939–1940, Bibliografía antropológica argentina correspondiente al año 1938–1940. *Boletín Bibliográfico de Antropología Americana* 3(2):117–125, 4(3):236–244, 5(1–3):19–28.

Carvalho Neto, Paulo de, 1950, Bases bibliográficas para el estudio sistemático de la antropología paraguaya. *Boletín Bibliográfico de Antropología Americana* 13:179–210.

———, 1955, Bibliografía afro-uruguya: informe preliminar, *Boletín Bibliográfico de Antropología Americana* 18:154–164.

———, 1955, Bibliografía afro-paraguaya: informe preliminar. *Boletín Bibliográfico de Antropología Americana* 18:164–170.

Castañeda, Carlos, and Jack A. Dabbs, 1939, *Guide to the Latin American Manuscripts in the University of Texas Library*. Cambridge, Mass.: Harvard University Press.

Castillo Tejero, Noemí, and Lorena E. Mirambell Silva, 1962, *Bibliografía antropológica: trabajos publicados en México, 1955–1962*. Mexico City.

Centro Latino-Americano de Pesquisas em Ciências Sociais, 1959, *Estratificación y movilidad social en Argentina: fuentes bibliográficas (1880–1958)*. Rio de Janeiro: Publicação no. 6.

———, 1959, *Estratificación y movilidad social en el Uruguay: fuentes bibliográficas (1880–1959)*. Rio de Janeiro: Publicação no. 5.

———, 1961, *Estratificación y movilidad sociales en Chile: fuentes bibliográficas (desde los orígenes históricos hasta 1960)*. Rio de Janeiro: Publicação no. 17.

Charno, Steven M., 1969, *Latin American Newspapers in United States Libraries: A Union List*. Austin, Tex.: University of Texas, Conference on Latin American History Publications, no. 3.

Chilcote, Ronald H. (comp. and ed.), 1970, *Revolutionary and Structural Change in Latin America. A Bibliography on Ideology, Development and the Radical Left*. Stanford, Calif.: The Hoover Institution Bibliographical Series, no. 40.

Childs, James B., 1932, *The Memorias of the Republics of Central America and the Antilles*. Washington, D.C.: Government Printing Office.

Clemence, Stella R., 1932–1936, *The Harkness Collection in the Library of Congress*, vol. 1 (*Calendar of Spanish Manuscripts Concerning Peru, 1531–1651*); vol. 2 (*Documents from Early Peru*). Washington, D.C.: U.S. Government Printing Office.

Cole, George W., 1907, *Bermuda in Periodical Literature*. Brookline, Mass.: The Riverdale Press.

————, 1907, *A Catalogue of Books Relating to the Discovery and Early History of North and South America Forming a Part of the Library of E. D. Church*. New York: Dodd, Mead & Company, Inc. (5 vols.).

Comas, Juan, 1941, Aportación a la bibliografía y estadística serológica racial americana. *Boletín Bibliográfico de Antropología Americana* 5(1–3):29–37.

————, 1948, *Bibliografía morfológica humana de América del Sur*. Mexico City: Instituto Indigenista Interamericano (2 vols.).

————, 1950, Bosquejo histórico de la antropología en México. *Revista Mexicana de Estudios Antropológicos* 11:97–192.

————, 1953, *Bibliografía selectiva de las culturas indígenas de América*. Mexico City: Instituto Panamericano de Geografía e Historia, Publication no. 166.

————, 1954, *Los congresos internacionales de Americanistas: síntesis histórica e index bibliográfica general, 1875–1952*. Mexico City: Instituto Indigenista Interamericano.

————, 1956, *Historia y bibliografía de los congresos internacionales de ciencias antropológicas: 1865–1954*. Mexico City: Universidad Nacional Autónoma de México, Instituto de Historia, Publicaciones, 1 Serie, no. 37.

————, 1958–1959, Bibliografía sobre las relaciones interraciales en América Latina desde 1940. *Boletín Bibliográfico de Antropología Americana* 20–21: 120–138.

————, 1958–1959, Recopilación bibliográfica de antropología física sobre América Central. *Boletín Bibliográfico de Antropología Americana* 20–21: 138–149.

Comhaire-Sylvain, Suzanne, 1956–1957, Publicaciones haitianas de interés antropológico e histórico en 1956. *Boletín Bibliográfico de Antropología Americana* 19–20:158–159.

Comitas, Lambros, 1968, *Caribbeana 1900–1965: A Topical Bibliography*. Seattle: University of Washington Press.

Consiglieri, Pedroso Zophimo, 1912, *Catálogo bibliografico das publicaçãoes relativas aos descobrimentos Portugueses*. Lisbon: Academia das Sciencias.

Cooper, John M., 1917, *Analytical and Critical Bibliography of the Tribes of Tierra del Fuego and Adjacent Territory*. Washington, D.C.: Smithsonian Institution, Bureau of American Ethnology, Bulletin no. 63.

Cox, Edward G., 1938, *A Reference Guide to the Literature of Travel*, vol. 2 (*The New World*). Seattle: University of Washington, Publications in Language and Literature.

Cruickshank, J. Graham, 1935, A Bibliography of Barbados. *Barbados Museum and Historical Society Journal* 2:155–165, 3:20–25.

Cumberland, Charles C., 1960, *The United States-Mexican Border: A Selective Guide to the Literature of the Region*. Ithaca, N.Y.: *Rural Sociology* (June), vol. 25, no. 2, Supplement.

Cundall, Frank, 1902, *Bibliographia Jamaicensis*. Kingston, Jamaica: The Institute of Jamaica.

————, 1909, *Bibliography of the West Indies (Excluding Jamaica)*. Kingston, Jamaica: The Institute of Jamaica.

Denevan, William M., 1971, *A Bibliography of Latin American Historical Geography*. Madison, Wis.: Pan American Institute of Geography and History.

Di Benedetto, Antonio, 1948, Bibliografía antropológica argentina: 1948. *Boletín Bibliográfico de Antropología Americana* 11:62–66.

Diccionario Enciclopedico Hispano-Americano, 1887–1910, Barcelona: Montaner y Simón (28 vols.).

Dillon, Dorothy Rita, 1952, *Latin America, 1935–1949: A Selected Bibliography* New York: United Nations, Bibliographical Series, no. 2.

Dirección General de Cartografía, 1961, *Diccionario Geográfico de Guatemala.* Guatemala City: Tipografía Nacional (2 vols.).

Dominguez Sánchez Bordona, Leonardo Jesús, 1935, *Manuscritos de América.* Madrid: Catalogo de Biblioteca de Palacio, tomo 9.

Dorsey, George Amos, 1898, *A Bibliography of the Anthropology of Peru.* Chicago: Field Columbian Museum, Publication no. 23, Anthropological Series, vol. 2, no. 2, pp. 55–206.

Dossick, Jesse J., 1967, *Doctoral Research on Puerto Rico and Puerto Ricans.* New York: New York University Press.

Espejo Nuñez, Julio V., 1962, Bibliografía de arqueología peruana (1956–1961). *Boletín Bibliográfico* (Lima) 32(1–2):138–186.

_____, 1964, Bibliografía arqueólogica de Chavín. *Boletín Bibligráfico* (Lima) 36(1–2):13–40.

Evans, G. Edward, 1970, A Guide to the Pre-1750 Manuscripts in the United States Relating to Mexico and the Southwestern United States, with Emphasis on Their Value to Anthropologists. *Ethnohistory* 17(1–2):63–90.

Ewald, Robert H., 1956, *Bibliografía comentada sobre antropología social guatemalteca, 1900–1955.* Guatemala City: Seminario de Integración Social Guatemalteca.

Febres Cordero G., Julio, 1950, Bibliografía sobre indigenismo en Cuba. *Revista de la Biblioteca Nacional* (Havana) 2nd series, 1(4):113–204.

Fernández-Caballero, Carlos F. S., 1970, *Aranduka ha Kuatuanee Paragui Rembiapocue: The Paraguayan Bibliography. A Retrospective and Enumerative Bibliography of Printed Works of Paraguayan Authors.* Asunción, Paraguay, and Washington, D.C.

Forster, David W., and Virginia Ramos Forster (comp.), 1970, *Manual of Hispanic Bibliography.* Seattle: University of Washington, Publications in Language and Literature, vol. 18.

Fuchs, Helmuth, 1964, *Bibliografía básica de Ethnología de Venezuela.* Seville: Universidad de Sevilla, Publicación del Seminario de Antropología Americana, no. 5.

Gallardo, Bartolomé José, 1968, *Ensayo de una biblioteca española de libros raros y curiosos.* Madrid: Biblioteca Nacional (4 vols.) [1863–1889].

García Granados, Rafael, 1952–1953, *Diccionario biográfico de historia antigua de México.* Mexico City: Instituto de Historio. (2 vols.).

García Icazbalceta, Joaquin, 1927, *Catálogo de la colección de manuscritos relativos a la historia de América.* Mexico City: Monografías Bibliográficas Mexicanas no. 4.

_____, 1954, *Bibliografía mexicana del siglo XVI.* Mexico City: Fondo de Cultura Económica [1886].

Gayangos, Pascual de, 1875–1893, *Catalogue of the Manuscripts in the Spanish Language in the British Museum*. London: The Trustees of the British Museum (4 vols.).

Gazin Gossel, Jacques, 1926, *Elements de bibliographie générale, méthodique et historique de la Martinique*. Fort-de-France, Martinique: Impr. Antillaise.

Genoves Taragaza, Santiago, and Juan Comas, 1964, *La antropología física en México 1943–1964: inventario bibliográfico*. Mexico City: Universidad Nacional, Cuadernos del Instituto de Investigaciones Historicas, Serie Antropológica 17.

Geoghegan, Abel Rodolfo, 1965, *Obras de referencia de América Latina*. Buenos Aires, Argentina: U.N.E.S.C.O.

Gibson, Charles, 1958, *Guide to the Hispanic American Historical Review, 1946–1955*. Durham, N.C.: Duke University Press.

Gibson, Gordon D., 1960, A Bibliography of Anthropological Bibliographies: The Americas. *Current Anthropology* 1(1):61–75.

Glass, John B., 1964, *Catálogo de la colección de códices*. Mexico City: Museo Nacional de Antropología, Instituto Nacional de Antropología e Historia.

Goldsmith, Peter H., 1915, *A Brief Bibliography of Books in English, Spanish and Portuguese Relating to the Republics Commonly Called Latin American, with Comments*. New York: The Macmillan Company.

Gómez Canedo, Lino, 1961, *Los archivos de la historia de América: periodo colonial español*. Mexico City: Instituto Panamericano de Geografía e Historia, Publication, no. 225. (2 vols.).

Gómez Ugarte, Elena, and Aurora Pagaza, 1937, *Bibliografía sumaria del Territorio de Quintana Roo*. Mexico City: D.A.P.P., Bibliografías Mexicanas no. 3.

Gray, Matilda Geddings, 1948, *A Collection of Books Pertaining to the Archaeology, Ethnology and Anthropology of Mexico, Guatemala and Central America with Particular Reference to Guatemala*. San Francisco.

Griffin, Charles C. (ed.), 1971, *Latin America: a Guide to the Historical Literature*. Austin, Tex.: University of Texas Press, Conference on Latin American History Publications, no. 4.

Grismer, Raymond Leonard, 1939, *A Reference Index to Twelve Thousand Spanish-American Authors: A Guide to the Literature of Spanish America*. New York: H. W. Wilson, Inter-American Bibliographical and Library Association, Publications Series 3, vol. 1.

Grismer, Raymond Leonard (ed.), 1941–, *A New Bibliography of the Literature of Spain and Spanish America, Including Many Studies on Anthropology, Archaeology . . . . and Other Subjects*. Minneapolis: Perine Book Company (vols. 1–4); St. Louis: John S. Swift (vol. 5); Dubuque: W. C. Brown (vol. 6–).

Gropp, Arthur E., 1941, *Guide to Libraries and Archives in Central America and the West Indies, Panama, Bermuda, and British Guiana*. New Orleans: Tulane University Press, Middle American Research Institute, Publication no. 10.

———, 1968, *A Bibliography of Latin American Bibliographies*. New York: Scarecrow Press, Inc.

———, 1971, *A Bibliography of Latin American Bibliographies: Supplement*. New York: Scarecrow Press, Inc.

Guerra, Francisco, 1950, *Bibliografía de la materia médica mexicana*. Mexico City: La Prensa Médica Mexicana.

Haggard, Juan Villasana, and Malcolm Dallas McLean, 1941, *Handbook for Translators of Spanish Historical Documents*. Austin, Tex.: University of Texas Press, Archives Collections.

Handbook of Latin American Studies, 1936–, Cambridge, Mass.: Harvard University Press (vols. 1–13); Gainesville, Fla.: University of Florida Press (beginning with vol. 14).

Hanson, Earl P., 1945, *Index to Maps of Hispanic America*, 1:1,000,000. Washington, D.C.: U.S. Government Printing Office.

Harrisse, Henry, 1866, *Biblioteca Americana Vetustissima: A Description of Works Relating to America. Published Between 1492 and 1551*. New York: G. P. Philes.

Heath, Dwight B., 1972, *Historical Dictionary of Bolivia*. Metuchen, N.J.: Scarecrow Press, Latin American Historical Dictionaries, no. 4.

Hedrick, Basil C., and Anne K. Hedrick, 1970, *Historical Dictionary of Panama*. Metuchen, N.J.: Scarecrow Press.

Hill, Roscoe R., 1945, *The National Archives of Latin America*. Cambridge, Mass.: Harvard University Press, Joint Committee on Latin American Studies, Miscellaneous Publications, no. 3.

Hilton, Ronald, 1956, *Handbook of Hispanic Source Materials and Research Organizations in the United States*, 2nd ed. Stanford, Calif.: Stanford University Press [1942].

Hispanic Society of America, 1910, *List of Printed Books in the Library of the Hispanic Society of America*. New York (20 vols.).

Hiss, Philip Hanson, 1943, *A Selective Guide to the English Literature on the Netherlands West Indies*. New York: The Netherlands Information Bureau.

Holmes, Ruth E. V., 1926, *Bibliographical and Historical Description of the Rarest Books in the Oliveira Lima Collection at the Catholic University of America*. Washington, D.C.: Catholic University of America, Library.

Humphreys, Robert A., 1958, *Latin American History: a Guide to the Literature in English*. London: Oxford University Press.

Icaza, Francisco A. D., 1969, *Diccionario autobiográfico de conquistadores y pobladores de Nueva España*. Guadalajara, Mexico (2 vols.).

Index to Latin American Periodicals, 1962——. Metuchen, N.J.: Scarecrow Press, Inc.

Instituto Nacional de Pesquisas de Amazonia, 1963, *Amazonia: Bibliografía, 1614–1962*. Rio de Janeiro, Brazil: Instituto Brasileiro de Bibliografía e Documentação.

Jiménez Moreno, Wigberto, 1937–1938, Materiales para una bibliografía etnográfica de la América Latina. *Boletín Bibliográfico de Antropología Americana* 1(1–2):47–77, 1(3):167–197, 2(1–3):289–421.

Johnson, Charles W., 1969, *México en el siglo XX: bibliografía política y social de publicaciones extranieras, 1900–1969*. Mexico City: Instituto de Investigaciones Sociales, Universidad Nacional Autónoma de Mexico.

Johnson, John J., et al., 1969, The Mexican-American: A Selected and Annotated Bibliography. Stanford, Calif.: Stanford University Center for Latin American Studies.

Jones, Cecil K., 1942, A Bibliography of Latin American Bibliographies. 2nd ed., rev. Washington, D.C.: U.S. Government Printing Office, Library of Congress, Latin American Series, no. 2.

Jones, Willis Knapp, 1944, Latin American Writers in English Translation: A Tentative Bibliography. Washington, D.C.: Pan American Union, Columbus Memorial Library, Bibliographical Series, no. 30.

Kemper, Robert V., 1971, Bibliografía comentada sobre la antropología urbana en América Latina. Boletín Bibliográfico de Antropología Americana 33–34:86–140.

Keniston, Haywood, 1920, List of Works for the Study of Hispanic-American History. New York: Hispanic Society of America, Hispanic Notes and Monographs, no. 5.

Ker, Annita M., 1940, Mexican Government Publications: a Guide to the More Important Publications of the National Government of Mexico, 1821–1936. Washington, D.C.: U.S. Government Printing Office.

King, James F., 1944, The Negro in Continental Spanish America: a Select Bibliography. Hispanic American Historical Review 24:547–559.

Konetzke, Richard, 1953–1962, Colección de documentos para la historia de la formación social de hispanoamérica, 1493–1810. Madrid: Consejo Superior (5 vols.).

Korkheimer, Hans, 1950, Guía bibliografía de los principales sitios arqueológicos del Perú. Boletín Bibliográfico (Lima) 20(3–4):181–234.

Larrea, Carlos Manuel, 1968, Bibliografía Científica del Eduador (Antropología-Etnografía-Arqueología-Prehistoria-Lingüística). 3rd ed. Quito: Corporación de Estudios y Publicaciones [1948].

Latcham, Ricardo E., 1915, Bibliografía chilena de la ciencias antropológicas. Revista de Bibliografía Chilena y Extranjera 3(6):148–185, 3(7):229–261.

Leclerc, Charles, 1878, Bibliotheca Americana: histoire, géographie, voyages, archéologie et linguistique des deux Amériques et des iles Philippines. 2nd ed. Paris: Maisonneuve et Cie [1867].

_____, 1881–1887, Bibliotheca Americana: historie, géographie, voyages, archéologie et linguistique des deux Amériques. Supplément No. 1–2. Paris: Maisonneuve et Cie. (2 vols.).

Lehmann, Henri, 1942, Bibliografía antropológica colombiana. Boletín Bibliográfico de Antropología Americana 6(1–3):42–46.

León, Nicolás, 1901, Apuntes para una bibliografía antropológica de México: somatología. Mexico City: Museo Nacional, Sección de Antropología y Etnografía.

_____, 1902–1908, Bibliografía mexicana del siglo XVIII. Mexico City: Boletín del Instituto Bibliográfico Mexicano (5 vols.).

León-Portilla, Miguel, et al., 1964, Historia documental de México. Mexico City: Universidad Nacional (2 vols.).

Library of Congress, 1945–1948, Guide to the Official Publications of the Other American Republics. Washington, D.C.: U.S. Government Printing Office (19 vols.).

Library of Congress, 1971, *National Directory of Latin Americanists.* 2nd ed. Washington, D.C.: Hispanic Foundation Bibliographical Series no. 12.

Lines, Jorge A., 1943, *Bibliografía antropológica aborigen de Costa Rica.* San José, Costa Rica: Universidad de Costa Rica, Facultad de Letras y Filosofía.

_____, 1967, *Anthropological Bibliography of Aboriginal Guatemala-British Honduras.* San José, Costa Rica: Tropical Science Center, Occasional Paper no. 6.

_____, 1967, *Anthropological Bibliography of Aboriginal Costa Rica.* San José, Costa Rica: Tropical Science Center, Occasional Paper no. 7.

Lines, Jorge A., Edwin M. Shook, and Michael D. Olien, 1965, *Anthropological Bibliography of Aboriginal Nicaragua.* San José, Costa Rica: Tropical Science Center, Occasional Paper no. 3.

_____, 1965, *Anthropological Bibliography of Aboriginal El Salvador.* San José, Costa Rica: Tropical Science Center, Occasional Paper no. 4.

_____, 1966, *Anthropological Bibliography of Aboriginal Honduras.* San José, Costa Rica: Tropical Science Center, Occasional Paper no. 5.

Luquiens, Frederick B., 1939, *Spanish American Literature in the Yale University Library: a Bibliography.* New Haven, Conn.: Yale University Press.

Manchester, Alan K., 1933, Descriptive Bibliography of the Brazilian Section of the Duke University Library. *Hispanic American Historical Review* 13(2):238–266, (4):495–523.

Mantilla Bazo, Victor, 1952, *Vivienda y planeamiento en América Latina: bibliografía preliminar.* Washington, D.C.: Unión Panamericana.

Marino Flores, Anselmo, 1945, Contribución a una bibliografía antropológica sobre los Tarascos. *Boletín Bibliográfica de Antropología Americana* 8.

_____, 1952–1953, Bibliografía antropológica del Estado de Guerrero. *Boletín Bibliográfico de Antropología Americana* 15–16:233–289.

Martin, Michael R., and Gabriel H. Lovett, 1968, *Encyclopedia of Latin-American History.* rev. ed. Indianapolis: The Bobbs-Merrill Company, Inc.

Martínez, Héctor, Miguel Cameo C., and Jesús Ramírez S., 1968, *Bibliografía indígena andina peruana (1900–1968).* Lima: Instituto Indigenista Peruano, Ministerio de Trabajo y Comunidades (2 vols.).

Martínez Rios, Jorge, 1961, *Bibliografía antropológica y sociológica del Estado de Oaxaca.* Mexico City: Instituto de Investigaciones Sociales, Universidad Nacional.

Martínez Solar, Benigno J., 1948, Bibliografía antropológica Argentina: 1946–1947. *Boletín Bibliográfico de Antropología Americana* 11:55–62.

Means, Philip Ainsworth, 1928, Biblioteca andina, Part One: The Chroniclers, or, the Writers of the Sixteenth and Seventeenth Centuries Who Treated of the Pre-Hispanic History and Culture of the Andean Countries. New Haven, Conn.: Yale University Press, *Transactions of the Connecticut Academy of Arts and Sciences* 29:271–525.

Mecham, John L., 1927, The Northern Expansion of New Spain, 1522–1822: a Selected Descriptive Bibliographical List. *Hispanic American Historical Review* 7(2):233–276.

Medina, José Toribio, 1898–1907, *Biblioteca hispano-americana, 1493–1810.* Santiago: Published by the Author (7 vols.).

Mendiburu, Manuel de, 1874–1890, *Diccionario historico-biográfico del Perú.* Lima: Imprenta de J. F. Solís (8 vols.).

Minkel, Clarence W., and Ralph H. Alderman, 1970, *A Bibliography of British Honduras, 1900–1970.* East Lansing, Mich.: Michigan State University, Latin American Studies Center, Research Report, no. 7.

Montane M., Julio C., 1963, *Bibliografía selectiva de antropología chilena: primera parte, Araucanos-Pehuenches-Chiloé y territorios adyacentes.* La Serena, Chile: Museo, Contribuciones arqueológicas, no. 2.

Monterforte Toledo, Mario, 1968, *Bibliografía sociopolítica latino-americana.* Mexico City: Universidad Nacional.

Monteiro, Palmyra V. M., 1967–1969, *A Catalogue of Latin American Flat Maps, 1926–1964.* Austin, Tex.: University of Texas, Institute of Latin American Studies, Guides and Bibliographies Series, no. 2 (2 vols.).

Moore, Richard E., 1967, *Historical Dictionary of Guatemala.* Metuchen, N.J.: Scarecrow Press, Inc.

Morse, Richard M., 1965, Recent Research on Latin American Urbanization: A Selective Survey with Commentary. *Latin American Research Review* 1(1): 35–74.

Moscov, Stephen, 1972, *An Annotated Bibliography of Paraguay.* Buffalo, N.Y.: State University of New York at Buffalo, Special Studies Series, no. 10.

Murdock, George P., 1960, *Ethnographic Bibliography of North America.* 3rd ed. New Haven, Conn.: Human Relations Area Files Press, Behavior Science Bibliographies.

Nichols, Madeline W., 1941, *A Bibliographical Guide to Materials on American Spanish.* Cambridge, Mass.: Harvard University Press.

Nogales, Luis G. (ed.), 1971, *The Mexican American: A Selected and Annotated Bibliography.* 2nd ed. Stanford, Calif.: Stanford University Press.

Noguera, Eduardo, 1937–1938, Bibliografía de los códices precolombinos y documentos indígenas posteriores a la conquista. *Anales de la Sociedad de Geografía e Historia* 14(2):230–240, 14(3):341–351.

Noriega, Felix F., 1923, *Diccionario geográfico de Costa Rica.* 2nd ed. San José, Costa Rica: Imprenta Nacional.

Okinshevich, Leo A., and Cecilia J. Gorokhoff, 1959, *Latin America in Soviet Writings, 1945–1958: A Bibliography.* Washington, D.C.: Library of Congress, Hispanic Foundation Bibliographical Series no. 5.

O'Leary, Timothy J., 1963, *Ethnographic Bibliography of South America.* New Haven, Conn.: Human Relations Area Files Press, Behavior Science Bibliographies.

Ortíz, Sergio Elías C., 1937, Contribución a la bibliografía sobre ciencias etnológicas de Colombia. *Idearium* (Supplement no. 1, Pasto, Colombia), pp. 1–66.

Palau y Dulcet, Antonio, 1948, *Manual del librero hispano-américano.* 2nd ed. Barcelona: Librería Anticuaria de A. Palau [1923–1927].

Pan American Union, Columbus Memorial Library, 1962, *Index to Latin American Periodical Literature, 1929–1960.* Boston: G. K. Hall and Company (8 vols.).

Parra, Manuel G., and Wigberto J. Moreno, 1954, *Bibliografía indigenista de México y Centroamérica, 1850–1950.* Mexico City: Instituto Nacional Indigenista, Memorias, vol. 4.

Paulotti, Osvaldo L., 1944, Bibliografía antropológica argentina, 1941–1942, 1943–1944. *Boletín Bibliográfico de Antropología Americana* 7(1–3):32–40.

Peña y Cámara, José María de la, 1955, *A List of the Spanish Residencias in the Archives of the Indies, 1516–1775.* Washington, D.C.: Library of Congress.

Peraza Sarausa, Fermin, 1970, *Revolutionary Cuba: A Bibliographical Guide, 1968.* Coral Gables, Fla.: University of Miami Press.

Perez Martínez, Hector, 1943, *Catálogo de documentos para la historia de Yucatán y Campeche.* Campeche, Mexico: Museo Arquelógico, Historico y Etnográfico de Campeche.

Pierson, Donald, 1945, *Survey of the Literature on Brazil of Sociological Significance Published up to 1940.* Cambridge, Mass.: Harvard University Press, Misc. Publications, no. 4.

Porter, Carlos Emilio, 1910, *Bibliografía chilena de antropología y etnología.* Buenos Aires: Coni Hnos.

_____, 1912, *Bibliografía chilena de ciencias antropológicas.* Santiago, Chile: Imprenta "Santiago."

Psuty, Norbert P., Wendell Beckwith, and Alan K. Craig, 1968, *1000 Selected References to the Geography, Oceanography, Geology, Ecology, and Archaeology of Coastal Peru and Adjacent Areas.* Washington, D.C.: Office of Naval Research, Geography Branch, The Paracas Papers, no. 1 (Master Bibliography).

Rabinovitz, Francine F., Felicity M. Trueblood, and Charles J. Salvo, 1967, *Latin American Political Systems in an Urban Setting: A Preliminary Bibliography.* Gainesville, Fla.: University of Florida, Center for Latin American Studies.

Ragatz, Lowell Joseph, 1970, *A Guide for the Study of British Caribbean History, 1763–1834. Including the Abolition and Emancipation Movements.* 2nd ed. New York: Da Capo Press [1932].

Rede, Leman Thomas, 1789, *Bibliotheca americana.* London: Printed for J. Debrett.

Reichel-Dolmatoff, Gerardo, 1949, *Bibliografía etnológica del Departmento del Magdelana.* Santa María, Colombia: Divulgación cultural del Instituto Etnológico del Magdalena, no. 3.

Rich, Obadiah, 1840–1846, *Bibliotheca Americana Nova.* London: Rich and Sons (3 vols.).

Rodrigues, José C., 1907, *Bibliotheca brasiliense*, Rio de Janeiro: Typ. do "Jornal do Comercio."

Royal Academy of History, 1951, *Mapas españoles de América, siglos XV–XVII.* Madrid.

Rubio y Muñoz-Bocanegra, Ángel, 1961, *Bibliografía de geografía urbana de América.* Río de Janeiro: Instituto Panamericano de Geografía e Historia, Publication, no. 220.

Rudolf, Donna K., and G. A. Rudolf, 1970, *Latin American Agriculture: A Bibliography on Pioneer Settlement, Agricultural History and Economics, Rural Sociology and Population (Including Immigration and Foreign Minorities), Agricultural Cooperatives and Credit from the Holdings of the Widener Library, Harvard University,* Milwaukee, Wis.: University of Wisconsin-Milwaukee, Latin America Center Special Studies Series, no. 1.

Rudolf, Donna K., and G. A. Rudolf, 1971, *Historical Dictionary of Venezuela.* Metuchen, N.J.: Scarecrow Press, Inc.

Sabin, Joseph, 1868–1936, *Bibliotheca Americana: a Dictionary of Books Relating to America, from its Discovery to the Present Time.* New York: Bibliographical Society of America (29 vols.).

Sable, Martin H., 1967, *A Guide to Latin American Studies.* Los Angeles: U.C.L.A. Latin American Center, Reference Series, no. 4 (2 vols.).

———, 1968, *Latin American Urbanization: a Guide to the Literature, Organizations and Personnel.* Los Angeles: U.C.L.A. Latin American Center.

———, 1970, *Latin-American Studies in the Non-Western World and Eastern Europe.* Metuchen, N.J.: Scarecrow Press, Inc.

Sánchez Alonso, Benito, 1927, *Fuentes de la historia española e hispanoamericana.* 2nd ed. Madrid: Publicaciones de la Revista de filologia española (2 vols.) [1919].

Saville, Marshall Howard, 1921, Bibliographic Notes on Uxmal Yucatán. *Indian Notes and Monographs* 9(2):55–131. New York: Museum of the American Indian.

———, 1928, Bibliographic Notes on Xochicalco, Mexico. *Indian Notes and Monographs* 6(5):119–180. New York: Museum of the American Indian.

———, 1928, Bibliographic Notes on Palenque, Chiapas. *Indian Notes and Monographs* 6(5):185–207. New York: Museum of the American Indian.

Schwab, Federico, 1936, Bibliografía de etnología peruana. *Boletín Bibliográfico* 9(1):1–26, 9(2):4–27, 9(3–4):101–115.

———, 1939, Bibliografía de antropología peruana, 1936–1937. *Boletín Bibliográfico* 8(1):48–85.

———, 1942, Bibliografía etnológica de la Amazonia peruana. *Boletín Bibliográfico* 12(3–4):205–271.

Sepulveda, Orlando, and Francisco Fernández, 1967, Bibliografía sistemática. In *Anuario de Sociología de los Pueblos Ibéricos.* Madrid: Instituto de Estudios Sindicales, Sociales y Cooperativas, vol. 1.

Shelby, Charmion C., (ed.), 1944, *Latin American Periodicals Currently Received in the Library of Congress and in the Library of the Department of Agriculture.* Washington, D.C.: Library of Congress, Latin American Series, no. 8.

Shook, Edwin M., Jorge A. Lines, and Michael D. Olien, 1965, *Anthropological Bibliography of Aboriginal Panama.* San José, Costa Rica: Tropical Science Center, Occasional Paper no. 2.

Spell, Lota M., 1954, *Research Materials for the Study of Latin America at the University of Texas.* Austin, Tex.: University of Texas Press, Latin American Studies, no. 14.

Steck, Francis B., 1943, *A Tentative Guide to Historical Materials on the Spanish Borderlands.* Philadelphia: Catholic Historical Society of Philadelphia.

Stewart, Thomas Dale, 1952, *A Bibliography of Physical Anthropology in Latin America, 1937–1948.* New York: Wenner-Gren Foundation for Anthropological Research, Inc.

Sundt, Roberto, 1917–1918, Bibliografía araucana. *Revista de bibliografía chilena y extranjera* (Santiago) 5:300–315, 6:3–21, 87–101, 182–213, 269–286.

Tauro, Alberto, 1946, Bibliografía indianista peruana. *Boletín Bibliográfico* (Lima) 16(3–4):283–308.

Teixidor, Felipe, 1937, *Bibliografía yucateca.* Mérida, Mexico: Museo Arqueológico e Historico de Yucatán, Publication, no. 1.

Tello, Julio César, 1927, Bibliografía antropológica del Perú. *Boletín Bibliográfico* 3(3):31–36.

Ternaux-Compans, Henri, 1837, *Bibliothèque américaine.* Paris: Arthus Bertrand.

Thomas, Henry, 1944, *Short-Title Catalogue of Spanish-American Books Printed Before 1601 Now in the British Museum.* London: British Museum, Department of Printed Books.

Toro, Josefina del, 1938, *A Bibliography of the Collective Biography of Spanish America.* Río Piedras, Puerto Rico: University of Puerto Rico, Bulletin Series 9, no. 1.

Trifilo, S. Samuel, 1959–1960, A Bibliography of British Travel Books on Argentina, 1810–1860. *The Americas* 15:133–143.

Tristan, José M., 1949, *Bibliografía maya yucateca.* Rochester, N.Y.: Mimeographed.

Uhle, Max, 1926, Bibliografía sobre etnología y arqueología del Ecuador. *Boletín de la Biblioteca Nacional* (Quito) n.s. 7:435–446.

————, 1929, Bibliografía ampliada sobre etnología y arqueología en el Ecuador. *Anales de la Universidad Central* (Quito).

University of California, 1928–1930, *Spain and Spanish America in the Libraries of the University of California: A Catalogue of Books.* Berkeley, Calif.: University of California Press, The Bancroft Library (2 vols.).

Valle, Rafael Heliodoro, 1937–1940, Bibliografía antropológica americana, 1936–1937, 1937–1938, 1938–1939, 1938–1940. *Boletin Bibliográfico de Antropología Americana* 1(4):267–287, 2(4):161–191, 3(2):195–219, 4(2):165–215.

————, 1937–1941, Bibliografía maya. *Boletín Bibliográfico de Antropología Americana* 1(1–2):1–22, 1(3):23–49, 1(4):45–70, 2(1–3):71–90, 2(4):91–118, 3(1):119–152, 3(2):153–202, 4(1):203–222, 4(2):223–258, 4(3):259–286, 5(1–3):287–404.

————, 1971, *Bibliografia Maya.* New York: Burt Franklin, Bibliography and Reference Series, no. 436 [1937–1941].

Vaughn, Denton R., 1970, *Urbanization in Twentieth-Century Latin America: A Working Bibliography.* Austin, Tex.: University of Texas, Institute of Latin American Studies and The Population Research Center.

Véliz, Claudio (ed.), 1968, *Latin America and the Caribbean: A Handbook.* New York: Frederick A. Praeger, Inc.

Viñaza, Cipriano Muñez y Manzano, Conde de la, 1892, *Bibliografía española de lenguas indígenas de América.* Madrid: Sucesores de Rivadeneyra.

Voorhoeve, Jan, and Antoon Donicie, 1963, *Bibliographie du Negro-Anglais du Surinam, avec un appendice sur les langues Creole parlées a l'intérieur du pays.* 'S-Gravenhage: M. Nijhoff, Koninklijk Instituut voor Taal-Land-en Volkenkunde, Bibliographical Series, no. 6.

Wagner, Henry R., 1937, *The Spanish Southwest, 1542–1794: an Annotated Bibliography.* Albuquerque, N.M.: Quivira Society Publication no. 7 (2 vols.) [1924].

————, 1940, *Nueva bibliografía mexicana del siglo XVI.* Mexico City: Antigua Libr. Robredo.

Warden, David Baillie, 1831, *Bibliotheca Americana, Being a Choice Collection of Books Relating to North and South America and the West Indies, Including Voyages to the Southern Hemisphere.* Paris: P. Renouard.

Watson, Gayle Hudgens, 1971, *Colombia, Ecuador and Venezuela: An Annotated Guide to Reference Materials in the Humanities and Social Sciences.* Metuchen, N.J.: Scarecrow Press, Inc.

Weaver, Jerry L. (ed.), 1969, *Latin American Development: A Selected Bibliography (1950–1967).* Santa Barbara, Calif.: Clio Press American Bibliographical Center, Bibliography and Reference Series, no. 9.

Welsh, Doris V., 1953, *A Catalog of the William B. Greenlee Collection of Portuguese History and Literature and the Portuguese Materials in the Newberry Library.* Chicago: Newberry Library.

Wilgus, Alva Curtis, 1966, *Histories and Historians of Hispanic America.* New York: Cooper Square Publishers [1942].

Zimmerman, Irene, 1961, *A Guide to Current Latin American Periodicals: Humanities and Social Sciences.* Gainesville, Fla.: Kalman Publishing Company.

————, 1971, *Current National Bibliographies of Latin America: A State of the Art Study.* Gainesville, Fla.: University of Florida Center for Latin American Studies.

APPENDIX C

Periodicals and monograph series on Latin America

GENERAL

Proceedings, International Congress of Americanists. (Issued every two years from the location of the Congress.)

ARGENTINA

Acta Praehistorica, Centro Argentina de Estudios Prehistóricos, Buenos Aires.
Actualidad Antropológica, Museo Etnográfico Municipal "Dámaso Arce" (supplement of *Etnia*), Olavarría.
Anales,· Instituto Étnico Nacional, Buenos Aires.
Anales de Arquelogía y Etnología, Universidad Nacional de Cuyo, Mendoza (formerly *Anales del Instituto de Etnología Americana,* 1940–1946).
Avulsa I.D.E.A., Instituto de Estudios Antropológicos, Buenos Aires.
Boletín, Departamento de Estudios Etnográficos y Coloniales, Santa Fe.
Boletín, Instituto Étnico Nacional, Buenos Aires.
Boletín, Museo Social Argentino, Buenos Aires.
Boletín, Sociedad Argentina de Antropología, Buenos Aires.
Boletín, Informativo de Investigaciones Sociológicas, Buenos Aires.
Cuadernos, Instituto Nacional de Antropología, Buenos Aires.
Cuadernos, Instituto Nacional de Investigaciones Folklóricas, Buenos Aires.
Cuadernos Informativo y Temático, Consejo Latinoamericano de Ciencias Sociales, Buenos Aires.
Estudios de Historia Social, Centro de Estudios de Historia Social, Universidad de Buenos Aires, Buenos Aires.
Etnia, Museo Etnográfico Municipal "Dámaso Arce," Olavarría.

Folia Lingüistica Americana, Buenos Aires.

Jornadas Internacionales de Arqueología y Etnografía, Universidad de Buenos Aires, Buenos Aires.

Notas, Instituto de Antropología, Universidad Nacional de Tucumán, Tucumán.

Notas del Museo (Antropología), La Plata.

Publicaciones, Instituto de Antropología, Universidad Nacional de Córdoba, Córdoba (formerly *Publicaciones del Instituto de Arqueología, Lingüística y Folklore "Dr. Pablo Cabrera"*).

Publicaciones, Sección de Antropología, Facultad de Filosofía y Letras, Universidad de Buenos Aires, Bueno Aires.

Publicaciones Especiales, Instituto de Antropología, Universidad Nacional de Tucumán, Tucumán.

Publicaciones (Serie A), Museo Etnográfico, Facultad de Filosofía y Letras, Universidad Nacional, Buenos Aires.

Revista, Instituto de Antropología, Universidad Nacional de Córdoba, Córdoba.

Revista, Instituto de Antropología, Universidad Nacional de Litoral, Rosario de Santa Fe.

Revista, Instituto de Antropología de Tucumán, Tucumán.

Revista, Instituto Nacional de Antropología, Buenos Aires.

Revista, Museo de La Plata, La Plata.

Revista de la Integración: Economía-Política-Sociología, Instituto para la Integración de América Latina, Buenos Aires.

Revista Latinoamericana de Sociología, Centro de Sociología Comparada, Instituto Torcuato Di Tella, Buenos Aires.

Runa: Archivo para las Ciencias del Hombre, Instituto de Antropología, Universidad de Buenos Aires, Buenos Aires.

Serie Monográfica, Asociación Argentina de Antropología, Córdoba.

Serie Técnica, Asociación Argentina de Antropología, Córdoba.

Servicio de Documentación Bibliográfica, Asociación Argentina de Antropología, Córdoba.

BELGIUM

Bulletin, Société des Américanistes de Belgique, Brussels.

Cultures et Développement, Servicio Europeo de Universitarios Latinoamericanos, Brussels.

BOLIVIA

Archivos Bolivianos de Folklore, Dirección Nacional de Antropología, La Paz.

Boletín, Sociedad Geográfica e Historia de Sucre, Sucre.

Boletín, Socieded Geográfica e Historia de Santa Cruz, Santa Cruz.

Boletín Bibliográfico Boliviano, La Paz.

Colección de Etnografía y Folklore, Dirección Nacional de Antropología, La Paz.

Estudios Andinos, Instituto Boliviano de Estudio y Acción Social, La Paz.

Notas Arqueológicas de Bolivia, Dirección Nacional de Antropología, La Paz.

Revista, Instituto de Sociología Boliviana, Sucre.

BRAZIL

América Latina, Centro Latino-Americano de Investigaciones en Ciências Sociales, Rio de Janeiro.

Anais, Museu Historico Nacional, Rio de Janeiro.

Arquivos do Museu, Museu Nacional, Rio de Janeiro.

Bibliografía, Centro Latino Americano de Pesquisas en Ciências Sociais, Rio de Janeiro.

Boletim, Instituto Joaquim Nebuco de Pesquisas Sociais, Recife.

Boletim, Museu Nacional, Rio de Janeiro.

Boletim, Museu Paraense Emilio Goeldi, Belem.

Boletim, Sociedade Brasileira de Genetica.

Boletim (Antropologia), Universidade de São Paulo, Faculdade de Filosofia, Ciências e Letras, São Paulo.

Boletim (Etnografia e Tupi-Guarani), Universidade de São Paulo, Faculdade de Filosofia, Ciências e Letras, São Paulo.

Cadernas Brasileiros, Rio de Janeiro.

Comunicações Avulsas, Universidade do Parana, Departamento de Antropologia, Curitiba.

Educação e Ciências Sociais, Centro Brasileiro de Pesquisas Educacionais, Rio de Janeiro.

Estudos de Antropologia, Sociedade de Antropologia de Minas Gerais, Belo Horizonte.

Estudos Linguísticos, Instituto de Idiomas Yázigi, Centro de Linguística Aplicada, São Paulo.

Orientação, Instituto de Geografia da Universidade de São Paulo.

Publicações, Instituto de Antropologia e Etnologia do Para, Belem.

Publicações, Museu Nacional, Serie Linguística Especial, Rio de Janeiro.

Relações Humanos, São Paulo.

Revista, Instituto Archaeologico, Historico e Geografico Pernambucano, Pernambuco.

Revista, Instituto de Estudos Brasileiros, Universidade de São Paulo, São Paulo.

Revista, Museu Julio de Castihos e Arquivo Historico do Rio Grande do Sul, Porto Alegre.

Revista, Museu Nacional, Rio de Janeiro.

Revista, Museu Paulista, São Paulo.

Revista de Antropologia, Associação Brasileira de Antropologia, Universidade de São Paulo, São Paulo.

Revista de Ciências Sociais, Universidade Federal do Ceará, Departamento de Sociologia, Fortaleza, Ceará.

Sociologia, São Paulo.

BRITISH HONDURAS

The Caribbean, Belize.

Caribbean Quarterly, Belize.

CHILE

Anales, Facultad Latinoamericana de Ciencias Sociales, Santiago.
Anales, (Etnología), Museo Nacional, Santiago.
Anales de la Universidad del Norte, Centro de Investigaciones Historicas y Arqueológicas, Museo Arqueológico de San Pedro de Atacama, Antofagasta.
Antropología: Revista del Centro de Estudios Antropológicos, Centro de Estudios Antropológicos, Departamento de Ciencias Sociales, Universidad de Chile, Santiago.
Archivos del Folklore Chileno.
Biblioteca de Lingüística Americana, Santiago.
Boletín, Museo Arqueológico de la Serena, La Serena.
Boletín, Museo Nacional de Historia Natural, Santiago.
Boletín C.E.L.A.P., Centro Latinoamericano de Población y Familia-Centro para el Desarrollo Económico y Social de América Latina, Santiago.
Boletín Informativo, Sociedad Chilena de Antropología, Santiago.
Boletín de Prehistoria de Chile, Departamento de Historia, Facultad de Filosofía y Educación, Universidad de Chile, Santiago.
Cuadernos de Sociología, Pontifica Universidad Católica de Chile.
Notas, Centro de Estudios Antropológicos, Universidad de Chile, Santiago.
Publicaciones, Museo de Etnología y Antropología, Santiago.
Revista, Museo Historico Nacional de Chile, Santiago.
Revista Latinoamericana de Estudios Urbano Regionales, E.U.R.E., Centro Interdisciplinario de Desarrollo Urbano y Regional, Universidad Católica de Chile, Santiago.
Trabajos Antropológicos, Sociedad Chilena de Antropología, Santiago.

COLOMBIA

Amazonia Colombiana Americanista, Sibundoy, Pasto, Bogotá.
Archivos, Academia Colombiana de Historia, Bogotá.
Boletín, Instituto de Antropología, Universidad del Cauca, Popayán.
Boletín Antropológico, Instituto Etnológico, Universidad del Cauca, Popayán.
Boletín de Antropología, Instituto de Antropología, Universidad de Antioquia, Medellín.
Boletín de Arqueología, Bogotá.
Boletín de Historia y Antgüedades, Bogotá.
Ciencias Sociales, Instituto Colombiano de Investigaciones Sociales, Medellín.
Cuadernos de Historia y Arqueología, Guayaquil.
Desarrollo Indoamericano, Barranquilla.
Divulgaciones Etnológicas, Instituto Colombiano de Antropología, Bogotá.
Investigaciones en Progreso en Colombia, Escuela Interamericana de Bibliotecología, Universidad de Antioquia, Medellín.
Monografías Sociológicas, Bogotá.
Noticias Sobre Reforma Agraria, Instituto Interamericano de Ciencias Agrícolas, Inter-American Center for Agrarian Reforms, Bogotá.

Publicaciones, Centro Interamericano de Vivienda, Serie Resumenes de Clase, Bogotá.
Publicaciones, Sociedad Colombiana de Etnología, Bogotá.
Revista, Instituto Etnológico Nacional, Bogotá.
Revista Colombiana de Antropología, Instituto Colombiana de Antropología, Bogotá.
Revista Colombiana de Folclor, Instituto Colombiano de Antropología, Bogotá.
Revista de las Indies, Bogotá.
Revista Interamericana de Bibliotecología, Escuela Interamericana de Bibliotecología, Universidad de Antioquia, Medellín.
Serie Socio-Economica, Centro de Investigaciones Sociales, Bogotá.

COSTA RICA

Anales, Academia de Geográfica e Historia de Costa Rica, San José.
Boletín, Museo Nacional de Costa Rica, San José.
Boletín Informativo, Museo Nacional de Costa Rica, San José.
Informes, Instituto Geográfico de Costa Rica, San José.
Revista, Archivos Nacionales, San José.
Revista de Costa Rica, San José. (Published 1919–1925, 1929).
Serie Etnología, Museo Nacional, San José.

CUBA

Antropológicas, Academia de Ciencias, Departamento de Antropología, Havana.
Bibliografía de América Latina, Havana.
Contribuciones, Academia de Ciencias, Departamento de Antropología, Havana.
Etnología y Folklore, Instituto de Etnología y Folklore, Academia de Ciencias de Cuba, Havana.
Revista, Junta Nacional de Arqueología y Etnología, Havana.

DOMINICAN REPUBLIC

Estudios Sociales, Centro de Investigación y Acción Social de la Compañía de Jesús, Santo Domingo.

ECUADOR

Boletín, Sociedad Ecuatoriana de Estudios Historicos Americanos, Quito.
Boletín Bibliográfico, Instituto Ecuatoriano de Folklore, Quito.
Boletín de Orientación e Información, Centro Misional de Investigaciones Científicas, Quito.
Cuadernos de Investigaciones Científicas, Centro Misional de Investigaciones Científicas, Quito.
Cuestiones Indígenas del Ecuador, Quito.

Humanitas: Boletín Ecuatoriano de Antropología, Instituto de Antropología, Universidad Central de Ecuador, Quito.
Informe, Instituto Ecuatoriano de Antropología y Geografía, Quito.
Llacta, Instituto Ecuatoriano de Antropología y Geografía, Quito.
Revista del Folklore Ecuatoriano, Instituto Ecuatoriano de Folklore, Quito.

EL SALVADOR

Anales, Museo Nacional "David J. Guzman," San Salvador.
Revista de Etnología, Arqueología y Lingüística. San Salvador.
Tzunpame, San Salvador.

ENGLAND

British Bulletin of Publications of Latin America, the West-Indies, Portugal and Spain. London.
Journal of Latin American Studies, Cambridge University Press, London.
New World Antiquity, London.

FRANCE

Americana, Editions de Malvina, Sainte-Pezenne.
Aportes, Instituto Latinoamericano de Relaciones Internacionales. Paris.
Archives, Société Américaine de France, Paris.
Bibliographie Américaniste, Société des Américanistes, Paris.
Bibliothèque Linguistique Américaine, Paris.
Cahiers des Amérique Latines, Institut des Hautes Études de l'Amérique Latine, University of Paris, Paris.
Caravelle: Cahiers de Monde Hispanique et Luso-Brésilien, Institut d'études híspaniques, hispano-américaines et luso-brésiliennes de l'Université, Paris.
Journal, Société des Américanistes, Musée de l'Homme, U.N.E.S.C.O. and CNRS, Paris.
Revue des Études Mayas-Quiches, Paris.
Trabajos: Boletín Informativo, Instituto Latinomericano de Relaciones Internacionales, Paris.
Travaux de l'Institut d'Études Latino-Américaines de Strasbourg, Institut d'Études Latino-Américaines, Palais Universitaire, Strausbourg.
Travaux, l'Institut Français d'Études Andines, Paris.

GERMANY

Arbeitsunterlagen zur Lateinamerika-Forschung, Sozialforschungsstelle an der Universität Münster, Dortmund.
Bibliotheca Ibero-Americana, Berlin.
Boletín Informativo, Asociación Alemana para la Investigación sobre América Latina, Cologne.

Boletín Informativo, Sozialforschungsstelle an der Universität Münster, Dortmund.

Estudios sobre la Economía Iberoamericana, Instituto Iberoamericano de Investigación Económica, University of Göttingen, Göttingen.

Humboldt, Übersee-Verlag, Hamburg.

Ibero-Amerikanische Bibliographie, Berlin and Bonn.

Ibero-Amerikanische Studien, Hamburg.

Information Dienst der Arbeitsgemeinschaft der Deutschen Latein-amerika-Institute, Köln.

Lateinamerika, Lateinamerika-Institutes der Universität Rostock, Rostock.

Süd-und-Mittelamerika, Berlin.

GUATEMALA

Anales, Sociedad de Geografía e Historia de Guatemala, Guatemala City.

Antropología e Historia de Guatemala, Instituto de Antropología e Historia, Guatemala City.

Boletín, Instituto Indigenista Nacional de Guatemala, Guatemala City.

Cuadernos, Seminario de Integración Social Guatemalteca, Guatemala City.

Cuadernos de Antropología, Instituto de Investigaciones Históricas, Universidad de San Carlos, Guatemala City.

Estudios Centroamericanos, Seminario de Integración Social Guatemalteca, Guatemala City.

Guatemala Indígena, Instituto Nacional Indigenista, Guatemala City.

Publicaciones, Seminario de Integración Social Guatemalteca, Guatemala City.

Revista, Museo Nacional, Sección de Arqueología, Guatemala City.

HAITI

Bulletin, Bureau d'Ethnologie, Port-au-Prince.

Les Cahiers du C.H.I.S.S.: Revue Haitienne de Sciences Sociales, Centre Haitien d'Investigation en Sciences Sociales, Port-au-Prince.

HONDURAS

Honduras Maya, Sociedad de Antropología y Arqueología de Honduras, Tegucigalpa.

Revista, Archivo y Biblioteca Nacionales de Honduras, Tegucigalpa.

ITALY

Terra Ameriga, Associazione Italiana Studi Americanistici, Genoa.

JAMAICA

Caribbean Quarterly, Department of Extra Mural Studies, University of the West Indies, Mona.

Journal of Caribbean History, Department of History, University of the West Indies, Mona.

New World Quarterly, New World Group Ltd., University of the West Indies, Mona.

Social and Economic Studies, Institute of Social and Economic Research, University of the West Indies, Mona.

MEXICO

Acción Indigenista, Instituto Nacional Indigenista, Mexico City.

Acta Americana, Sociedad Interamericana de Antropología y Geografía, Mexico City.

Acta Antropológica, Escuela Nacional de Antropología e Historia, Mexico City.

América Indígena, Instituto Indigenista Interamericano, Mexico City.

Anales, Instituto Nacional de Antropología e Historia, Mexico City.

Anales, Museo Nacional de Arqueología, Historia y Etnología, Mexico City.

Anales de Antropología, Sección de Antropología, Instituto de Investigaciones Historicas, Universidad Nacional Autónoma de México, Mexico City.

Anuario, Escuela Nacional de Antropología e Historia, Mexico City.

Anuario Indigenista, Instituto Indigenista Interamericano, Mexico City (formerly *Boletín Indigenista*).

Bibliotecas y Archivos, Escuela Nacional de Biblioteconomía y Archivonomía, Mexico City.

Boletín, Centro de Investigaciones Antropológicas de México, Mexico City.

Boletín, Instituto Nacional de Antropología e Historia, Mexico City.

Boletín Bibliográfico de Antropología Americana, Comisión de Historia, Instituto Panamericano de Geografía e Historia, Mexico City.

Cuadernos (Serie Antropológica), Instituto de Investigaciones Historias, Universidad Nacional Autónoma de México, Mexico City.

Cuadernos Americanos, Mexico City.

Cuadernos Mayas, Mérida.

Desarollo: Estudios sobre Estructuración Social, Instituto Mexicano de Estudios Sociales, Mexico City.

Ediciones Especiales, Instituto Indigenista Interamericano, Mexico City.

Estudios de Cultura Maya, Seminario de Cultura Maya, Universidad Nacional Autónoma de México, Mexico City.

Estudios de Cultural Nahuatl, Seminario de Cultura Nahuatl, Universidad Nacional de México, Instituto de Historia, Mexico City.

Estudios de Historia Novohispaña, Instituto de Investigaciones Historicas, Universidad Nacional Autónoma de México, Mexico City.

I.C.A.C.H., Instituto de Ciencias y Artes de Chiapas, Tuxtla Gutiérrez, Chiapas.

Latino América, Centro de Estudios Latinoamericanos, Mexico City.

Memorias, Instituto Nacional Indigenista, Mexico City.

Mesoamerican Notes, Department of Anthropology, University of the Americas, Puebla.

Mexican Folkways, Mexico City.

Prehistoria, Departamento de Prehistoria, Instituto Nacional de Antropología e Historia, Mexico City.

Revista Interamericana de Sociología, Asociación Mexicana de Sociología, Mexico City.

Revista Mexicana de Estudios Antropológicos, Sociedad Mexicana de Antropología, Mexico City.

Revista Mexicana de Sociología, Instituto de Investigaciones Sociales, Universidad Nacional Autónoma de México, Mexico City.

Serie de Vocabularios Indígenas "Marino Silva y Aceves," Summer Institute of Linguistics, Mexico City.

Tlalocan, La Casa de Tlaloc, Mexico City.

Tlatoani, Escuela Nacional de Antropología e Historia, Mexico City.

Yan (Ciencias Antropológicas), Centro de Investigaciones Antropológicas, Mexico City.

Yikal Maya Than, Mérida.

NETHERLANDS

Boletín Bibliográfico, Center of Latin American Studies and Documentation, University of Amsterdam, Amsterdam.

Boletín de Estudios Latinoamericanos, Centro de Estudios y Documentación Latinoamericanos, Amsterdam.

Boletín Informativo Sobre Estudios y Documentación Latinoamericanos en Europa, Centro de Estudios y Documentación Latinoamericanos, Amsterdam.

NICARAGUA

Anales, Instituto Nicaragüense de Antropología y Arqueología, Managua.

Nicaragua Indígena, Instituto Indigenista Nacional, Managua.

Revista, Academia de Geografía e Historia de Nicaragua, Managua.

PANAMA

Boletín, Museo Chiricano, Colegio Felix Olivares C., David.

Hombre y Cultura, Centro de Investigaciones Antropológicas de la Universidad Nacional, Panama City.

Lotería, Panama City.

Panama Archaeologist, Archaeological Society of Panama, Balboa Heights, Canal Zone.

PARAGUAY

Boletín, Sociedad Científica del Paraguay y del Museo Dr. Andres Barbero, Etnográfico e Historico Natural, Asunción.

Revista, Centro de Estudios Antropológicos del Ateneo Paraguayo, Asunción.

Revista Paraguaya de Sociología, Centro Paraguayo de Estudios Sociológicos, Asunción.

Suplemento Antropológico, of the *Revista del Ateneo Paraguayo,* Centro de Estudios Antropológicos del Ateneo Paraguayo, Asunción.

PERU

Andina, Departamento de Ciencias Históricas y Geográficas, Universidad Nacional Federico Villarreal, Lima.
Antropología, Universidad Nacional del Centro, Huancayo.
Archivo Peruanos de Folklore, Cuzco.
Arqueológicas, Museo Nacional de Antropología y Arqueología, Lima.
Boletín Bibliográfico, Universidad Nacional Mayor de San Marcos, Lima.
Boletín del Seminario de Arqueología, Instituto Riva-Agüero, Pontificia Universidad Católica del Perú, Lima.
Cuadernos de Antropología, Centro de Estudiantes de Antropología, Universidad Nacional Mayor de San Marcos, Lima.
Etnología y Arqueología, Instituto de Etnología y Arqueología, Universidad Nacional Mayor de San Marcos, Lima.
Folklore Americano, Lima.
Historia e Cultura, Lima.
Monografías Andinas, Lima.
Perú Indígena, Instituto Indigenista Peruano, Lima.
Publicaciones, Instituto de Etnología y Arqueología, Universidad Nacional Mayor de San Marcos, Lima.
Revista, Archivo Nacional del Perú, Lima.
Revista, Museo e Instituto Arqueológico, Cuzco.
Revista, Museo Nacional, Lima.
Revista, Sección Arqueológica de la Universidad Nacional del Cuzco, Cuzco.
Revista de Arqueología, Lima.
Revista de Ciencias Políticas y Sociales, Instituto Latinoamericano de Ciencias Políticas y Sociales, Lima.
Revista de Etnografía, Lima.
Revista Histórica Iqueña, Ica.
Serie Monografías Etnológicas, Universidad Nacional Mayor de San Marcos, Lima.
Serie Monográfica, Plan Nacional de Integración de la Población Aborígena, Lima.

PUERTO RICO

Caribbean Review, Hato Rey.
Caribbean Studies, Institute of Caribbean Studies, University of Puerto Rico, Río Piedras.
Current Caribbean Bibliography, Caribbean Regional Library, Hato Rey.
Revista de Ciencias Sociales, El Colegio de Ciencias Sociales, Universidad de Puerto Rico, Río Piedras.

SPAIN

Aconcagua, Madrid.
El Americanismo en las Revistas: Antropología, Universidad de Sevilla, Sevilla.

Anales, Instituto de Etnografía Americana, Mendoza.
Anuario de Estudios Americanos, Sevilla.
Anuario de Sociología de los Pueblos Ibéricos, Asociación de Sociólogos de Lengua Española y Portuguesa, Instituto de Cultura Hispanica, Madrid.
Archivo Ibero-Americano, Madrid.
Boletín, Centro de Estudios Americanistas, Sevilla.
Boletín Americanista, Barcelona.
Estudios Americanos, Sevilla.
Publicaciones, Escuela de Estudios Hispano-Americano, Sevilla.
Publicaciones, Seminario de Antropología Americana, Sevilla.
Revista de Indias, Madrid.

SWITZERLAND

Bulletin, Société Suisse des Americanistes Schweizerische Amerikanisten-Gesellschaft, Musée et Institut d'Ethnographie, Geneva.
Estudios Sociológicos Latino-Americanos, Freiburg.

TRINIDAD

Caribbean Historical Review, Port-of-Spain.
Caribbean Quarterly, Port-of-Spain.

UNITED STATES

American Universities Field Staff Reports, South American Series, New York.
The Americas: A Quarterly Review of Inter-American Cultural History, Academy of American Franciscan History, Washington, D.C.
Aztlán: Chicano Journal of the Social Sciences and the Arts, Chicano Center, U.C.L.A., Los Angeles.
Cerámica de Cultura Maya, Department of Anthropology, Temple University, Philadelphia.
Ciencias Sociales, Pan American Union, Washington, D.C.
Contributions to American Archaeology, Carnegie Institution of Washington, Washington, D.C.
Cuban Studies Newsletter, Center for Latin American Studies, University of Pittsburgh, Pittsburgh, Pa.
El Grito, a Journal of Contemporary Mexican-American Thought, Quinto Sol Publications, Berkeley, Calif.
Estudios Andinos, Instituto Boliviano de Estudio y Acción Social, Chicago.
Folklore Americas, Center for the Study of Comparative Folklore and Mythology, U.C.L.A., Los Angeles.
Hispanic American Historical Review, Baltimore.
Ibero-Americana, University of California, Berkeley, Calif.
Inter-American Review of Bibliography, Pan American Union, Washington, D.C.
Journal of Inter-American Studies and World Affairs, Center for Advanced International Studies, University of Miami, Coral Gables, Fla.

Journal of Mexican American History, University of California at Santa Barbara, Santa Barbara, Calif.

Katunob, Department of Anthropology and Sociology, Colorado State College, Greeley, Colo.

Latin American Bulletin, Center for Latin American Studies, Arizona State University, Tempe, Ariz.

Latin American Monographs, University of Florida, Gainesville, Fla.

Latin America in Periodical Literature, U.C.L.A., Los Angeles.

Latin American Research Briefs, Land Tenure Center of the University of Wisconsin, Madison, Wis.

Latin American Research Review, Latin American Studies Association, University of Texas Press, Austin, Tex.

Latin American Studies, Latin American Center, U.C.L.A., Los Angeles.

Latin American Urban Research, Sage Publications, Beverly Hills, Calif.

Luzo-Brazilian Review, University of Wisconsin Press, Madison, Wis.

Maya Research, New York and New Orleans.

Maya Society Quarterly, Baltimore.

Monographs, Institute of Latin American Studies, University of Texas, Austin, Tex.

Ñawpa Pacha, Institute of Andean Studies, University of California, Berkeley, Calif.

Nispa Ninku, Inter-University Committee on Andean Studies, Cornell University, Ithaca, N.Y.

Notes on Middle American Archaeology and Ethnology, Carnegie Institution of Washington, Washington, D.C.

Papers of the New World Archaeological Foundation, Brigham Young University, Provo, Utah.

Publications, Institute of Social Anthropology, Smithsonian Institution, Washington, D.C.

Publications, Middle American Research Institute, Tulane University, New Orleans.

Reference Series, Latin American Center, U.C.L.A., Los Angeles.

Revista Interamericana de Ciencias Sociales, Department of Social Affairs, Pan American Union, Washington, D.C.

Social Sciences Monographs, Pan American Union, Washington, D.C.

URUGUAY

Amerindia, Centro de Estudios Arqueológicos y Antropológicos Americanos Dr. Paul Rivet, Montevideo.

Boletín, Sociedad de Antropología del Uruguay, Montevideo.

Boletín Uruguayo de Sociología, Montevideo.

Comunicaciones Antropológicas, Museo de Historia Natural de Montevideo, Montevideo.

Cuadernos de Antropología, Centro de Estudios Arqueológicos y Antropológicos Americanos, Montevideo.

Revista, Sociedad de los Amigos de la Arqueología de Montevideo, Montevideo.

U.S.S.R.

América Latina, Instituto de América Latina, Moscow.

VENEZUELA

Acta Venezolana, Grupo de Caracas de la Sociedad Interamericana de Antropología y Geografía, Caracas.

América Unida, Departamento de Estudios Latinoamericanos y Relaciones Internacionales, Escuela de Ciencias Sociales, Universidad de Oriente, Cumaná.

Antropológica, Instituto Caribe de Antropología y Sociología de La Fundación La Salle de Ciencias Naturales, Caracas.

Anuario, Instituto de Antropología e Historia, Universidad Central de Venezuela, Caracas.

Archivos Venezolanos de Folklore, Instituto de Antropología e Historia, Universidad Central de Venezuela, Caracas.

Boletín, Instituto de Antropología e Historia del Estado de Aragua, Museo de Arqueología, Maracay.

Boletín, Instituto de Folklore, Caracas.

Boletín Indigenista Venezolano, Comisión Indigenista Nacional, Ministerio de Justicia, Caracas.

Boletín Informativo, Departamento de Antropología, Instituto Venezolano de Investigaciones Científicas, Caracas.

Boletín Informativo de Antropología, Asociación Venezolana de Sociología, Caracas.

Ciencias Sociales, Escuela de Ciencias Sociales, Universidad de Oriente, Cumaná.

Cuadernos de Antropología, Universidad de los Andes, Departamento de Antropología, Mérida.

Economía y Ciencias Sociales, Facultad de Economía, Universidad Central de Venezuela, Caracas.

Folia Antropológica, Museo de Ciencias Naturales, Caracas.

Lenguas Indígenas de Venezuela, Comisión Indigenista Nacional, Caracas.

Publicaciones, Grupo de Caracas de la Sociedad Interamericana de Antropología y Geografía, Caracas.

Revista Venezolana de Sociología y Antropología, Escuela de Sociología y Antropología, Universidad Central de Venezuela, Caracas.

Serie de Fuentes Históricas, Instituto de Antropológica e Historia, Universidad Central de Venezuela, Caracas.

APPENDIX D

Biographies and autobiographies of Latin Americans

Barnet, Miguel (ed.), 1968, *The Autobiography of a Runaway Slave: Esteban Montejo:* New York: Pantheon Books.

*Cochran, Thomas C., and Ruben E. Reina, 1962, *Entrepreneurship in Argentine Culture: Torcuato Di Tella and S.I.A.M.* Philadelphia: University of Pennsylvania Press (Paperback edition entitled *Capitalism in Argentine Culture: A Study of Torcuato Di Tella and S.I.A.M.*).

Della Cava, Ralph, 1970, *Miracle at Joaseiro.* New York: Columbia University Press.

Guiteras-Holmes, Calixta, 1961, *Perils of the Soul: The World View of a Tzotzil Indian.* New York: The Free Press.

Hilger, M. Inez, 1966, *Huenun Ñamku: An Araucanian Indian of the Andes Remembers the Past.* Norman, Okla.: University of Oklahoma Press.

Hudson, Wilson M. (ed.), 1951, *The Healer of Los Olmos and Other Mexican Lore.* Dallas, Tex.: Texas Folklore Society, no. 24.

*Jesus, Carolina Maria de, 1963, *Child of the Dark: The Diary of Carolina Maria de Jesus.* New York: Signet Books [1960].

*Lewis, Oscar, 1959, *Five Families: Mexican Case Studies in the Culture of Poverty.* New York: Basic Books, Inc.

*_____, 1961, *Children of Sánchez: Autobiography of a Mexican Family.* New York: Random House, Inc.

*_____, 1964, *Pedro Martínez: A Mexican Peasant and His Family.* New York: Random House, Inc.

*_____, 1965, *La Vida: A Puerto Rican Family in the Culture of Poverty— San Juan and New York.* New York: Random House, Inc.

* Indicates that the publication is available in paperback edition.

*_____, 1970, *A Death in the Sánchez Family*. New York: Vintage Books [1969].

Mintz, Sidney W., 1960, *Worker in the Cane: A Puerto Rican History*. New Haven, Conn.: Yale University Press.

Moises, Rosalio, Jane Holden Kelley, and William Curry Holden, 1971, *The Tall Candle: The Personal Chronical of a Yaqui Indian*. Lincoln, Nebr.: University of Nebraska Press.

*Pozas, Ricardo, 1962, *Juan the Chamula: An Ethnological Re-Creation of the Life of a Mexican Indian*. Berkeley, Calif.: University of California Press [1952].

Monographs on Latin American societies and subcultures (in English)

MIDDLE AMERICA

British Honduras

Carey Jones, N. S., 1953, *The Pattern of a Dependent Economy*. Cambridge: Cambridge University Press.

Parsons, James A., 1969, *Mennonite Settlements in British Honduras*. Berkeley, Calif.: University of California, Department of Geography.

Taylor, Douglas MacRae, 1951, *The Black Carib of British Honduras*. New York: Viking Fund Publications in Anthropology, no. 17.

Thompson, J. Eric S., 1930, *Ethnology of the Mayas of Southern and Central British Honduras*. Chicago: Field Museum of Natural History Publications, no. 274, Anthropological Series, vol. 17, no. 2 pp. 27–213.

Waddell, D. A. G., 1961, *British Honduras: A Historical and Contemporary Survey*. London: Oxford University Press.

Costa Rica

Biesanz, John, and Mavis Biesanz, 1944, *Costa Rican Life*. New York: Columbia University Press.

Goldrich, Daniel, 1966, *Sons of the Establishment: Elite Youth in Panama and Costa Rica*. Skokie, Ill.: Rand McNally & Company.

Loomis, Charles P., *et al.,* 1953, *Turrialba: Social Systems and Social Change*. New York: The Free Press.

Olien, Michael D., 1970, *The Negro in Costa Rica: The Role of an Ethnic Minority in a Developing Society*. Winston-Salem, N.C.: Wake Forest University, Overseas Research Center, Developing Nations Monograph Series, no. 3.

Orso, Ethelyn, 1970, *Hot and Cold in the Folk Medicine of the Island of Chira, Costa Rica.* Baton Rouge, La.: Louisiana State University, Latin America Studies Institute, Monograph and Dissertation Series, no. 1.

Richardson, Miles, and Barbara Bode, 1969, *Popular Medicine in Puntarenas, Costa Rica: Urban and Societal Features.* New Orleans: Tulane University, Middle American Research Institute, Publication no. 24, pp. 249–275.

Sariola, Sakari, 1954, *Social Class and Social Mobility in a Costa Rican Town.* Turrialba, Costa Rica: Inter-American Institute of Agricultural Sciences.

Skinner, Alanson, 1920, Notes on the Bribri of Costa Rica. *Indian Notes and Monographs* 6(3):37–106. New York: Museum of the American Indian.

Stone, Doris, 1949, *The Boruca of Costa Rica.* Cambridge, Mass.: Harvard University, Papers of the Peabody Museum of American Archaeology and Ethnology, vol. 26, no. 2.

_____, 1962, *The Talamancan Tribes of Costa Rica.* Cambridge, Mass.: Harvard University, Papers of the Peabody Museum of American Archaeology and Ethnology, vol. 43, no. 2.

Wagner, Philip L., 1958, *Nicoya: A Cultural Geography.* Berkeley, Calif.: University of California, Publications in Geography, vol. 12, no. 3, pp. 195–250.

El Salvador

Adams, Richard N., 1957, *Cultural Surveys of Panama-Nicaragua-Guatemala-El Salvador-Honduras.* Washington, D.C.: Pan American Sanitary Bureau, Scientific Publications, no. 33.

Guatemala

Adams, Richard N., 1957, *Cultural Surveys of Panama-Nicaragua-Guatemala-El Salvador-Honduras.* Washington, D.C.: Pan American Sanitary Bureau, Scientific Publications, no. 33.

_____, 1970, *Crucifixion by Power: Essays on Guatemalan National Social Structure, 1944–1966.* Austin, Tex.: University of Texas Press.

Bunzel, Ruth, 1952, *Chichicastenango: A Guatemalan Village.* Seattle: University of Washington Press.

Carter, William E., 1969, *New Lands and Old Traditions: Kekchi Cultivators in the Guatemalan Lowlands.* Gainesville, Fla.: University of Florida Press, Latin American Monographs, Second Series, no. 6.

Colby, Benjamin N., and Pierre L. van den Berghe, 1969, *Ixil Country: A Plural Society in Highland Guatemala.* Berkeley, Calif.: University of California Press.

Correa, G., 1960, *The Spirit of Evil in Guatemala.* New Orleans: Tulane University, Middle American Research Institute, Publication no. 19, pp. 37–103.

Ebel, Roland H., 1969, *Political Modernization in Three Guatemalan Indian Communities.* New Orleans: Tulane University, Middle American Research Institute Publications.

Gillin, John, 1951, *The Culture of Security in San Carlos: A Study of a Guatemalan Community of Indians and Ladinos.* New Orleans: Tulane University, Middle American Research Institute, Publication No. 16.

Gonzalez, Nancie L. Solien, 1969, *Black Carib Household Structure: A Study of Migration and Modernization.* Seattle: University of Washington Press.

La Farge, Oliver, 1947, *Santa Eulalia: The Religion of a Cuchumatan Indian Town*. Chicago: University of Chicago Press.

McBryde, Felix Webster, 1934, *Sololá: A Guatemalan Town and Cakchiquel Market-Center*. New Orleans: Tulane University, Middle American Research Institute, Studies in Middle America, no. 5, pp. 45–153.

_____, 1945, *Cultural and Historical Geography of Southwest Guatemala*. Washington, D.C.: Smithsonian Institution, Institute of Social Anthropology, Publication no. 4.

*Nash, Manning, 1967, *Machine Age Maya: The Industrialization of a Guatemalan Community*. 2nd ed. Chicago: University of Chicago Press [1958].

Oakes, Maud, 1951, *Beyond the Windy Place: Life in the Guatemalan Highlands*. New York: Farrar, Straus & Giroux, Inc.

*_____, 1969, *The Two Crosses of Todos Santos: Survivals of Mayan Religious Ritual*. Princeton, N.J.: Princeton University Press, Bollingen Series, no. 27 [1951].

Reina, Ruben E., 1960, *Chinautla, A Guatemalan Indian Community: A Study in the Relationship of Community Culture and National Culture*. New Orleans: Tulane University, Middle American Research Institute, Publication no. 24, pp. 55–130.

*_____, 1966, *The Law of the Saints: A Pokomam Pueblo and Its Community Culture*. Indianapolis: The Bobbs-Merrill Company, Inc.

Roberts, Bryan R., 1972, *Organizing Strangers: The Careers and Politics of Poor Families in Guatemala City*. Austin, Tex.: University of Texas Press.

Rodas N., Flavio, Ovidio Rodas C., and Laurence F. Hawkins, 1940, *Chichicastenango: The Kiche Indians*. Guatemala City: Unión Tipográfica.

Tax, Sol, 1953, *Penny Capitalism: A Guatemalan Indian Economy*. Washington, D.C.: Smithsonian Institution, Institute of Social Anthropology, Publication no. 16.

Tumin, Melvin M., 1952, *Caste in a Peasant Society: A Case Study in the Dynamics of Caste*. Princeton, N.J.: Princeton University Press.

Wagley, Charles, 1941, *Economics of a Guatemalan Village*. Menasha, Wis.: American Anthropological Association Memoir, no. 58.

_____, 1949, *The Social and Religious Life of a Guatemalan Village*. Menasha, Wis.: American Anthropological Association Memoir, no. 71.

Whetten, Nathan L., 1961, *Guatemala: The Land and the People*. New Haven, Conn.: Yale University Press, Caribbean Series, no. 4.

Wisdom, Charles, 1940, *The Chorti Indians of Guatemala*. Chicago: University of Chicago Press.

Honduras

Adams, Richard N., 1957, *Cultural Surveys of Panama-Nicaragua-Guatemala-El Salvador-Honduras*. Washington, D.C.: Pan American Sanitary Bureau, Scientific Publications, no. 33.

---

* Indicates books available in paperback editions. The date of the most recent edition is given. Dates in brackets indicate the date in which it was first published.

Conzemius, Eduard, 1932, *Ethnographical Survey of the Miskito and Sumu Indians of Honduras and Nicaragua*. Washington, D.C.: Smithsonian Institution, Bureau of American Ethnology, Bulletin no. 106.

Von Hagen, Victor Wolfgang, 1943, The Jicaque (Torrupán) Indians of Honduras. *Indian Notes and Monographs*, miscellaneous no. 53, New York: Museum of the American Indian. pp. 1–98.

Mexico

Avila, Manuel, 1969, *Tradition and Growth: A Study of Four Mexican Villages*. Chicago: University of Chicago Press.

Bailey, Helen Miller, 1958, *Santa Cruz of the Etla Hills*. Gainesville, Fla.: University of Florida Press.

Beals, Ralph L., 1933, *The Acaxee: A Mountain Tribe of Durango and Sinaloa*. Berkeley, Calif.: University of California, Ibero-Americana, no. 6.

———, 1943, *The Aboriginal Culture of the Cáhita Indians*. Berkeley, Calif.: University of California, Ibero-Americana, no. 19.

———, 1945, *The Contemporary Culture of the Cáhita Indians*. Washington, D.C.: Smithsonian Institution, Bureau of American Ethnology, Bulletin no. 142.

———, 1945, *Ethnology of the Western Mixe*. Berkeley, Calif.: University of California, Publications in American Archaeology and Ethnology, no. 42.

———, 1946, *Cherán: A Sierra Tarascan Village*. Washington, D.C.: Smithsonian Institution, Institute of Social Anthropology, Publication no. 2.

Belshaw, Michael, 1966, *Economic and Social Problems of a Tarascan Village*. New York: Columbia University Press.

Bennett, Wendell C., and Robert M. Zingg, 1935, *The Tarahumara: An Indian Tribe of Northern Mexico*. Chicago: University of Chicago Press.

Berlin, Brent, Dennis E. Bredlove, and Peter Raven, 1972, *Principles of Tzeltal Plant Taxonomy: An Introduction to the Botanical Ethnography of a Mayan Speaking People of Highland Chiapas*. New York: Seminar Press, Inc.

Blaffer, Sarah C., 1972, *The Black-Man of Zinacantan: A Central American Legend*. Austin, Tex.: University of Texas Press.

Brand, Donald D., 1951, *Quiroga: A Mexican Municipio*. Washington, D.C.: Smithsonian Institution, Institute of Social Anthropology, Publication no. 11.

*Cancian, Frank, 1965, *Economics and Prestige in a Maya Community: The Religious Cargo System in Zinacantan*. Stanford, Calif.: Stanford University Press.

———, 1972, *Change and Uncertainty in a Peasant Economy: The Maya Corn Farmers of Zinacantan*. Stanford, Calif.: Stanford University Press.

Carrasco, Pedro, 1957, *Tarascan Folk Religion*. New Orleans: Tulane University, Middle American Research Institute, Publication no. 17, pp. 1–64 [1952].

*Chiñas, Beverly, 1973, *Isthmus Zapotecs: Sex Roles in Cultural Context*. Case Studies in Cultural Anthropology. New York: Holt, Rinehart and Winston, Inc.

Colby, Benjamin N., 1966, *Ethnic Relations in the Chiapas Highlands*. Santa Fe, N.M.: Museum of New Mexico Press.

Collier, Jane F., 1968, *Courtship and Marriage in Zinacantan*. New Orleans: Tulane University, Middle American Research Institute, Publication no. 25, pp. 139–201.

Covarrubias, Miguel, 1946, *Mexico South: The Isthmus of Tehuantepec.* New York: Alfred A. Knopf.

Crumrine, Lynn Scoggins, 1969, *Ceremonial Exchange as a Mechanism in Tribal Integration Among the Mayos of Northwest Mexico.* Tucson, Ariz.: University of Arizona, Anthropological Papers, no. 14.

Crumrine, N. Ross, 1964, *The House Cross of the Mayo Indians of Sonora, Mexico: A Symbol of Ethnic Identity.* Tucson, Ariz.: University of Arizona Press.

*Diaz, May N., 1966, *Tonalá: Conservatism, Responsibility and Authority in a Mexican Town.* Berkeley, Calif.: University of California Press.

Driver, Harold E., and Wilhelmine Driver, 1963, *Ethnography and Acculturation of the Chichimeca-Jonaz of Northeast Mexico.* Bloomington, Ind.: Indiana University, Publications of the Research Center in Anthropology, Folklore, and Linguistics, vol. 26.

Erasmus, Charles J., 1967, Culture Change in Northwest Mexico. In Julian H. Steward (ed.), *Contemporary Change in Traditional Societies,* vol. 3 (*Mexican and Peruvian Communities*), pp. 1–131. Urbana, Ill.: University of Illinois Press.

Fisher, Glenn, 1957, *Directed Culture Change in Nayarit, Mexico: An Analysis of a Pilot Project in Basic Education.* New Orleans: Tulane University, Middle American Research Institute, Publication 17, pp. 65–176 [1953].

Foster, George M., 1966, *A Primitive Mexican Economy.* Seattle, Wash.: University of Washington Press [1942].

————, 1948, *Empire's Children: The People of Tzintzuntzan.* Washington, D.C.: Smithsonian Institution, Institute of Social Anthropology, Publication no. 6.

————, 1967, *Tzintzuntzan: Mexican Peasants in a Changing World.* Boston: Little, Brown & Company.

Friedrich, Paul, 1970, *Agrarian Revolt in a Mexican Village.* Englewood Cliffs, N.J.: Prentice-Hall, Inc.

Fromm, Erich, and Michael MacCoby, 1970, *Social Character in a Mexican Village: A Sociopsychoanalytic Study.* Englewood Cliffs, N.J.: Prentice-Hall, Inc.

Gann, Thomas W. F., 1918, *The Maya Indians of Southern Yucatan and Northern British Honduras.* Washington, D.C.: Smithsonian Institution, Bureau of American Ethnology, Bulletin no. 64.

Griffen, William B., 1959, *Notes on Seri Indian Culture, Sonora, Mexico.* Gainesville, Fla.: University of Florida Press, Latin American Monographs, no. 10.

————, 1969, *Culture Change and Shifting Populations in Central Northern Mexico.* Tucson, Ariz.: University of Arizona, Anthropological Papers, no. 13.

Gwaltney, John L., 1970, *The Thrice Shy: Cultural Accommodation to Blindness and Other Disasters in a Mexican Community.* New York: Columbia University Press.

Hancock, Richard H., 1959, *The Role of the Bracero in the Economic and Cultural Dynamics of Mexico: A Case Study of Chihuahua.* Stanford, Calif.: Stanford University Press.

Hill, A. David, 1964, *The Changing Landscape of a Mexican Municipio: Villa Las Rosas, Chiapas.* Chicago: University of Chicago, Department of Geography, Research Paper no. 91.

Hinton, Thomas B., 1959, *A Survey of Indian Assimilation in Eastern Sonora.* Tucson, Ariz.: University of Arizona, Anthropological Papers, no. 4.

*Iwánska, Alicja, 1971, *Purgatory and Utopia: A Mazahua Indian Village of Mexico.* Cambridge, Mass.: Schenkman Publishing Company.

Johnson, Jean B., 1950, *The Opata: An Inland Tribe of Sonora.* Albuquerque, N.M.: University of New Mexico, Publications in Anthropology, no. 6.

*Kearney, Michael, 1972, *The Winds of Ixtepeji: World View and Society in a Zapotec Town.* Case Studies in Cultural Anthropology. New York: Holt, Rinehart and Winston, Inc.

Kelly, Isabel, 1965, *Folk Practices in North Mexico: Birth Customs, Folk Medicine, and Spiritualism in the Laguna Zone.* Austin, Tex.: University of Texas Press, Latin American Monograph no. 2.

Kelly, Isabel, and Angel Palerm, 1952, *Tajín Totonac: Part I. History, Subsistence, Shelter and Technology.* Washington, D.C.: Smithsonian Institution, Institute of Social Anthropology, Publication no. 13.

Kelly, Isabel T., *et al.,* 1956, *Santiago Tuxtla, Vera Cruz: Culture and Health.* Mexico City: Institute of Inter-American Affairs.

La Farge, Oliver, and Douglas Byers, 1931, *The Year Bearer's People.* New Orleans: Tulane University, Middle American Research Institute, Publication no. 3.

Leslie, Charles M., 1960, *Now We are Civilized: A Study of the World View of Zapotec Indians of Mitla, Oaxaca.* Detroit, Mich.: Wayne State University Press.

*Lewis, Oscar, 1951, *Life in a Mexican Village: Tepoztlán Restudied.* Urbana, Ill.: University of Illinois Press.

*_____, 1960, *Tepoztlán: Village in Mexico.* Case Studies in Cultural Anthropology. New York: Holt, Rinehart and Winston, Inc.

Madsen, Claudia, 1966, *A Study of Change in Mexican Folk Medicine.* New Orleans: Tulane University, Middle American Research Institute, Publication no. 25.

Madsen, William, 1957, *Christo-Paganism: A Study of Mexican Religious Syncretism.* New Orleans: Tulane University, Middle American Research Institute, Publication no. 19, pp. 105–180.

_____, 1960, *The Virgin's Children: Life in an Aztec Village Today.* Austin, Tex.: University of Texas Press.

*Modiano, Nancy, 1973, *Indian Education in the Chiapas Highlands.* Case Studies in Education and Culture. New York: Holt, Rinehart and Winston, Inc.

Nader, Laura, 1964, *Talea and Juquila: A Comparison of Zapotec Social Organization.* Berkeley, Calif.: University of California, Publications in American Archaeology and Ethnology, vol. 48, no. 3, pp. 195–296.

Nash, June C., 1970, *In the Eyes of the Ancestors: Belief and Behavior in a Mayan Community.* New Haven, Conn.: Yale University Press.

Nelson, Cynthia, 1971, *The Waiting Village: Social Change in Rural Mexico.* Boston: Little, Brown & Company.

Nutini, Hugo G., 1968, *San Bernardino Contla: Marriage and Family Structure in a Tlaxcalan Municipio.* Pittsburgh, Pa.: University of Pittsburgh Press.

Owen, Roger C., 1959, *Marobavi: A Study of an Assimilated Group in Northern Sonora.* Tucson, Ariz.: University of Arizona, Anthropological Papers, no. 3.

Parsons, Elsie Clews, 1936, *Mitla, Town of the Souls and Other Zapoteco-speaking Pueblos of Oaxaca, Mexico.* Chicago: University of Chicago Press.

Pennington, Campbell W., 1963, *The Tarahumar of Mexico: Their Environment and Material Culture.* Salt Lake City, Utah: University of Utah Press.

_____, 1969, *The Tepehuan of Chihuahua: Their Material Culture.* Salt Lake City, Utah: University of Utah Press.

Pi-Sunyer, Oriol, 1967, *Zamora: A Regional Economy in Mexico.* New Orleans: Tulane University, Middle American Research Institute, Publication no. 29, pp. 95–180.

*_____, 1973, *Zamora: Change and Continuity in a Mexican Town.* Case Studies in Cultural Anthropology. New York: Holt, Rinehart and Winston, Inc.

Redfield, Robert, 1930, *Tepoztlán, A Mexican Village: A Study of Folk Life.* Chicago: University of Chicago Press.

_____, 1941, *The Folk Culture of Yucatán.* Chicago: University of Chicago Press.

*_____, 1950, *A Village That Chose Progress: Chan Kom Revisited.* Chicago: University of Chicago Press.

*Redfield, Robert, and Alfonso Villa Rojas, 1962, *Chan Kom: A Maya Village.* abridged ed. Chicago: Phoenix Books [1934].

Ritzenthaler, Robert E., and Frederick A. Peterson, 1956, *The Mexican Kickapoo Indians.* Milwaukee, Wis.: Milwaukee Public Museum, Publications in Anthropology, no. 2.

*Romney, Kimball, and Romaine Romney, 1966, *The Mixtecans of Juxtlahuaca, Mexico.* New York: John Wiley & Sons, Inc.

Scholes, France V., and Ralph L. Roys, 1968, *The Maya Chontal Indians of Acalan-Tixchel: A Contribution to the History and Ethnography of the Yucatán Peninsula.* Norman, Okla.: University of Oklahoma Press [1948].

Schmieder, O., 1930, *The Settlements of the Tzapotec and Mije Indians, State of Oaxaca, Mexico.* Berkeley, Calif.: University of California, Publications in Geography, vol. 4.

Spicer, Edward H., 1954, *Potam: A Yaqui Village of Sonora.* Menasha, Wis.: American Anthropological Association Memoir, no. 77.

Stanislawski, Dan, 1950, *The Anatomy of Eleven Towns in Michoacán.* Austin, Tex.: University of Texas, Latin American Studies, no. 10.

Starr, Frederick, 1900–1902, *Notes Upon the Ethnography of Southern Mexico.* Davenport, Iowa: Proceedings of the Davenport Academy of Natural Science, vols. 8 and 9.

Steininger, G. Russell, and Paul van de Velde, 1971, *Three Dollars a Year, Being the Story of San Pablo Cuayo Venados, a Typical Zapotecan Indian Village that Hangs on a Slope of the Sierras in Southwestern Mexico.* Detroit, Mich.: Blaine Ethridge Books [1938].

Taylor, Paul S., 1933, *A Spanish-Mexican Peasant Community: Arandas in Jalisco, Mexico.* Berkeley, Calif.: Ibero-Americana, no. 4.

Tozzer, Alfred, 1907, *The Comparative Study of the Mayas and the Lacandones.* New York: Archaeological Institute of America.

*Turner, Paul R., 1972, *The Highland Chontal.* Case Studies in Cultural Anthropology. New York: Holt, Rinehart and Winston, Inc.

Van Zantwijk, R. A. M., 1967, *Servants of the Saints: The Social and Cultural Identity of a Tarascan Community in Mexico*. Assen, Netherlands: Van Gorcum and Company.

Villa Rojas, Alfonso, 1945, *The Maya of East-Central Quintana Roo*. Washington, D.C.: Carnegie Institution of Washington, Publication no. 559.

Vogt, Evon Z., 1969, *Zinacantan: A Maya Community in the Highlands of Chiapas*. Cambridge, Mass.: Belknap Press of Harvard University Press.

*_____, 1970, *The Zinacantecos of Mexico: A Modern Maya Way of Life*. Case Studies in Cultural Anthropology. New York: Holt, Rinehart and Winston, Inc.

West, Robert C., 1948, *Cultural Geography of the Modern Tarascan Area*. Washington, D.C.: Smithsonian Institution, Institute of Social Anthropology, Publication no. 7.

Whetten, Nathan L., 1948, *Rural Mexico*. Chicago: University of Chicago Press.

*Whiteford, Andrew H., 1964, *Two Cities of Latin America: A Comparative Description of Social Classes*. New York: Anchor Books [1960].

Wilkie, Raymond, 1971, *San Miguel: A Mexican Collective Ejido*. Stanford, Calif.: Stanford University Press.

Nicaragua

Adams, Richard N., 1957, *Cultural Surveys of Panama-Nicaragua-Guatemala-El Salvador-Honduras*. Washington, D.C.: Pan American Sanitary Bureau, Scientific Publications, no. 33.

Conzemius, Eduard, 1932, *Ethnographical Survey of the Miskito and Sumu Indians of Honduras and Nicaragua*. Washington, D.C.: Smithsonian Institution, Bureau of American Ethnology, Bulletin no. 106.

Helms, Mary W., 1971, *Asang: Adaptations to Culture Contact in a Miskito Community*. Gainesville, Fla.: University of Florida Press.

Panama

Adams, Richard N., 1957, *Cultural Surveys of Panama-Nicaragua-Guatemala-El Salvador-Honduras*. Washington, D.C.: Pan American Sanitary Bureau, Scientific Publications, no. 33.

Biesanz, John, and Mavis Biesanz, 1955, *The People of Panama*. New York: Columbia University Press.

Goldrich, Daniel, 1966, *Sons of the Establishment: Elite Youth in Panama and Costa Rica*. Skokie, Ill.: Rand McNally & Company.

Guzman, Louis E., 1956, *Farming and Farmlands in Panama*. Chicago: University of Chicago, Department of Geography, Research Papers, no. 44.

Nordenskiöld, Erland, 1938, *An Historical and Ethnographical Survey of the Cuna Indians*. Göteborg: Göteborg Museum Etnografiska Avdelningen, Comparative Ethnographical Studies, no. 10.

Stout, D. B., 1947, *San Blas Cuna Acculturation: An Introduction*. New York: Viking Fund Publications in Anthropology, no. 9.

Wassén, Henry, 1949, *Contributions to Cuna Ethnography*. Göteborg: Etnografiska Museet, Ethnologiska Studier, no. 16.

Young, Philip D., 1971, *Ngawbe: Tradition and Change Among the Western Guaymí of Panama*. Urbana, Ill.: University of Illinois Studies in Anthropology, no. 7.

SOUTH AMERICA

Argentina

*Cochran, Thomas C., and Ruben E. Reina, 1962, *Entrepreneurship in Argentine Culture: Torcuato Di Tella and S.I.A.M.* Philadelphia: University of Pennsylvania Press (Paperback edition entitled *Capitalism in Argentine Culture: A Study of Torcuato Di Tella and S.I.A.M.*).

Eidt, Robert C., 1971, *Pioneer Settlement in Northeast Argentina*. Madison, Wis.: University of Wisconsin Press.

Fillol, Thomas, 1961, *Social Factors in Economic Development: The Argentine Case*. Cambridge, Mass.: M.I.T. Press.

Pendle, George, 1961, *Argentina*. 2nd ed. London: Oxford University Press.

Taylor, Carl, 1948, *Rural Life in Argentina*. Baton Rouge, La.: Louisiana State University Press.

Winsberg, Morton D., *Colonia Baron Hirsch: A Jewish Agricultural Colony in Argentina*. Gainesville, Fla.: University of Florida, Social Sciences Monograph, no. 19.

Bolivia

*Buechler, Hans, and Judith-Maria Buechler, 1971, *The Bolivian Aymara*. Case Studies in Cultural Anthropology. New York: Holt, Rinehart and Winston, Inc.

Carter, William E., 1964, *Aymara Communities and the Bolivian Agrarian Reform*. Gainesville, Fla.: University of Florida Press, Social Sciences Monographs, no. 24.

Heath, Dwight B., Charles J. Erasmus, and Hans C. Buechler, 1969, *Land Reform and Social Revolution in Bolivia*. New York: Frederick A. Praeger, Inc.

*Holmberg, Allan R., 1969, *Nomads of the Long Bow: The Sirionó of Eastern Bolivia*. Garden City, N.Y.: Natural History Press [1950].

Karsten, Rafael, 1967, *The Toba Indians of the Bolivian Gran Chaco*. Oosterhout N.B., The Netherlands: Anthropological Publications [1923].

La Barre, Weston, 1948, *The Aymara Indians of the Lake Titicaca Plateau, Bolivia*. Menasha, Wis.: American Anthropological Association Memoir, no. 68.

Leonard, Olen E., 1948, *Canton Chullpas: A Socio-Economic Study in the Cochabamba Valley of Bolivia*. Washington, D.C.: United States Department of Agriculture, Foreign Agricultural Reports, no. 27.

_____, 1952, *Bolivia: Land, Peoples, and Institutions*. New York: Scarecrow Press, Inc.

Osborne, Harold, 1964, *Bolivia: A Land Divided*. 3rd ed. London: Oxford University Press.

Scheffler, Harold W., and Floyd G. Loundsbury, 1971, *A Study in Structural Semantics: The Sirionó Kinship System*. Englewood Cliffs, N.J.: Prentice-Hall, Inc.

Brazil

Azevedo, Fernando de, 1950, *Brazilian Culture: An Introduction to the Study of Culture in Brazil.* New York: The Macmillan Company.

Azevedo, Thales de, 1963, *Social Change in Brazil.* Gainesville, Fla.: University of Florida Press, Latin American Monograph Series, no. 22.

*Basso, Ellen, 1973, *The Kalapalo Indians of Central Brazil.* Case Studies in Cultural Anthropology. New York: Holt, Rinehart and Winston, Inc.

*Chagnon, Napoleon A., 1968, *Yąnomamö: The Fierce People.* Case Studies in Cultural Anthropology. New York: Holt, Rinehart and Winston, Inc.

Costa Eduardo, Octavio da, 1948, *The Negro in Northern Brazil: A Study in Acculturation.* Seattle: University of Washington Press.

Fernandes, Florestan, 1969, *The Negro in Brazilian Society.* New York: Columbia University Press.

Forman, Shepard, 1970, *The Raft Fishermen: Tradition and Change in the Brazilian Peasant Economy.* Bloomington, Ind.: Indiana University Latin American Series.

Freye, Gilberto, 1963, *The Mansions and the Shanties: The Making of Modern Brazil.* New York: Alfred A. Knopf [1946].

*_____, 1963, *New World in the Tropics: The Culture of Modern Brazil.* New York: Vintage Books [1945].

*_____, 1964, *The Masters and the Slaves: A Study in the Development of Brazilian Civilization.* abridged ed. New York: Alfred A. Knopf [1946].

Fuji, Yukio, and T. Lynn Smith, 1959, *The Acculturation of the Japanese Immigrants in Brazil.* Gainesville, Fla.: University of Florida, Latin American Monograph Series, no. 8.

Galjart, Benno, 1968, *Itaguaí: Old Habits and New Practices in a Brazilian Land Settlement.* Wageningen, Netherlands: Center for Agricultural Publishing and Documentation.

Hack, H., 1959, *Dutch Group Settlement in Brazil.* Amsterdam: Royal Tropical Institute, no. 132, Department of Cultural and Physical Anthropology, no. 61.

*Harris, Marvin, 1971, *Town and Country in Brazil.* New York: W. W. Norton & Company, Inc. [1956].

*Henry, Jules, 1964, *Jungle People: A Kaingáng Tribe of the Highlands of Brazil.* New York: Vintage Books [1941].

Hutchinson, Harry W., 1957, *Village and Plantation Life in Northeastern Brazil.* Seattle: University of Washington Press.

*Huxley, Francis, 1966, *Affable Savages: An Anthropologist Among the Urubu Indians of Brazil.* New York: Capricorn Books [1956].

Johnson, Allen W., 1971, *Sharecroppers of the Sertão: Economics and Dependence on a Brazilian Plantation.* Stanford, Calif.: Stanford University Press.

Landes, Ruth, 1947, *The City of Women.* New York: Macmillan.

*Lévi-Strauss, Claude, 1964, *Tristes Tropiques.* abridged ed. New York: Atheneum Publishers [1955].

Maybury-Lewis, David, 1967, *Akwẽ-Shavante Society.* London: Clarendon Press.

*_____, 1968, *The Savage and the Innocent.* Boston: The Beacon Press [1965].

*Meggars, Betty J., 1971, *Amazonia: Man and Culture in a Counterfeit Paradise.* Chicago: Aldine Publishing Company.

Morse, Richard M., 1958, *From Community to Metropolis: A Biography of São Paulo, Brazil.* Gainesville, Fla.: University of Florida Press.

Murphy, Robert F., 1958, *Mundurucú Religion.* Berkeley, Calif.: University of California, Publications in Archaeology and Ethnology, no. 49.

_____, 1960, *Headhunter's Heritage: Social and Economic Change Among the Mundurucú Indians.* Berkeley, Calif.: University of California Press.

Murphy, Robert, and Buell Quain, 1955, *The Trumai Indians of Central Brazil.* Seattle: University of Washington Press.

Nimuendajú, Curt, 1939, *The Apinayé.* Washington, D.C.: The Catholic University of America Press.

_____, 1942, *The Šerente.* Los Angeles: Southwest Museum, Publication of The Frederick Webb Hodge Publication Fund, vol. 4.

_____, 1946, *The Eastern Timbira.* Berkeley, Calif.: University of California Press.

_____, 1952, *The Tukuna.* Berkeley, Calif.: University of California, Publications in American Archaeology and Ethnology, vol. 45.

Oberg, Kalervo, 1949, *The Terena and the Caduveo of Southern Mato Grosso, Brazil.* Washington, D.C.: Smithsonian Institution, Institute of Social Anthropology, Publication no. 9.

_____, 1953, *Indian Tribes of Northern Mato Grosso, Brazil.* Washington, D.C.: Smithsonian Institution, Institute of Social Anthropology, Publication no. 15.

_____, 1957, *Toledo: A Municipio on the Western Frontier of the State of Parana.* Rio de Janeiro: U.S.O.M.

Pierson, Donald, 1942, *Negroes in Brazil: A Study of Race Contact in Bahia.* Chicago: University of Chicago Press.

_____, 1951, *Cruz das Almas: A Brazilian Village.* Washington, D.C.: Smithsonian Institution, Institute of Social Anthropology, Publication no. 12.

Ramos, Arthur, 1939, *The Negro in Brazil.* Washington, D.C.: The Associated Publishers.

Rivière, Peter, 1969, *Marriage Among the Trio: A Principle of Social Organization Among a South American Forest People.* New York: Oxford University Press.

*_____, 1972, *The Forgotten Frontier: Ranchers of Northern Brazil.* Case Studies in Cultural Anthropology. New York: Holt, Rinehart and Winston, Inc.

Rodrigues, José Honório, 1967, *The Brazilians: Their Character and Aspirations.* Austin, Tex.: University of Texas Press.

Schurz, William, 1961, *Brazil the Infinite Country.* New York: E. P. Dutton & Co., Inc.

Shirley, Robert W., 1971, *The End of a Tradition: Culture Change and Development in the Municipio of Cunha, Sao Paulo, Brazil.* New York: Columbia University Press.

Smith, T. Lynn, 1963, *Brazil: People and Institutions.* 3rd ed. Baton Rouge, La.: Louisiana State University Press.

Smith, T. Lynn, and Alexander Marchant (eds.), 1951, *Brazil, Portrait of Half a Continent.* New York: Dryden Press.

*Stein, Stanley J., 1970, *Vassouras: A Brazilian Coffee County, 1850–1890: The Roles of Planter and Slave in a Changing Plantation Society*. New York: Atheneum Publishers [1957].

*Wagley, Charles, 1964, *Amazon Town: A Study of Man in the Tropics*. New York: Alfred A. Knopf [1953].

*―――――, 1971, *An Introduction to Brazil*. rev. ed. New York: Columbia University Press [1963].

*Wagley, Charles (ed.), 1963, *Race and Class in Rural Brazil*. 2nd ed. New York: U.N.E.S.C.O. [1952].

Wagley, Charles, and Eduardo Galvão, 1949, *The Tenetehara Indians of Brazil*. New York: Columbia University Contributions to Anthropology, no. 35.

Watson, James B., 1952, *Cayuá Culture Change: A Study in Acculturation and Methodology*. Menasha, Wis.: American Anthropological Association, Memoir no. 73.

Willems, Emilio, 1967, *Followers of the New Faith: Culture Change and the Rise of Protestantism in Brazil and Chile*. Nashville, Tenn.: Vanderbilt University Press.

Willems, Emilio, and Giocondo Mussolini, 1953, *Buzios Island: A Caiçara Community in Southern Brazil*. Seattle: University of Washington Press.

Chile

Butland, Gilbert J., 1953, *Chile: An Outline of Its Geography, Economics and Politics*. rev. ed. London: Royal Institute of International Affairs.

―――――, 1957, *The Human Geography of Southern Chile*. London: Institute of British Geographers, Publication no. 24.

Faron, Louis C., 1961, *Mapuche Social Structure: Institutional Reintegration in a Patrilineal Society of Central Chile*. Urbana, Ill.: University of Illinois Studies in Anthropology, no. 1.

―――――, 1964, *Hawks of the Sun: Mapuche Morality and Its Ritual Attributes*. Pittsburgh, Pa.: University of Pittsburgh Press.

*―――――, 1968, *The Mapuche Indians of Chile*. Case Studies in Cultural Anthropology. New York: Holt, Rinehart and Winston, Inc.

Hilger, Sister Inez, 1957, *Araucanian Child Life and Its Cultural Background*. Washington, D.C.: Smithsonian Institution, Miscellaneous Collection, vol. 133.

Lambert, Charles J., 1952, *Sweet Waters: A Chilean Farm*. London: Chatto and Windus, Ltd.

Lothrop, Samuel K., 1928, *The Indians of Tierra del Fuego*. New York: Museum of the American Indian, vol .10.

McBride, George Mc., 1936, *Chile: Land and Society*. New York: American Geographical Society Research Series, no. 19.

Titiev, Mischa, 1951, *Araucanian Culture in Transition*. Ann Arbor, Mich.: University of Michigan, Museum of Anthropology, Occasional Papers, no. 15.

Willems, Emilio, 1967, *Followers of the New Faith: Culture Change and the Rise of Protestantism in Brazil and Chile*. Nashville, Tenn.: Vanderbilt University Press.

Colombia

Crist, Raymond E., 1952, *The Cauca Valley, Colombia: Land Tenure and Land Use*. Baltimore: Waverly Press.

Fals-Borda, Orlando, 1955, *Peasant Society in the Colombian Andes: A Sociological Study of Saucío*. Gainesville, Fla.: University of Florida Press.

————, 1969, *Subversion and Social Change in Colombia*. New York: Columbia University Press.

Goldman, Irving, 1963, *The Cubeo: Indians of the Northwest Amazon*. Urbana, Ill.: University of Illinois Studies in Anthropology, no. 2.

Lipman, Aaron, 1969, *The Colombian Entrepreneur in Bogotá*. Coral Gables, Fla.: University of Miami Press, Hispanic American Studies, no. 22.

Parsons, James J., 1968, *Antioqueño Colonization in Western Colombia*. rev. ed. Berkeley, Calif.: University of California, Ibero-Americana, no. 32 [1949].

Reichel-Dolmatoff, Gerardo, 1971, *Amazonian Cosmos: The Sexual and Religious Symbolism of the Tukano Indians*. Chicago: University of Chicago Press [1969].

Reichel-Dolmatoff, Gerardo, and Alicia Reichel-Dolmatoff, 1961, *The People of Aritama*. Chicago: University of Chicago Press.

*Richardson, Miles, 1970, *San Pedro, Colombia: Small Town in a Developing Society*. Case Studies in Cultural Anthropology. New York: Holt, Rinehart and Winston, Inc.

Savage, Charles, 1964, *Social Reorganization in a Factory in the Andes*. Ithaca, N.Y.: Society for Applied Anthropology, Monograph no. 7.

Smith, T. Lynn, 1967, *Colombia: Social Structure and the Process of Development*. Gainesville, Fla.: University of Florida Press.

Smith, T. Lynn, Justo Rodríguez Díaz, and Luis Roberto Garcia, 1945, *Tabio: A Study in Rural Social Organization*. Washington, D.C.: United States Department of Agriculture, Office of Foreign Agricultural Relations.

West, Robert C., 1957, *The Pacific Lowlands of Colombia: A Negroid Area of the American Tropics*. Baton Rouge, La.: Louisiana State University Studies, Social Science Series, no. 8.

*Whiteford, Andrew H., 1964, *Two Cities of Latin America: A Comparative Description of Social Classes*. New York: Doubleday & Company, Inc., Anchor Books [1960].

Whitten, Norman E., Jr., 1973, *Black Frontiersmen: A South American Case*. Cambridge, Mass.: Schenkman Publishing Company, Inc.

Ecuador

Barrett, Samuel A., 1925, *The Cayapa Indians of Ecuador*. Indian Notes and Monographs 40. New York: Museum of the American Indian (2 vols.).

Beals, Ralph L., 1966, *Community in Transition: Nayón, Ecuador*. Los Angeles: University of California at Los Angeles, Latin American Center, Latin American Studies, no. 2.

Collier, John, Jr., and Aníbal Buitrón, 1949, *The Awakening Valley*. Chicago: University of Chicago Press.

Ferndon, Edwin N., Jr., 1950, *Studies in Ecuadorian Geography*. Santa Fe, N.M.: Monographs of the School of American Research, no. 15, pp. 1–86.

Karsten, Rafael, 1923, *Blood Revenge, War, and Victory Feasts Among the Jibaro Indians of Eastern Ecuador.* Washington, D.C.: Smithsonian Institution, Bureau of American Ethnology, Bulletin no. 79.

————, 1935, *The Head-Hunters of Western Amazonas: The Life and Culture of the Jibaro Indians of Eastern Ecuador and Peru.* Helsingfors, Finland: Finska vetenskaps-societen, Commentationes humanarium litterarum, vol. 7, no. 1.

Leonard, Olen E., 1947, *Pichilinque: A Study of Rural Life in Coastal Ecuador.* Washington, D.C.: United States Department of Agriculture, Office of Foreign Agricultural Relations.

Linke, Lilo, 1960, *Ecuador: Country of Contrasts.* 3rd ed. London: Oxford University Press.

Parsons, Elsie Clews, 1945, *Peguche: A Study of Andean Indians.* Chicago: University of Chicago Press.

Salz, Beate R., 1955, *The Human Element in Industrialization: A Hypothetical Case Study of Ecuadorean Indians.* Menasha, Wis.: American Anthropological Association, Memoir no. 85.

Stirling, Matthew W., 1938, *Historical and Ethnographical Material on the Jivaro Indians.* Washington, D.C.: Smithsonian Institution, Bureau of American Ethnology, Bulletin no. 117.

Von Hagen, Victor W., 1939, *The Tsátchela Indians of Western Ecuador. Indian Notes and Monographs,* miscellaneous no. 51. New York: Museum of the American Indian.

Whitten, Norman E., Jr., 1965, *Class, Kinship and Power in an Ecuadorian Town: The Negroes of San Lorenzo.* Stanford, Calif.: Stanford University Press.

————, 1973, *Black Frontiersmen: A South American Case.* Cambridge, Mass.: Schenkman Publishing Company, Inc.

Guyana

*Despres, Leo A., 1967, *Cultural Pluralism and Nationalist Politics in British Guiana.* Skokie, Ill.: Rand McNally & Company.

Fock, Niels, 1963, *Waiwai: Religion and Society of an Amazonian Tribe.* Copenhagen: The National Museum (Nationalmuseets Skrifter, Etnografisk Raeke, no. 8).

Gillin, John, 1936, *The Barama River Caribs of British Guiana.* Cambridge, Mass.: Papers of the Peabody Museum of Archaeology and Ethnology, vol. 14, no. 2.

Glasgow, Roy Arthur, 1970, *Guyana: Race and Politics Among Africans and East Indians.* The Hague: Martinus Nijhoff.

Jayawardena, Chandra, 1963, *Conflict and Solidarity in a Guianese Plantation.* London: London School of Economics, Monographs in Social Anthropology, no. 25.

Roth, Walter E., 1915, *An Inquiry into the Animism and Folk-Lore of the Guiana Indians.* Washington, D.C.: Smithsonian Institution, Thirtieth Annual Report of the Bureau of American Ethnology, 1908–1909, pp. 103–386.

————, 1924, *An Introductory Study of the Arts, Crafts, and Customs of the Guiana Indians.* Washington, D.C.: Smithsonian Institution, Thirty-Eighth Annual Report of the Bureau of American Ethnology, 1916–1917, pp. 25–720.

Roth, Walter E., 1929, *Additional Studies of the Arts, Crafts, and Customs of the Guiana Indians with Special Reference to Those of Southern British Guiana.* Washington, D.C.: Smithsonian Institution, Bureau of American Ethnology, Bulletin no. 91.

Smith, Raymond T., 1956, *The Negro Family in British Guiana: Family Structure and Social Status in the Villages.* London: Routledge & Kegan Paul Ltd.

————, 1962, *British Guiana.* London: Oxford University Press.

Yde, Jens, 1965, *Material Culture of the Waiwái.* Copenhagen: National Museum, Ethnographical Series, vol. 10.

Paraguay

Fretz, Joseph Winfield, 1962, *Immigrant Group Settlements in Paraguay: A Study in the Sociology of Colonization.* North Newton, Kan.: Bethel College.

Hack, H., 1958, *Primavera: A Communal Settlement of Immigrants in Paraguay.* Amsterdam: Royal Tropical Institute.

Keiderling, Wallace F., 1962, *The Japanese Immigration in Paraguay.* Gainesville, Fla.: University of Florida Press.

Krause, Annemarie Elizabeth, 1952, *Mennonite Settlement in the Paraguayan Chaco.* Chicago: University of Chicago, Department of Geography, Research Papers, no. 25.

Pendle, George, 1967, *Paraguay: A Riverside Nation.* 3rd ed. London: Oxford University Press.

Raine, Philip, 1956, *Paraguay.* New Brunswick, N.J.: Rutgers University Press.

Reh, Emma, 1946, *Paraguayan Rural Life: Survey of Food Problems.* Washington, D.C.: Institute of Inter-American Affairs.

Service, Elman R., and Helen S. Service, 1954, *Tobatí: Paraguayan Town.* Chicago: University of Chicago Press.

Stewart, Norman R., 1967, *Japanese Colonization in Eastern Paraguay.* Washington, D.C.: National Academy of Sciences, National Research Council, Foreign Field Research Program Report, no. 30.

Peru

Adams, Richard N., 1959, *A Community in the Andes: Problems and Progress in Muquiyauyo.* Seattle: University of Washington Press.

Astiz, Carlos A., 1969, *Pressure Groups and Power Elites in Peruvian Politics.* Ithaca, N.Y.: Cornell University Press.

Castillo, Herman, Teressa Castillo, and Arcenio Revilla, 1964, *Carcas: The Forgotten Community.* Ithaca, N.Y.: Cornell University, Socio-Economic Development of Andean Communities, Report no. 1.

Dew, Edward, 1969, *Politics in the Altiplano: The Dynamics of Change in Rural Peru.* Austin, Tex.: University of Texas, Latin American Monographs, no. 15.

Doughty, Paul L., 1968, *Huaylas: An Andean District in Search of Progress.* Ithaca, N.Y.: Cornell University Press.

Fejos, Paul, 1943, *Ethnography of the Yagua.* New York: Viking Fund Publications in Anthropology, no. 1.

Ford, Thomas R., 1955, *Man and Land in Peru.* Gainesville, Fla.: University of Florida Press.

Gillin, John, 1947, *Moche: A Peruvian Coastal Community.* Washington, D.C.: Smithsonian Institution, Institute of Social Anthropology, Publication no. 3.

Hammel, E. A., 1969, *Power in Ica: The Structural History of a Peruvian Community.* Boston: Little, Brown & Company (A revision of *Wealth, Authority and Prestige in the Ica Valley, Peru,* 1962).

Karsten, Rafael, 1935, *The Head-Hunters of Western Amazonas: The Life and Culture of the Jibaro Indians of Eastern Ecuador and Peru.* Helsingfors, Finland: Finska vetenskaps-societen, Helsingfors, Commentationes humanarium litterarum, vol. 7, no. 1.

Miller, Solomon, 1967, Hacienda to Plantation in Northern Peru: The Processes of Proletarianization of a Tenant Farmer Society. In Julian H. Steward (ed.), *Contemporary Change in Traditional Societies,* vol. 3 (*Mexican and Peruvian Communities*), pp. 133–225. Urbana, Ill.: University of Illinois Press.

Owens, R. J., 1963, *Peru.* London: Oxford University Press.

Stein, William W., 1961, *Hualcan: Life in the Highlands of Peru.* Ithaca, N.Y.: Cornell University Press.

Stephens, Richard H., 1971, *Wealth and Power in Peru.* New York: Scarecrow Press, Inc.

Tschopik, Harry, 1947, *Highland Communities of Central Peru: A Regional Survey.* Washington, D.C.: Smithsonian Institution, Institute of Social Anthropology, Publication no. 5.

————, 1951, *The Aymara of Chucuito, Peru, I: Magic.* New York: Anthropological Papers of the American Museum of Natural History, vol. 44, pt. 2.

Tullis, F. La Mond, 1970, *Lord and Peasant in Peru: A Paradigm of Political and Social Change.* Cambridge, Mass.: Harvard University Press.

Surinam

Groot, Silvia W. de, 1969, *Djuka Society and Social Change: History of an Attempt to Develop a Bush Negro Community in Surinam, 1917–1926.* Assen, Netherlands: Van Gorcum and Company.

Herskovits, Melville J., and Frances S. Herskovits, 1934, *Rebel Destiny: Among the Bush Negroes of Dutch Guiana.* New York: McGraw-Hill, Inc.

Kahn, Morton C., 1931, *Djuka, the Bush Negroes of Dutch Guiana.* New York: The Viking Press Inc.

Speckmann, Johan Dirk, 1965, *Marriage and Kinship Among the Indians in Surinam.* Assen, Netherlands: Van Gorcum and Company.

Waal Malefijt, Annemarie de, 1963, *The Javanese of Surinam: Segment of a Plural Society.* Assen, Netherlands: Van Gorcum and Company.

Uruguay

Pendle, George, 1963, *Uruguay.* 3rd ed. New York: Oxford University Press.

Venezuela

Bolinder, Gustaf, 1957, *Indians on Horseback.* London: Dennis Dobson.

Bonilla, Frank, 1970, *The Failure of Elites.* Cambridge, Mass.: M.I.T. Press.

*Chagnon, Napoleon A., 1968, *Yąnomamö: The Fierce People.* Case Studies in Cultural Anthropology. New York: Holt, Rinehart and Winston, Inc.

Lieuwen, Edwin, 1961, *Venezuela.* New York: Oxford University Press.

McCorkle, Thomas, 1965, *Fajardo's People: Cultural Adjustment in Venezuela, and the Little Community in Latin American and North American Contexts.* Los Angeles: University of California at Los Angeles, Latin American Studies Series, no. 1.

*Peattie, Lisa Redfield, 1970, *The View from the Barrio.* Ann Arbor, Mich.: University of Michigan Press [1968].

Petrullo, Vincenzo, 1939, *The Yaruros of the Capanaparo River, Venezuela.* Washington, D.C.: Smithsonian Institution, Bureau of American Ethnology, Bulletin no. 123, Anthropological Papers, no. 11.

Powell, John Duncan, 1971, *Political Mobilization of the Venezuelan Peasant.* Cambridge, Mass.: Harvard University Press.

Ray, Talton, 1969, *The Politics of the Barrios of Venezuela.* Berkeley, Calif.: University of California Press.

Schwerin, Karl H., 1966, *Oil and Steel: Processes of Karinya Culture Change in Response to Industrial Development.* Los Angeles: University of California at Los Angeles, Latin American Studies Series, no. 4.

Watson, Lawrence C., 1968, *Guajiro Personality and Urbanization.* Los Angeles: University of California at Los Angeles, Latin American Studies Series, no. 10.

Wilbert, Johannes, 1972, *Survivors of El Dorado: Four Indian Cultures of South America.* New York: Frederick A. Praeger, Inc.

THE CARIBBEAN

Bahamas

Otterbein, Keith F., 1966, *The Andros Islanders: A Study of Family Organization in the Bahamas.* Lawrence, Kan.: University of Kansas, Social Science Series, no. 14.

Barbados

Greenfield, Sidney M., 1966, *English Rustics in Black Skin: A Study of Modern Family Forms in a Pre-Industrial Society.* New Haven, Conn.: College and University Press.

Carriacou

Smith, Michael G., 1962, *Kinship and Community in Carriacou.* New Haven, Conn.: Yale University Press.

Cuba

*MacGaffey, Wyatt, and Clifford R. Barnett, 1965, *Twentieth Century Cuba: The Background of the Castro Revolution.* New York: Doubleday & Company, Inc., Anchor Books (Original title: *Cuba: Its People, Its Society, Its Cultures*) [1962].

Nelson, Lowry, 1950, *Rural Cuba.* Minneapolis, Minn.: University of Minnesota Press.

Nelson, Lowry, 1972, *Cuba: The Measure of a Revolution.* Minneapolis, Minn.: University of Minnesota Press.
Ortiz Fernández, Fernando, 1947, *Cuban Counterpoint: Tobacco and Sugar.* New York: Alfred A. Knopf.

Grenada

Smith, M. G., 1965, *Stratification in Grenada.* Berkeley, Calif.: University of California Press.

Haiti

Courtlander, Harold, 1960, *The Drum and the Hoe: Life and Lore of the Haitian People.* Berkeley, Calif.: University of California Press.
Courtlander, Harold, and Rémy Bastien, 1966, *Religion and Politics in Haiti.* Washington, D.C.: Institute for Cross-Cultural Research.
Deren, Maya, 1970, *Divine Horsemen: Voodoo Gods of Haiti.* New York: Chelsea House Publishers [1952].
De Young, Maurice, 1958, *Man and Land in the Haitian Economy.* Gainesville, Fla.: University of Florida, Latin American Monographs, no. 3.
*Herskovits, Melville J., 1971, *Life in a Haitian Valley.* New York: Doubleday & Company, Inc., Anchor Books [1937].
*Leyburn, James G., 1966, *The Haitian People.* New Haven, Conn.: Yale University Press Paperback [1941].
Métraux, Alfred, *et al.,* 1951, *Making a Living in Marbial Valley (Haiti).* Paris: U.N.E.S.C.O., Occasional Papers in Education, no. 10.
Métraux, Alfred, 1960, *Haiti: Black Peasants and Voodoo.* New York: Universal Books.
*_____, 1972, *Voodoo in Haiti.* New York: Schocken Books [1959].

Jamaica

Barrett, Leonard E., 1968, *The Rastafarians: A Study in Messianic Cultism in Jamaica.* Río Piedras, Puerto Rico: University of Puerto Rico, Institute of Caribbean Studies, Caribbean Monograph Series, no. 6.
Beckwith, Martha W., 1929, *Black Roadways: A Study of Jamaican Folk Life.* Chapel Hill, N.C.: University of North Carolina Press.
Bell, Wendell, 1964, *Jamaican Leaders: Political Attitudes in a New Nation.* Berkeley, Calif.: University of California Press.
Blake, Judith, 1961, *Family Structure in Jamaica: The Social Context of Reproduction.* New York: The Free Press.
Clarke, Edith, 1957, *My Mother Who Fathered Me: A Study of the Family in Three Selected Communities in Jamaica.* London: George Allen & Unwin Ltd.
Cumper, George E., 1949, *The Social Structure of Jamaica.* Mona, Jamaica: University College of the West Indies.
Henriques, F. M., 1968, *Family and Colour in Jamaica.* 2nd ed. London: MacGibbon and Key [1953].
Kerr, M., 1952, *Personality and Conflict in Jamaica.* Liverpool, England: University of Liverpool Press.

Roberts, George W., 1957, *The Population of Jamaica: An Analysis of Its Structure and Growth*. London: Cambridge University Press.

Leeward Islands

Harris, David R., 1965, *Plants, Animals, and Man in the Outer Leeward Islands, West Indies: An Ecological Study of Antigua, Barbuda and Anguilla*. Berkeley, Calif.: University of California, Publications in Geography, no. 18.

Martinique

*Horowitz, Michael M., 1967, *Morne-Paysan: Peasant Village in Martinique*. Case Studies in Cultural Anthropology. New York: Holt, Rinehart and Winston, Inc.

Netherlands Antilles

Keur, John Y., and Dorothy L. Keur, 1960, *Windward Children: A Study of Human Ecology of the Three Dutch Windward Islands in the Caribbean*. Assen: Van Gorcum and Company.

Puerto Rico

Anderson, Robert W., 1965, *Party Politics in Puerto Rico*. Stanford, Calif.: Stanford University Press.

*Brameld, Theodore, 1966, *The Remarking of a Culture: Life and Education in Puerto Rico*. New York: John Wiley & Sons, Inc., Science Editions [1959].

Caplow, Theodore, Sheldon Styker, and Samuel E. Wallace, 1964, *The Urban Ambience: A Study of San Juan, Puerto Rico*. Totowa, N.J.: The Bedminster Press.

Cochran, Thomas C., 1959, *The Puerto Rican Businessman: A Study in Cultural Change*. Philadelphia: University of Pennsylvania Press.

Hatt, Paul K., 1952, *Backgrounds of Human Fertility in Puerto Rico*. Princeton, N.J.: Princeton University Press.

Hill, Reuben, *et al.*, 1959, *The Family and Population Control: A Puerto Rican Experiment in Social Change*. Chapel Hill, N.C.: University of North Carolina Press.

*Landy, David, 1965, *Tropical Childhood: Cultural Transmission and Learning in a Rural Puerto Rican Village*. New York: Harper Touchbooks [1959].

Lewis, Gordon K., 1963, *Puerto Rico: Freedom and Power in the Caribbean*. New York: Monthly Review Press.

Rogler, Charles C., 1940, *Comerío: A Study of a Puerto Rican Town*. Lawrence, Kans.: University of Kansas Press.

Rosario, José Colombán, 1935, *The Development of the Puerto Rican Jíbaro and His Present Attitude Towards Society*. San Juan, Puerto Rico: University of Puerto Rico, Monographs, Social Science Series, no. 1.

Steward, Julian (ed.), 1956, *People of Puerto Rico: A Study in Social Anthropology*. Urbana, Ill.: University of Illinois Press.

Tumin, Melvin M., and Arnold S. Feldman, 1961, *Social Class and Social Change in Puerto Rico*. Princeton, N.J.: Princeton University Press.

Trinidad

Herskovits, Melville J., and Frances S. Herskovits, 1947, *Trinidad Village*. New York: Alfred A. Knopf.

Klass, Morton, 1961, *East Indians in Trinidad: A Study of Cultural Persiştence*. New York: Columbia University Press.

Malik, Yogendra K., 1971, *East Indians in Trinidad: A Study in Minority Politics*. New York: Oxford University Press.

Niehoff, Arthur, and Juanita Niehoff, 1960, *East Indians in the West Indies*. Milwaukee, Wis.: Milwaukee Public Museum, Publications in Anthropology, no. 6.

Rodman, Hyman, 1971, *Lower-Class Families: The Culture of Poverty in Negro Trinidad*. New York: Oxford University Press.

Rubin, Vera, and Marisa Zavalloni, 1969, *We Wish To Be Looked Upon: A Study of the Aspirations of Youth in a Developing Society*. New York: Teachers College Press, Center for Education in Latin America.

Simpson, George E., 1965, *The Shango Cult in Trinidad*. Río Piedras, Puerto Rico: Institute of Caribbean Studies, Caribbean Monograph Series, no. 2.

Virgin Islands

Campbell, Albert A., 1943, *St. Thomas Negroes: A Study of Personality and Culture*. American Psychological Association, Psychological Monographs, vol. 55, no. 5.

Western Caribbean

Parsons, James J., 1956, *San Andrés and Providencia: English-Speaking Islands in the Western Caribbean*. Berkeley, Calif.: University of California, Publications in Geography, vol. 12, no. 1, pp. 1–84.

LATIN AMERICANS IN THE UNITED STATES

Barker, George C., 1972, *Social Functions of Language in a Mexican-American Community*. Tucson, Ariz.: University of Arizona, Arizona Anthropological Papers Series, no. 22.

*Clark, Margaret, 1959, *Health in the Mexican-American Culture: A Community Study*. Berkeley, Calif.: University of California Press.

Edmonson, Munro S., 1957, *Los Mantos: A Study of Institutional Values*. New Orleans: Tulane University, Middle American Research Institute, Publication no. 23, pp. 1–72.

Fagen, Richard R., Richard A. Brody, and Thomas J. O'Leary, 1968, *Cubans in Exile: Disaffection and the Revolution*. Stanford, Calif.: Stanford University Press.

Gamio, Manuel, 1931, *The Mexican Immigrant: His Life Story*. Chicago: University of Chicago Press.

*Gonzalez, Nancie L., 1969, *The Spanish-Americans of New Mexico: A Heritage of Pride*. rev. ed. Albuquerque, N.M.: University of New Mexico Press [1967].

*Madsen, William, 1964, *Mexican-Americans of South Texas.* Case Studies in Cultural Anthropology. New York: Holt, Rinehart and Winston, Inc.

Mills, Charles W., Clarence Senior, and Rose Goldsen, 1950, *The Puerto Rican Journey.* New York: Harper & Row, Publishers.

Padilla, Elena, 1958, *Up From Puerto Rico.* New York: Columbia University Press.

*Rubel, Arthur J., 1966, *Across the Tracks: Mexican Americans in a Texas City.* Austin, Tex.: University of Texas Press.

Sanchez, George, 1940, *Forgotten People: A Study of New Mexicans.* Albuquerque, N.M.: University of New Mexico Press.

Saunders, Lyle, 1954, *Cultural Differences and Medical Care: The Case of the Spanish-Speaking People of the Southwest.* New York: Russell Sage Foundation.

Spicer, Edward H., 1940, *Pascua: A Yaqui Village in Arizona.* Chicago: University of Chicago Press.

Tuck, Ruth, 1956, *Not With the Fist: Mexican-Americans in a Southwest City.* New York: Harcourt Brace Jovanovich, Inc.

WEST INDIANS IN GREAT BRITAIN

Calley, Michael, 1965, *God's People: West Indian Penetecostal Sects in England.* London: Oxford University Press.

Davison, R. H., 1962, *West Indian Migrants.* London: Oxford University Press.

_____, 1966, *Black British.* London: Oxford University Press.

Glass, Ruth, 1960, *Newcomers: The West Indians in London.* London: George Allen & Unwin Ltd.

Little, K. L., 1948, *Negroes in Britain: A Study of Racial Relations in English Society.* London: Routledge & Kegan Paul Ltd.

Peach, Ceri, 1968, *West Indian Migration to Britain.* London: Oxford University Press.

Name index

Abdu'r-Rahman, 58
Acamapichtli, 42–43
Acosta, José de, 146, 150
Adams, Frederick U., 260, 264
Adams, Richard N., 127, 157, 159, 170, 176–182, 188, 288, 305
Alvarado Tezozómoc, Fernando, 150
Anderson, Gallatin, 200
Anonymous Conqueror, 150, 151
Aponte Figueroa, Juan de, 68
Arriaga, Pablo José de, 79
Atahuallpa, 50, 54
Atkinson, William C., 57, 58
Augelli, John P., 88, 90, 101, 106
Ávila, Francisco de, 151
Azevedo, Thales de, 171

Bagu, Sergio, 80
Baily, Samuel L., 104
Baker, Paul T., 12
Barrett, Samuel A., 155
Barthel, Thomas S., 53
Basauri, Carlos, 159
Bastide, Roger, 117
Beals, Ralph L., 64, 69, 157, 163, 279, 284
Becker, Howard P., 161
Bernal, Ignacio, 23, 150, 156
Betanzos, Juan de, 151
Biesanz, John B., 202, 279, 280
Biesanz, Mavis, 202, 279, 280
Blaffer, Sarah C., 157
Blanchard, R., 94
Bode, Barbara, 208
Bolívar, Simón de, 74
Bonilla, Frank, 288
Borah, Woodrow, 108, 109
Brasseur de Bourbourg, C. E., 152
Breese, Gerald, 285
Brundage, Burr C., 50
Buechler, Hans C., 205, 278
Bunzel, Ruth, 208
Burgess, Ernest, 161
Burma, John H., 140
Bushnell, G. H. S., 33

Caddy, John, 153
Caldwell, Joseph R., 5
Cámara Barbachano, Fernando, 157
Cancian, Frank, 157
Caplow, Theodore, 280
Cappanari, Stephen, 200
Carlos III, of Spain, 152
Carr, Robert F., 156
Carroll, Thomas F., 278
Casas, Bartolomé de las, 77
Caso, Alfonso, 43
Catherwood, Frederick, 153

Cavazzi, G. A. da Montecuccolo, 83
Chagnon, Napoleon A., 229
Chevalier, François, 278
Chonchol, Jacques, 278
Cieza de León, Pedro de, 151
Clifton, James A., 194
Cobean, Robert H., 156
Cochran, Thomas C., 130, 187, 288, 310, 311
Coe, Michael D., 19, 26, 30, 31, 33, 48, 49, 148, 156
Coe, William R., 30
Cohen, Lucy M., 135
Cole, Fay-Cooper, 160
Collier, June, 157
Collins, Robert O., 84
Columbus, Christopher, 59, 71, 75, 145
Comas, Juan, 157
Cortés, Hernán, 64, 80, 149, 150
Costa Pinto, Luis A., 171
Crevenna, Th., 159, 280, 283
Crowther, Samuel, 261, 263
Curtin, Philip, 85

Dávalos, Eusebio, 156
Davidson, Basil, 82, 83
Davis, Kingsley, 195, 296
Delgado O., Carlos, 227
Deshon, Shirley, 201
Despres, Leo A., 132, 137
Dew, Edward, 278
Diaz, May N., 217
Díaz del Castillo, Bernal, 149, 150
Diaz-Guerrero, Rogelio, 224
Dibble, Charles E., 148
Dobyns, Henry F., 108, 110
Dobele, William A., Jr., 297
Donnelly, Ignatius, 154
Dotson, Floyd, 199, 280, 289
Dotson, Lillian Ota, 289
Doughty, Paul L., 291
Durán, Fray Diego, 149, 150
Durkheim, Émile, 161

Eca, Raul, d', 71
Eggan, Fred, 160
Enríquez B., Eliecer, 282
Erasmus, Charles, 207, 278
Estrada, Emilio, 20
Evans, Clifford, 20
Exquemelin, Alexander O., 88

Fallas, Carlos Luis, 260
Fals Borda, Orlando, 278
Faron, Louis C., 90, 91, 93, 111, 112, 159, 245
Ferdinand, of Spain, 59, 75

397

Subject index